Jazz

E i g h t h   E d i t i o n

Paul O. W.
Tanner

University of California
Los Angeles

David W.
Megill

Mira Costa College

Maurice
Gerow

University of California
Los Angeles

Brown & Benchmark
PUBLISHERS

Madison, WI Dubuque Guilford, CT Chicago Toronto London
Mexico City Caracas Buenos Aires Madrid Bogotá Sydney

Book Team

Publisher *Rosemary Bradley*
Acquisitions Editor *Chris Freitag*
Publishing Services Coordinator *Peggy Selle*
Proofreading Coordinator *Carrie Barker*
Art Editor *Rita L. Hingtgen*
Photo Editor *Rose Deluhery*
Permissions Coordinator *Lou Ann Wilson*
Production Manager *Beth Kundert*
Production/Imaging and Media Development Manager *Linda Meehan Avenarius*
Production/Costing Manager *Sherry Padden*
Visuals/Design Freelance Specialist *Mary L. Christianson*
Marketing Manager *Kirk Moen*
Copywriter *Sandy Hyde*

Brown & Benchmark
PUBLISHERS

Executive Vice President and General Manager *Bob McLaughlin*
Vice President of Business Development *Russ Domeyer*
Vice President of Production and New Media Development *Victoria Putman*
National Sales Manager *Phil Rudder*
National Telesales Director *John Finn*

A Times Mirror Company

Cover and interior design by Wood Street Studio

Cover photograph © Charles Thatcher/Tony Stone Images

Copyedited by Bruce R. Owens, A–R Editions, Inc.; Proofread by Janet Reuter

Library of Congress Catalog Card Number: 95–83647

ISBN 0–697–28807–2

Printed in the United States of America by Times Mirror Higher Education Group, Inc.,
2460 Kerper Boulevard, Dubuque, IA 52001

10 9 8 7 6 5 4 3 2 1

Basal Text *10/12 Times Roman*
Display Type *Helvetica Light*
Typesetting System *Macintosh™ QuarkXPress™*
Paper Stock *50# Restore Cote*
Production Services *A–R Editions, Inc.*

Contents

6

Boogie-Woogie (the 1920s and 1930s) 71

7

Swing (1932–1942) 77

8

Bop (1940–1950) 101

9

Cool (1949–1955) 117

10

Hard Bop, Funky/Straight-Ahead Jazz (circa 1954–) 129

11

Free Form, Avant-Garde 145

12

Crossover, Third Stream, Latin Jazz 163

13

Crossover, Jazz Fusion 171

Listening Guides

Recorded Demonstrations

Photographs

Preface

This edition of *Jazz* focuses on presenting a clear, chronological account of the evolution of jazz in a manner that is easily accessible to students. The historical framework offered in this edition is used to introduce the individuals who shaped jazz as it developed into America's signature art form and, at the same time, to support individual instructors in their own presentation of jazz styles and eras.

Features for the eighth edition include the following:

The listening experiences of the reader are the focus; and more than fifty listening guides, including those for commercially available listening collections (Smithsonian, New World Records, and Folkways), are presented.

This edition is accompanied by a two-cassette (or CD) set of original jazz recordings, all with accompanying listening guides in the text.

Listening software will also be available to help guide students interactively through the listening examples.

The text has been reorganized to better reflect how courses are taught. The new restructuring has been designed to support both students' learning and professors' course organization.

Technical material from previous editions has been gathered in the appendices so that it is easily accessible but not overwhelming for the uninitiated student.

The instructor's manual includes example scores of earlier jazz styles as well as organizational materials.

Chapters have been updated to include recent accomplishments by contemporary jazz artists.

New Internet opportunities are now offered to extend the effectiveness of the text. You can correspond with the author (dwmegill@yar.miracosta.cc.ca.us), visit a World Wide Web site (http://www.miracosta.cc.ca.us—look under the music department), or subscribe to a listserv (jazz-l@spock.miracosta.cc.ca.us), where students and professors around the world who use this book can extend their classrooms to discuss their study of jazz.

The new organization of the text and the guided listening examples are designed to introduce students to the stylistic eras of jazz and to expose the fluid nature of stylistic change. The first chapter, "Listening to Jazz," is designed to help students learn how to approach jazz through critical listening skills. The presentation is meant to be appropriate for the general appreciation student through its sparing use of technical terms and examples.

Knowing that musical notation and the technical language of music can unnecessarily intimidate new students to music, we have moved those elements to easily accessible appendices. For students with more preparation, Appendix A contains a more technical discussion of chapter 1, complete with notational examples. Appendix B contains notational examples for the discussions offered in chapters 2 through 8.

The accompanying musical examples include recordings by Bessie Smith, Billie Holiday, Joe "King" Oliver, Scott Joplin, Art Tatum, Louis Armstrong, Meade Lux Lewis, Duke Ellington, Benny Goodman, Coleman Hawkins, Charlie Parker, Dizzy Gillespie, Lester Young, Count Basie, Miles Davis, Horace Silver, Ornette Coleman, John Coltrane, Joe Zawinul, Weather Report, Chick Corea, the Yellowjackets, Fletcher Henderson, Charles Mingus, Thelonious Monk, the Modern Jazz Quartet, Wynton Marsalis, Art Blakey, and the New York Voices.

To help students identify additional recordings found on the *Smithsonian Collection of Classic Jazz*, the cited recordings are identified by "S." Likewise, examples found on the New World Records collection are identified by "NW" (this collection can be obtained from 3 East 54th St., New York,

New York 10022). Another important collection for early jazz influences is the Folkways Jazz series, identified by "F.J."

In some cases, we recommend listening examples that are not readily available in these major collections. We do so only because we believe that these are the best examples of the material being discussed. Our dialogue with professors of jazz history makes clear that individualized listening lists are an important part of most course offerings. We expect that professors will know best how to substitute for these recordings if these prove to be not readily available.

We would like to thank the reviewers for this edition:

Charles Blancq
University of New Orleans

George Bouchard
Nassau Community College
Hermina Watthall Butcher
Randolph Macon Woman's College
David Manuel Garcia
Bridgewater State College
Brad Madson
Jefferson College

Jazz

CHAPTER 1

Listening to Jazz

"Jazz is considered by many to be America's greatest contribution to music. Its impact on American society has been enormous and its influence on world culture has been far reaching. Its message has been direct, vital, and immediate, enabling it to hurdle cultural, linguistic, and political barriers."[1]

What Is Jazz?

What is jazz? What are the unique characteristics that distinguish it from other types of musical composition and performance? Throughout its chronology, jazz has freely imported influences from diverse cultural and musical elements, forming a type of music that has been accepted as uniquely American. "The American popular song is inextricably and profoundly linked with jazz, the one serving—along with the blues—as the basic melodic/harmonic material on which the other could build."[2]

Jazz is both indigenous to this country and the most democratic music ever devised. Performers in an improvised jazz ensemble are equal partners in the developing musical expression. As the music unfolds, the musical leadership may shift several times as the players contribute their own expressive ideas. Jazz is defined by this balance between the individual voices that constitute an ensemble and the collective expression unique to that ensemble.

In its early development, all music not clearly classical was generally considered jazz, thereby putting jazz, country and western, rock and roll, and all popular and other types of music into one category. As jazz developed, the lines between it and the other musics in America became much clearer. In fact, even the distinction between "good" and "bad" jazz seems to have settled into a general consensus, but this consensus has seldom developed free of controversy. The newer musical expression often served as a reaction to the jazz status quo.

The music of America has many faces. Few of these musical expressions survive a temporary popularity, but jazz ultimately matured in a way that wove it into the American fabric itself. It is often called "America's classical music," and it has proven to be an appropriate subject of study in colleges and universities around the world. Although there was other musical activity during this time—such as country and western, blues, rhythm and blues, and the popular songs of musical theater—only jazz claimed a dominant foothold in the American identity.

Jazz embodies the irony of how a music can move from such lowly origins as the heartfelt expressions of American slaves, the music of the church, and the dance hall to the American academy and the concert stage.

This musical and cultural phenomenon was not to be replicated until the advent of rock and roll, which now appears to have an equal amount of cultural energy to etch itself, as jazz did, into the American identity.

At Bob Reisner's Open Door, Greenwich Village, New York, ca. 1953. (Left to right): Charles Mingus, Roy Haynes, Thelonious Monk, and Charlie "Bird" Parker.

Photo by Bob Parent

Understanding jazz requires an understanding of the jazz performer. Unlike music of the Western European tradition, which traces the history of musical composition, jazz traces its history through the performance of individuals. Jazz is about personal, unique expressions, and those performers most remembered by history have always stood above others in the power of their personal expressions. These expressions have always depended on the unique balance of the technical and aesthetic prowess of the performers themselves.

Because jazz is defined by the personal voices of its performers and only secondarily by its composers, it is misleading to force the musical styles used to define jazz into overly rigid categories. The stylistic similarities among players of a particular era are useful in understanding the evolution of jazz, but they are only a shadow of the individual creative voices that propelled jazz's evolution. Along with many others, author-critic Henry Pleasants has tried to identify the origins of jazz: "The influence of a variety of indigenous musical styles originating in the Negro communities of New Orleans and other American cities, in the Negro communities of the rural South, and in the Negro or mixed communities of the Caribbean islands and some areas of South America in the early decades of the twentieth century has been felt and reflected in the popular music of most of the civilized world."[3]

Pleasants's statement, emphasizing the contribution of African Americans and the geographical origins of jazz, is only partially correct. Jazz was fired in a more complex crucible. It required all the musical and cultural forces at work in America to reach its ultimate definition: the crosscurrent of the western European harmonic system and song form as well as the expressive melodic and rhythmic elements of the African heritage. It also required the American cultural context with all its contributing forces, both (arguably) good and bad.

Pleasants does, however, invalidate several of the misconceptions concerning jazz:

Prevalent assumptions are: (1) that the distinguishing feature of jazz is syncopation; (2) that the distinguishing feature of jazz is improvisation; (3) that jazz cannot be played from notes; and (4) that jazz is a Negro music and can be played properly only by Negroes. All are easily disposed of: (1) If syncopation were the distinctive element in jazz, then much European music would be jazz. (2) Improvisation was common in European music well into the 19th century, and most church organists improvise to this day without producing anything that sounds like jazz. (3) The time has long passed when an astigmatic jazz musician could get by without spectacles. (4) While the Negro has certainly been the decisive contributor to jazz, there is no jazz in Africa that was not brought there by Americans or Europeans, white, black and mixed.[4]

Jazz is about the balance between **improvisation** and composition. Although jazz is best known for being improvisational, it is certainly more than that. In fact, some of the distinctive characteristics of certain jazz periods involve just this balance. Some periods, such as bebop and free form, used a high degree of improvisation and only a small amount of precomposed material. On the other hand, the swing era's big bands used highly structured arrangements that left little room for improvisation, although even within these large bands small groups (e.g., the Benny Goodman orchestra) played improvisational jazz. However, even these small groups included an overall plan of some kind that guided the performance. For example, the strains of two- and three-part harmony played by the clarinet, piano, and vibraphone on "Avalon" could not possibly have been performed unless they had been previously contrived.[5]

To be a discriminating jazz listener, one must assess the level and appropriateness of the improvisation in any given style. To expect a highly improvised performance from a highly precomposed style can lead only to a disappointing listening experience. Pursuing the example of "Avalon" further helps clarify this point. The Goodman big band may have used highly composed arrangements, but not all big bands did the same. Kansas City bands, such as the early Count Basie band, used a much less formal approach to big-band performance. Their "riffing" style was often developed in an improvisatory manner, unlike the more specifically notated arrangements of bands such as Goodman. The performances of each of these bands reflect the manner in which their arrangements were created: one structured very loosely and openly and the other controlled and more complex. Each approach had its advantages but also precluded the assets of the other.

But an even finer distinction can be made in this example. The Basie band actually later became known as one of the most precise ensembles in big-band history, a development that required Basie to shift to more spe-

---

What Is Jazz?

"Jazz I regard as an American folk music; not the only one but a very powerful one which is probably in the blood and feeling of the American people more than any other style."

—George Gershwin

"It is difficult to give a definition of Jazz. Those offered are as varied and numerous as those who have played or listened to it."

"Who invented jazz? The city of New Orleans did."

—From a display at the New Orleans Jazz Museum

cific arrangements than he used with his earlier ensembles. So, even within the work of one musician, the balance between improvisation and composition is shifting. This balance is subtly at work even in the process of improvisation itself. While performers improvise, they make compositional decisions that cannot be edited because they are made in real time rather than before the performance began. The excitement of improvisation must be balanced against the possible complexity that an edited composition allows. Again, there are advantages to both, and listeners must align their expectations with the compositional/improvisational balance offered by the performance.

As mentioned, musicians must be allowed to define jazz from period to period and not to force it into any one narrowly defined category. Doing so lets one enjoy both the wider breadth of the jazz tradition and the individuals who define it. One's understanding of various jazz styles then comprises only very general descriptors,

not specific mandates for performers to follow. Such an inclusive jazz definition helps one approach the history of jazz honestly and allows future jazz expressions more room to breathe.

An important first step to understanding jazz is recognizing that jazz is not static within its own tradition. This must be established before trying to distinguish it from the other musical traditions in America, a task that at first seems obvious but that ultimately proves more elusive than one would expect. What characteristics are common to most all jazz and are not typical of other musical traditions? It is much easier to recognize something as jazz than to state how one knows it is jazz and not something else. The more technical musical activities understood only by the practitioners of music somehow signal to even the untrained listener that it is jazz rather than some other musical style. Actually, the musical elements of jazz are very similar to those used in other musical styles. Also, most of the musical forms

Jazz Interpretation

The main characteristic of jazz is the individual musician's interpretation of his or her material, whether it be originally written for a jazz group or from a popular tune, an aria or a classical theme, using the elements of jazz such as improvisation, syncopation, blues scale, etc. A jazz musician absorbs the material and models it according to his ideas and talents, "forming the link between the composer and the audience." The tradition of interpretive jazz has as its source the musical style of slaves singing as they worked in the field, worshiped in church, or celebrated during their free time. A specific interpretation can be identified only by comparison to other styles. It might include such jazz elements as blues scales and harmony, smears, fall, bend, growls, flutters, vibrato, glissandos, or differing tone colors in muted brass instruments. Also possible are pitch variations, one-half valved notes, and "tricks" used by early jazzmen. These musicians sometimes guarded their individual styles, many times using a cloth over the valves to hide their technique. Many early jazzmen refused to record because they feared their techniques would be stolen by other musicians.

Improvisation

The art of improvisation is as old as music itself, for early musicians, like early jazz players, were both composers and performers.

Improvised music, which has occurred in all musical systems of the world, evolves into written music, thus completing a cycle from spontaneous creativity to traditional repetition of written

melodies. Every development of a new form and style of music has in its beginning elements of improvised material. Improvisational music dominated the polyphonic music of the fifteenth century, and was the essential element of eighteenth century music for harpsichord and piano, as played by Johann Sebastian Bach and his contemporaries. A resurgence of improvised music came in the form of jazz in the latter decades of the nineteenth century, after lying dormant.

Jazz became the foremost improvisational style at the turn of the twentieth century, evolving from many different types of music, especially the Negro music in and around the city of New Orleans.

Syncopation

Syncopation occurred in early jazz, characterizing a style of musical performance different from any heard before. While improvising on a given theme was not unique to jazz, the elements of music used by these early jazz musicians in their own colorful style was singular. Syncopation is the deliberate upsetting of the normal pulse of meter, accent or rhythm. It is felt as a contradiction or disturbance between the underlying pulse and the actual pulse of music and is created by sustaining or stressing notes or by adding rests in unsuspected places.

The best description of this use of unestablished rhythm is ". . . a jazz performance using syncopation makes it swing."

—From a display at the New Orleans Jazz Museum

(or structures) of jazz are not new to American music. However, jazz is still recognizably different, its most distinctive attribute being the manner in which all these elements and forms are performed and the improvised context in which this jazz interpretation is carried out.

The interpretation of music in the jazz style originally came about when African Americans attempted to express themselves on European musical instruments. These early instrumentalists tended to think of their musical lines in terms of how they would be treated vocally. Eventually, the attitude developed that *what* was played was not as important as *how* it was played.

In jazz interpretation, the player restricts interpretive ideas to his or her conception of the melody, coloring it by the use of rhythmic effects, dynamics, and any other slight alterations that occur to him or her while performing. The player remains enough within such melodic restrictions to allow a listener to recognize the melody easily, regardless of the player's interpretation. Almost any kind of melodic line can be performed with jazz interpretation. Most jazz musicians will agree that to write down an exact jazz interpretation is next to impossible, and all will agree that only a musician who has played jazz can even approximate the notation.

Critical Listening

"There need be no mystery about jazz, but each listener has a right, even a duty, to be discriminating."[6]

To appreciate music, the listener must be actively involved, and understanding and enjoyment go hand in hand. Passive listening will not bring intelligent musical enjoyment. Rather, such enjoyment is fostered through active participation that includes understanding, careful listening, and emotional response. The thrust of all musical learning should be to develop a sensitized awareness of those expressive elements of music that will foster a wide range of musical interests and activities and a variety of musical pleasures.

Listening Techniques

The primary aim in listening to a composition is to focus attention on the various musical events as they unfold—not an easy task. Mental concentration of a high order is needed. The mind is so conditioned to hearing music as a background **accompaniment** to daily activities—in the dentist's office or at the supermarket—that it is difficult to devote full attention to listening to music.

In daily living, one encounters many spatial relationships—high walls and low walls, houses and garages, sidewalks and streets, country and urban vistas—that are immediately visual and easily identified. In listening to music, one must forget the visual and learn to concentrate on the nonvisual elements.

Another difference is that music moves in time, and time relationships are less obvious in daily living. For example, a painting can be viewed at leisure and its parts observed in relationship to the whole, but not so when listening to a musical composition, when memory becomes important. The mind must remember at one point what has transpired so that one part of a piece of music can be compared or contrasted with another part.

Finally, if one is to learn more about the structure of music, it is important to develop the ability to separate juxtaposed musical sounds and to focus attention on a single musical element. For example, when identifying the **ostinato** bass employed in boogie-woogie playing, one must be able to shut out the right-hand piano sounds to recognize what the left hand is realizing at the keyboard.

What to Listen for in Jazz

Sounds Associated with Jazz

In classical music, each instrument has an "ideal" sound or tone, or at least there is a consensus as to what the ideal sound is. The jazz musician, though, finds such conformity of little importance. As long as the sound communicates well with peers and listeners, the jazz musician appreciates the individuality of personal sounds. This situation, in which personal expression is more important than aesthetic conformity, often causes listeners not accustomed to jazz to question the sounds that they hear.

Certain sounds peculiar to jazz have their origins in oral tradition and are the result of instrumentalists attempting to imitate vocal techniques. Jazz singers and instrumentalists use all the tone qualities employed in other music and even increase the emotional range through the use of growls, bends, slurs, and varying shades of **vibrato,** employing any device they can to assist their personal interpretation of the music. Jazz musicians have always had a great affinity with good singers, especially those whose interpretation closely resembles their own. Such singers include the early great blues singers (to be discussed later) and other talented performers such as Bing Crosby, Ella Fitzgerald, Billie Holiday, Frank Sinatra, Sarah Vaughan, Billy Eckstine, and Betty Carter.

Distinctive jazz **instrumentation** produces unique sounds. For example, a featured saxophone section or a **rhythm section** is seldom found in other types of music. Although it is a mistake to claim that mutes are indigenous to jazz (mutes were used in the 1600s), it is true that a larger variety of mutes are used in jazz.

To many listeners, the sounds of jazz are personified and identified through the musical interpretation of specific artists. Listeners who have not heard much jazz are often surprised that the well-initiated can recognize a soloist after hearing only a few notes—at least within the listener's preferred style. Talented jazz musicians seem to

Sarah Vaughan.
Courtesy of Ray Avery

have their own personal vibrato, attack, type of melodic line, choice of notes in the **chord**—indeed, their own sound. On the other hand, very few classical connoisseurs can say for sure who is conducting a standard work, let alone identify the individual soloists or section leaders.

Listen to the taped demonstrations to hear how a classically played melody (demonstration 1) can be given a jazz interpretation (demonstration 2). Demonstration 3 then offers a possible improvisation of that same melody.

Jazz Interpretation and Improvisation

What is the jazz "idiom"? Classical music and jazz music differ primarily in idiom. A classical musician plays the notes, but the playing lacks the idiomatic execution usually found in jazz. The European system of musical notation cannot represent this kind of expression. "The conventional symbols could, in other words, indicate in a general way *what* should be played, but could not indicate *how* it should be played."[7] Idiomatic expression in jazz is the result of African American musicians interjecting African music into European music.

Improvisation is similar to interpretation but without melodic restriction. When jazz players improvise, they usually use the original melody or the chords that support the melody as a point of departure for inventing a new melodic line while the chords remain fairly constant. However, as discussed in chapter 14, there is a contemporary style called free form, or free improvisation, in which the player's only restriction is to compose lines related to the musical sounds made by the other musicians in the group.

Improvisation did not come into being with jazz, nor is the technique confined solely to jazz, as some authorities state. In principle, jazz improvisation is no different than the time-honored improvisational techniques used in classical music. It is only the way in which individual idioms are used that distinguishes them from each other. The Greeks improvised two thousand years ago,[8] and at one time improvisation was extremely important in baroque and classical music.

J. S. Bach, Mozart, Beethoven, Liszt, and many others were superb improvisers. Therefore, listeners who say they cannot understand jazz because of improvisation also cannot understand much of the great traditional classical music. Today, improvisation in classical music can be heard performed by groups such as the Improvisation Chamber Ensemble.[9] Although jazz is not the only musical idiom that uses improvisation, it is certainly one that places improvisation in high regard.

Rhythm

"Rhythm is the most magnetic irresistible force among all the elements of music."[10]

An emphasis on rhythm has always been an integral part of jazz, one reason being that for many years jazz was considered primarily dance music. Jazz players have found that a steady, unbroken beat is necessary not only for dancing but also for developing the emotional pitch identified with jazz, even though in some cases the pulse is merely implied rather than obvious.

The jazz player does not always play exactly in rhythm with the pulse. He or she sometimes feels the need to be slightly ahead of (on top of) the beat and sometimes to be slightly behind the beat. This is more a feeling than something that can be measured accurately, and it varies from one style and from one individual to another. Throughout the development of most jazz, performers have felt that they needed this pulse to play what they considered jazz. However, recent experiments in jazz have not used a steady beat. (These experiments in rhythm are discussed further in chapter 11.) For years it was thought that all jazz must be played with a steady beat, but this attitude changed when new, uneven-beat groups (**meters**) began to be used in performing well-accepted jazz works. Pianist Dave Brubeck first brought newer meters to public notice with an extremely popular recording of Paul Desmond's "Take Five."[11] Most jazz, however, still uses even meters.

Jazz also makes use of a specific type of rhythmic treatment called **syncopation**, which places accents between the basic beats in the music. Jazz uses this so much that it has become one of its identifying characteristics. Syncopation is responsible to a great extent for the "swing feel" most often associated with jazz.

Form

The word **form** in music describes the overall structure of a musical composition or performance. Perceiving and understanding the elements of form presents a greater challenge in listening to music than in considering visual art. In music, the various parts of a composition are presented in time, and a listener can compare them by memory only. Many jazz pieces have relatively simple forms, such as the blues, which has a single musical section made up of three smaller **phrases.** During the entire performance, this musical section is repeated many times.

Repetition is the presentation of the same musical material in two or more parts of a composition. **Contrast,** on the other hand, is the introduction of different musical material. From earliest times, repetition of a melody has played a vital role in prolonging a game, dance, or story. A similar reason for repetition is found in work songs, in which repetition of the melody depends on the amount of work to be done by those singing the song. When contrasting musical ideas are introduced, a new section of the form begins. The repetitions and contrasts tend not only to build the performance but also to give a feeling of balance and symmetry to the composition as a whole. If you understand

Paul Desmond.
Lee Tanner/The Jazz Image

the principles of repetition and contrast, you can sharpen your listening focus by anticipating the parts that are repeated and those that are contrasted and thus will have a much better idea of what to listen to and for. Consequently, you will enjoy the music more as it unfolds.

Listening Guidelines

As you continue your study of jazz, we suggest that you concentrate on some specific points while you listen, remembering that any jazz performance can have a blend of any of the following:

1. What are the general stylistic characteristics that make the style identifiable? For example, is the music fast? Does it have a swing feel, or does it have a rock-and-roll feel? Does it seem agitated or subdued?

2. What instruments are used, and how do the instrumentalists interact? Do they work closely together in a way that would require a previously written arrangement, or do they interact spontaneously?

3. What makes the performance a personal one? Does the singer or instrumentalist use any unique tone or inflections? Are there melodic or rhythmic clues that would distinguish this performer from

another? Does the performance focus more on virtuoso technique or expressive content?

4. How do the bass player, drummer, and rhythm player (guitar, piano, and so on) interact? Which has the more dominant role? How do their balance and their roles differ from other styles? How does the drummer (if present) use the drum set differently for this style?

5. What other types of music possibly influence what you are hearing? Are there any classical, rock, country, gospel, rhythm and blues, or world music influences? From what jazz style is the performance derived?

6. Is there any obvious musical form (e.g., standard song form), or are the performers also improvising the form?

7. Is the melody singable, or is it designed more appropriately for the instrument playing it? Do the melodies played or sung overlap, or are they harmonized?

8. What is the musical focus of the performance? The performer? The composition? The group as a whole?

9. What is the social context for this style? Is it a reaction to previous musical styles? Is there a social message?

For a more technical approach to listening to jazz, see Appendix A.

Summary

A listener must decide whether a specific performance contains enough recognizable jazz elements to make it jazz. Identical melodies can be played or sung in a jazz or another musical style. A good example is "Empty Bed Blues" as sung on the Leonard Bernstein record *What Is Jazz?*[12] The melody is sung by both Sherry Ostrus and Bessie Smith. Miss Ostrus's interpretation lacks jazz elements, whereas Miss Smith uses the jazz elements discussed here. There can be no question in any listener's mind which rendition is jazz.

In traditional classical music, the composer remains the focal point. In general, a performer of classical music follows the conductor (and what the conductor understands the composer to have intended). On the other hand, in a jazz performance, if the performer does not integrate something of his or her personality and background into the music, the audience (which is itself a part of the performance) justifiably feels cheated. In classical music, *how* a work is performed is rarely considered as important as the work itself. In jazz, the work itself is never really as important as the way in which it is played. Even more unusual is that, in jazz, the way a performer plays determines *what* he or she plays. That is, both the strong and the weak aspects of an individual's abilities on an instrument cause stylistic directions to appear in the playing, and in turn these directions dictate both *what* and *how* he or she plays, and the *what* and the *how* tend to merge. For example, what Charlie Parker played on "Parker's Mood," "Bird Gets the Worm," or "Merry Go Round" was precisely how he played the saxophone[13] (NW, 271, "Parker's Mood," side 1, band 4); there is no way of separating style from content. This approach—this attitude—distinguishes jazz from most other music.

Perhaps Bryce Jordan has one of the clearest definitions of jazz: "Jazz, then, is not a composer's art. The particular melody and harmonies which formed the basis of a performance, improvised or arranged, are of secondary importance. Rather jazz is the art of the performer, the performing ensemble, the arranger. And the quality of the art is dependent upon their creative ideas."[14]

For Further Study

1. If you were asked to describe why you prefer a particular type of music, what would you say?

2. Listen to "Silver" from the album *Collaboration* by the Modern Jazz Quartet with Laurindo Almeida (Atlantic Records, 1429) and answer the following:

   a. Is the ensemble a large group or a small combo?

   b. See how many of the following instruments you can identify in the tune: violin, vibraphones, saxophone, oboe, piano, percussion (drums and others), string bass, and amplified guitar.

3. Listen to the Modern Jazz Quartet's rendition of the very familiar carol "God Rest Ye Merry Gentlemen" (*The Modern Jazz Quartet at Music Inn*, Atlantic Records, 1247). Describe as many of the jazz ingredients as you can, including specific instrumental sounds.

4. Benny Goodman Trio and Coleman Hawkins on saxophone use jazz interpretation and jazz improvisation in the same composition. Listen to "Body and Soul" (S, side C, band 6) and identify the places where you find interpretation and improvisation. Do the same with Coleman Hawkins (S, side C, band 7).

Notes

1. Robert Hickok, *Exploring Music* (Dubuque, Iowa: Wm. C. Brown, 1989), 22.

2. Gunther Schuller, *The Swing Era* (London: Oxford University Press, 1989), 5n.

3. From Henry Pleasants, *Serious Music and All That Jazz;* 1969. Reprinted by permission of Simon & Schuster, Inc.

4. Ibid., 62.

5. Benny Goodman, "Avalon," *Benny Goodman Carnegie Concert.*

6. Dom Cerulli, Burt Korall, and Mort Nasatir, *The Jazz Word* (New York: Ballantine Books, 1960), 36.

7. From Henry Pleasants, *Serious Music and All That Jazz;* 1969. Reprinted by permission of Simon & Schuster, Inc.

8. Leroy Ostransky, *The Anatomy of Jazz* (Seattle: University of Washington Press, 1960), 50.

9. Improvisation Chamber Ensemble, *Studies in Improvisation*, RCA Victor Red Seal Records, LSC-2558.

Listening Guide Form

Melody
Parts with jazz interpretation
Parts improvised
All parts improvised
Uses blue tones

Tempo
Slow
Moderate speed
Fast
Extremely fast

Meter
$\frac{2}{4}$
$\frac{3}{4}$
$\frac{4}{4}$ (flat four)
Other (identify)

Rhythm
Syncopated patterns very fast

Harmony
Relaxed (not complex)
Uses IV to I
Tense (complex)
Chord progressions

Texture
Vertical (homophonic)
Horizontal (polyphonic)
Both

Tone color
Solo spots played by:
Banjo
Clarinet
Cornet (trumpet)
Guitar
Percussion
Piano
Saxophone
String bass
Trombone
Other (identify)

Form
Twelve-bar blues
AABA
ABAB
Other (identify)

Size of group
Small (two to eight players)
Large, with sections

Mood or feeling tone
Frantic, driving
Happy
Low key, understatement
Rough, aggressive
Soulful
Sweet, calm, smooth
Other (identify)

Era or style

Piano style
Left hand (bass part in $\frac{2}{4}$ rhythm)
Left hand (walking bass)
Left hand (chordal)
Other (identify)

Other jazz influences
Classical
Contemporary large band
Electronic
Free form
Liturgical
Rock
Popular

The following is an example, using demonstration 12, of Early New Orleans Dixieland.

Melody
Parts with jazz interpretation
Parts improvised
Uses blue tones

Tempo
Moderate speed

Meter
$\frac{4}{4}$ (flat four)

Rhythm
Syncopated but not fast

Harmony
Relaxed (not complex)
Uses IV to I
Blues chord progression

Texture
Horizontal (polyphonic)

Tone color
Solo spots played by clarinet

Form
AABA

Size of group
Small

Mood or feeling tone
Happy

Era or Style
Early New Orleans Dixieland

Piano style
No piano

Other jazz influences
Just Early New Orleans
Dixieland

---

10. Schuller, The Swing Era, 223.
11. Dave Brubeck Quartet, *Time Out*, Columbia Records, CL-1397, and *Time Further Out*, Columbia Records, CS-8490; Don Ellis Orchestra, *Live at Monterey*, Pacific Jazz Records, PJ-10112, and *Live in 32/3/4 Time*, Pacific Jazz Records, PJ-10123; Elvin Jones Quartet, "That Five-Four Bag," *The Definitive Jazz Scene*, vol. 3.
12. Leonard Bernstein, *What Is Jazz?* Columbia Records, 919.
13. Charlie Parker, "Parker's Mood," "Bird Gets the Worm," and "Merry Go Round," *Charlie Parker Memorial Album*, vol. 1, Savoy Records, MG-12000.
14. Homer Ulrich, *Music: A Design for Listening*, 2d ed. (New York: Harcourt, Brace & World, 1962), 449.

Jazz Heritages

Jazz in America came about through a blending

of African and European musical heritages.

African and European

The union of the African and European musical cultures did not take place and then abruptly cease. The continuation of this blending is shown not only by the addition of more complex rhythms from Africa in the 1940s but also by the innovation of present-day third-stream music that uses the European musical forms and harmonic system. Too often it is stated that jazz is the music of the African American. However, this belief falsely implies (1) that only African Americans can play jazz, thereby excluding such white musicians as Goodman, Teagarden, Beiderbecke, and Evans, and (2) that African Americans are successful in no other kind of music.

There are far too many excellent musicians to begin listing the talented nonjazz African American artists, both composers and performers. However, the point should be made that each new style (or era) in jazz was pioneered by an African American musician. Although any talented player of any race can probably learn to play the different styles, and although race has nothing to do with developing a style after its innovation, the African American was and is the innovator.

Mrs. William Grant Still (Verna Arvey), the wife of an outstanding African American classical composer, discussed this question as it related to her husband and George Gershwin:

It was with considerable surprise that I read in a recent book [Music in the Twentieth Century, by William W. Austin, New York: W. W. Norton, 1966] by a Cornell University professor, the statement that "Gershwin's Rhapsody helped inspire William Grant Still to make use of Jazz and Negro folk song in his symphonies and operas." Surprise, because it seemed so unrealistic to assume that a Negro composer could have been motivated by a white composer who had made no secret of his own devotion to Negro musicians and their music.

For Gershwin's indebtedness has been well documented over the years, and it does no disservice to his memory to acknowledge it, since he himself did just that during his lifetime. One of these acknowledgments came when on August 30, 1926 he autographed a copy of his Rhapsody in Blue to W. C. Handy. "For Mr. Handy," he wrote respectfully (for at the time the beloved Father of the Blues was almost twice his age), "Whose early 'blue' songs are the forefathers of this work. With admiration and best wishes."

Those people who lived—as did Gershwin—through the exciting Twenties in New York can attest to the presence of both Gershwins (George and Ira) at nearly every place where Negroes were performing, or even enjoying themselves at parties.[1]

Duke Ellington and his orchestra at the Fifth Avenue Presbyterian Church in New York City on December 26, 1965.

Bettmann Archive

13

Music from Africa

Music was by far the most vital and demonstrative form of expression in the life of Africans. From morning until night, from the cradle to the grave, everything was done to the rhythm of their music. The art form was passed down by word of mouth from one generation to the next and was a means of preserving tribal traditions, ambitions, and lore.

Music performed a vital role in maintaining the unity of the social group. Singing the same songs in the same way at the same time bound individuals together and established a strong group feeling. Whether religious or secular, improvised or traditional, the music of Africans was a powerful influence in their lives.

In Africa, music was for a whole community, and everyone from youngest to oldest participated. Music was so interwoven with work, play, and social and religious activities that to isolate one phase from its role in the total life of the people is difficult. Africans themselves did not consider their music an art, which is seldom taken seriously in their birthplace. Innovators such as Charlie Parker have always suffered from this fact.

Many of the daily activities within a tribe were accompanied by the pulse and beating of a drum. It was a part of religious ceremonies and special occasions such as births, deaths, and weddings. Drums, ranging in size from very small hand drums to great tree drums (sometimes fifteen feet high) were used to frighten wild beasts and to bolster courage in times of emergency. The drum served as one fundamental means of coordinating the movements of the wonderful rhythmic native dances, aided hunting parties, and played an important part in sport and physical exhibitions.

African slaves brought these traditions to the United States and nurtured them in the woe and hardship of slavery. Obviously, the slaves did not intentionally invent a new music at this point; rather, the new music arose unconsciously from the transplantation of the African culture and the African Americans' struggle for survival.

African Rhythms

One common misconception about the origins of jazz is that its rhythms came from Africa. Actually, it is only the *emphasis* on rhythm that can truly be designated African, not the direct influence of any specific rhythmic pattern.[2] Three important points to keep in mind concerning Africans and rhythmic sounds are that (1) religion, very important in the cultures of Africans, is a daily way of life, not just a Sunday activity; (2) African religions are greatly oriented toward ritual—their sincerest form of expression; and (3) African rituals have always involved a great deal of dancing, so rhythmic sounds have always been very important in the lives of Africans.

This does not mean that European music is not rhythmic. A very short excursion into Bach, for example, reveals that if his inventions are not played rhythmically, they are not played well. At the time when the chief exponents of jazz were generically closest to their African ancestry, the rhythms used by these jazz performers were very simple, far removed from the complex pattern combinations used by the natives in Africa. The rhythm used by these early jazz players generally consisted of quarter notes evenly spaced in the measure of music without syncopation or accent. At this time, the very complex African rhythms should have been most influential on their performance!

However, emphasis on rhythm is such a natural element in African life that even African languages are very rhythmically oriented. Because of their rhythmic cultures, Africans were interested in Spanish music. Some researchers even state that Spanish music is so rhythmical mainly because Spain was once conquered by the Moors from North Africa. Thus, it is conceivable that slaves in America heard something from their past in this particular branch of European music. In a pamphlet entitled *Afro-American Music*, William Tallmadge writes of African penetration into Spain:

This penetration occurred during the Mohammedan conquest [758–1492], and accounts for much of the highly individualistic and non-European rhythmic character of Spanish music. Spanish fandangos, tangos, habaneras, etc., were derived from African antecedents. This Spanish music readily amalgamated with the music of the African slaves who were shipped to Latin American countries as early as 1510. Afro-Spanish music influenced the music in North America in two ways: through Spanish possessions in America and through the importation of slaves into America from Spanish colonies. Since New Orleans played such an important part in the early development of jazz, it should be mentioned that Spain controlled that city from 1763 to 1803.

It was soon discovered that slaves adjusted themselves to conditions in North America much better if they were first shipped to the West Indies and acclimatized there before being sent on. Latin American influences have, therefore, been a factor in Afro-American music from earliest times. "Jelly Roll" Morton, a jazz pioneer, once stated that Spanish rhythms were a part of jazz. In connection with that statement one might point out that the traditional bass pattern of [one strain of] the "St. Louis Blues" is a tango. Latin American rhythms continue to exert an influence on the progress of jazz, as these rhythmic patterns are employed in many contemporary styles.[3]*

There is no doubt that the Moorish conquest considerably changed the music of Spain, Portugal, and southern France. Therefore, European music brought to the United States had already been influenced by Africa.

---

[3]*From William Tallmadge, *Afro-American Music*. Music Educators National Conference, 1957, Washington, D.C. Reprinted by permission.

Many slaves who were first brought to America were first kept on the Caribbean islands (which were French or Spanish possessions before they became British) for months and sometimes for years and thus were heavily exposed to French or Spanish music before ever arriving in the United States.

European Influences

The melodic feature of jazz is inherited directly from European music. The **diatonic** and **chromatic** scales used in jazz are the same as those used for centuries by European composers (Africans used a **pentatonic** scale).

The harmonic sonorities also derive from European sources: polkas, **quadrilles**, hymns, and marches. This does not dispute the fact that Africans had varying pitches in their drums, reeds, and logs, but the sense of harmony absorbed by jazz is strictly that of the European school.

The African Americans who first sang gospel music, work songs, and so on satisfied the desire to imitate rich

Creole Music

A segregation movement was initiated about ten years after the end of the Civil War. The **Creoles**—people with

Call and Response

The **call-and-response pattern** heard recurrently in jazz can be traced directly to African tribal traditions. In its original form, the call and response was a ritual in which a leader shouted a cry to which the group responded.[4] A common, present-day form is a congregation's response to a minister or another leader. One hears the influence of the call-and-response pattern constantly in jazz. One example is the musical instance called **trading fours**, in which two improvising instrumentalists play solo parts on alternating four bars. In short, they are responding to each other's musical thoughts.[5] This interplay can be heard on many jazz recordings. Listen to Stanley Turrentine on tenor saxophone and Kenny Burrell on guitar as they use a minor blues tune to go so far as to alternate single measures of improvisation.[6] At one spot in "Casa Loma Stomp," the complete brass and saxophone sections alternate with one measure apiece (NW, 217, side 1, band 2).[7]

Another example is when a solo instrument "calls" and is then responded to by the background melodic and/or percussive figures of the other members of the band or of a specific section of the band. Listen to the entire band responding to Count Basie's piano in "Queer Street."[8] On the swing part of the cassette with this book, the clarinet solo is answered by the trombone section; later, the saxophone section is answered by the brass section. In Manny Albam's "Blues Company," Oliver Nelson and Phil Woods on saxophones are answered by trombones.[9] In Benny Goodman's "King Porter Stomp," Goodman's clarinet has the brass section as a background, whereas the saxophone section is the background for Harry James's trumpet solo. Later in the same selection, the brass and saxes alternate measures.[10]

European melody and harmony. On the other hand, nothing in European music could compare with their oral sonority and the vitality of their music, so blessed with rhythmic tradition.

The musical forms of Europe became standard in jazz works. The twelve-bar strains, such as those found in the blues, are directly traceable to very early European music. Most jazz is constructed in a theme-and-variations form that is symmetrical. Africans, however, were not concerned with symmetry of form. In fact, if their music resulted in a symmetrical construction, they considered it crude and unimaginative.

African Americans in the Early Colonies

The evolution of African music in the colonies depended greatly on the particular colony to which the slaves were brought. In the Latin-Catholic colonies, their musical life was allowed more latitude. Latin planters were not too concerned with the activities of slaves as long as the work was done. Thus, slaves were allowed to play their drums, sing, and dance when not working. The British Protestants, on the other hand, tried to convert the slaves to Christianity. The slaves in these colonies were required to conceal their "pagan" musical inheritance. (It is interesting to speculate on how the resulting music would have sounded if the slaves from Africa had been taken to some part of Asia. For example, if African and Japanese music had influenced each other centuries ago, what would have been the result? Would it resemble any music we know today?)

Congo Square

The name **Congo Square** is frequently mentioned in many accounts of jazz. Congo Square was a large field in New Orleans where slaves were allowed to gather on Sunday to sing, dance, and play their drums in their traditional native manner. (The name was changed to Beauregard Square in 1893. In 1974, plans were finalized for the area to be part of the very impressive Louis Armstrong Park.) The principal significance of Congo Square to the history of jazz is that it gave this original African music a place to be heard where it "could influence and be influenced by European music."[11] When the famous dances of Congo Square began around 1817, the backgrounds of the participants produced a music that was often a cross between French and Spanish with African rhythms.

Negro and French or Spanish ancestry—were ostracized from white society and joined the ranks of the African Americans. Prior to segregation, the Creoles had the rights and privileges of whites, which included conservatory training for musicians. The combination of the musical talents of conservatory-trained Creoles and the spontaneous oral tradition of African Americans resulted in an interchange of musical expression, and the music that evolved from this assimilation was an early form of jazz.

The unfavorable aspects of this segregation movement are still apparent today, as pointed out by Charles Suber:

There is a sociological reason why more black student musicians are not involved in jazz. That reason lies in the images retained by many black educators, school administrators, and community leaders. Jazz means slavery, sporting houses, "natural rhythm" and sin and damnation. Jazz stands for those unpleasant things that could "reduce endowments" or "debase our cultural standards."[12]

An interesting point is that so much of the musical instruction in the United States propagates the theory that the music originating from European culture typifies what is good in the arts; yet the Europeans accepted jazz as an art form long before the Americans. It is often felt that jazz players are unregimented individualists who play together cohesively with a mutual feeling; these opposing concepts (individuality and unity) can be viewed as representing the freedom of America.

Most jazz historians leave a considerable gap between the activities at Congo Square and the first known jazz band led by Buddy Bolden at the turn of the twentieth century. Actually, there was no gap because this period was filled by the Creole music in New Orleans. It was natural that this music was mainly French and Spanish and much more advanced (at least by European standards) than the music of the first jazz bands. Henry Pleasants points to the similarities of jazz and early European music:

What I want to stress, however, is not the differences separating the two idioms, but the similarities. The differences are, indeed, startling and disturbing to those who think of the traditional European criteria as immutable, so startling and disturbing that they have tended to overshadow and obscure the similarities. But it is in the similarities that I see a fertile area for the reconciliation of long standing incompatibility and for a fruitful give-and-take in music education.

This reconciliation is easier the further back we go in European musical history. The most common form of jazz has always been theme and variations, advanced and refined in bebop to something closer to chaconne or passacaglia. The jazz band arrangement or original composition bears an unmistakable resemblance to the concerto grosso of the eighteenth century. Without its distinctive rhythmic and phrasing characteristics, the jazz combo is indistinguishable from the Baroque chamber group.

Let me be precise about this. If I were a teacher today, trying to give my students an insight into seventeenth- and eighteenth-century musical conventions, I would suggest that they study sympathetically the conventions of jazz. How to fill in a bass line in continuo playing, for example; how to improvise from a figured bass. Every jazz pianist and every jazz bass player does it, and the best of them do it superbly. Or how to apply ornaments and embellishments. Every jazz musician does it, and the best of them do it every bit as well as it was done in the seventeenth and eighteenth centuries, and probably better. And the embellishments, I hasten to add, are essentially the same.

If I were a singing teacher trying to assist my pupils to a mastery of seventeenth- and eighteenth-century practices, I would have them listen to Frank Sinatra, Sarah Vaughan, Ella Fitzgerald, and Peggy Lee. If you want to know what appoggiatura and rubato are all about, listen to Sinatra. No one has ever used them better than he. If you want to study the mordent, listen to Bing Crosby. If you want to know about the portamento and slurs and melodic deviation, listen to Sarah Vaughan. None of these singers, I may assume, think in those terms. They may not use those terms, but they do use those devices. And what makes their use of them so instructive is the spontaneity. They use tempo rubato, appoggiatura, mordent, slur, portamento, and so on not because they are told that someone else used them two or three hundred years ago, but because they feel they are appropriate or even essential to the articulation of text and melodic line, which is precisely why they came into use in the first place.[13]*

Field Hollers (Cries)

West Africa had no art music by European standards, only functional music used for work, love, war, ceremonies, or communication. American slaves were often not allowed to talk to one another in the fields while working, but garbled singing was permitted. They established communication between themselves by **field hollers**, or cries, that whites could not understand. The outstanding element of the field cry that is constantly used in jazz is the bending of a tone,[14] which is simply the overexaggerated use of a slide or slur. A tone is bent (slurred) upward to a different tone or pitch, downward to another pitch, upward to no specific tone, or downward to no specific tone. Examples of the four typical ways of employing this feature in jazz follow (for the notation of these examples, see Appendix B):

1. Example 6A demonstrates the bending of a note upward to a specific pitch (demonstration 0 on the accompanying cassette).

2. Example 6B uses a blues cliché to show the bending of a note downward to a specific pitch (demonstration 0).

3. Example 6C illustrates the bending of a note upward to no specific pitch (demonstration 0).

---

[13]*From Henry Pleasants, "Afro-American Epoch—Emergence of a New Idiom," in *Music Educators Journal*, Vol. 57, No. 1, September, 1970. Reprinted by permission.

4. Example 6D illustrates the bending of a note downward to no specific pitch (demonstration O). As it is demonstrated here, this is called a "fall-off." Every jazz fan has heard ensemble endings with this type of bending.

The adaptation of these effects allowed the musician a freedom of embellishment not available in European music.

Work Songs

Some African American songs were born on the banks of the Mississippi to the accompaniment of work tasks associated with the riverboats. Others were born in the mines of Virginia, in the cotton fields of the South, and in the labor gangs of prison camps in Texas and Georgia.

The singing of these songs had one thing in common: They were sung without instrumental accompaniment and were associated with a monotonous, regularly recurring physical task. Also, the singing was sprinkled with grunts and groans inspired by the physical effort of straining muscular activity. Many years later, these sounds became a distinguishing feature of both vocal and instrumental jazz.

Rex Harris has described work songs as "tribal songs which started life in West Africa."[15] In addition, he stated that they were used "to ease the monotony of a regular task and to synchronize a word or exclamation with a regularly repeated action."[16] An example of this type of work song is the "Song of the Volga Boatman," probably the best known of all work songs. The grunt indicates the exact time when concerted action is to take place—in this case, when pulling on the oars. (Circus workers standing in a circle hammering huge tent stakes are another example of accomplishing a difficult task through rhythmic coordination; for notation example 7, see Appendix B.)

A good work-song leader was essential in coordinating the workers. He not only caused the work to be more efficiently done but also helped to make time pass. Huddie Ledbetter (Leadbelly) is reputed to have been one of the best leadmen ever, and recordings are available to prove it.[17]

Though work songs varied according to their use, the main contribution of the work song to jazz was the emphasis on rhythm and meter.

Religious Music

Spirituals

"The impact of Christianity on the African Americans was, of course, the origin of the spiritual; owing to the fact that practically all of the missionary work was done by nonconformist ministers, their evangelical hymns set the style and flavour of the spiritual as we know it today."[18] Around 1800 there occurred in America a religious mass movement known as the Great Awakening. **Spirituals** and revival **hymns** that carried a great amount of emotion were sung at camp meetings. Spirituals, often called "hymns with a beat," were the first original songs created by Protestant African American slaves on American soil.

Spirituals are an excellent example of the blend of African and European cultures and can be easily traced back to 1780, but most seem to have originated between 1790 and 1883. The slaves added their own rhythmic emphasis to any music taught to them, liturgical or otherwise. The better-known spirituals of today are the type that were generally heard in large concert halls. Examples are the familiar "Swing Low, Sweet Chariot" and "Nobody Knows the Trouble I've Seen." The European influence of more emphasis on melody and harmony than on rhythm is obvious in these songs.

The greatest number of spirituals performed in the 1800s employed a call-and-response pattern[19] in which there was great emphasis on rhythm, with hand clapping and foot stomping—an example of the West African influence on European liturgy—in a set pattern of emphasis on the second and fourth beats. As Borneman states, "The accent was shifted from the strong to the weak beat."[20] Piano players executed this rhythmic accentuation with the left hand and brought it to ragtime music.

There are many similarities between popular songs and rhythms and religious music in African American church services today. Methodist John Wesley once defended such similarities: "Why should the devil be the only one to make pleasing music?"[21]

Early African American church music can be divided into three categories:

1. Many of the selections were improvised, made up at the moment by the preacher and his congregation; they would be remembered and eventually notated. Many of these were based on the blues chord progression because of its simplicity and because it seemed natural and flowing.

2. Some African American congregations would adopt European church music and add not only their own rhythmic concepts but also their own variations.

3. In many cases, African ritual music was altered so that it could be used in these services in America.

The fervent participation in their "syncopated hymns" is something very remote from the Western conception of reverent quietude as an expression of worship, but hymns without beat are to the Negro religion without God. It is as natural, and no more naive, for them to sing hymns in this style as it was for Renaissance painters to portray Christ in Italian dress and environment.[22]

The spiritual, besides being a type of folk song, made its contribution to the development of the popular song and to vocal jazz. Although the singing of African Americans attracted little attention in the period before the Civil War, their singing of spirituals began to arouse interest and widespread attention after the war. It is interesting to note that the first collection of American spirituals, *Slave Songs of the United States*,[23] was published in 1867. The collection contains many errors in notation because, in the words of the editors, "their notations could only approximate, not accurately reproduce, the characteristic traits of the music in actual performance."[24]

The singing of spirituals was primarily a group activity performed in a religious setting or on a plantation. There is evidence that spirituals were used in work situations as well. A good example is "Michael, Row the Boat Ashore," one of the songs found in the 1867 collection. Often the song leader would be joined by the chorus singing the refrain (call-and-response pattern).

African Americans also participated in camp meetings, singing the same hymns and revival songs as the whites. In addition, however, they practiced a ceremony after religious services that had a direct influence on the preservation of the spiritual in its traditional performance style. This ceremony, called the "shout" (or "holy dance"), included a group of singers and shouters who would stand to one side singing the spiritual and clapping hands with great fervor while another group would shuffle and dance in a circle with a monotonous thumping of their feet. The swing element in the spiritual was kept alive through this rhythmic intensity of performance.

It is important to recognize the two trends that occurred in the development of spirituals in the middle 1800s. One movement adopted the forms and techniques of European art music, whereas the other conserved the traditional folk character by retaining the characteristics of the African tribal influences. The former spread rapidly through harmonized arrangements sung by choirs and concert performances by trained soloists. The latter, a style much like the shout or holy dance, was cultivated in rural areas or small communities, attracting little attention from outsiders. This type of African American vocal singing used traits that are fundamentally of African origin.

Gospel

In 1921, at a convention of African American Baptists, Thomas A. Dorsey was so inspired by the leading gospel singers that he decided to devote his life to the composition and singing of gospel music. His five-hundred-odd songs became so popular that in 1973 he was designated "The Father of Gospel Music" by the publication *Black World*.[25] His composition "There Will Be Peace in the Valley," was written for Mahalia Jackson. He also composed the most popular gospel song of all time, "Precious Lord, Take My Hand."

By 1940, gospel music became so popular in the Holiness Churches that these singers were prompted to become professionals and to go on tours. By 1948, Sister Rosetta Tharpe was singing before as many as thirty thousand people in stadiums and parks. She had an unusual ability to raise audiences to new emotional heights through her moaning techniques and shaking head.

In 1950, Mahalia Jackson recorded "Move On Up a Little Higher," and the Ward Singers recorded "Surely, God Is Able." Both sold over a million copies, thus establishing gospel music in the mainstream of American music.

Gospel music, to be better understood, has to be experienced in person. By tradition, when gospel music is performed in African American churches, it is important that the audience respond. In fact, the performer's skill is measured by the amount of active support, or "talking back," that comes from the listeners. Often a singer becomes so caught up in the intensity of the moment that he or she begins to improvise and embellish the melodic lines by bending, sliding, or adding tones, all enhancing the intense feeling generated by mutual emotional release.

Some gospel ensembles consist of groups of men who sing unaccompanied and supply their rhythm by slapping their thighs or hands in time to the music. Other ensembles are composed of women who sing with piano accompaniment and clap their hands for rhythmic accentuation.

The melody of a gospel song can be embellished in several ways. These techniques are used mostly by individual soloists or a soloist backed by a vocal ensemble. One of the most popular techniques is to use a passing tone, that is, one inserted between two tones that are a third apart. Another technique is to add one tone either above or below the last tone of the phrase, and yet another is to use several "extra" tones sung in rapid succession either stepwise or by skips.

Gospel singing has been freely adapted by performers of other types of music and is, in a sense, a synthesis of many American vocal styles dating back at least to the Fisk Jubilee Singers. It must be remembered that spirituals and gospel songs are not necessarily musical works of yesterday, as the thoughts and lyrics contained in them are often contemporary. A fine set of recordings (four sides) includes a collection of gospel songs recorded between 1926 and 1968.[26] In fact, gospel and jazz are still partners in vocal groups such as Take 6.[27]

Spirituals sometimes contained symbolic references to the railways or rivers that led to freedom or to heaven, and sometimes the songs gave directions for escaping from slavery. Most spirituals and gospel songs refer to biblical characters such as Daniel, Moses, Joshua, and Gabriel. Many are well-known choral and nonjazz instrumental melodies (e.g., "Nobody Knows the Trouble I've Seen" and "Swing Low, Sweet Chariot"), and others are standard dixieland and other jazz pieces (e.g., "When the Saints Go Marching In" and "A Closer Walk with Thee").

Gospel songs and spirituals are often considered religious forms of the blues. Blues singer T-Bone Walker agrees:

Of course, the blues comes a lot from the church, too. The first time I ever heard a boogie-woogie piano was the first time I went to church. That was the Holy Ghost Church in Dallas, Texas. That boogie-woogie was a kind of blues, I guess. Then the preacher used to preach in a bluesy tone sometimes. . . . Lots of people think I'm going to be a preacher when I quit this business because of the way I sing the blues. They say that it sounds like a sermon.

The visitor to a church in Harlem, or on Chicago's South Side, will not find a great contrast to the ecstatic atmosphere that might be found at a jazz concert or in a jazz club. He will find the identical rhythms, the same beat, and the same swing in the music. Frequently, he will find jazz instruments—saxophones, trombones, drums; he will hear boogie-woogie bass lines and blues structures and see enraptured people who beat time with their hands and sometimes even begin to dance.[28]

In the early Catholic churches, participation in the services by even the most faithful worshipers was limited.

In the Latin-Catholic colonies, slaves often worshiped a combination of Catholic saints and voodoo deities:

On the English and Protestant side, the question is as diverse as are the numerous sects of the reformed churches. The Protestant churches are less rigid than the Catholic church: one listens to the sermon and then freely sings hymns. It is this freedom which allows one to celebrate God according to one's own conscience which was to encourage a host of Negroes into the Protestant religions. Furthermore, God, among the Protestants, is praised in everyday language and not in the dead language, Latin. This permitted the Negroes to sing to God according to their hearts and according to some of their own traditions. The ancestral rhythm was reborn, transfiguring a religion.[29]

Methodist hymns were the most emotional, but even these were too somber for the slaves; therefore, improvisation gradually began to creep into hymn singing. "The hymn book of the day stressed part-singing which harmonized only by accident."[30] This accidental vocal harmonization indicates that the voice lines were invented independently of each other. In music, this is known as **polyphonic** (horizontal) construction, and this approach to the creation of musical line was carried over into dixieland music and was later employed in more contemporary jazz styles. Polyphonic music makes use of two or more melodies that work well together but that also seem independent of one another. By contrast, **homophonic** music is more like singing a harmonizing melody to an existing melody. Both melodies are essentially the same only at different pitches. (For notational examples 8A and 8B of polyphonic and homophonic music, see Appendix B.)

Often, some confusion arises regarding the difference between spirituals and gospel songs. Although the two terms are often used interchangeably, gospel songs are usually considered religious songs that recount passages from the scriptures, whereas spirituals are considered hymns.[31]

In 1867, a choral group from Fisk University in Nashville, Tennessee, left school to do a series of concerts to raise money for their college. This group, called the Fisk Jubilee Singers (*jubilee* is another name for a very spirited, joyful hymn), traveled all over the United States, England, and Europe, carrying spirituals, gospel songs, and work songs to an international audience. Examples of this type of singing today are heard in the records of Mahalia Jackson.[32] Generally, most gospel music is very simple in melody and harmony, and the excitement comes from the jazz type of rhythmic pulse.

Mahalia Jackson and the African American Church

Gospel music as an art form was all but ignored until the recognition—or, rather, the great triumphs—of Mahalia Jackson. Jackson never performed in a jazz situation,

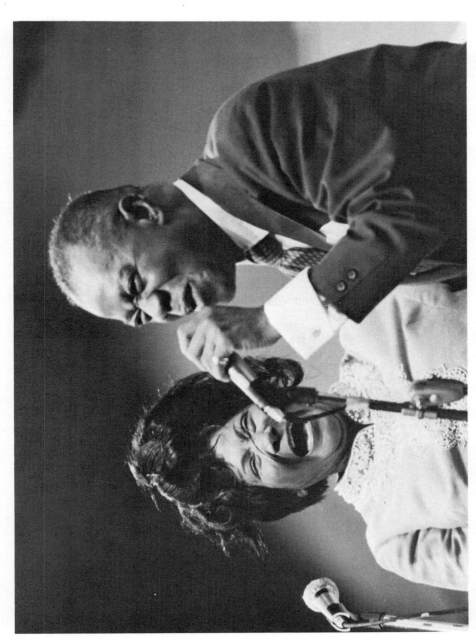

Mahalia Jackson with Louis Armstrong.
Courtesy of Les McCann

and she sang only songs that she believed served her religious feelings. She believed so profoundly in her religious convictions that she felt entirely free to expose her emotions as sincerely as any singer had ever done.

Francis Ward, writing about Jackson in the *Los Angeles Times*, said, "The earliest important musical influence in her life was blues singer Bessie Smith whose recording of 'Careless Love' was a favorite of Miss Jackson's and from which she learned much about the phrasing of African American folk music. Despite Bessie Smith's influence, Miss Jackson never sang blues or any kind of jazz, only gospel."[33]

For many years, Jackson's singing was not accepted in middle-class African American churches, as her music was a reminder of a lifestyle that parishioners seemed to want to forget. However, record sales grew, and she primed the world for the many gospel singers who eventually followed. Jackson went on to become one of the most stirring, most sought-after singers in the world. She died of heart disease in Chicago on January 27, 1972.

When a gospel group gets up on stage before an audience, two things become important to them. They want to sing well and to express some religious convictions so that they can reach the souls of the listeners. When the soul of an audience is reached, you will very often see the people shouting, crying, screaming, clapping as a genuine response to the music.

Although many Gospel groups write some of their own material, most of the songs making up the repertoires of these singers are old spirituals and religious songs that date back to slavery. These songs have been passed down from generation to generation and the people have sung them in church since early childhood. There are about fifteen or twenty "Gospel standards" that are sung by hundreds of choirs, quartets and groups throughout the country. It is therefore important for a group or singer to create his own sound.[34]

The worldwide penchant for spiritual music has not dampened since the early tours by the Fisk Jubilee Singers, a fact aptly demonstrated by Albert McNeil's Jubilee Singers, who have given concerts to standing ovations in twenty-five countries. Some African American churches today still believe that association with jazz is wicked, an attitude that may account for the lack of African American jazz critics. However, because of the sacred works of Duke Ellington and many other fine jazz composers, this attitude has moderated considerably.[35] In an interview with Leonard Feather, singer Vi Redd explained that:

the church was people's only hope in the midst of all the discrimination and oppression, so their ties to it remained very close and they felt obliged to go along with whatever precepts it dictated.

I was brought up in this environment, but not as strictly as some of the other children, perhaps because my father was a musician. Some of the kids I associated with were not even allowed to have a record player in the house. They used to come over to my place to listen to King Cole Trio records. That was their only opportunity to listen to jazz.

Her [Mahalia Jackson's] music has the same harmonic structure, the same feeling, in many of those gospel songs. By the same token, Milt Jackson is a product of the sanctified church. Sarah Vaughan, Dinah Washington and a lot of the greatest jazz artists came directly out of a church background; yet the people in the church, in all sincerity, still refuse to accept it when it's known as jazz.[36]

Milt Jackson, a leading jazz vibraphonist, was asked many times about the origin of his "funky" style. His answer was always that it came from the church. When asked about "soul" in jazz, he replied, "What is soul in jazz? It's what comes from inside."[37] Good contemporary jazz players often record music that clearly is church music, such as Stanley Turrentine's recording of "I Told Jesus."[38] Even the most casual listening to Ray Charles will reveal the obvious relationship between jazz and African American church music.[39]

Marching Bands

At first, African American music in the United States was vocal, being accompanied by a rhythm of clapping, stomping, and beating on virtually anything available. Then gradually, after the Civil War, African Americans were able to make some instruments and to buy pawned and war surplus instruments. Marching bands began to influence

Marching band in New Orleans.
Courtesy of Ray Avery

their music. (Military bands, important in all French settlements, also influenced the development of jazz.)

There were many other bands in the New Orleans area as well. Every secret society or fraternity, for example, had its own band, and there were bands for hire that were not affiliated with any organization. Most of the early jazz players started their careers in such bands, playing marches, polkas, quadrilles, and so on (NW, 269, "Castle Walk," side 1, band 2; NW, 269, "Castle House Rag," side 1, band 1; NW, 269, "Memphis Blues," side 1, band 3).

At the turn of the twentieth century, the most publicized use of marching bands was for funerals. These bands were used not only in New Orleans but also in the Southeast and as far west as Oklahoma. Such bands, usually composed of five or six players, should be considered a separate type of musical aggregation in contrast to large modern bands. Nonetheless, these small marching bands played an important part in the early development of jazz.

For a funeral procession, the African American band would drone a traditional funeral march on the way to the cemetery. After the burial ceremony, the band would march two or three blocks from the cemetery with only a conservative drumbeat. The band would then break into a jazz type of march, such as "Didn't He Ramble" or "When the Saints Go Marching In." The reasoning behind this established plan was that the traditional funeral music elicited mourning, whereas the later use of the more rhythmic music signified that the departed was going to a happier place—a cause for rejoicing.

When the band began to play a livelier version of the march, its followers would gradually respond more to the music. Their responses were often in the form of clapping, stomping, or any physical rhythmic movement leading toward dancing. In those early days, a band often marched directly from the street into a hall, where the same music accompanied dancing.[40]

The most common instrumentation used by these bands consisted of cornet, trombone, clarinet, tuba, banjo, and drums. One of the first leaders of a jazz marching band is thought to have been Buddy Bolden, who is usually credited with establishing the set instrumentation for these bands. Bolden combined brass-band music with ragtime, quadrilles, and blues in the first stages of jazz. The small size of these marching bands made the groups adaptable for various functions such as advertising campaigns, weddings, serenades, and so on. A group might also perform in a horse-drawn wagon, an activity that generated the name **tailgate trombone** to describe how the trombone player sat at the end of the wagon in order to have sufficient room for the trombone slide.

Because this music lent itself so well to dancing, much of the early jazz repertoire developed from marches.

The transformation of straightforward marches into jazz may be compared with the process which took place when hymns were changed into spirituals. . . . This jazzing of marches was achieved partly by the trick of shifting the accent from the strong to the weak beat and partly by allowing solo players to "decorate" the melody they were playing—solo improvisation; or several players to indulge in their extemporization simultaneously—**collective improvisation.**[41] [Boldface added]

The regularity of march music could have easily influenced early jazz; today, people often "swing" as they march. The integration of the playing of the conservatory-trained Creoles with the self-taught African Americans produced well-played marches with the freedom of an oral tradition.

Most important to jazz are the emphasis on rhythm taken from African music, the harmonies taken from European music, and the melodies added by the improvisations from American culture. All these elements fuse to make jazz an American music rather than the music solely of the African Americans, who were (and remain) its pioneers and innovators.

Summary

Jazz began with a blending of African and European musical cultures. From Africa came the emphasis on rhythm and the call-and-response patterns. The European influences encompass the kind of melodies, harmonies, and forms used in jazz.

The Creoles demonstrated a combination of conservatory training and the oral tradition from Africa that proved to play an important part in the origins of jazz. Work songs emphasized rhythm and meter, but the foundations of jazz seemed to emanate more from religious services than from any other source.

■ First and Second Lines

When the bands marched down the street, their enthusiasm was enhanced by their "second lines," found in every band. The "first line," or **front line** (not an actual line), was composed of the players of instruments. Those composing the second line were young people who danced and clapped and generally encouraged their heroes in the first line. One of the second line's duties was to carry the instrument cases. Another, more unusual obligation was to protect the first line from competitive agitators from other bands. Of course, the goal of each member of the second line was to move up to the first line someday.

An important lesson to be learned from this chapter is that although the musical materials may have been pulled from Western European roots, the pioneers and innovators of jazz were mainly African American musicians.

For Further Study

1. American jazz came about through a blend of the musical cultures of Africa and Europe. Discuss the influences on early jazz made by Africans and those made by Europeans.

2. Explain why it is incorrect to say that jazz rhythms came from Africa.

3. Explain the importance of Congo Square and other similar places in the South to the development of jazz.

4. Compare and contrast spiritual songs to gospel songs and to modern liturgical jazz.

5. Describe the following and discuss their contribution to early jazz:

   a. Field hollers
   b. Work songs
   c. Spirituals
   d. Marching bands

6. Give the instrumentation most commonly used in the early marching bands.

7. What is the difference between the construction of homophonic (vertical) harmony and polyphonic (horizontal) harmony?

8. Pretend that you are pounding railroad spikes as you sing the work song "I Got to Roll." Notice the places in the music where the singers give a half-shout or grunt. (This song is found on page 544 of Alan Lomax's The Folk Songs of North America [Doubleday], a splendid resource for background material on spirituals, work songs, ballads, and blues.)

Additional Reading Resources

Brooks, Tilford. *America's Black Musical Heritage.*

Haskins, Jim. *Black Music in America.*

Roach, Hildred. *Black American Music: Past and Present.*

Roberts, John Storm. *Black Music of Two Worlds.*

Note: Complete information, including name of publisher and date of publication, is provided in this book's bibliography.

Notes

1. Verna Arvey, "Afro-American Music Memo," *Music Journal* 27, no. 9 (November 1969): 36.

2. "Royal Drums of the Abatusi," *History of Classic Jazz.*

3. William Tallmadge, *Afro-American Music,* (Washington, D.C.: Music Educators National Conference, 1957).

4. Ethnic Folkways Library, 01482B, vol. 1, Secular.

5. Santos Brothers, "Beat the Devil," *Jazz for Two Trumpets,* Metro Jazz Records, E1015.

6. Kenny Burrell, "Chittlins Con Carne," *Three Decades of Jazz,* vol. 1.

7. Glen Gray, "Casa Loma Stomp," *The Jazz Story,* vol. 4.

8. Count Basie, "Queer Street," Columbia Records, 36889.

9. Manny Albam, "Blues Company," *The Definitive Jazz Scene,* vol. 2.

10. Benny Goodman, "King Porter Stomp," *The Great Benny Goodman,* Columbia Records, CL-820; *Big Band Jazz,* Smithsonian Collection of Recordings, cassette 3, band 2.

11. Marshall Stearns, *The Story of Jazz* (London: Oxford University Press, 1958), 38.

12. Charles Suber, "The First Chorus," *Down Beat* 36, no. 9 (May 1969): 4.

13. Henry Pleasants, "Afro-American Epoch—Emergence of a New Idiom," *Music Educators Journal* 57, no. 1 (September 1970): 35–36.

14. "Field Cries or Hollers," Album 8, Library of Congress Recording.

15. Rex Harris, *Jazz* (Baltimore: Penguin Books, 1956), 34.

16. Ibid. 30.

17. *Leadbelly,* Columbia Records, C-30035.

18. Harris, *Jazz,* 47.

19. Stearns, *Story of Jazz,* 93.

20. Ernest Borneman, "The Roots of Jazz," in *Jazz,* ed. Nat Hentoff and Albert J. McCarthy (New York: Holt, Rinehart & Winston, 1959), 17.

21. André Francis, *Jazz* (New York: Grove Press, 1960), 20.

22. Avril Dankworth, *Jazz: An Introduction to Its Musical Basis* (London: Oxford University Press, 1968), 49.

23. William Francis Allan, Charles Pickard Ware, and Lucy McKim Garrison, *Slave Songs of the United States* (New York: Peter Smith, 1867).

24. Gilbert Chase, *America's Music from the Pilgrims to the Present* (New York: McGraw-Hill, 1955), 243.

25. Horace Clarence Boyer, "An Overview: Gospel Music Comes of Age," *Black World* 23, no. 1 (November 1973).

26. *The Gospel Sound,* Columbia Records, KG 31086/KG-31595.

27. Take 6, *Take 6,* Reprise Records, 9 25670-2.

28. Joachim Berendt, *Jazz Book: From New Orleans to Rock and Free Jazz,* trans. Dan Morgenstern (Westport, Conn.: Lawrence Hill & Co., 1975.

29. Francis, *Jazz,* 20.

30. Stearns, *Story of Jazz,* 63.

31. Francis, *Jazz,* 20.

32. Mahalia Jackson, "If We Ever Needed the Lord Before," *Come On Children, Let's Sing,* Columbia Records, CS8225; *Mahalia Jackson,* Columbia Records, CL 644.

33. Francis Ward, "Mahalia Jackson, Renowned Gospel Singer, Dies at 60," *Los Angeles Times,* 28 January 1972.

34. Charles Hobson, "Gospel," *Sounds and Fury* 1, no. 4 (February 1966): 30.

35. Dave Brubeck, *The Light in the Wilderness,* Decca Records, DX3A-7202; Duke Ellington, *Concert of Sacred Music,* RCA Victor Records, LSP-3582; Duke Ellington, *Third Sacred Concert,* RCA Victor Records, APL 1-0785; Lalo Schifrin and Paul Horn, *Jazz Suite on the Mass Texts,* RCA Victor Records, LSP-3414.

36. Leonard Feather, "End of the Brainwash Era," *Down Beat* 36, no. 16 (August 1969): 71.

37. Joachim Berendt, *Jazz Book: From New Orleans to Rock and Free Jazz*, trans. Dan Morgenstern (Westport, Conn.: Lawrence Hill & Co., 1975).

38. Stanley Turrentine, "I Told Jesus," *Salt Song*, CTI Recordings, 6010.

39. Ray Charles, "America," *A Message from the People*, ABC Records, ABCX 755/TRC.

40. Olympia Brass Band of New Orleans, *New Orleans Street Parade*, BASF Recordings, 20678.

41. Harris, *Jazz*, 57.

CHAPTER 3

The Blues

"As Ray Charles says, everybody can understand the blues, regardless of whether they've had them, or were born with them or born without. It doesn't matter."[1]

Bessie Smith.
Courtesy of Columbia Records and the Estate of Carl Van Vechten

Before we discuss the blues, listen to the recording of the hymnlike melody on demonstration 8 (notational example 9A in Appendix B), which uses the blues harmonic construction. Now listen to this same hymnlike melody on demonstration 9 (notational example 9B in Appendix B) as it is given a jazz interpretation. Let us analyze the blues construction.

The blues is neither an era in the chronological development of jazz nor a particular style of playing or singing jazz. Because of the great variety of individual styles used by those who are referred to as "blues" singers, it can be said that there is no single set manner of interpreting this type of jazz that should be labeled a blues style. General research has pictured the blues as something sung by "old" people accompanied by guitar; yet, from the mid-1920s through the 1930s, young energetic singers in Kansas City were accompanied by complete jazz bands.

The blues has been played and sung in every era in the development of jazz and can be performed with many interpretations. Any recorded anthology of jazz in general, or of blues in particular, shows this great variety of styles.[2] Blues can be slow and sad like a dirge, or it can be happy and rollicking. Blues is as important today in jazz as it ever was. Many modern jazz selections still use the basic blues progression with expanded harmonies. Charlie Parker's "Another Hair Do" is a good example of blues in bop, and Milt Jackson's "Bags' Groove" is played in both cool and funky styles, showing minor blues to be apropos in a contemporary setting.[3] Notice on the cassette that accompanies this book the blues melody that progresses through demonstrations of each era. The same blues tune is used in each case, showing the flexibility of this form. Note that no matter how frantic sounding the music may become (e.g., the bop), the same blues structure is very apropos.

The Origin

When African and European music first began to merge, the slaves sang very sad songs about their extreme suffering. The singing was in unison, no chords were determined, and no specific form was designated. At this time, the name "blues" was not in popular use. After the Civil War, however, blacks could perform their music more openly, and, as it united with European music, the blues began to take on a specific musical form. At first this form consisted of the three vocal phrases (AAB) and eight musical measures (each measure had four pulses, or beats; see example 3.2A). The number of musical measures varied between eight, twelve, and sixteen, the most popular being twelve. The chords or harmonies that supported the vocal line also became standardized, and these harmonies supported the three sung phrases. (For a more detailed discussion of the blues form, see Appendix B.)

Slight variations and embellishments may be used to alter this form. If, however, the basic construction does not use the chord progression, the music is *not technically in the blues* format. Therefore, many melodies that have the word "blues" in the title and that are often spoken of as being the blues are not the blues because they lack the blues harmonic construction. The well-known "Bye, Bye Blues," "Limehouse Blues," and "Wabash Blues" are examples. Regardless of their titles and the fact that they are often placed in the blues category, the harmonic progressions of these songs are not constructed in the blues pattern. One of the most famous melodies with a blues title is "The St. Louis Blues," but of the three strains found in this music only two are constructed in the blues pattern. However, "the blues" is bigger than the technical form that normally defines it, and it also has an affective definition that comes more from the manner in which the music is performed than from the form, notes, or harmonies that are sung or played. Let us first look at the music itself and then follow it with the performers who made the blues come alive.

Blue Notes

One characteristic associated with the blues is the **blue tonalities,** which, in the authors' opinion, resulted from the West Africans' search for comparative tones not in the Western European or pentatonic scales.[4] The easiest way to explain blue tonalities without the use of a piano is to use a diagram such as the one in example 3.1.

Western diatonic and chromatic music includes all the tones indicated on the piano keyboard. If the tonal center (C) is arbitrarily used as the basis for discussion, the tones marked with an X are included in the pentatonic scale of the West Africans. As is noted, the West African scale has neither the third or seventh tone nor the flat third or flat seventh. Therefore, imitating either of these tones requires that the pitch be sounded about midway between the tone E-flat and E-natural and between B-flat and B-natural, causing what is called a blue tonality. Because no keys on the piano correspond to these blue tonalities (or blue notes), pianists must obtain the blues effect by striking these two keys at the same time.

Blue notes, or "blue areas," cannot be designated as concretely as stated in this explanation. Jazz players have always had a tendency to bend and twist notes as an additional means of self-expression. Long ago, lowering the fifth note of the chord became a standard device comparable to other blue notes. The use of the flatted fifth can be traced back to early players such as Bubber

Miley in the 1920s. Musicians have always compromised normal musical practice in an effort to find personal expression.

One possible reason a blues tune does not feel as melancholy when performed at a faster tempo is that there is less time to bend the blues notes around in a dramatic fashion. The blues players used these blue areas so much that the scale used by these players permanently included these new blue notes.

Before the field cry, with its bending of notes, musicians had not considered exploring the area of the blue tonalities on instruments. Blue tonalities and note bending can be heard on many records by early jazz brass bands (FI, "Didn't He Ramble," vol. 3). In fact, blue notes are heard in work songs, spirituals, and all styles of jazz. Tin Pan Alley (the popular music publishing industry) has used this element excessively. One can also find the use of blue notes in the works of many twentieth-century classical composers. Blue notes as performed in the blues were of melodic origin and reflected the oral tradition. The European developments placed blue notes in their harmonic structures within their compositions.

Both wind and string instruments offered an opportunity to use blue notes. The string player could pull on the string with the left hand to make a note slightly higher in pitch, whereas the wind player could move the pitch slightly by making changes in the **embouchure** (mouth position). These slight adjustments would create a pitch that falls between two notes on the piano. This out-of-tuneness helped create that blue-note feeling.

Blues Lyrics

The meter of the blues lyrics is generally written in **iambic pentameter.**[5] For example, in "I hate to see the ev'nin' sun go down," the first line is generally repeated (a throwback to the African call and response) and then followed by an original third line. The repetition of the first line gives the singer the necessary time to improvise a third line. Very often the lyrics of the blues do not seem to fit the music, but good blues singers "would stress certain syllables and almost eliminate others so that everything falls into place neatly and surely."[6] Each line of the lyrics consists of four measures of music. Because the lyrics seldom use the four measures completely, the remainder of each four-measure segment of the strain is completed by an instrumentalist. These areas within the strain are known as **fill-ins** (see examples 3.2A and 3.2B). Listen to the saxophone fill-ins for Billie Holiday on "Fine and Mellow" (demonstration 11), the trombone performing the same function for Bessie Smith on "Empty Bed Blues" (demonstration 10), and Louis Armstrong playing the fill-ins on Bessie Smith's "St. Louis Blues" and "Lost Your Head Blues" (S, side A, bands 3 and 4).

Example 3.1

Pentatonic Scale   X   X   X X X   X

Western Scale   1   2   3   4   5   6   7   8

Eb&E   Bb&B

The approximate blue pitches

Example 3.2A The Usual Format Showing Fill-in Areas

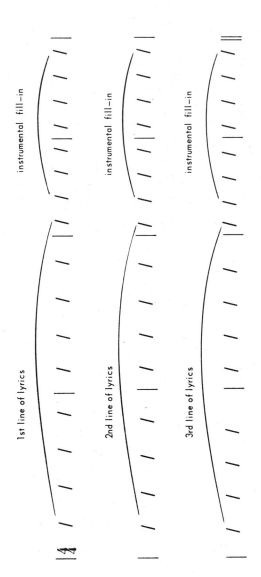

Fill-ins were the first means by which some jazz instrumentalists were heard on records. In this way, some of the more talented players, such as Louis Armstrong, began to build a broader reputation. (Armstrong can be heard playing fill-ins on some Bessie Smith recordings.) The fill-ins gradually developed in importance and interest to the point where they were often called **breaks.** Their importance was emphasized by the fact that the entire musical organization often stopped playing to feature the solo instrument filling in the break.

The blues, as they are sung, use lyrics that are usually concerned with unhappy situations: being out of work, hungry, broke, away from home, lonely, or brokenhearted because of an unfaithful lover. Consequently, their melancholy lyrics usually describe the blues emotion: "I'm laughin' to keep from cryin'," "Nobody knows you when you're down and out," "I've got the blues so bad, it's hard to keep from cryin'," and so on.

"By their very etymology the blues are songs of abandon, despair, or lyric sadness. However, content soon goes beyond form, and in the same mold all kinds of sentiments have been cast. Today, given blues are gay, ironic, sarcastic, vengeful. They were slow; they may now be fast (as in boogie-woogie) and even, in modern

Example 3.2B

The blues a - round me if it's night or day

instrumental fill—in

The blues a - round me if it's night or day

instrumental fill—in

Un - less you love me they won't go a - way.

instrumental fill—in

*Iambic pentameter markings.

Listening Guide

Bessie Smith
"Lost Your Head Blues"*

Bessie Smith singing "Lost Your Head Blues" with Louis Armstrong playing fill-ins on trumpet:

:00 Four-bar introduction. Open trumpet solo by Louis Armstrong.

:11 First chorus, sung by Bessie Smith, backed by muted trumpet. The first vocal phrase, "I was with you baby when you didn't have a dime," is followed by trumpet fill-in.

:21 The second vocal phrase of the blues chorus, which repeats the same lyric phrase.

:30 The third and final vocal phrase, which has a new lyric phrase that responds to the first two phrases: "And since you got plenty money you have throwed your good gal down."

:44 Second blues chorus. The structure is the same in both harmonies and lyric phrases, but the lyrics themselves are new.

1:17 Third blues chorus. This and the remaining choruses follow the same pattern established in the first two choruses.

1:50 Fourth blues chorus.

2:22 Fifth blues chorus with a more lyical phrasing used by Smith.

2:54 End.

*Smithsonian Collection, side A, band 4 (CD 1, track 11).

---

jazz, very fast."[7] Most people recognize the blues only by melancholy lyrics, and as a consequence many jazz listeners do not know that the blues can also be happy, swinging tunes. The great variety in this one form allows some entertainers to base their entire repertoire on blues.

Interpretation of the blues by instrumentalists and singers varied all over the United States as early as the latter part of the nineteenth century,[8] a fact that helps support those who contend that jazz did not originate in any one area of the country.

The word *blue* has been associated with melancholia as far back as Elizabethan times. Washington Irving is credited with first using the term "the blues" in 1807. By 1910, the word *blues* was in fairly wide use. Some writers state that the first written-down blues was "Dallas Blues," published in 1912 by Hart Wand, a white violinist from Oklahoma City (NW, 217). But it is unclear which blues tune was "first," and consequently no individual city or state can claim the origin of the blues.

W. C. Handy, an Alabaman who was called the Father of the Blues, wrote "The Memphis Blues" in 1909 as a political campaign song. His two most famous songs with "blues" in the titles are "The Memphis Blues" and "St. Louis Blues." Handy proved that money could be made from writing and publishing blues tunes. Around 1917, blues became more popular as ragtime began to fade. The first blues recording was Mamie Smith's "Crazy Blues" in 1920; it sold seventy-five thousand copies in the first month and a million copies in the first six months.

A common misconception is that the blues originated with work songs. Actually, work songs were functional, whereas blues songs were usually quite emotional and had no specific function. The consensus among authorities who write about jazz is that the blues was important in the development of jazz. This musical form has never lost its importance, and it is heard as frequently today as it was in all the previous eras of jazz. Blues performances in general are filled with subtleties. Recent adaptations, such as rhythm and blues in 1945 and rock and roll in 1955, seem fairly devoid of subtleties, but the durability of the form is evident as it continues to survive through all adaptations.

Country and Urban Blues

"I guess all songs is folk songs. I never heard no horse sing 'em."9

The period from 1930 on is divided primarily between singers and instrumentalists. The singers include such talented artists as Joe Turner, Jimmy Rushing, Joe Williams, and Jimmy Witherspoon. The problem with listing the best blues instrumentalists is that they were also singers (e.g., Louis Armstrong, Jack Teagarden, and Ray Charles). It is an oddity that in the beginnings of jazz, instrumentalists copied vocal techniques but that later some of the best jazz singers imitated instrumental jazz. Consequently, some of the best jazz singers were also instrumentalists.

City blues seems to be more rhythmic, more crisp, than country blues. Most country blues singers accompanied themselves on guitar, whereas urban blues performers often used fairly elaborate accompaniment, including that of jazz musicians like Louis Armstrong.

Huddie Ledbetter, known as Leadbelly, was discovered on a prison farm in Louisiana by John and Alan Lomax. He has been quoted as saying that he was born in 1885 in Louisiana and raised in Texas. He became a guide for Blind Lemon Jefferson and learned twelve-string guitar technique from him. Ledbetter spent a considerable amount of time in prison and became known as a valuable leadman for work songs. The Library of Congress contains 144 songs recorded by Ledbetter between 1933 and 1940 under the supervision of the Lomaxes. Some recordings can be heard today on Folkways Records and some on Columbia Records. Ledbetter seldom played softly, as he felt that blues tunes were meant to be danced to or worked to. His blues and folk songs gained him much popularity and led to many tours and concerts. Huddie Ledbetter died in 1949 in New York. His "Good Night, Irene" became extremely popular even among people who knew nothing about him.

Big Bill Broonzy's recordings span a thirty-one-year period. Broonzy, who directly influenced Josh White and many others, composed about three hundred songs. One of the most famous of his records, *Troubled in Mind* (Folkways Records), has lyrics in the eight-bar

American Popular Music

Of all the contributions made to music by Americans, the one most taken to heart by the entire world is American popular music. It has been a vital part of the country's heritage since colonial times, when its first popular composer, William Billings, wrote the first great war song during the Revolution. From that point, the contributions to the development of American popular music have been numerous. The African slaves brought their rhythms and musical practices, and immigrants brought ballads, dances, and melodies from their countries, all of which were fused into something new—a distinct art form that reflected the American way of life to the world.

Many different kinds of songs became popular during the first half century of American independence: songs that emerged from the Revolution (many based on melodies that came from England); the singing commercials of street vendors who sold wares from their wagons; and popular songs that described everyday experiences about city and country living, politics, and love. Most popular, though, were the sentimental ballads.

Listening Guide

Jelly Roll Morton
*"Dead Man Blues"**

:00 Introduction: A funeral march with trombone lead.
:14 Ensemble: Listen for the standard blues chord sequence over the established dixieland instrumental format. Listen for the loose interweaving instrumental lines that make up the polyphonic dixieland style.
:35 Clarinet solo for a blues chorus.
:57 Trumpet solo for two blues choruses.
1:20 Second chorus of trumpet solo.
1:41 Clarinet trio: Accents by the rest of the band on the fourth beat of every other measure that anticipate the riffing that will become important in later big bands.
2:02 Clarinet trio with trombone playing a solo legato line.
2:23 Ensemble in the dixieland polyphonic style.
2:45 Tag played by the clarinet trio.
2:49 End.

*Smithsonian Collection, side A, band 7.

Huddie Ledbetter.
Courtesy of Orin Keepnews

blues construction that have inspired many downtrodden persons to have hope:

Troubled in mind, I'm blue.
But I won't be blue always.
The sun's gonna shine
In my back do' someday.[10]*

Singing the Blues

Blues Singers

The history of the blues and the story of blues singers are complete studies in themselves, deserving of the fine volumes written about them. Students of the blues and blues singers will be aided greatly by the historically important Library of Congress recordings. The aim of this book, however, is to point out a very few singers who were important in this field.

All types of blues, from the early to the present-day forms, have greatly influenced how jazz players perform, but certain singers have been heard more than others and

Ma Rainey.
Courtesy of Orrin Keepnews

Publishing Popular Music

A brief description is provided here of the printed outlet for vocal jazz, namely, the sheet music publishing industry.

Before 1880, the most important song publishers were located in such cities as New York, Chicago, Pittsburgh, Detroit, Milwaukee, and San Francisco. By the middle of the 1890s, however, Union Square in New York City became the center of the largest concentration of song publishers in the country.

The method of selling songs to the public was unique even for those days. The song pluggers would do almost anything to get an audience. Some would visit the shops that sold sheet music and play the tunes on the piano all day. Others would travel by truck through the city streets, singing their songs through megaphones to attract the people.

By 1900 the "Street of Song" moved from Union Square to 28th Street between Fifth and Sixth Avenues. This location was baptized **Tin Pan Alley** by a journalist who heard a piano being played with strips of paper stuffed between the piano strings, producing a tinny effect. Here the song plugger was king, demonstrating newly published songs on the piano, and the million-copy sale of sheet music became a common event.

Around 1930, with the advent of recordings, radio, and talking motion pictures, Tin Pan Alley, with its techniques of writing and selling songs, became obsolete.

thus have had more influence. "The great blues singers of the twenties and the early thirties bred the jazz men, but they also bred a line of itinerant musicians who sang and played only the blues."[1] Today, in retrospect, it is impossible to separate blues from jazz as performed in the past or the present.

After World War I, the African American population migrated in great numbers to large northern cities. These people wanted the type of entertainment they were accustomed to, and so there was a demand for blues singers. Because recordings of African American singers were bought and heard only by African Americans, a collection of what were called "race records" developed. When whites eventually began to hear these records, sometimes fragile 78 rpm records became collector's items, sometimes selling for over one hundred dollars each.

Two blues periods can be discerned, the first from the latter part of the nineteenth century to about 1930 and the second from about 1930 to the present. The early period is usually divided between performers who sang "country," or "rural," blues and those who sang "city," or "urban,"

blues. The best-known early male blues singers were Big Bill Broonzy, Robert Johnson, Josh White, Blind Lemon Jefferson, Huddie Ledbetter ("Juliana Johnson," FJ, 2801), Son House, and Lightnin' Hopkins (NW, 261), who were followed by Albert King, T-Bone Walker, B. B. King, and others. The early urban blues singers were mostly women: Ma Rainey, Chippie Hill, Mamie Smith, Trixie Smith, and, most famous of all, Bessie Smith.

Early rural blues was created by African American singers in solo form accompanied by guitar, harmonica, or both. These itinerant singers converged on the cities of the South and Midwest in the 1890s in search of work. Eventually, the influence of female blues singers in the cities made its impact on Tin Pan Alley as another type of American popular song: the blues.

W. C. Handy, a composer of early published blues, introduced this type of rural folk song as "the blues." The blues became popular not only as Handy's creation but also in the performances of such blues singers as Gertrude "Ma" Rainey, who recorded fifty records,[12] and her pupil Bessie Smith.

Both Ma Rainey and Bessie Smith were professional vaudeville singers who took great pride in their ability to sing popular songs (vaudeville blues was popular music composed by Tin Pan Alley professionals). These singers used a song style that was smooth; the words were well-enunciated and the overall delivery was somewhat dramatic.

Usually, the women who sang vaudeville blues were accompanied not by a guitar or another instrument but by a small jazz combo in which the piano played the underlying beat and a solo horn improvised on the fill-ins during a pause in the vocal line. If a solo pianist provided the accompaniment, the style of playing consisted of a stride bass line with improvised fill-ins.

Bessie Smith

Bessie Smith was born in Tennessee in 1894. She made her first recording, "Downhearted Blues," in 1923, selling eight-hundred thousand copies to an almost exclusively African American public and becoming the best-known blues singer of the 1920s. Smith had a large voice and showed a wonderful talent for interpreting lyrics personally. Even today, when one listens to her recordings, it is easy to feel the deep emotion that she communicated to her contemporaries. Her repertoire was varied, and her personal feelings show on her recordings—sometimes sad, other times happy and full of humor.

Smith would interpret any given song by reshaping it to her own special vocal style and to her own feelings about the text. She would infuse the melodic line by embellishment, that is, melodic and rhythmic changes with a special type of word emphasis. Through her unique style of singing, she not only became known as the Empress of the Blues but also served as a model for the blues and jazz singers who followed.

By the end of her first recording year (1923), Smith had sold over two million records and by 1927 four million. She recorded 160 songs and literally saved Columbia Records from bankruptcy at that time. Smith also made a movie short—quite a breakthrough for an African American singer whose market was primarily ethnic. She earned a great deal of money and spent as much. By 1930, public interest in her began to wane, some say because she would not adjust to more modern song material. But listening to Bessie Smith records, one can feel that the blues was very personal to her and that she sang these songs with great sincerity[13] (S, side A, bands 3 and 4).

Smith was always selective in choosing her accompanying musicians, among whom were Clarence Williams, Fletcher Henderson, Louis Armstrong, Don Redman, Coleman Hawkins, James P. Johnson, Jack Teagarden, Benny Goodman, Charlie Green, and Buster Bailey.

She died penniless in 1937 in an automobile accident. At the time of her death, about ten million of her records had been sold. With her great gift of communication, Bessie Smith set the standard for all future singing of the blues.

Ma Rainey, Bessie Smith, and other singers trained on the minstrel circuits. Sadly, many black minstrels were copies of white minstrels—truly imitations of imitations—and their performances often did not reveal the artistry they were capable of. Ma Rainey, called the Mother of the Blues, was born in 1886, yet recordings of her work are still available on the Riverside and Folkways labels. Reissues of Bessie Smith's work are now available on the Columbia label. Technical mastery on these records is very good, and the records are quite important for historical documentation. They are also fine recordings for mere listening pleasure.

Ethel Waters

Ethel Waters made a name for herself in the early 1920s by making records and appearing in black nightclubs. Her repertoire broadened from blues to jazz styles of singing and then to pop. She made records with swing bands such as Benny Goodman and the Dorsey Brothers. In addition, she starred in successful Broadway musicals and appeared in films and television shows.

Waters was born an illegitimate child and married for the first time when she was fourteen. Starting as a cleaning lady, she managed to work her way up as a singer in Harlem nightclubs and in vaudeville. Her singing style influenced singers such as Mildred Bailey, Connee Boswell, Ella Fitzgerald, Pearl Bailey, Lena Horne, and Sarah Vaughan. Waters died in 1977.

Listening Guide

Bessie Smith (singing)
"St. Louis Blues"*

:00 Chord on reed organ and muted trumpet.
:03 First strain: Vocal (Bessie Smith) accompanied by fill-ins on the muted trumpet (Louis Armstrong); listen for the standard blues chord sequence that is repeated.
:18 Repeat of first vocal phrase "I hate to see the evening sun go down."
:32 Third responding phrase of the blues chorus.
:48 Repeat of the first chorus with new lyrics: Vocal with trumpet fill-ins; this section breaks the 12-bar blues pattern with 16 measures that set up the return to the next section.
1:31 Middle section: Vocal with trumpet fill-ins; leaves the standard blues chord sequence—16 measures.
2:26 Last section: Returns to the blues structure with trumpet fill-ins.
3:07 End.

*Smithsonian Collection, side A, band 3.

"Lover Man" and "Travelin' Light." But if popular music means selling a great number of records, she never really entered the popular field. There can never be any doubt, however, that she was a singer of jazz.

There is a kind of jazz song style that is neither all improvised nor all embellishment but a little of each. The French jazz critic André Hodeir uses the term *para-phrase* to describe this song style. Holiday excelled at both paraphrase and invention. She is aptly described by the cliché "a legend in her own time." Whereas early instrumentalists copied singers (or at least oral stylings), Holiday's singing style seemed to stem mainly from her favorite instrumentalist, tenor saxophonist Lester Young, whom she dubbed "The Prez."

Besides Young, Holiday was undoubtedly influenced by Bessie Smith and Louis Armstrong. Singers are influenced by their background, but this background does not always lead to a predictable conclusion. Leonard Feather speaks of this unpredictability:

> It would be a gigantic oversimplification to pretend that social conditions alone shaped her life, formed her vocal style, led to her death. Ella Fitzgerald had to endure a family background and childhood not greatly different from Billie's. Each was a product of a breaking or broken family; both suffered through years of poverty; both were at the mercy of Jim Crow. In Ella's case these conditions led to a career that started her on an upward curve at the age of 16, to a success story that has never been touched by scandal, and to the achievement of economic security and creature comforts far beyond her most optimistic childhood aspirations. Yet during the same time span, these conditions in Billie's case led to marijuana at 14, a jail term as a prostitute at 15, and heroin addiction from her middle 20s.[14]

One of the most frustrating aspects of Holiday's career must have been that the public was unwilling to accept black and white musicians performing together on the same bandstand, even though musicians *en masse* were her fans. Because of this attitude, some of her best employment situations were short lived. Musicians enjoyed hearing her sing blues, lovely ballads, novelty tunes, and gripping stories of lynching such as "Strange Fruit," written by a poet named Lewis Allen. This stark, graphic song deservedly attracted attention even after being rejected and banned in some important circles.

It is said that Holiday matured while listening to recordings of Bessie Smith and Ethel Waters. But, as stated before, the instrumentalists she seemed to admire most—Louis Armstrong and Lester Young—definitely influenced her through their simplicity and economy. To these wonderful models she added her own feelings, her own lifestyle, and the results were truly most intimate and personal.

Holiday did not record as many blues tunes as many fans think. Her style and her conceptions often led listeners to feel that she was singing blues when the song was some fairly banal pop tune. Most successful female singers, knowingly or unknowingly, have been

---

Listen to her famous recording of "Stormy Weather" and you will feel very deeply the mood she projects of a woman who has lost her man. This recording is a good example of how her singing emphasizes the consonants *n*, *m*, and *l*.

Waters was different from most blues singers. She noted herself that she was not a shouter. Her singing style was smoother than most blues singers, and her tones and vibrato were unique.

Billie Holiday

Billie Holiday must be considered apart from others in the jazz field. It is true that many artists defy categorization, a fact to be applauded, but Holiday crossed musical lines while sticking with her individual singing style. She sang many blues tunes, such as "Fine and Mellow," and could compete most admirably with this one vehicle. If the blues is a "feeling," then she used the blues on most of her songs. In addition, Holiday was deeply into the popular field with beautiful renditions of songs like

---

Listening Guide

Demonstration 1
(cassette 1, side A, track 1; CD 1, track 1)

Bessie Smith (singing)
"Empty Bed Blues"

Charlie Green, trombone

:00 Four-measure introduction by trombone and piano; the trombone plays a tailgate style.

:11 First vocal chorus: 12 measures of fill-ins by trombone throughout the recording. First lyric phrase, "I woke up this morning with a awful achy head."

:23 Second phrase of blues chorus with repeat of first lyric phrase.

:34 Third lyric phrase responds to the repeated first phrase, "My new man had left me just a room and an empty bed." This completes the standard 12-bar blues chorus.

:45 Second vocal chorus. This chorus, like the rest to follow, is also a standard 12-bar chorus.

1:18 Third vocal chorus. Listen for the trombone growls and the different accompaniment patterns used by the piano: 12 measures.

1:24 Trombone growls continue.

1:53 Fourth vocal chorus. Continued variation in the piano accompaniment: 12 measures.

2:26 Fifth vocal chorus. Piano uses ragtime feel as accompaniment: 12 measures.

3:01 End.

Billie Holiday

Billie Holiday was born in Baltimore in 1915 but matured on the streets of New York. She was discovered by John Hammond in a club in New York's Harlem when she was eighteen years old. She recorded with Benny Goodman as early as 1933, but her best recordings, well over one hundred sides (songs), were made in 1935 with a select group of New York musicians conducted by Teddy Wilson. It should be kept in mind that these masterpieces were accomplished under unusual conditions. The tunes were new to Holiday (who did not read music), and they were new to the other musicians as well, yet beautiful improvisations and interpretations were achieved. (Most of these records are available now on repressings by Columbia Records.)

Holiday died in 1939, having worked with many bands, including those of Count Basie, Artie Shaw, and Paul Whiteman. She earned a lot of money during her career but died possessing only seventy cents. Saddest of all, she never realized how many people loved her and her singing.

Listening Guide

Demonstration 2 (cassette 1, side A, track 2, CD 1, track 2)

Billie Holiday (singing)
"Fine and Mellow"

:00 Unison instrumental introduction: 4 measures.

:12 First vocal chorus, which starts with the first lyric phrase.

:22 Second lyric phrase of the first chorus.

:34 Final lyric phrase, which responds to the first repeated lyric phrase.

:46 Second vocal chorus. Listen for the piano fill-ins. Long notes are played by the other instrumentalists.

1:22 Third vocal chorus. The alto sax begins to offer fill-ins with the piano.

1:58 Fourth vocal chorus opens with "stop time," in which the band stops playing. As the chorus continues, listen for the increasing fill-in activity in the band.

2:33 Fifth vocal chorus.

3:09 End.

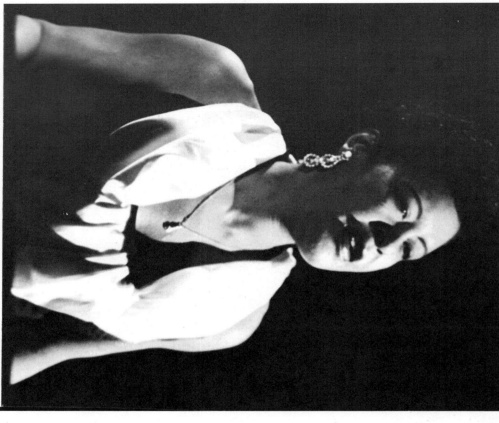

Billie Holiday.
Courtesy of Ray Avery

influenced by the jazz singing of Billie Holiday[15] (S, "He's Funny That Way," side C, band 8; NW, 295, "I Can't Get Started," side 1, band 1; NW, 295, "The End of a Love Affair," side 2, band 8).

Ray Charles

The man who gave R and B its fresh thrust was a blind, Georgia-born bard named Ray Charles, one of the most hauntingly effective and versatile Negro singers in the history of pop music.

Negroes have always rigorously maintained a distinction between gospel and blues—the sacred and profane—despite the affinity of their sounds. But Charles boldly brought them together, blending foot-stamping orgiastic jubilation shouts with the abrasive, existentialist irony of "devil songs." He even carried over the original gospel tunes and changed the words to fit the emotion. "Lord" became "you," or "baby," and it didn't matter if the bulk of the prayerful text remained the same. Thus Clara Ward's rousing old gospel song, "This Little Light of Mine," became Charles's "This Little Girl of Mine." (A wonderful identification!) Old timers who had once been forced to choose between the two genres were offended. "I know that's wrong," said Bluesman and former Preacher Big Bill Broonzy. "He should be singing in a church."

But Charles's innovation brought waves of gospel talent into the blues field, and at the same time offered blues performers a chance to employ the climactic cadences and mythic ritual of black evangelism. . . . Most important, once Charles broke the barrier between gospel and blues, the way was open for a whole cluster of ingredients to converge around an R and B core and form the potent musical mix now known as soul.[16*]

Other Jazz Vocalists

Vocal jazz flowered during the swing era. Singers had to be well versed in a wide range of styles to hold their positions as soloists with the big bands. They had to be able to realize the earthy sounds of the blues, the dreamy sounds of love ballads, and that indefinable swing technique.

Connee Boswell is deserving of mention here, as she and her sisters opened the door for many other vocal groups. Boswell wrote not only the vocal arrangements but also the instrumental parts, making her, with Mary Lou Williams, one of the first women arrangers/composers in jazz.

It is interesting that many of the better jazz singers are known primarily for their instrumental prowess. Obvious examples are Louis Armstrong, Jack Teagarden, and Clark Terry, with his style of **scat singing.** Conversely, some excellent instrumentalists are known primarily for their singing. For example, much of the listening public is not even aware of the talented piano work of Sarah Vaughan or Nat Cole.

B. B. King considers the blues a contemporary experience, a living music rather than a folk art. He plays electric guitar, as did T-Bone Walker (NW, 261). King's album *Live and Well* on ABC Records shows the great freedom that was typical of early blues performers.[17] Many rock superstars have acknowledged their debt to King's lyrical guitar virtuosity.

Because this book does not discuss or even mention all the talented blues personalities, the following resources are suggested. An important two-record set of early music in the United States is Arhoolie's *The Roots of American Music*,[18] which presents both city and country blues as well as examples of Cajun (Clifton Chenier), gospel, and other types of music. The Folkways and Riverside record companies have made truly remarkable efforts to preserve the sounds of important pioneers in music. Few researchers have delved more deeply into blues than Samuel B. Charters, whose book *The Country Blues* is a standard among jazz musicologists.[19] Three other books of merit must be suggested: *Urban Blues* by Charles Keil, *The Meaning of the Blues* by Paul Oliver, and *Blues People* by LeRoi Jones.[20]

Gospel and Liturgical Jazz

A more recent trend in jazz is labeled gospel jazz. Although this style encompasses eighty years of development in the art, it is directly traceable to the early religious and blues roots.

The Pentecostal Church was perhaps the first to pave the way for gospel singing, but the individual who affected the acceptance so definitely was a jazz piano player named Georgia Tom, who, after he was "saved," became Thomas A. Dorsey. His compositions are favorites today of proponents of this style of music.

Modern **liturgical** jazz must also be included in the discussion of religious music. Music of this type has been performed, in churches of various denominations, in the United States as well as other countries. Because all types of contemporary music are performed in various religious services, these works can now be added to the important repertoire of religious works of past centuries. In 1971, Leonard Bernstein's "Mass" premiered at the opening of the John F. Kennedy Center for the Performing Arts in Washington, D.C. Press coverage was favorable. Critic David E. Anderson of United Press International called it a "powerful experience." Paul Hume of the *Washington Post* stated that the central message of "Mass," and its crucial challenge is the place and function of religion in a world of violence. Anderson agreed that Bernstein's message was "one of hope."[21]

Mary Lou Williams was another great composer who used her talent writing lengthy religious scores, including "St. Martin de Porres" and "Mary Lou's Mass."[22]

Many recorded compositions use the jazz elements in strict conformity to the **Mass.**[23] Other performances are based on the historic liturgy of John Wesley and the Methodist Church and underscored by original contemporary music. These performances usually consist of jazz

---

[16*]Reprinted by permission from *Time*, The Weekly Newsmagazine; © Time Inc., 1968.

played in all portions of the service except during the actual sermon. This jazz is given serious thought and is well written and performed for these specific services, which are well received by congregations and considered appropriate and in good taste. Sometimes they are called liturgical jazz services, sometimes jazz masses, and sometimes jazz-rock masses. (Although Duke Ellington's 1965 concert at Grace Cathedral in San Francisco seemed to include jazz and ecclesiastical elements, it consisted mostly of "Ellingtonia.")

Of the many significant works, one that stands out is the *Jazz Suite on the Mass Texts* by Lalo Schifrin and Paul Horn. The freest portion of this work, the "Credo," consists of an unusual use of voices and Horn improvising on the alto saxophone. Actually, one of the problems in the acceptance of this music is its "free" quality; it seems in opposition to the inhibited, controlled performance of most church music. The beginnings of jazz and present-day liturgical jazz services prove that the supposed antithesis between jazz and liturgy is not valid. In 1970, Gerald Gipson of the University of Missouri wrote this about the controversy:

Can a musical language that is so charged with emotions and extra-musical connotations be admitted as a part of the church service?

To pass judgment on this question is difficult; there are as many arguments for as there are against. It must be remembered that jazz is a form of music alien to the church. Churchgoers are used to hymns and unison readings that have been so much a part of worship for years. They hesitate to make changes, partly out of fear and partly out of custom of thought. At times their attitude seems almost lackadaisical. There is fear of being embarrassed by the demonstrativeness of jazz by the person accustomed to the disciplined routine church service. Still jazz has a religious origin. The spirituals of the Negro slaves of yesterday show the authentically religious roots of jazz. . . . Is this so-called embarrassment real on the part of the puritanical when we remember the emotion-packed sermons of the revivals, the public confession of sin, and the public adoration of Christ? . . . Services keyed to the thinking and problems of modern man should be offered as should music geared to the thinking of a modern world. . . . When jazz first made the crossover between the sacred and the secular, it was more of a folk cult than a commercial empire. The unnamed and unhonored jazz musicians of the earliest days never dreamed that jazz would become the idol that it is now. An example of the new thinking in modern music is Duke Ellington, who has performed in numerous jazz liturgies and written a great deal of music for this purpose. Dave Brubeck (The Light in the Wilderness) has also been fundamental in the organization of good jazz liturgical music.

There seems to be a need for an awakening. It is necessary to utilize the wants and desires of a modern people so that our churches will grow stronger instead of weaker.[24]

Reverend Norman J. O'Connor, director of the New York Paulist Fathers' office for radio and television, says

of the Schifrin-Horn *Jazz Suite*, "At a moment in our lives when music is finding a new life in the church, this work turns our eyes from the past—where they have lingered too long—to the present and to the future. How could it be that (until now) liturgical music could fail to grow and incorporate the values of our world?"[25]

Charles Weisenberg has also commented on the place of jazz in modern church services:

Jazz has roots in the religious service through its association with the Negro spiritual. The contemporary use of jazz in church is thus not a new adventure. It is important to note that J. S. Bach, whose music is used in many church services, composed in a contemporary style. There is certainly no reason why 20th century contemporary music, whether or not it is jazz, cannot be suitably prepared for church use.[26]

The union of church and jazz should surprise no one. (There is an anonymous saying: "Each Sunday Buddy Bolden went to church and that's where he got his idea of jazz music.") Because the beginnings of jazz were in the church, it is only natural that modern liturgical jazz settings should also be acceptable in churches. The authors of this book have personally been involved in such services and feel that jazz can express solemnity, peacefulness, dedication, vitality, rejoicing, and any other sentiment embraced by the church. One thing that must be remembered, however, is that for this type of service to be successful the jazz must enhance the service; it must reinforce the emotions but not become the main attraction. It is true that it is next to impossible for a person to leave a jazz service untouched, as surely happens in many standard services.

Summary

There is no era designated as a blues era, and there are many individual blues styles. Over the years, the blues performances settled into a specific chord progression.

The so-called blue notes originally resulted from the West Africans' search for comparative tones not included in western European or pentatonic scales. Blues lyrics, although very flexible, were ideally composed in iambic pentameter. Three lines of lyrics, the first two being similar, are traditional.

There has always been a great interchange of ideas among blues singers and instrumentalists.

The two easily determined periods of blues are from the latter part of the nineteenth century to about 1930 and from 1930 to the present. Most of the early urban blues singers were women, whereas most of the rural blues singers were men.

Blues feelings, blues stylings, and the blues construction are all as important today as they have ever been.

The identification of a jazz singer dates back to the late 1920s with Al Jolson, though the jazz community quite naturally never seriously regarded the talented

Jolson a jazz singer. It is easy to look back and say that Louis Armstrong, Jack Teagarden, Billie Holiday, and Ray Charles were jazz singers; they phrased in the jazz idiom on jazz materials. Today, this issue is more problematic, in that the usually dependable hindsight cannot help solve the immediate dilemma: Is a singer a jazz singer if the repertoire is associated with jazz? If jazz interpretation is employed? Is improvisation the main dividing line, as is often said about instrumentalists individually or bands collectively? One of the best examples by which to discuss this dilemma is Ella Fitzgerald. Surely, she belonged to this elite group of sensitive vocal talent, yet she often recorded albums composed of strictly popular sounds done with beautiful timbre, intonation, and personal phrasing. The rationale has to be that even our best jazz singers do not always sing jazz any more than our finest jazz instrumentalists always perform in this genre.

For Further Study

1. Select a blues melody, such as the first twelve measures of "St. Louis Blues," and adapt a sonnet or original poem to this melody.

2. Sing the spiritual "Lord, Lord, Lord," shown on page 203. What melodic characteristics in this spiritual suggest a blues melody?

3. Give some titles of blues melodies that do not follow the usual harmonic construction but have the word *blues* in their titles.

4. In your own words, describe the "blue tonality." How does a pianist obtain the effect of blue tonality at the keyboard?

5. Listen to "In the House Blues" as sung by Bessie Smith (*The Story of the Blues*, Columbia, G30540) and answer the following:

   a. Is there an introduction?

   b. Do the lyrics follow the iambic pentameter plan (i.e., the first line repeats, whereas the third line is original)?

   c. How many times does she sing the blues song?

   d. What instrument accompanies her? What instruments play the fill-ins?

   e. When you hear the melody sung, do you hear the singer interpolate the blue notes?

6. The twelve-bar blues became standard with instrumental ensemble musicians during the 1920s. No further instruction was necessary once an experienced jazz musician was told "blues in B-flat." This structure, with its set harmonic pattern, became the norm. Listen to "Dippermouth Blues" (demonstration 13). After the four-measure introduction, answer the following: How many ensemble-improvised choruses (twelve measures each) are there? How many choruses did the clarinet and cornet play? Do you hear the "stop-time" device used by the ensemble?

7. Describe the differences between a folk song and a popular song.

8. Select a blues melody with text. Have each student or the class as a whole learn to sing the blues song; then, with each repetition, add some new element of either the melody or the rhythm. Have all the other students listen actively and critically to those changes made. A tape recorder can be a very good aid for the participants.

9. Select three or four different recordings of jazz singers. Encourage students to listen for the specific techniques used by the artist to achieve her or his effects. Encourage students to copy the jazz phrases on paper or reproduce them vocally.

10. Feel the excitement of a gospel selection by responding physically while listening. This may be accomplished through syncopated hand clapping, which is an integral part of gospel performance. Respond to the music by tapping the foot on beats 1 and 3 and clapping the hands on beats 2 and 4.

11. After listening to Ella Fitzgerald's "One Note Samba" on the album *Fitzgerald and Pass*, select a song that is very familiar, such as "De Lovely" or "Great Feelin'" by Scott Fredrickson, and make up your own scat rendition. Try to select a variety of vowels and consonants that do not follow the familiar "shoo-bee-doo-bee-doo-bee-doo." Create a musical line with form and sense to it. After the scat syllables have been created, repeat the song and start to make creative alterations by changing the rhythmic patterns. Next, alter the melody. Perhaps a portion of melody can be sung as written and another portion altered.

Suggested Additional Listening

Bailey, Mildred. *Greatest Performances 1929-1946*. Columbia Records, C31-22.

The Blues: Folkways Jazz, vol. 2.

The Blues: History of Classic Jazz, vol. 3.

Carmen McRae and the Great American Music Hall. Blue Note Records, LA-709-H2.

The Essential Jimmy Rushing. Vanguard Records, 65/66.

Jazz Singers: Folkways Jazz, vol. 4.

Mean Mothers/Independent Women's Blues. Rosetta Records, RR1300.

Negro Folk Songs for Young People. Folkways, SC 7533.

The Roots of the Blues. New World Records, 252.

Singers and Soloists of the Swing Bands, Smithsonian Collection of Recordings.

Sorry But I Can't Take You/Woman's Railroad Blues. Rosetta Records, RR1301.

Washington, Dinah. *Dinah Jams*. Trip Records, TLP-5500.

When Malindy Sings—Jazz Vocalists 1938–1961. New World Records, 295.

Additional Reading Resources

Albertson, Chris. *Bessie*.

Balliett, Whitney. "Miss Holiday." In *Dinosaurs in the Morning*, 74–80.

Bernstein, Leonard. *The Joy of Music*, 95–111.

Broonzy, William, and Bruynogle, Yannick. *Big Bill Blues*.

Charters, Samuel B. *The Country Blues*.

Chilton, John. *Billie's Blues*.

Harris, Rex. *Jazz*, 34–42.

Hentoff, Nat, and McCarthy, Albert. *Jazz: New Perspectives on the History of Jazz*.

Holiday, Billie, and Dufty, William. *Lady Sings the Blues*.

Jones, LeRoi. *Blues People*.

Keil, Charles. *Urban Blues*.

Oliver, Paul. *Bessie Smith* (King of Jazz Series).

———. *The Meaning of the Blues*.

Pleasants, Henry. *The Great American Popular Singers*.

Smith, Charles Edward. "Billie Holiday." In *The Jazz Makers*, 276–95.

Stearns, Marshall. *The Story of Jazz*, 14, 75–81, 196–98.

Ulanov, Barry. *Handbook of Jazz*, chap. 1.

Note: Complete information, including name of publisher and date of publication, is provided in this book's bibliography.

Notes

1. Mike Toombs (quoting B. B. King), *San Diego Union*, 11 August 1989, D-4.

2. *Many Faces of the Blues*, Savoy Records, MG12125; Bessie Smith, *Empty Bed Blues*, Columbia Records, G39450; *The Story of the Blues: Jazz Odyssey*, vols. 1–3; Port of Harlem Jazzmen, "Port of Harlem Blues," Albert Ammons, "Boogie Woogie Stomp," Meade Lux Lewis, "Honky Tonky Train Blues," Ed Hall, "Profoundly Blue," Josh White, "Milk Cow Blues," Sidney de Paris, "The Call of the Blues," and Sidney Bechet, "Blue Horizon," *Three Decades of Jazz (1939–1949)*.

3. Charlie Parker, "Another Hair Do," *Charlie Parker Memorial Album*, vol. 1, Savoy Records, MG-12000; Milt Jackson, "Bags' Groove," Horace Silver, "Senor Blues," and Lou Donaldson, "Blues Walk," *Three Decades of Jazz (1949–1959)*; Jimmy Smith, "Back at the Chicken Shack," Kenny Burrell, "Chittlins Con Carne," Lee Morgan, "The Sidewinder," and Stanley Turrentine, "River's Invitation," *Three Decades of Jazz (1959–1969)*; McCoy Tyner, "Flapstick Blues," *The Definitive Jazz Scene*, vol. 1.

4. Marshall Stearns, *The Story of Jazz* (London: Oxford University Press, 1958), 15.

5. Leonard Bernstein, *The Joy of Music* (New York: Simon & Schuster, 1959), 109.

6. Rex Harris, *Jazz* (Baltimore: Penguin Books, 1956), 39.

7. André Francis, *Jazz* (New York: Grove Press, 1960), 17.

8. Marshall Stearns, "Sonny Terry and His Blues," in *The Art of Jazz*, ed. Martin T. Williams (London: Oxford University Press, 1959), 9.

9. Charles Keil (quoting Big Bill Broonzy), *Urban Blues* (Chicago: University of Chicago Press, 1966), 37.

10. "Troubled in Mind," Words and music by Richard M. Jones. © 1926, 1937 by MCA Music, a division of MCA, Inc. © renewed 1953 and assigned to MCA Music, a division of MCA, Inc. © 1971 by MCA Music, a division of MCA, Inc., 445 Park Ave., New York, N.Y. 10022. Used by permission. All rights reserved.

11. Ralph J. Gleason, "Records," *Rolling Stone* (May 1971): 45.

12. Ma Rainey, Milestone Records, M-47021.

13. Bessie Smith, *Empty Bed Blues*, Columbia Records, G39450; *The Empress*, Columbia Records, G30818; *The Bessie Smith Story*, Columbia Records, C1855.

14. Leonard Feather, "Billie Holiday: The Voice of Jazz," *Down Beat* 29, no. 3 (February 1962): 18.

15. Billie Holiday, *The Golden Years*, Columbia Records, C3L-21, C3L-40; *The Billie Holiday Story*, Decca Records, DXSB7161; *Lady Day*, Columbia Records, CL637; *Billie Holiday*, Mainstream Records, s/6000; *Strange Fruit*, Atlantic Records, 1614; *Singers and Soloists*, Smithsonian Collection of Recordings.

16. James Baldwin, "No Music Like That Music," from *The Fire Next Time*. Reprinted by permission from *Time*, Time Inc., 1968.

17. B. B. King, *Live and Well*, ABC Records, S-6031; *Best of B. B. King*, ABC Recordings, 767.

18. *The Roots of American Music*.

19. Samuel Charters, *The Country Blues* (New York: Doubleday, 1958).

20. Charles Keil, *Urban Blues* (Chicago: University of Chicago Press, 1966); Paul Oliver, *The Meaning of the Blues* (New York: Macmillan, Collier Books, 1960); LeRoi Jones, *Blues People* (New York: William Morrow, 1963); Melody from Dresden Hymn Book, 1954, arranged by Johann Sebastian Bach, *Anniversary Collection of Bach Chorales*, ed. Walter E. Buszin (Chicago: Hall & McCreary, 1935), 6.

21. "Bernstein's 'Mass' Wins Music Critics Acclaim," *Los Angeles Times*, 9 September 1971.

22. *Mary Lou's Mass*, Mary Records, 102.

23. Geoffrey Beaumont, *20th Century Folk Mass*, Fiesta Recordings, FLP-25000; Joe Masters, *The Jazz Mass*, Columbia Records, CS9398.

24. Gerald L. Gipson, "The Church and Jazz," *Music Journal* 28, no. 4 (1970): 38.

25. Dan L. Thrapp, *Los Angeles Times*, 24 April 1966.

26. Charles M. Weisenberg, "On Brubeck and Others," *Frontier* 2, no. 9 (July 1960): 24.

Ragtime (1900–1917)

"Oh go 'way man, I can hypnotize dis nation,

I can shake de earth's foundation wid de Maple

Leaf Rag."[1]

Listening Guide

Demonstration 3
(cassette 1, side A, track 3; CD 1, track 3)

Ragtime

:00 to :28   Two choruses of piano solo (tuba, banjo, and drums play $\frac{2}{4}$ rhythm).

Ragtime music has been considered by some to be outside the jazz tradition because it is completely composed before it is performed. But, as was pointed out in chapter 1, if jazz must be improvised to be considered jazz, then most of the music generally conceded to be jazz could not be classified as such. Even without being improvised, ragtime has the "improvisatory feel" that seems so essential to jazz. On the other hand, some consider ragtime to be another name for early jazz.[2] (For an introduction to ragtime, listen to demonstration 3.)

The Birth of Ragtime

Ragtime is often said to have originated in Sedalia, Missouri, because a large number of such players performed there. However, a great deal of ragtime was played before these performers migrated to Sedalia in the late nineteenth century. (When reform government came to Sedalia in 1901, however, all ragtime activity there ceased.) Ragtime, then, predated jazz if Buddy Bolden is considered the one who brought the elements of jazz, or at least of dixieland jazz, together.

Ragtime had a direct impact on the development of jazz, but because of its juxtaposition chronologically to Early New Orleans Dixieland, ragtime can best be considered a piano style that developed as a result of special conditions.

Because pianists were not used in the first dixieland bands (which evolved from marching bands), the pianists developed a solo style of playing. A piano player was hired in place of a six- or seven-piece band, forcing the player to develop a technique that provided a full sound. The left hand had to play both the bass notes and the chords, leaving the right hand free for highly syncopated melodic lines. This playing was much more difficult than merely accompanying a vocalist or instrumentalist, in which case a pianist was responsible only for the bass notes with the left hand and the chords with the right. In fact, the extreme difficulty of the technique caused many academic piano players to completely

Fats Waller.
Courtesy of Orrin Keepnews

oppose the "unusual" style of ragtime. (For notational examples that demonstrate the difficulty of ragtime interpretation, see Appendix B.)

The accompaniment consists of the bass part confined to the first and third beats and the chords played on the second and fourth beats, or **offbeats**. Because of the physical action of the left hand, it became the practice for pianists to accent these offbeats, a technique that led to the new rhythmic style of the following era.

The intricate syncopation used in ragtime compositions could well have been the reason this music was called ragtime, or "ragged time." This is only one of many versions of the origin of the name *ragtime*, and as in the case of the name *jazz*, it is impossible to say which explanation is correct.

Ragtime was a refreshing change from the usual songs that often had commonplace melodies and predictable rhythmic feeling. Unlike many of the blues tunes and some of the spirituals, the mood of ragtime is happy. The country welcomed this happy music because it had just experienced the long depression of the 1890s.

The general public first became aware of ragtime during a series of world's fairs held in Chicago, Omaha, Buffalo, St. Louis, and other cities where peripatetic piano players from the Midwest and the South found employment along the midways. Ragtime flourished for over twenty years. When the music publishing industry (Tin Pan Alley) began to sell "rags," the music was too difficult for uninitiated pianists to play; it had to be considerably simplified if it were to sell. Ragtime players frequently earned substantial income teaching ragtime style.

The ragtime players then began to migrate to Sedalia, Missouri. Though it was later said that ragtime was born in Sedalia, these players merely drifted into the town because of employment opportunities. One player, Tom "Million" Turpin, owned a series of clubs in Sedalia and sponsored many ragtime players. Turpin's "Harlem Rag" (1897) is reputed to be the first rag ever published (although some say William Krell's "Mississippi Rag," also published in 1897, was first). When reform came to Sedalia in 1901, many ragtime players moved to St. Louis, which then became the ragtime center.

Much controversy exists about who composed what rag. Possibly, some rags were a compilation of ideas "borrowed" from many players, and the player who had the knowledge to notate the rag on music manuscript received credit for the composition. It is interesting that typical ragtime selections were composed in a definite format that showed a European influence with its concern for balance and form. Each selection included four themes (or melodies), and each theme had equal stress, or equal importance, within the composition. Examples are "Tiger Rag" and "Maple Leaf Rag." This fairly rigid form was probably borrowed from the construction of marches. Ragtime players, both black and white, were expected to be good readers, and sheet music was one of the principal means of disseminating ragtime music.

Listening Guide

Demonstration 4
(cassette 1, side A, track 4; CD 1, track 4)
Scott Joplin (piano playing)
"Maple Leaf Rag"

:00 A: Establishes the main recognizable theme.
:22 A: Repeat of A forecasts Joplin's involvement with form.
:45 B: New theme demonstrates further attraction to syncopation.
1:06 B: Repeat of the second theme.
1:28 A: Reiteration of the A theme helps the ear hold the form together.
1:50 C: Playing in a higher register causes the third theme to seem brighter in spite of the fact that the tempo stays firm.
2:12 C: Repeat of the third theme.
2:33 D: Syncopation becomes even more daring.
2:54 D: Repeat sounds like improvisation, which of course it is not.
3:17 End.

Jelly Roll Morton

The best-known ragtime piano player was Jelly Roll Morton (Ferdinand de Menthe). In his Library of Congress recordings and on his calling card, Morton claims that he originated jazz in 1902 as well as ragtime, swing, and just about everything else in this area of music. He may not have been that important, but he was surely at the top among ragtime players. Morton had no peer as a soloist[5] (S. "Maple Leaf Rag," side A, band 2), and he also performed successfully with a variety of bands[4] (S. "Grandpa's Spells," side A, band 8; S. "Dead Man's Blues," side A, band 7).

The most prolific composer of ragtime music was Scott Joplin, a schooled musician who published about fifty rags (some say he composed about three hundred). The most famous, "Maple Leaf Rag" (1899), sold hundreds of thousands of copies in the first ten years of publication (demonstration 15). Many jazz critics are not aware that Joplin wrote a symphony and two operas, one of which, *Treemonisha*, is still performed today.

A monument in honor of Joplin was erected in Sedalia at the site of the old Maple Leaf Club. When the movie *The Sting* was released in 1973, some of the

Scott Joplin.
Bettmann Archive

Jelly Roll Morton
*"Maple Leaf Rag"**

:00 Introduction: driving very hard, influencing a future era to come (swing).

:11 The A strain shows Morton to be a master of syncopation.

:27 Introduction reenters, helping to hold framework together.

:33 B strain as a relief from A, usually called a bridge.

:52 The A strain again but with noticeable additions in both hands.

1:13 Interestingly contrasting section (C).

1:34 Repeat of the C section with new variations.

1:53 New strain (D) vacillates between a tango and a swing feeling.

2:12 Repeat of the D strain, this time in most acceptable stride style.

2:32 End.

*Smithsonian Collection, side A, band 2.

Jelly Roll Morton.
Courtesy of Ray Avery

citizens of Sedalia expressed concern about the popularity of ragtime. They were worried that Joplin's tunes would be associated only with the film and that the composer and the city itself would be lost to obscurity. (In hindsight, more recognition could have been given Joplin and his music when he was living there instead of sixty years later.)

Two other very fine ragtime composers are deserving of mention here: James Scott and Joseph Lamb.

As soon as their finances permitted, some ragtime pianists formed their own orchestras: Jelly Roll Morton formed Jelly Roll Morton and His Red Hot Peppers, Jelly Roll Morton's Stomp Kings, and Jelly Roll Morton's Jazz Band. Some already established jazz bands then added piano players: Lil' Hardin, later to be Lil' Armstrong, joined King Oliver's orchestra. As the ragtime bands had to have piano players as leaders, this trend carried over to bands not so involved with ragtime. This was especially true in the Southwest, where Bennie Moten, Count Basie, Jay McShann, and many other piano players were leaders.

Morton was an ideal ragtime bandleader. He was an excellent piano player, a creative and knowledgeable **arranger,** and a fair singer. He had an extremely attractive, outgoing personality. In fact, Morton was the first jazz musician who is thought to have precisely planned what each musician was to play on his recordings, thus opening the way for recorded arrangements of jazz. The recordings on which he plays piano and talks with folklorist Alan Lomax are important in the history of jazz to the 1930s.[5] "In Jelly Roll Morton, we recognize for the first time in jazz that the personality of the performing musician is more important than the material contributed by the composer."[6] Because ragtime players were becoming bandleaders, the need for players to be more schooled in music became obvious.

When the piano players began to play with other instrumentalists, the two music styles, dixieland and ragtime, began to merge. There are many recorded examples of bands playing rag tunes that were primarily meant to be played on a piano. Listen, for example, to Paul Mares's recording of "Maple Leaf Rag," the New Orleans Rhythm Kings' recording of "Tiger Rag," and others[7] (FJ, vols. 3 and 6).

Two important changes resulted from the merging of dixieland and ragtime. First, the basic melodic concept of the rags was changed and second, the rhythmic accentuation indigenous to the rags was carried over into dixieland jazz. As a consequence, a new repertoire was added to the music of the jazz bands, which began to play the rags but altered the form. The first melody became a **verse,** the second and third melodies were omitted completely, and the fourth became a repeated chorus and the basis for improvisation.[8]

The rhythm of the bands changed from a flat-four (four equal pulsations in each measure) to a two-four ($\frac{2}{4}$) rhythm (four beats to a measure with accents on beats 2

Listening Guide

James P. Johnson
"Carolina Shout"*

Entire selection is a piano solo:
:00 Introduction: 4 bars.
:05 Section A: First chorus—sixteen bars.
:25 Section A: Repeat of First chorus.
:45 Section B: Starts out with a vamplike part but develops—16 bars.
1:04 Section C: Third type of chorus—16 bars.
1:24 Section C: Repeat of section C.
1:45 Section B: Improvisation on section B theme—16 bars.
2:01 Section D: New theme—16 bars.
2:20 Repeat of section D theme.
2:39 Coda: 4 bars.
2:44 End.

*Smithsonian Collections, side A, band 12 (CD 1, track 12).

Art Tatum

Art Tatum was possibly the best—surely the most versatile—piano player in the history of jazz. It is impossible (thankfully) to put Tatum in a stylistic category, but stride was certainly one of his favorites. Tatum worked occasionally with a small group, but he felt this was confining, so he usually played alone. He seemed so far ahead of other players technically and harmonically that he was merely listened to in awe. Tatum was very instrumental in bringing advanced harmonies into jazz. He was almost completely blind, but some maintain that his only handicap was his virtuosic technique—Tatum could not possibly harness his rapid flow of thoughts in order to play with simplicity.

Of course, he often proved this wrong. His followers would be Bud Powell, Oscar Peterson, and Paul Smith.

and 4). These measured offbeats correspond to the action of the left hand of the ragtime pianists.

Stride Piano

As we have seen, jazz bands ignored the original construction of the rags. Piano players were no longer compelled to play alone; consequently, the piano was considered a part of the jazz band's instrumentation. Also, as tempos were increased, the relaxed feeling of the early ragtime gave way to virtuoso displays, and improvisation, not present in early ragtime, began to gain importance in piano music. The culmination of these developments resulted in what is known as stride piano, an extension of ragtime. There are three basic differences between stride piano—playing and ragtime:

1. Stride players were not at all concerned with ragtime form. They played popular tunes of the day and any other kind of music that appealed to them.

2. Original ragtime was a composed music, whereas stride players were often very proficient improvisers and used this element in their performance.

3. The feeling of stride music was intense because, in general, stride pianists played faster and with much more drive than the more relaxed players of ragtime.

James P. Johnson

James P. Johnson, composer of the famous tune "Charleston" (among many others), is considered to be the father of stride piano. There are many fine recorded examples of his performances[9] (S, "Carolina Shout," side A, band 12; FJ, "Snowy Morning Blues," vol. 9). Closely akin to Johnson, and usually discussed in superlatives, is Willie "The Lion" Smith. However, perhaps the most entertaining and exciting stride piano player was Thomas "Fats" Waller, a student of Johnson. Waller mugged and clowned incessantly, and if a purist found this disturbing, he merely had to concentrate on the piano playing to hear true artistry and a most energetic rhythmic pulse[10] (S, "I Ain't Got Nobody," side C, band 3; FJ, "Handful of Keys," vol. 9; FJ, "Squeeze Me," vol. 11). Waller began to accompany blues singers on recordings in 1922. He was Bessie Smith's accompanist on tour and worked for a short time in Fletcher Henderson's orchestra. In 1927 he formed a solo act. His records sold well, and he even performed in motion pictures.

Art Tatum's recordings include some of the best stride piano on record[11] (S, "Willow Weep for Me," side C, band 11). Some musicians never have the opportunity to record their achievements for posterity, but this cannot be said of Tatum. He was hired by Norman Granz for two days of recording in December 1953 and for two days in April 1954. The result was a set of thirteen long-playing records (twenty-six sides) that was released to the public in 1974 on Pablo Records, truly a historic event for Tatum followers in particular and for jazz fans in general.[12]

Another collection of previously unreleased recordings of Tatum received a Grammy Award from the National Academy of Recording Arts and Sciences as the best solo album of 1973.[13] The collection was

which is a piano that is altered to sound much older than it is so that the ragtime sounds more authentic. This is accomplished in various ways. One way is to put thumbtacks in all the felts of the piano hammers. Other ways include laying a light chain across the strings or putting newspaper, aluminum foil, or something similar over the strings.[15] Most of these adjustments, however, are harmful to the piano felts.

Another good ragtime source is the repressing of old master recordings by such players as Morton, Joplin, and others[16] (S, "Grandpa's Spells," side A, band 8; S, "Dead Man's Blues," side A, band 7; S, "Black Bottom Stomp," side A, band 6; FJ, vols. 5, 9, and 11). Many good ragtime and stride players made piano rolls that can be purchased, and recordings made from rolls are satisfactory[17] (S, "Maple Leaf Rag," side A, band 2).

Another important source consists of recordings of old-timers, such as the two-record set called *The Eighty-Six Years of Eubie Blake*, played by Eubie Blake.[18] Blake, at age ninety-eight, received the Medal of Freedom from President Reagan in October 1981. After charming the nation as a composer and performer for over seventy-five years, James Hubert Blake died on February 12, 1983, at the age of one hundred.

Interest in authentic ragtime began to wane because some players played the style so fast and aggressively that the original relaxed feeling dissipated. As a result, stride playing became more popular. Also, the dixieland players had destroyed the important ragtime form. Since 1920, however, revivals of this style continue to bring talented composers and players to public notice.

The public was more aware of ragtime in 1973 than during any time since 1920 because of the popular motion picture *The Sting*. Throughout the movie, Scott Joplin's rags established the mood for the period in which the movie was set, and the composer's name once again became a household word. Marvin Hamlisch, the musician who adapted the Joplin rags for the movie, received an Oscar Award for the best movie score of the year. As he accepted the award, Hamlisch acknowledged his absolute indebtedness and gratitude to Scott Joplin and his genius. Joplin (who died frustrated and penniless in 1917) was given screen credits as well.

It is interesting to note that although *The Sting* was set in 1936, ragtime had not been popular since 1920 and that although ragtime had not been played at all in 1936, the music was still apropos for the movie. It is also interesting that a quiet revival of ragtime had preceded the movie. It was common during 1971 and 1972 to hear students in college practice rooms working on the intricacies of "Maple Leaf Rag." After the release of the film in 1974, students turned their efforts to "The Entertainer," a piece used extensively in the movie. The authors feel that the revival preceded the movie and that the makers of the movie used the music because of the revival. The important point, however, is that ragtime is once again popular, to the delight of its present-day practitioners.

recorded on a portable home-recording device by a young friend of Tatum. Some songs were recorded in an apartment and others in various after-hours clubs. The title of the album, *God Is in the House*, was taken from a remark made by Fats Waller when Tatum entered a club where Waller was playing. The remark reveals a respect for Tatum that is common among musicians.

Oscar Peterson, though also difficult to label stylistically, often ventures into some of the best stride piano on record. He is a talented and versatile musician. Basie and Ellington, too, often went into authentic stride piano during improvisation. Stride can also be heard in an interesting manner in the $\frac{5}{4}$ excursions of Johnny Guarnieri.[14]

Ragtime Lives On

Ragtime, then, was a style of solo piano playing that coexisted with Early New Orleans Dixieland jazz. It influenced the interpretation of jazz by shifting the rhythm from a flat $\frac{4}{4}$ to a $\frac{2}{4}$ interpretation and by additions to the jazz repertoire, such as "Maple Leaf Rag" and "Tiger Rag."

Ragtime is still played today, and recordings are available from several sources. One source consists of recordings of ragtime played today on a **tack piano,**

Art Tatum.
Courtesy of Ray Avery

Listening Guide

Demonstration 5
(cassette 1, side A, track 5; CD 1, track 5)

Art Tatum (piano)
"Elegie"

:00	Starts immediately on the original theme.
:11	Repeat and continuation of original theme.
:23	Arpeggio to anticipate personal additions to theme.
:32	Vamp to introduce faster tempo.
:37	Introduction of new harmonic aspects.
:53	Sustained-chord interlude.
:57	Addition of still newer harmonies.
1:05	Trill in left hand and transition into stride style.
1:10	Extended stride style.
1:47	Back to original theme plus Tatum arpeggios.
1:51	Ritard.
2:00	Sounds as if Tatum is about to stop.
2:22	End.

At the beginning of this chapter it was mentioned that some authorities do not consider ragtime to be jazz. To illustrate this point, in 1974 the Academy of Recording Arts and Sciences gave an award to a ragtime record without placing it in any specific award category. *The Red Back Book* won a Grammy Award for being the best **chamber music** record of 1973. Its competition included string quartets, classical piano duos, and woodwind trios.

Listen once again to the musical example of ragtime (demonstration 3) on the accompanying cassette (example 2A in Appendix A is the basis of an interpretation showing ragtime style).

Summary

Ragtime is a composed music played within certain accepted forms that resemble those used in traditional marches. This is not to say that some exponents of this style were not capable of excellent improvisation.

Ragtime displayed a definite separation of the hands at the piano: the left hand played both bass and chords and the right hand the melodic parts. The syncopation in ragtime compositions was advanced for the time, making the music difficult for less proficient pianists.

Stride piano developed directly from ragtime, and it was more aggressive, more improvisational, and less formal. Some of the greatest jazz pianists (such as Art Tatum and Fats Waller) were so expert at performing in the stride style that, regardless of their other talents, they have been included in this chapter.

It appeared for a few years that ragtime was to be relegated to history; however, it is accepted today not only for its nostalgic value but also as regular concert fare.

For Further Study

1. Compare the musical role of a ragtime pianist with that of a pianist in an instrumental ensemble.
2. How did the techniques of the pianist's left hand (playing alternately bass parts and chords) influence the flat-four rhythm played in early dixieland music?
3. Listen to "Grandpa's Spells" as played by Jelly Roll Morton (S, side A, band 8) and discover the offbeat accents in the left hand. Is this left-hand technique continuous, or does it change at times? If there are changes, what are they?
4. Now listen to "Kansas City Stomp" by Jelly Roll Morton (*The King of New Orleans Jazz,* Dixieland Jazz, RCA Victor, LPM-1649) and compare the ragtime rhythm that Morton used in his piano playing with that used in his instrumental rendition of "Kansas City Stomp."
5. Usually, how many different themes or melodies are there in ragtime compositions?
6. As a result of the merging of ragtime and dixieland, what happened to ragtime's melodic design and dixieland's rhythm?
7. What is stride piano?
8. Listen to "Carolina Shout" (S, side A, band 12). Is the tempo of the music like a stately march, or is it faster? Listen to the left hand. Is it the "oompah" of the earlier ragtime pianists, or is it broken up with irregular, shifting beat patterns?

Suggested Additional Listening

Classic Jazz Piano Styles.
Johnson, James P. *Father of Stride Piano.* Columbia Records, CL 1780.
———. *1917–1921: Rare Piano Rolls,* vol. 1. Biograph Records, 1003Q.
Joplin, Scott. *Joplin.* Biograph Records, 1013/4Q.
Kansas City Piano. Decca Records, DL-9226.
Maple Leaf Rag: Ragtime in Rural America. New World Records.
Morton, Jelly Roll. *The Immortal Jelly Roll Morton.* Milestone Records, MLP 2003.
———. *New Orleans Memories.* Atlantic Records, 2-308.
———. *Stomps and Joys.* RCA Victor Records, LPV-508.
New England Conservatory Ragtime Ensemble. "The Red Back Book," by Gunther Schuller and The New England Conservatory Ragtime Ensemble (playing Scott Joplin music), Angel Records, S-36060.
Waller, Fats. *African Ripples.* RCA Victor Records, LPV-562.
———. *1934–1935.* RCA Victor Records, LPV-516.

Additional Reading Resources

Blesh, Rudi. *Classic Piano Rags.*
Blesh, Rudi, and Janis, Harriet. *They All Played Ragtime.*
Dance, Stanley. *The World of Earl Hines.*
Gammond, Peter. *Scott Joplin and the Ragtime Era.*
Harris, Rex. *Jazz,* 60–72.
Hentoff, Nat, and McCarthy, Albert. *Jazz.*
Hodeir, André. *Jazz: Its Evolution and Essence.*
Kimball, Bob, and Bolcum, Bill. *Reminiscing with Sissle and Blake.*
Kirkeby, Ed. *Ain't Misbehavin': The Story of Fats Waller.*
Rose, Al. *Eubie Blake.*
Shapiro, Nat, and Hentoff, Nat, eds. *The Jazz Makers,* 3–17.
Stearns, Marshall. *The Story of Jazz.*
Ulanov, Barry. *Handbook of Jazz.*

Note: Complete information, including name of publisher and date of publication, is provided in this book's bibliography.

Notes

1. "Maple Leaf Rag" (1903). Music by Scott Joplin, words by Sydney Brown.
2. Guy Waterman, "Ragtime," in *Jazz,* ed. Nat Hentoff and Albert J. McCarthy (New York: Holt, Rinehart & Winston, 1959), 107.
3. *Jelly Roll Morton,* Mainstream Records, S/6020.
4. *Jelly Roll Morton, The King of New Orleans Jazz,* RCA Victor Records, LPM-1649.

5. Jelly Roll Morton, *The Saga of Jelly Roll Morton*, Riverside Records, 9001–9012; *Smithsonian Collection of Classic Jazz*.

6. Joachim Berendt, *Jazz Book: From New Orleans to Rock and Free Jazz*, trans. Dan Morgenstern, Westport, Conn.: Lawrence Hill & Co., 1975.

7. Paul Mares, "Maple Leaf Rag," *Folkways Jazz*, vol. 6; New Orleans Rhythm Kings, "Tiger Rag," *Folkways Jazz*, vol. 3; Joe King Oliver, "Snake Rag," *Folkways Jazz*, vol. 3; New Orleans Feetwarmers, "Maple Leaf Rag," *Folkways Jazz*, vol. 11; Papa Celestin, "Original Tuxedo Rag," *Jazz Odyssey*, vol. 1.

8. Waterman, "Ragtime," *Jazz*, 7.

9. James P. Johnson, "Keep off the Grass," *Jazz Odyssey*, vol. 3; "Black Bottom Dance" and "Mr. Freddie Blues," *Piano Roll Hall of Fame*.

10. Fats Waller, *Ain't Misbehavin'*, RCA Victor Records, LPM-1246; "Mama's Got the Blues," *History of Classic Jazz*, vol. 8; "Handful of Keys," *Folkways Jazz*, vol. 11: "Draggin' My Poor Heart Around," *Jazz Odyssey*, vol. 11; "Do It Mr. So-and-So" and "If I Could Be with You," *Piano Roll Hall of Fame*; "The Flat Foot Floogie," *The Jazz Story*, vol. 3; *The Complete Fats Waller*, Bluebird Records, 2AXM-5511.

11. Art Tatum, *The Art of Tatum*, Decca Records, DL 8715; *Piano Discoveries*, vols. 1 and 2, 20th Fox Records, Fox 3032/3; "Too Marvelous for Words," *Smithsonian Collection of Classic Jazz*.

12. *The Tatum Solo Masterpieces*, Pablo Recordings, 2625 703.

13. Art Tatum, *God Is in the House*, Onyx Recordings, ORI 205.

14. Johnny Guarnieri, *Breakthrough in 5/4*, Bet Records, BLPS-1000.

15. Phil Moody, *Razz-Ma-Tazz*, Urania Records, UR 9009; Joshua Rifkin, *Scott Joplin Ragtime*, Nonesuch Records, H-71248.

16. Jelly Roll Morton, "Grandpa's Spells," *Piano Roll Hall of Fame*; "Perfect Rag," *History of Classic Jazz*, vol. 2; "Big Fat Ham" and "Black Bottom Stomp," *Folkways Jazz*, vol. 5; "Tom Cat Blues" and "Wolverine Blues," *Folkways Jazz*, vol. 9; "Kansas City Stomps," *Folkways Jazz*, vol. 11; "London Blues," *Jazz Odyssey*, vol. 1; "Someday Sweetheart," *Jazz Odyssey*, vol. 2; Scott Joplin, "The Cascades," *History of Classic Jazz*, vol. 2; "Original Rags," *Folkways Jazz*, vol. 11; *History of Classic Jazz*, vol. 2; *The Jazz Story*, vol. 2; *Reunion in Ragtime*, Stereoddities Records, S/1900.

17. *Piano Roll Hall of Fame and Piano Roll Ragtime*, Sounds Records, 1201; Jelly Roll Morton, *Rare Piano Rolls*, Biograph Records, 1004Q; Fats Waller, *Rare Piano Rolls*, vols. 1 and 2, Biograph Records, 1002Q, 1005Q.

18. Eubie Blake, *The Eighty-Six Years of Eubie Blake*, Columbia Records, C2S-847.

Dixieland (1900–1920s)

"The life span of a musical masterpiece may encompass a number of generations, but music, being a reflection of society, is subject, like any other art, to social obsolescence. It may endure, metaphorically speaking, in libraries, on records and in the occasional archeological revival, but it will not satisfy a changing society's changing musical requirements."[1]

Listening Guide

Demonstration 6
(cassette 1, side A, track 6; CD 1, track 6)

Early New Orleans Dixieland

:00 Ensemble chorus (trumpet, clarinet, trombone); tuba, banjo, and drums keep $\frac{4}{4}$ rhythm.

:23 Clarinet solo (one chorus, low register).

:47 Ensemble chorus (same as first chorus).

1:13 End.

Early New Orleans Dixieland (1900–1920)

The transition between jazz eras is gradual and overlapping. In some cases, a new era arises as a reaction to a previous one. In others, the transition may be slow and not immediately recognizable. We have chosen to designate each era of jazz by its most commonly used name, and the dates given for each era are approximate because no style of jazz started or stopped at a given point. (For an introduction to Early New Orleans Dixieland jazz, listen to demonstration 6.)

Too often, both musicians and lay listeners tend to identify their tastes with specific eras in jazz and to ignore all other styles. Generally speaking, it is only the jazz *fans* who want *their* style to remain as the one authentic way to play jazz; the musicians seldom want this themselves. Such clichés as "I don't know much about it but I know what I like" are used to defend this attitude, but most humanities teachers agree that people *like* what they *know*. A deeper understanding of the unfamiliar areas of this art form will help one develop better discernment and more enjoyment. The intolerant attitude of some musicians who state that the only true jazz is the style in which they and their favorite performers are involved shows an extremely narrow outlook that is usually based on a minimum of "outside" listening.

In fact, the labels used to describe most eras are somewhat misleading and tend to encourage an oversimplification of the diversity within that era. As we use these labels throughout this book, we encourage you to view them as general descriptors rather than totally inclusive of all the musical activity during that era. Most musicians do not restrict themselves to one era or style of jazz; their style may even vary within a given

Louis Armstrong.
Courtesy of Ray Avery

improvised chorus. However, the various styles do have certain characteristics that differentiate them, and the use of labels can help focus the discussion.

New Orleans

The era of jazz discussed in this chapter is called Early New Orleans Dixieland jazz not because New Orleans was the only geographical origin of this type of music but because, at the beginning of the twentieth century, New Orleans bred more jazz and more notable jazz musicians than any other era. However, when considering New Orleans as the birthplace of jazz, we must keep two facts in mind: (1) slaves were brought first to Virginia in 1619, and they brought with them their musical traditions, thereby producing, through the merging of their music with European music, the first faint beginning of jazz and (2) the first instrumental jazz was recorded in New York about three hundred years later (1917).

The more in-depth the research, the more difficult it becomes to claim one city as the origin of this art form. W. C. Handy said that music that was later called jazz was played in Memphis around 1905 but that the performers did not know until about 1917 that New Orleans had the same kind of music.[2] However, jazz critic Dan Morgenstern writes, "Jazz: one of the great and wonderful mysteries of our age. New Orleans: the cradle of this mystery. You don't agree? Have you a better myth? Have you Louis Armstrong?"[3] The word *early* is included in this label to differentiate between the dixieland music played from approximately 1890 to 1920 from the jazz developed in Chicago after 1920. The dixieland music performed in New Orleans today, however, often includes elements of all the jazz eras since 1920.

The historical background of New Orleans, an exciting city that keeps alive many of its early customs and traditions, provided a receptive environment for jazz to develop and grow. For the first forty-six years, New Orleans was a French possession. It was then ceded to Spain in 1764 and remained a Spanish possession for the next thirty-six years, when it once again came under French rule. In 1803 it came to the United States as part of the Louisiana Purchase. This heterogeneous atmosphere was tolerant of all races and was a natural setting for the music of West Africa and Europe to meet and to merge. New Orleans was and is an exciting city with great activity of all sorts, both business and pleasure.

Oddly enough, recognition of jazz players in New Orleans by the New Orleans press has always been quite poor ever since the art form took shape at the turn of the twentieth century. The New Orleans musicians "testify that it is easier to get national and international recognition of their talents than it is to get the attention of the *Times-Picayune* and the *States & Items* . . . when their talents are adequately fossilized, their instruments museum pieces, and the musical forms they are creating safely a part of jazz history, they probably will show up on the cover of the *Picayune* Sunday supplement."[4]

The Oral Tradition

It was said earlier that early jazz combined the techniques of formally trained Creole musicians with the techniques of African Americans whose playing was based on oral tradition. There is no better example of playing based on the oral tradition than that heard on any Louis Armstrong record when he sings first and then plays the melody. His phrasing in each instance is identical. This is an example of how the instrument is used as an extension of the voice.

Charles "Buddy" Bolden, who led one of the earliest marching bands, is usually credited with establishing the fixed instrumental combination used in this era.[5] The first jazz instrumentation was a logical outgrowth of that used in the marching bands and in the music halls—the same instruments were used. In its beginnings, this music was generally a creation of African Americans, with the exception of a few whites such as drummer Jack "Papa" Laine, who led a band as early as 1891. But soon the music was being created by both African Americans and whites. It should be noted, however, that the African American musicians did much more to foster these beginnings and to continue its development. Bolden was eighteen years old when the African type of dancing in Congo Square every Sunday came to an end. He was a cornet player in his brass band and was a member of a "shouting congregation" in his church. Obviously, he was heir to many of the early influences leading toward jazz. His band played ragtime melodies, marches, quadrilles, and a great amount of the blues. Bolden stopped playing entirely in 1907, a fact that points out the diversity of this music at an early date. Unfortunately, there are no recordings of Bolden.

Small bands playing dixieland music developed concurrently with ragtime. Dixieland and ragtime influenced each other and were influenced a great deal by the same sources. The same players were often involved in both, and ultimately the two styles merged. In their beginnings, however, early dixieland music used no piano, whereas early ragtime was primarily piano music. Eventually, though, ragtime bands developed.

All Early New Orleans Dixieland bands did not sound the same. In New Orleans there were at least thirty quite well known bands in just the first decade of the twentieth century. It was only natural that the bands varied according to personnel, just as jazz groups do today.

Another important point is that a given jazz band altered its style according to each job. The music played in some African American clubs was considered far too "rough" for the white dances, where the musicians would have to adjust to a more "sweet" style.

Listening Guide

Demonstration 7
(cassette 1, side A, track 7; CD 1, track 7)

King Oliver's Creole Jazz Band (playing)
"*Dippermouth Blues*" (also called "*Sugarfoot Stomp*")

:00	Introduction: Ensemble
:05	Two ensemble choruses: 2 cornets, clarinet, trombone; rhythm played by piano, bass, banjo, and drums—$\frac{4}{4}$ rhythm. True collective improvisation with Oliver on lead cornet. Trombone slides into each chorus.
:37	Two choruses of clarinet solo (Johnny Dodds). The rest of the band plays what is called "stop time"; it seems to make the solo more dominant.
1:09	Ensemble chorus, same pattern as first chorus.
1:26	Three choruses of cornet solo by Oliver; note his use of the plunger as a mute for his instrument. The clarinet and trombone also play as in an ensemble chorus, except now they are very soft.
2:12	Vocal break ("Oh play that thing!").
2:14	Ensemble chorus similar to the first chorus, but a short tag is added on the end.
2:32	End.

In any discussion of New Orleans at the turn of the century, the name **Storyville** figures prominently. In 1896 a New Orleans alderman, Sidney Story, sponsored a civic ordinance confining the red-light district to a thirty-eight-block section adjoining Canal Street. Undoubtedly, Mr. Story was humiliated when the area came to be called Storyville. Some of the larger night spots in this section hired small bands, but mainly solo piano players were employed. However, there was much activity for street bands. Before the Navy closed Storyville in 1917, the district made important contributions to the beginnings of jazz. Contrary to what some writers claim, Storyville was not as important to the origins of jazz as were the religious services.

Instrumental Obligations

There is a certain amount of solo work in dixieland music, but from its very beginnings each of the frontline players (cornet, clarinet, and trombone) had a definite obligation to fulfill in ensemble playing.

Because by usual standards it is the loudest instrument in the orchestra, the cornet (or trumpet) played the melody. The cornet player was allowed to "decorate" the melody according to individual interpretation. The melody, however, was usually not altered to the point where it became unrecognizable to the lay listener. The clarinet player had a dual role: to play a harmony part, a countermelody above the melodic line carried by the trumpet (a natural task for the clarinet because it can be played at a higher pitch than the trumpet), and to create momentum (because the clarinet can be played with more agility than can the two other melodic instruments).

The role delegated to the trombone was to play the most important note in the chord to help clarify the change in harmonies.[6] The banjo, tuba, and drums played straight rhythm parts as they had in the marching bands. No piano was used in these first dixieland groups because they were often the same group that played in the street marches, where a piano could not be used. For this same reason the tuba rather than the string bass was used. (For a notational example of Early New Orleans Dixieland, see Appendix B.)

Another identifying feature of the music of this era was that the rhythm section played in a flat four; that is, with no accents—four even beats to a measure (or bar).[7] This is contrary to the belief of many dixieland advocates who believe that all dixieland music uses a $\frac{2}{4}$ rhythm with accented afterbeats. One need only to listen to recordings of the King Oliver band (typical of this era) for confirmation that these rhythm sections played with no regularly accented beats[8] ("Dippermouth Blues," demonstration 7).

Some people believe that Latin rhythm was an element added to jazz in the 1940s by the orchestras of Dizzy Gillespie, Stan Kenton, and others or in the 1960s, when the bossa nova became popular. Actually, the addition of Latin rhythm can be traced to the beginnings of jazz. One example of Latin rhythm in early jazz is the tango section of "St. Louis Blues" written by W. C. Handy in 1914.

Another important aspect was that the front-line players conceived their parts polyphonically (horizontally), as shown in example 8A in Appendix B. It should be noted that the direct roots of the counterpoint in modern jazz are from the music of the dixieland bands and very early classical music, as both used the polyphonic approach in construction.

The customary structure of a dixieland format consists of an ensemble chorus, the solo choruses, and a return to the ensemble. The case is often stated that all dixieland music is composed of improvisational playing. But it can be pointed out that during ensemble playing that included improvisation, patterns were often established in which a player repeated the same part on the last chorus of the arrangement that was played on the opening chorus. Thus, these choruses were played from memory rather than by strict improvisation. In spite of this, this type of music has a feeling of spontaneity.

Joe ("King") Oliver and his orchestra. Left to right: Baby Dodds, Honore Dutrey, Oliver, Louis Armstrong, Bill Johnson, Johnny Dodds, and Lil' Armstrong.

Courtesy of Orrin Keepnews

One of the most interesting aspects of dixieland music is the rhythmic complexity caused by collective improvisation, in which conventional chord changes become secondary to creative interaction and instrumental independence. (For a notational example of this syncopated type of interaction, see Appendix B, example 14.)

The King

In this phase of jazz, one musician was designated by his peers to be the "King." He was always a trumpet player. For example, Freddie Keppard succeeded Bolden as king (NW, 269, "Stock Yard Strut," side 1, band 6). Keppard left New Orleans in 1912 and played in Los Angeles in 1914, Coney Island (New York) in 1915, and Philadelphia in 1918. These facts surely dispute the "up-the-river" legend, perpetuated by many jazz writers, that jazz came up the river by steamboat directly to Chicago from New Orleans. (Other famous New Orleans players,

e.g., trombonist Kid Ory, went to Los Angeles before going to Chicago.)

The last trumpeter to be called king was Joe "King" Oliver. The type of jazz played by Oliver exemplifies that performed before and during World War I. It is extremely difficult, however, to obtain recordings that have the exact instrumentation and approach to performance that was popular before 1920 (no instrumental jazz was recorded before 1917). By the time Oliver went into recording studios, his style had been somewhat influenced by the activity in Chicago. He was using two trumpets (Louis Armstrong on a second trumpet) and a piano (Lil' Hardin Armstrong). Nevertheless, his recording output around 1923 (thirty-seven numbers in all) is considered a cornerstone in traditional jazz.

The Early New Orleans Dixieland bands relied more on ensemble than on solo improvisation, certainly less improvisation than Chicago Style Dixieland. Still, every member of a band like Oliver's was a star and capable of good solo improvisation. Yet everyone's solos were considerably shorter than those by Oliver himself. Oliver was the leader and hence the featured attraction. Proof of the esteem in which present-day musicians hold Oliver is that whenever the tune "Dippermouth Blues" is played, the trumpet player must always play Oliver's choruses, note for note, or he is not considered to be even playing the right number. Interestingly, Oliver was actually improvising when he recorded the tune[9] (demonstration 7).

Sidney Bechet

Sidney Bechet was as important as any one musician coming out of New Orleans with the exception of Louis Armstrong. Perhaps the reason he is not better known is that he spent so much of his great career in France. Nevertheless, he has influenced clarinet and soprano saxophonists to the present day. John Coltrane has acknowledged this, as would any other soprano saxophonist.

Dixieland Spreads Out

Jazz seemed to become more permanent as it became less localized. Oliver moved to Chicago, as did many other well-known musicians and bands. The Original Dixieland Jazz Band went to Chicago in 1916, then on to New York in 1917. In fact, the Original Dixieland Jazz Band was the first band to record instrumental jazz instead of merely playing background for blues singers (1917). This was also the first group to perform in New York, where they opened at Reisenweber's Cafe (near Columbus Circle) in 1917, and the first jazz band to go to Europe (1919).

The band consisted of a group of young white musicians who listened very intently to and absorbed what the black bands in the New Orleans area were playing. They copied these bands until their own style began to develop.[10] Some jazz critics imply that this band's music and that of the New Orleans Rhythm Kings was more toward barnyard sounds and clowning. It should be kept in mind, however, that the imitation of barnyard animals was as much "in" at that time as electronic distortion would be years later. The Original Dixieland Jazz Band even recorded a piece called "Barnyard Blues."[11] No matter what a listener's stylistic preferences, it would be impossible to deny the great energy and exuberance of the Original Dixieland Jazz Band.

Early Recording Process

Early jazz recordings were made under rather difficult conditions. The musicians played toward a large megaphone that was reduced at one end to a stylus on a wax disc. The players were placed around the room according to how their individual sounds would affect the stylus. For example, the clarinet was the closest because its sound did not carry as well as the trumpet's did. (Young Louis Armstrong was very proud that he was stationed much farther away than anyone else, so "big" was his sound on the cornet.) On the other hand, cymbals on the drums were very hard to record, as were sticks on the snare drum. And it was not until the early 1950s, because of pressure by Duke Ellington to record Jimmy Blanton, that the recording industry solved the problems of recording basses. From today's perspective, it is truly a wonder that there was any kind of a respectable blend or balance on those early recordings, as the players stood or sat in some strange configuration unlike that to which they were accustomed in a club or ballroom.

One of the newer methods of making records is called "direct to disc." There are complaints that using this method required that a complete recording be made with no patching, no erasing, no unsatisfactory solos, no missed notes—no mistakes of any kind. It is seldom realized that recording was always done that way until the advent of tape in the 1950s. All masterpieces up to then were recorded exactly as described (direct to disc).

Listening Guide

Sidney Bechet
"Blue Horizon" *

Entire selection is a clarinet solo, all 12-bar blues choruses:

:00 Chorus 1: Sidney Bechet plays low-register clarinet. His phrasing follows the same pattern used in standard blues lyrics.

:42 Chorus 2: A little higher into the chalumeau register. Listen for the call and response with the trombone player.

1:27 Chorus 3: Listen for the riff pattern used by the other instrumentalists.

2:11 Chorus 4: Into the medium and high registers. Bechet uses inflections, such as scoops and slurs, like those used by blues singers.

2:57 Chorus 5: Bechet brings this chorus down in register and sets up the higher energy of the next chorus.

3:42 Chorus 6: Long, sustained, high register with a steady emphasized beat in the rest of the band.

4:27 Clarinet retards and plays out the 12 bars with a fermata at the end.

* Smithsonian Collection, Side A, band 11 (CD 1, track 11).

Original Dixieland Jazz Band. Left to right: Tony Spargo, Eddie Edwards, Harry Barth, Larry Shields, Nick La Rocca, and Russell Robinson.

Courtesy of Leo Walker

Louis Armstrong (1901–1971)

If the one most influential musician in the entire span of jazz had to be chosen, the choice would be Louis Armstrong. "His heritage permeates all of jazz to this day . . . all that we may hear today has been touched by his genius."[12]

The myth has always been that Daniel Louis Armstrong was born on July 4, 1900. However, extensive research has uncovered his baptism papers at the Sacred Heart of Jesus Church in New Orleans stating that he was actually born on August 4, 1901. Armstrong was born in a poor neighborhood in New Orleans, and his parents were separated when he was very young. His father worked in a factory, and his mother was a cleaning woman. Armstrong was placed in the Colored Waifs Home for boys at age thirteen (because he playfully fired a revolver in the air while celebrating New Year's Eve),

and he remained there for eighteen months. At the Waifs Home, Peter Davis taught him to play the bugle and then the cornet. He joined the band and the chorus and played for social affairs outside the home.

After leaving the Waifs Home, he first played with an orchestra of youngsters under Joe Lindsay. Joe Oliver, the king of New Orleans trumpet players around 1917, took an interest in Armstrong and made him his protégé. When Oliver left for Chicago in 1918, he placed Armstrong in his chair with a band directed by trombonist Kid Ory. Armstrong stayed with Ory for eighteen months and then joined Fate Marable's orchestra on a Mississippi steamboat in 1920. He was briefly married when he was eighteen years old.

In 1922 Oliver sent for Armstrong to join him in Chicago at the Lincoln Gardens. Armstrong married Lil' Hardin (the second of four wives) in 1924. She was the pianist with Oliver, but she encouraged Armstrong to

Listening Guide

Louis Armstrong
"Hotter Than That"

:00	Introduction by the ensemble.
:09	Trumpet solo (Louis Armstrong).
:25	Trumpet break.
:27	Trumpet solo.
:41	Clarinet break into solo.
:43	Clarinet solo.
:59	Clarinet break.
1:01	Clarinet solo.
1:17	Scat singing backed by guitar only.
1:31	Vocal break.
1:33	Scat singing—note rhythmic complexity.
1:49	Guitar and voice alternate short breaks.
2:07	Piano interlude.
2:12	Trombone solo.
2:27	Trumpet break.
2:29	Ensemble (standard established dixieland format).
2:35	Trumpet break.
2:40	Ensemble.
2:42	Guitar break.
2:44	Trumpet break.
2:46	Guitar break.
2:50	End.

*Smithsonian Collection, side B, band 3.

organize his own band. However, Armstrong always remained grateful to Oliver and considered him his idol. Another of Armstrong's early idols was B. A. Rolfe, a white virtuoso trumpeter who later conducted a Paul Whiteman-type radio orchestra and who was never associated with the mainstream of jazz. Armstrong heard in Rolfe a good tone and sensible control of melodic thoughts. (In Armstrong's opinion, both of these elements are missing in the performance of most contemporary jazz players.) One of Armstrong's greatest thrills was at his first recording session, when the engineer placed him twenty feet behind the other musicians (including King Oliver) because Armstrong's tone was so powerful.

Armstrong left the Oliver band in 1924, and the band declined. Oliver did make some good recordings in 1926 and 1927. Armstrong joined Fletcher Henderson at the Roseland Ballroom in New York in 1924. At this time he recorded frequently with Clarence Williams's Blue Five accompanying singers. With Henderson, he accompanied Bessie Smith and Ma Rainey. He was a remarkable influence in the Fletcher Henderson band. Because of his spirit and inspiration, he was a true catalyst.

In 1925 he returned to Chicago and was billed as the World's Greatest Trumpet Player. Also in 1925, he started to record under his own name. The next four years are notable for the Hot Five and Hot Seven records. With these records (classics in this music), jazz was turning from ensemble-oriented to solo-oriented music.

By 1926 Armstrong was considered the greatest trumpet player who had ever lived. His tone, stamina, range, creativeness, and technique were envied by all jazz performers. At that early age, he became the ideal, the model of how to play jazz improvisation. In 1929 he headed for New York again—this time with his own band. Here he continued to record and play nightly on radio as well, which helped to spread his fame. In 1930 he was in Hollywood, and in 1931 he returned to Chicago. Then he went to England and Europe, where he was, of course, a tremendous success. Armstrong was the first jazz player to achieve international fame. His career remained very solid throughout the swing era and even included several motion pictures. He had a large swing band that was usually led by someone else— Louis Russell, for example. The band was usually only a showcase for the talents of Armstrong himself. His big-band phase was neither as productive nor as creative as the earlier and later small-band phases. He seemed to be most comfortable with the small-band format.

Armstrong's career hit a new high in 1947. He returned to using a combo, which included at one time or another Jack Teagarden, Earl Hines, Cozy Cole, Barney Bigard, Sid Catlett, Arvell Shaw, Dick Cary, Billy Kyle, Joe Darrensbourg, Tyree Glenn, and Trummie Young. With his All Stars, Armstrong toured the world in the 1950s and 1960s and became known as the Ambassador of Good Will. As late as 1964, he had his biggest record

success, "Hello Dolly." Fortunately, he lived to be both wealthy and famous. He died on July 6, 1971.

Armstrong was the first great jazz soloist. Here is Martin Williams's assessment of Armstrong (with which most other writers agree):

Armstrong's music has affected all our music, top to bottom, concert hall to barroom. No concert composers here or abroad write for brass instruments the way they used to, simply because Armstrong has shown that brass instruments, and the trumpet in particular, are capable of things that no one thought them capable of before he came along. Our symphonists play trumpet with a slight, usually unconscious vibrato that is inappropriate to Beethoven or Schubert because Armstrong has had one. "Louis changed our whole idea of the band," said Henderson's chief arranger at the time, Don Redman. So did he change everyone's idea of every band, and every soloist's idea of himself. From that, the era and the style took its name: swing. From the Henderson band itself came the Benny Goodman style, and, directly or indirectly, most of the popular big bands of the Swing Era. American music was not the same after it became swing, and what made it different was the influence of Armstrong.[13]

In the 1920s, playing high C on the trumpet was considered quite extraordinary, unlike today. Armstrong, however, often amazed his audiences by playing one hundred high C's (with the band shouting out the count on each one). Then Armstrong would soar upward to a high F. In the 1920s and 1930s, that alone was an incredible feat, but Armstrong would follow this display with an outstanding version of a blues tune of the day. The moment was one to be remembered.

Armstrong was also considered one of the best jazz singers. He was very concerned with pleasing his audiences, and he became a great showman and even a comedian. Too often, praise for Armstrong is divided between Armstrong the artist and Armstrong the entertainer, as if artists do not entertain. It is almost inconceivable that the man who was probably America's greatest natural musician, the man who was so personally responsible for a way of playing and listening to music, should be remembered as an affable clown. Is it possible that without Armstrong there would have been no jazz? There may have been jazz, but it truly would have developed in an entirely different way than it did. Armstrong always felt that even if music was one's whole life, it was meaningless if it could not be presented to and appreciated by the public.

It must be gratifying to their fans to know that during their lifetimes both Armstrong and Ellington received the public acclaim they deserved. Armstrong was undoubtedly one of the best-known and most highly respected musical personalities in the world. He was probably the first to be recognized as an artist (around 1925) in a music that was at that time considered merely entertainment. Today's researchers benefit greatly from the fact that Armstrong's recordings are a real documentation of his career and his permanent worth. The most mentioned solos are "West End Blues," "Savoy Blues," "Potato Head Blues," "Hotter Than That," "Weather Bird," "Muggles," "Beau Koo Jack," "I'm Not Rough," "Cornet Chop Suey," "Struttin' with Some Barbeque," "Heebie Jeebies," and "Mahogany Hall Stomp."

In Armstrong were combined well-developed technique, rhythmic feel, intuition, good tone, and high register as well as personal warmth and an ability to communicate. Each solo, no matter how deep into improvisation, sounds cohesive and well planned but still spontaneous. In spite of being a great improviser, Armstrong's chief talent was his ability to inject rhythmic feeling into a melodic line, whether that melodic line was improvised or written. The tunes that he recorded were often quite banal until he transformed them into a worthwhile listening experience.

He was a genius at improvisation, and his improvisations showed more than anything else that simplicity leads directly to communication. As great as his trumpet playing was, Armstrong's chief asset was his ability to communicate.

Although he often seemed gregarious and extroverted, Armstrong could play a blues that was lovely and sad at the same time. Almost every player who improvises plays phrases that can be traced back to Armstrong and his influence, and the whole world has benefited. Somehow, he almost single-handedly set the stage for the jazz soloist, maybe the stage for jazz itself. Most musicians agree that Armstrong was the leader that all other jazz players followed. "Daniel Louis Armstrong, the man from whom has flowed so much good music and so much good-will that the world will never fully realize just how deeply it is in his debt."[14] Armstrong's approach to jazz and to life has never been out of style. Somehow Armstrong made everybody happy!

Chicago Style Dixieland (the 1920s)

"For the first time in my life I was playing with musicians who could swing—was like flying without an airplane."[15]

In 1917 the closing of Storyville, a district in New Orleans where a great number of musicians were employed, shifted the heart of the jazz scene to Chicago. By 1918 many musicians had left New Orleans, and when Congress passed the Volstead Act in 1919, prohibiting the sale and consumption of alcoholic beverages, employment for jazz musicians in New Orleans came to a real halt. Quite a few jazz players drifted to Chicago, where demand for their music and a still-active nightclub atmosphere fostered the further development of jazz.

The Roaring Twenties

There was a growing demand for jazz in Chicago during the Roaring Twenties. Chicago was a prosperous city with many opportunities for employment because of the railroads, stockyards, and mills. Many workers in

---

Listening Guide

Demonstration 8 (cassette 1, side A, track 8; CD 1, track 8)

Chicago Style Dixieland

:00 Introduction (trombone glissando leading into following chorus).
:05 Ensemble chorus (trumpet, clarinet, trombone, tenor sax); string bass, guitar, piano, and drums keep $\frac{2}{4}$ rhythm.
:19 Trumpet solo (1 chorus).
:34 Trombone solo (1 chorus).
:48 Ensemble chorus (same as first chorus).
1:03 End.

Chicago had migrated from the South and wanted the type of entertainment they had left behind. King Oliver came to Chicago in 1918 and went to work immediately at the Royal Gardens with Johnson's Creoles from 8 P.M. to 1 A.M., and then went to the Dreamland Cafe and worked until 6 A.M. (For an introduction to Chicago Style Dixieland, listen to demonstration 8.)

In 1920 the nation's leading entertainer was Al Jolson, and Bessie Smith was a big success in the Atlanta, Georgia, area. In September of that year, the first radio broadcast took place. Radio soon became a part of many households and did much to popularize jazz in general and some jazz artists in particular. In the 1920s recordings were as important as they are today. Although jazz could be heard in several cities, most of the recording was done in New York (with blues singers) or on the outskirts of Chicago.

In Los Angeles in 1921, New Orleans trombonist Kid Ory recorded what most historians feel were the first instrumental jazz records by a black band. In 1923 Ory scored another first with his radio broadcasts. Kid Ory trombone solos may sound very rough and dated today, but at the time his playing was so modern that he is credited with freeing the trombone from playing glorified tuba parts and allowing the instrument such choices as long flowing lines and even improvisation with the aid of a plunger mute[16] (NW, 269, "Ory's Creole Trombone," side 1, band 7; NW, 269, "Society Blues," side 1, band 8). Kid Ory was also a recognized jazz composer. His most famous work became a dixieland standard, "Muskrat Ramble."

In New York around 1924, Fletcher Henderson was organizing recording sessions and accompanying blues singers. Chicago Style Dixieland seeped into New York, too. Trumpeter Red Nichols, trombonist Miff Mole, and saxophone-clarinet player Jimmy Dorsey each recorded records that have become jazz classics[17] (FJ, "Original Dixieland One Step," vol. 7).

In Detroit around 1927, a band named McKinney's Cotton Pickers featured a fine young saxophonist-arranger, Don Redman. Jean Goldkette had a fairly commercial type of orchestra in spite of the fact that his personnel included such jazz greats as Bix Beiderbecke, Frankie Trumbauer, and Pee Wee Russell.

And in Los Angeles, a former New Orleans Rhythm Kings drummer, Ben Pollack, organized a Chicago Style Dixieland band. Pollack used mainly Chicago musicians like Benny Goodman plus a Texas clique like the Teagardens.

(The jazz activity in Kansas City in the 1920s is discussed in chapter 7 because it was more truly swing jazz.)

To appreciate Chicago Style Dixieland, one must have a sense of the times. It was the Roaring Twenties, what F. Scott Fitzgerald called "the Jazz Age." There were straw hats and arm bands, Model T and Model A Fords and Stutz Bearcats, raccoon coats, and

speakeasies. Gangsters ruled Chicago during this period, and with the musicians playing in the saloons, there is no question that these same racketeers had a great deal to say about the careers of the musicians.

In spite of the fact that Chicago was almost entirely in the hands of gangsters, these were happy times for the general public. The emphasis was on having fun. In fact, musicians today call dixieland music "happy music." World War I was over, and the big stock market crash of 1929 was of course not foreseen. Life seemed to be a party. New dances such as the **Charleston** and **Black Bottom** were invented to suit the new energetic music.

Chicago of the gangster period, the Golden Era, saw the first Vitaphone "talkie" movie, Al Jolson's The Jazz Singer, from Warner Brothers opening in November 1926. Thirteen months later, the Negro weekly the Chicago Defender commented on a new-fangled "Amplivox" in a South Side restaurant. It was a machine that reproduced Louis Armstrong's scatting vocal of "Heebie Jeebies." Few musicians recognized the potential popularity of the primitive juke box. And even fewer anticipated the eventual sale of $600 million in records annually, and the millions in fees and royalties payable to the musicians and singers for their services on records.[18]

The Two Dixieland Styles

Both Chicago Style Dixieland and New Orleans Dixieland used cornet, trombone, clarinet, and drums. The piano was now used in both styles, and the **string bass** had replaced the tuba. The last two changes occurred because the bands that played for dancing no longer played for marching. However, there are several technical features that distinguish Chicago Style Dixieland:

1. A saxophone (usually a tenor saxophone) was added.
2. The guitar replaced the banjo.
3. Fairly elaborate (by comparison) introductions and endings were common.
4. Ease and relaxation in playing style gave way to tension and drive.
5. Individual solos became more important.
6. Rhythm changed from $\frac{4}{4}$ to $\frac{2}{4}$.

Listen to the accompanying cassette to hear and compare the two different ways of performing dixieland jazz. Demonstration 6 is Early New Orleans Dixieland and demonstration 8 Chicago Style Dixieland.

The players of the Chicago era preferred the guitar to the banjo. Banjo players made the shift to guitar quite easily, mainly because the type of guitars first played in bands were four-stringed instruments and tuned like banjos. The addition of the tenor saxophone gave more body to ensemble playing and added solo color. When one more player is added to an ensemble of twenty or so, the change could go unnoticed. But in early dixieland the front line was only three players; to add another musician to these three made a decided difference.

The Original Dixieland Jazz Band added a baritone saxophone and an alto sax in 1920. The role of the saxophone in ensemble playing was comparable to that of the clarinet, except that its harmony line (or countermelody) was directly under the melodic line of the cornet.

As mentioned before, the rhythmic feel in Early New Orleans Dixieland—four even beats in each measure—was changed in Chicago Style Dixieland to measures with accents on the second and fourth beats (or the offbeats) and was called $\frac{2}{4}$ rhythm in jazz. The reason for the change was that the bands, no longer used for marching, could hire piano players who had been playing ragtime with its accented offbeats. The jazz drummer was now influenced by the addition of the piano, and he began to accent beats 2 and 4. Listen to young drummer Gene Krupa toward the end of the Chicagoans' record of "Nobody's Sweetheart." Krupa, playing in the Chicago style at that time, plays **rim shots** on beats 2 and 4. He is accenting these beats as loudly as he can without putting a hole in his drum (FJ, "Nobody's Sweetheart," vol. 6). The bass player followed the left hand of the piano and played only on beats 1 and 3. The guitar player played on 2 and 4 or, at least, accented beats 2 and 4 to adjust to the piano. (For notational examples (numbers 13, 14, 15, and 16), showing the difference between the rhythm sections in both styles, see Appendix B.)

This shift of the accents to beats 2 and 4 has held throughout most jazz eras. It has even become a signature of the "swing" feel of jazz. In fact, jazz-oriented people even now clap their hands or snap their fingers on beats 2 and 4 instead of on 1 and 3.

Chicago

During the 1920s Louis Armstrong and Earl "Fatha" Hines began a long association, indicating that Armstrong influenced not only all wind players but also piano players[19] (S, "Weather Bird," side B, band 5).

Armstrong was considerably involved in Chicago jazz during the 1920s, and his recordings with the Hot Five and Hot Seven are truly jazz classics[20] (S, "Sweethearts on Parade," side B, band 6; S, "I Gotta Right to Sing the Blues," side B, band 7; S, "Potato Head Blues," side B, band 1; S, "Struttin' with Some Barbecue," side

---

Earl Hines

Earl "Fatha" Hines developed what was called "trumpet-style" piano playing because he played with a melodic style similar to that of his friend Louis Armstrong, instead of that of ragtime or boogie-woogie. This trumpet-style piano had also been used by Jelly Roll Morton and others. But Hines, with his fantastic technique, made great use of octaves and tremolos in the right hand. His fast double time foreshadowed the coming of Charlie Parker and Dizzy Gillespie.

Hines opened the Grand Terrace on Chicago's south side in 1928 when he was only twenty-three years old. After 1939 his band became a proving ground for young players, as did Stan Kenton's band a few years later. After all the young bop-oriented players began to leave him, he did record in 1945, there was no bop influence in his band at all. Hines tried a large band (twenty-four musicians) for a while, then disbanded entirely in 1948. He performed for three years with Armstrong's All Stars and then went out on his own again with small groups in the 1950s and early 1960s.

Earl Hines.
Courtesy of Bob Asen, Metronome Magazine

Listening Guide

Demonstration 9 (cassette 1, side A, track 9; CD 1, track 9)

Louis Armstrong (playing)
"West End Blues"

:00 Armstrong on solo trumpet cadenza as introduction.

:15 Ensemble chorus. Trumpet plays melody; clarinet and trombone mainly play sustained notes as harmony. Rhythm plays $\frac{4}{4}$ with piano, banjo, bass, and drums.

:50 Trombone solo by Fred Robinson. Rhythm section plays $\frac{4}{4}$ except drummer, who attains special effects by hitting blocks and other various items.

1:24 Voice (Armstrong) and low-register clarinet (Johnny Strong) alternate measures; rhythm in $\frac{4}{4}$.

1:58 Earl Hines plays a piano solo.

2:11 Hines (on piano) goes into his recognizable style of octaves in the right hand, mainly double time.

2:33 Ensemble chorus—trumpet, clarinet, and trombone all play long sustained notes; $\frac{4}{4}$ rhythm.

2:45 Trumpet goes into more of a solo while others continue their sustained notes.

2:56 Hines plays a short solo piano interlude.

3:05 Trumpet, then other ensemble instruments join in.

3:16 End.

B, band 2). But Armstrong is a good example of a musician who cannot and should not be categorized so narrowly. He had been a member of King Oliver's band earlier and then later had a famous swing band. His last band was a dixieland group, one of the most enjoyable in the history of jazz.[21]

The period of the 1920s brought many professionally trained instrumentalists into jazz. Until this time, jazz had been a mainly black art form. The only formally trained black musicians, with the exception of a few piano players, were the Creole performers. With the advent of Chicago Style Dixieland, large numbers of white players with formal musical training entered the jazz field.

As is the case with every new style of jazz, Chicago Style Dixieland brought into jazz many youngsters who were avid fans of the jazz groups who had moved into Chicago. A high school clique called the "Austin High Gang" formed an important nucleus in the development

of this style. Among these young players were Pee Wee Russell, Dave Tough, Bud Freeman, Gene Krupa, Eddie Condon, Mezz Mezzrow, and their friends Benny Goodman, Bix Beiderbecke, Muggsy Spanier, and Bunny Berigan—a group of talented young players for the jazz roster. A jazz historian could never find more enthusiasm than these young Chicago players had for their brand of music. However, by comparison with other styles of jazz, the recordings of these musicians simply do not exemplify either their energetic feeling or their musical technique.

As Benny Goodman grew up in the hurried pace of Chicago in the 1920s, he patterned his early efforts after Jimmy Noone of New Orleans and Frank Teschemacher of Chicago's Austin High Gang, but he soon surpassed his models and went on to become the "King" of the swing era.

One of the best and most popular groups in the Chicago era was the New Orleans Rhythm Kings

Left to right: Howdy Quicksell, Tommy Gargano, Paul Mertz, Don Murray, Bix Beiderbecke, and Tommy Dorsey.

Courtesy of Leo Walker

Listening Guide

Bix Beiderbecke/Frankie Trumbauer
*"Singin' the Blues"**

:00	Four measures: Introduction with cornet and sax in thirds.
:06	Trumbauer on C melody sax playing solo for 14 measures—a combination of interpretation and improvisation.
:31	Two-measure break on sax.
:35	Sax solo continues for 14 measures.
1:01	Two-measure break on sax.
1:05	Beiderbecke plays his solo on cornet for 14 measures.
1:30	Two-measure break; Beiderbecke goes into double time for the first measure.
1:33	Beiderbecke continues his solo for 16 measures.
2:03	Third chorus ensemble for 8 measures.
2:18	Clarinet solo for 6 measures.
2:29	Two measures of clarinet break.
2:33	Ensemble on the second half of the tune for 9 measures.
2:50	Guitar takes a 1-measure break (Eddie Lang).
2:52	Ensemble on out to end; Beiderbecke pushes the ensemble harder.
3:03	End.

*Smithsonian Collection, side B, band 8.

(though they never played in New Orleans)[22] (FJ). This group influenced and inspired many young musicians in the Chicago area. It should be noted that combos such as this one and the members from Austin High School played in downtown Chicago, whereas Armstrong and Oliver reigned on the south side of town. Whereas the Original Dixieland Jazz Band denied (falsely) being influenced by black musicians, the New Orleans Rhythm Kings stated that they did whatever they could to sound like Oliver and others. It also appears that the New Orleans Rhythm Kings were a link between the New Orleans players and the roster of players entering jazz in the Chicago days. They were actually more important as an influence than as individual players; in other words, those players they influenced often surpassed them.[23]

Bix Beiderbecke

Leon "Bix" Beiderbecke was born in 1903 and lived for only twenty-eight years. His talent was such that his name on a record alone makes it a collector's item. It is said that his style was fairly well formed from listening to records of the Original Dixieland Jazz Band and others before he had heard Armstrong. In Chicago he listened to Oliver, Armstrong, and the New Orleans Rhythm Kings. Some historians state that Beiderbecke developed his style from listening to Emmet Hardy, who played on the riverboats that stopped at Davenport, Iowa, Beiderbecke's hometown. Beiderbecke's first employment was with a group called the Wolverines, whose first recordings were made in 1924[24] (FJ, "Jazz Me Blues," vol. 6).

Until Bix Beiderbecke came to Chicago, the best white trumpet player was Francis Spanier, a youngster who followed Armstrong every hour possible. Armstrong nicknamed him "Muggsy." His recordings are some of the best examples of the way these young players attempted to play. The music has great vitality and creativeness, and yet it was meant to be and truly is "fun" listening.[25]

Beiderbecke worked for a while with his close friend saxophonist Frankie "Tram" Trumbauer. Trumbauer soon became dedicated to looking after Beiderbecke's welfare, guiding him to the big bands of Jean Goldkette and Paul Whiteman, where top salaries were to be had. Some of Beiderbecke's best records were done with small combos "outside" his regular job with Whiteman. Especially notable are those with Trumbauer.[26] Debussy's influence can be heard in some of Beiderbecke's piano compositions, the best known of which is "In a Mist." On the cornet, Beiderbecke never seemed to let his style become as dramatic or sensual as Armstrong's. Instead, his cornet music is usually described as poetic, fluid, moving, and sensitive—if words can ever truly describe music (FJ, "Somebody Stole My Gal"; FJ, "Margie," vol. 6).

Many writers refer to Beiderbecke as the first "cool" artist. (For a discussion of cool jazz, see chapter 9.) It is true that even though he could move an

Pure Jazz

Although jazz has undergone many changes since its inception, some bands today play jazz almost as it was played at the turn of the twentieth century. The Early New Orleans Dixieland style had a great revival in the early 1940s. Prominent in this movement was Lu Watters and his Yerba Buena Jazz Band (based in Oakland, California). This band, like others in the movement, did everything possible to re-create King Oliver's style. The advocates of this style of jazz refer to their music as the "real" or "pure" jazz. This "purist" jazz school is fairly intolerant, as are other jazz schools. But how, and at what point, with all the borrowings that transpire in jazz and other musical styles, could there be purity?

ensemble almost by himself, he usually did not play with the frenzy of most of the Chicago Style trumpets. This situation could be compared to that of Miles Davis during the bop era, when Dizzy Gillespie's virtuosic style was in vogue.

Summary

Even though the type of jazz known as dixieland started one hundred years ago, mainly in New Orleans, it is still with us. As a "played-by-ear" combination of European melodies, African rhythms, and European brass marching band sounds, it was, and is, colorful, exciting, and carefree. Dixieland is still being played and listened to. The members of dixieland bands perform their music as if the music itself is fun. Maybe that is why it is still so popular.

To this day, Chicago Style Dixieland music has not lost its appeal, primarily because of its rhythmic concept. When dixieland is played today, it is almost always Chicago Style. Many musicians are not even aware of the fact that there is more than one style of dixieland.

Though there are clubs and societies dedicated to the preservation of dixieland music, it is seldom played exactly as it was in the 1920s. The musicians have lived through other jazz eras, all of which have become part of their musical personalities. Of course, jazz musicians have always been more concerned about playing with good expression than about playing "authentically." However, many seventeen- and eighteen-year-old musicians accept the Chicago Style as the best way to express themselves and play it very well.[27] Today, this tradition is carried on most admirably by such groups as The World's Greatest Jazz Band and The Dukes of Dixieland and by individuals like Bobby Hackett.[28]

The Chicago Style was perpetuated by large orchestras such as the Dorsey Brothers and Bob Crosby, the latter of whom built a reputation on a big-band version of this small-band style.[29] In larger orchestras, complete sections play written parts based on lines originally invented for one instrument. This is an example of one style of jazz influencing the styles that followed.

Although Armstrong certainly did not exemplify Chicago Style Dixieland trumpet players, he was extremely important to jazz in this time span. His association with Earl Hines began in Chicago in the 1920s, and he recorded many classics with his Hot Five and Hot Seven groups.

Recording companies have not reproduced Chicago Style Dixieland records with nearly the same enthusiasm that they have Early New Orleans Dixieland, blues singers, and swing bands. Of the records that are available, there is more to be said for the soloists than for the ensemble passages.[30] This seems incongruous when one hears the excellence of ensembles on exceptional records like those of Muggsy Spanier.

Some writers feel that the jazz age ended about 1927. Although jazz did continue, the large bands began to absorb the better jazz players (e.g., Beiderbecke joined the famous Paul Whiteman Orchestra). By the end of the 1920s, the heart of the jazz scene had again moved, this time from Chicago to New York.

For Further Study

1. Discuss why New Orleans was important in the development of jazz at the beginning of the twentieth century.

2. At first, early dixieland music used no piano. What was the instrumentation of these bands?

3. Discuss the influence of Storyville on jazz.

4. Discuss the role each instrument assumed in the overall sound of Early New Orleans Dixieland ensembles.

5. What was the overall plan or design of the music?

6. Listen to the recorded example of the original melody played in Early New Orleans Dixieland style (demonstration 12) and answer the following:
   a. Do you hear the steady pulse of the flat-four rhythm? Which instruments realize this musical characteristic?
   b. In this dixieland arrangement, which instrument is realizing the solo chorus part?
   c. In the return section, which instrument is playing the melody?

7. Who recorded the first instrumental jazz records by a black band?

8. Describe Chicago during the Roaring Twenties.

9. Musically, in what ways did Chicago Style Dixieland music differ from Early New Orleans Dixieland?

10. In what ways did ragtime piano playing influence the rhythm of Chicago Style Dixieland music?

11. In this era, what instruments were added and what instruments replaced instruments used in Early New Orleans Dixieland ensembles? Why did these changes take place?

12. Gradually, short solo spots crept into jazz ensembles. Listen to "Maple Leaf Rag" by Paul Mares and his Friars' Society Orchestra (*Folkways Jazz*, vol. 6). Identify the instruments that you hear in brief solo spots. Does the piano have an opportunity to play solo? Is there a string bass?

13. Listen to Bix Beiderbecke and His Gang play "Margie" (*Folkways Jazz*, vol. 6). In the opening statement of the melody, which instrument is featured? Is this a good example of the $\frac{2}{4}$ rag rhythm? Notice that a bass sax is used in place of a tenor sax.

Suggested Additional Listening

Bechet, Sidney. *Master Musician*. Bluebird Records, 2 AXM-5516.

Beiderbecke, Bix. *Bix Beiderbecke and the Chicago Cornets* (4 sides).

———. *The Bix Beiderbecke Legend*. RCA Victor Records, LPM-2323.

Chicagoans (1928–1930).

Chicago Ramblers. Jazz of the 1920's.

Crosby, Bob. *Stomp Off, Let's Go*. Ace of Hearts Records, AH-29.

Dukes of Dixieland. *At the Jazz Band Ball*. RCA Victor Records, LSP-2097.

Encyclopedia of Jazz on Records, vols. 1 and 2.

Folkways Jazz, vols. 5–7.

Hackett, Bobby. *The Hackett Horn*. Epic Records, EE 22004.

History of Classic Jazz, vols. 4, 6, 7, and 9.

Jazz at Preservation Hall, vol. 2.

The Jazz Odyssey, vol. 2.

The Jazz Story, vols. 1 and 2.

King Oliver's Jazz Band, Smithsonian Collection of Classical Jazz, R-001.

The Original Dixieland Jazz Band. RCA Victor Records, LPU-547.

Ruedebusch, Dick. Mister Trumpet. Jubilee Records, 5015.

———. Meet Mr. Trumpet. Jubilee Records, 5008.

Louis Armstrong

Autobiography. Decca Records, DX-155.
Best of Louis Armstrong. Audio Fidelity Records, 6132.
Essential Louis Armstrong. Verve Records, V-8569.
Folkways Jazz, vols. 2, 4, 5, and 7.
Hello Dolly. Kapp Records, 3364.
Louis Armstrong. Audio Fidelity Records, 6241.
Louis Armstrong. RCA Victor Records, VPM-6044.
Louis Armstrong and Earl Hines. Columbia Records, CL 853.
Louis Armstrong in Memoriam. Everest Records, 3312.
Louis Armstrong in the Thirties and Forties. RCA Victor Records, LSP 2971.
Louis Armstrong Jazz Classics. Decca Records, 8284.
Louis Armstrong Plays W. C. Handy. Columbia Records, CL 591.
Louis Armstrong Story. vols. 1–4. Columbia Records, CL 851-52-53-54.
Louis Armstrong, V.S.O.P. Columbia Special Products, JEE-20019.
Rare Batch of Satch. RCA Victor Records, LPM 2322.
Rare Items. Decca Records, 79225.
Satchmo at Pasadena. Decca Records, 8041.
Satchmo at Symphony Hall. Decca Records, DXS 7195.
Satchmo on Stage. Decca Records, 8330.
Smithsonian Collection of Classic Jazz, vols. 2 and 3.
Young Louis Armstrong: The Sideman. Decca Records, 79233.

Additional Reading Resources

Allen, Walter C., and Rust, Brian. King Joe Oliver.
Berendt, Joachim. The New Jazz Book, 4–12, 32–35.
Berton, Ralph. Remembering Bix: A Memoir of the Jazz Age.
Buerkle, Jack V., and Barker, Danny. Bourbon Street Black.
Dexter, Dave. The Jazz Story, 6–19, 30–55.
Feather, Leonard. The Book of Jazz, 30–38.
Francis, André. Jazz, 27–34.
Harris, Rex. Jazz, 77–93, 189–96.
Hentoff, Nat, and McCarthy, Albert. Jazz: New Perspectives on the History of Jazz, 21–43, 139–69.
Schuller, Gunther. Early Jazz: Its Roots and Musical Development, 63–88, 175–94.
Stearns, Marshall. The Story of Jazz, 33–60.
Sudhalter, Richard M., and Evans, Phillip R. Bix: Man and Legend.
Williams, Martin T., ed. The Art of Jazz, 59–73.

Note: Complete information, including name of publisher and date of publication, is provided in this book's bibliography.

Notes

1. From Henry Pleasants, Serious Music and All That Jazz; 1969. Reprinted by permission of Simon & Schuster, Inc.

2. Joachim Berendt, Jazz Book: From New Orleans to Rock and Free Jazz, trans. by Dan Morgenstern (Westport, Conn. Lawrence Hill & Co., 1975.)

3. Dan Morgenstern, "The Meaning of New Orleans," Down Beat 36, no. 12 (June 1969): 13.

4. Charles Suhor, "Jazz and the New Orleans Press," Down Beat 36, no. 12 (June 1969): 19.

5. Barry Ulanov, Handbook of Jazz (New York: Viking Press, 1959), 8.

6. One example is in the tune "Indiana." The first chord is composed of the notes F, A, C, and D, and the second chord moves to F-sharp, A, C, and D. The natural resolution for the trombone player is from F to F-sharp, pointing out to the other players that the chord has changed and that this is the change that has occurred.

7. Larry Gushee, "King Oliver's Creole Jazz Band," The Art of Jazz, ed. Martin Williams (London: Oxford University Press, 1959), 45.

8. King Oliver's Savannah Syncopaters, "Snag It," Introduction to Jazz, ed. Rev. A. L. Kershaw, Decca Records, DL8244.

9. King Oliver, King Oliver, Epic Records, LA16003; "Jazzin' Babies Blues," Jazz Odyssey, vol. 1; "New Orleans Stomp" and "Where Did You Stay Last Night?" Jazz Odyssey, vol. 2; "Working Man's Blues," Folkways Jazz, vol. 2; "Snake Dance," "Dippermouth Blues," and "High Society," Folkways Jazz, vol. 3; "Sugarfoot Stomp," Folkways Jazz, vol. 5; "Sweet Lovin' Man," Folkways Jazz, vol. 6; "Froggie Moore," History of Classic Jazz.

10. Original Dixieland Jazz Band, "At the Darktown Strutters' Ball," Jazz Odyssey, vol. 1; The Original Dixieland Jazz Band, RCA Victor Records, LPV-547.

11. Original Dixieland Jazz Band, "Barnyard Blues," Jazz Odyssey, vol. 1.

12. Gunther Schuller, The Swing Era (London: Oxford University Press, 1989), 196.

13. Martin T. Williams, "For Louis Armstrong at 70," Down Beat 37, no. 13 (July 1970): 22.

14. Leonard Feather, "The Real Louis Armstrong," Down Beat 29, no. 5 (March 1962): 23.

15. Max Kaminsky, My Life in Jazz (New York: Harper and Row, 1963), 32.

16. Kid Ory, "Weary Blues," History of Classic Jazz, vol. 10.

17. Red Nichols, "Ida," The Jazz Story, vol. 2.

18. Dave Dexter, The Jazz Story: From the Nineties to the Sixties; 1964. By permission of Prentice-Hall, Inc., Englewood Cliffs, N.J.

19. Louis Armstrong and Earl Hines, Columbia Records, CL 853; Earl Hines, The Father Jumps, Bluebird Records, AXM 2-5508; "Piano Man," Singers and Soloists of the Big Bands, Smithsonian Collection of Recordings; Big Band Jazz, Smithsonian Collection of Recordings.

20. Louis Armstrong and His Hot Five, Columbia Records, CL 851; Singers and Soloists of the Swing Bands, Smithsonian Collection of Recordings.

21. Louis Armstrong Plays W. C. Handy, Columbia Records, CL 391.

22. New Orleans Rhythm Kings, "Livery Stable Blues," History of Classic Jazz, vol. 4; Dave Dexter, The Jazz Story, 34.

23. New Orleans Rhythm Kings, "Tin Roof Blues," Introduction to Jazz, Della Records, DL 8244.

24. The Wolverines, "Royal Garden Blues," History of Classic Jazz, vol. 7; Bix Beiderbecke and the Wolverines, Riverside Records, RLP 12-133.

25. Muggsy Spanier, "Muskrat Ramble," History of Classic Jazz, vol. 9.

26. The Bix Beiderbecke Story, vols. 1–3, Columbia Records, CL 844 6.

27. The Windjammers, *Jammin' with the Windjammers,* Argo Records, LP-4047.

28. *The World's Greatest Jazz Band,* Atlantic Records, 1570; *The Dukes of Dixieland,* Audio Fidelity Records, 5962, 5976; Harmony Music Records, 11149; Bobby Hackett, "Struttin' with Some Barbecue," *The Jazz Story,* vol. 2.

29. Bob Crosby, *Stomp It Off, Let's Go,* Mono Records, AH 29; *Greatest Hits,* Decca Records, 74856; "Maryland My Maryland," *The Jazz Story,* vol. 4; *Mardi Gras Parade,* Monmouth-Evergreen Records, 7026.

30. *The Best of Dixieland.*

Boogie-Woogie (the 1920s and 1930s)

"Elements of this style became known later as boogie-woogie, but much of it must have existed from the first time that a Negro, without orthodox instruction, worked out his own thoughts on the piano."[1]

Listening Guide

Demonstration 10
(cassette 1, side A, track 10; CD 1,
track 10)

Boogie-Woogie

:00 to :36 Two choruses on solo piano (note the left hand is playing 8 beats to the bar while utilizing what is known as the "wagon wheels" pattern); drums play 8 rhythm.

Boogie-woogie is another stage in the evolution of jazz, and like ragtime it is a piano style that was important in the development of jazz. The term *boogie-woogie* itself is very descriptive. Although historically the term is used by Rousas Rushdoony in reference to ancient rites in Morocco,[2] the musical association is the feeling created by playing eight beats to the bar. This style of piano playing came into prominence during an economic crisis—the Great Depression of the early 1930s. Jazz again faced a situation in which a full style of piano playing was needed as a substitute for hiring a band. (For an introduction to boogie-woogie, listen to demonstration 10.)

Ostinato Bass

The most identifying feature of boogie-woogie is the eight beats to a measure that are played as an ostinato, the term for a melodic figure that recurs throughout the music. The ostinato is a structural device that works as a stylistically cohesive element of the composition.

In boogie-woogie piano playing, the ostinato phrase is always in the bass. It is very possible, however, to hear boogie-woogie played by a big band when the ostinato is not present; there will still be eight beats to the bar. Distinguished from jazz played in the even $\frac{4}{4}$ rhythm of Early New Orleans Dixieland or the $\frac{2}{4}$ rhythm of ragtime and Chicago Dixie Style Dixieland, boogie-woogie employs eight beats to the bar in the ostinato.

There are two distinct methods of boogie-woogie playing. In both, the right hand is kept free for melodic interpretation or improvisation. The difference between the two methods occurs in the use of the left hand. In one the left hand plays full, moving chords and in the other a **walking bass** line outlines the chords in a melodic fashion. (For notational examples of these two methods of playing boogie-woogie bass, see example 18 in Appendix B.)

Meade Lux Lewis.
Courtesy of Bob Asen, Metronome Magazine

Boogie-woogie has also been called "8 over 4," a description that comes from the eight notes that the left hand of the piano plays in the normal four-beat measure. Although the music might be written in the usual four-beat time signature, the feel of the music emphasizes the eight-beat time. (For notational examples of 8-over-4 playing, see example 19 in Appendix B.)

Although the right hand can play an interesting melodic line, the main feature of this style is rhythmic virtuosity. The left hand and the right hand operate so independently that boogie-woogie often sounds like it is being performed by two pianists instead of one. The style is extremely taxing physically, as it is usually played loudly with tensed muscles, a most tiring means of performing. The **riff** emphasis, typical of Kansas City (to be discussed in chapter 7), is often heard in the right hand of the boogie-woogie player as the left hand busies itself with the ostinato. Boogie-woogie is generally, but not always, played in the blues form.

The Players

Boogie-woogie was usually played by untrained pianists. Ragtime had incorporated European influences, but it appears as though boogie-woogie piano players worked out their style without any thought of European concert tradition. Many could not read music, so they simply listened and developed this full style of playing. Most of the time, boogie-woogie players were comfortable playing only this one style of jazz. However, Pete Johnson, who was surely the number one boogie-woogie pianist in Kansas City, was also a fine stride player. He really showed his versatility when he accompanied blues singer Joe Turner hour after hour.[3]

Although it is true that boogie-woogie reached its peak of popularity during the depression of the early 1930s, the style surely was not invented then. The first time that the word boogie appears to have been used on a record was in 1928 by Chicago's Pine Top Smith as he recorded "Pine Top's Boogie"[4] (NW, 259, side 1, band 4). Huddie Ledbetter claimed that he first heard this type of playing in 1899, Bunk Johnson (an early New Orleans trumpeter) said 1904, Jelly Roll Morton said 1904, and W. C. Handy said 1909. This music has also been called "Western rolling," "fast Western," and "Texas style," indicating that its origin was in the western part of the country, although Florida has also been named as a birthplace.

There were three fairly defined generations of boogie-woogie players. The earlier pianists were active primarily in the 1920s: Jimmy Yancey, Cow Cow Davenport, and Pine Top Smith[5] (NW, 259, Jimmy Yancey, "The Mellow Blues," side 2, band 3; NW, 259, "Tell 'Em About Me," side 2, band 4; FJ, "Yancey Stomp," vol. 10). The middle group, popular during the early 1930s, consisted of Meade Lux Lewis, Albert Ammons, Joe Sullivan, Clarence Lofton, and Pete Johnson[6] (S, "Honky Tonk Train," side C, band 4; NW, 259, side 1, band 6; FJ, vols. 9 and 10). The last group included such players as Freddie Slack, Cleo Brown, and Bob Zurke.

Listening Guide

Demonstration 11
(cassette 1, side A, track 11; CD 1, track 11)

Meade Lux Lewis (playing)
"Honky Tonk Train"

:00 Piano solo throughout; trill for short introduction.
:02 Chorus 1: Left hand playing "full moving chords" pattern, right hand playing melodically and very independently.
:19 Chorus 2: Lewis shows his control by playing 6 beats with the right hand while playing 8 beats with the left (this occurs often on this record).
:36 Chorus 3.
:53 Chorus 4: Picks up last small idea from previous chorus and expands on it.
1:10 Chorus 5: Uses trills and shows extreme independence of hands.
1:27 Chorus 6: Shows a small thought, then develops a technical display.
1:44 Chorus 7: Many full chords and use of the "6 against 8" as in chorus 2.
2:02 Chorus 8: similar to chorus 7.
2:19 Chorus 9.
2:36 Chorus 10: Getting softer, seems to be tapering down, preparing to stop.
2:57 End.

Rent Parties

Rent parties were actually all-night jam sessions. The word was passed around that a musician, or sometimes a friend, could not come up with the rent payment. A piano would be rolled into the apartment, and musicians would drop in and play. On a table would be a hat that acted as a pot for contributions. Much more often than not, when dawn's early light made its appearance, the necessary rent money had accrued. For the musicians, these sessions were often learning experiences, but at times cutting contests developed, much to the audiences' approval.

Origin

Max Harrison states that this style of piano playing developed from a guitar technique used in mining, logging, and turpentine camps.[7] When three guitar players performed together, one picked out an improvised melody, the second played rhythmic chords, and the third played a bass line. To imitate three guitars at one time, piano players had to develop a very full style by having the right hand play the melodic improvisation and the left hand substitute for the other two guitars. By playing the eight faster notes in the left hand, the piano player can give the impression that the three guitar parts are all there. The result is that both a bass line and the chords are outlined by the left hand, leaving the right hand free to play an improvisation. (For notational examples of how the harmonies are outlined with the left hand, see example 20 in Appendix B.)

Although boogie-woogie is considered a definite piano style, it has been successfully adapted by large bands such as those of Will Bradley, Lionel Hampton, Tommy Dorsey, Count Basie, Harry James, Glenn Miller, and others.[8] The eight beats to the bar created by the ostinato bass is considered its most important feature. This rhythmic component exemplifies the fact that jazz players are always searching for new means of expression. However, having been created within a fairly limited set of circumstances (the guitar origin), regardless of the rhythmic interest, this style's range of expression is not very wide. Boogie-woogie has never really disappeared (one major revival occurred as late as 1938), though it is not prominent today.

Summary

Boogie-woogie music has not evolved further because, if it were to change rhythmically, it would no longer be considered boogie-woogie. It could progress harmonically, but, because of the very mechanics of performing this style, most players are comfortable only with quite simple harmonies. In fact, since the beginnings of this style, the standard chord sequence has been the blues chord progression, and this is still true today.

The boogie-woogie revival around 1938 was so popular that almost all performing groups had at least one number in their repertoire. Some boogie-woogie pianists toured and even played in such notable concert halls as Carnegie Hall. Pete Johnson, Meade Lux Lewis, and Albert Ammons perform a boogie-woogie trio on the *Spirituals to Swing* album, which was recorded live at Carnegie Hall.[9] It seems that when three of these stylistic players perform at the same time, they almost try to outshout one another. In their exuberance they even lose the eight-to-the-bar feeling. The revival was a boon to these players but did not serve to help the style evolve further.

For Further Study

1. Define the term *boogie-woogie* as applied to piano technique.
2. In this style of piano technique, how many beats are in each measure?
3. Describe two methods of boogie-woogie playing.
4. Listen to "Yancey Stomp" by pianist Jimmy Yancey (FJ, vol. 10).
5. Listen to "Honky Tonk Train" (demonstration 20) and decide whether the left-hand ostinato bass is in the walking bass style or the chordal bass style.

Suggested Additional Listening

Boogie-Woogie. Folkways Jazz, vol. 10.
Boogie Woogie. History of Classic Jazz, vol. 5.
Boogie Woogie Piano: Original Recordings 1938–40. Columbia Records, KC-32708.
Boogie-Woogie Rarities.
Cuttin' the Boogie. New World Records, 259.
Pitchin' Boogie. Milestone Records, MLP-2018.

Additional Reading Resources

Hentoff, Nat, and McCarthy, Albert, eds. *Jazz*, 107–35.
Williams, Martin T., ed. *The Art of Jazz*, 95–108.

Note: Complete information, including name of publisher and date of publication, is included in this book's bibliography.

Notes

1. Marshall Stearns, *The Story of Jazz* (London: Oxford University Press, 1958), 168.
2. Rousas J. Rushdoony, *The Politics of Pornography* (Sandton City, Sandton, South Africa: Valiant Publishers, 1975), 98.
3. Joe Turner and Pete Johnson, "Roll 'Em Pete," Columbia Records 35959; "Johnson and Turner Blues," *Jazz of Two Decades*, EmArcy Records, DEM-2.
4. Pine Top Smith, "Pine Top's Boogie," *Encyclopedia of Jazz on Records*, vol. 1.
5. Jimmy Yancey, "The Fives," *History of Classic Jazz*, vol. 5.
6. Meade Lux Lewis, "Far Ago Blues," *History of Classic Jazz*, vol. 5; Albert Ammons, "St. Louis Blues," *Folkways Jazz*, vol. 10; Joe Sullivan, "Little Rock Getaway," *Folkways Jazz*, vol. 9; Clarence Lofton, "Brown Skin Gal," *Folkways Jazz*, vol. 10; "Blue Boogie," *History of Classic Jazz*, vol. 5; Pete Johnson, "Let 'Em Jump," *Folkways Jazz*, vol. 10; "Lone Star Blues," *History of Classic Jazz*, vol. 5.
7. Max Harrison, "Boogie Woogie," in *Jazz*, ed. Nat Hentoff and Albert McCarthy (New York: Holt, Rinehart & Winston, 1959), 107.
8. Will Bradley, "Beat Me Daddy, Eight to the Bar," Columbia Records, 35530; Lionel Hampton, "Hamp's Boogie Woogie,"

Decca Records, 71828; Tommy Dorsey, "Boogie-Woogie," RCA Victor Records, 26054; Count Basie, "Boogie-Woogie," *The Best of Basie*, Roulette Records, RE118; Harry James, "Boo Woo," Columbia Records, 35958; Glenn Miller, "Bugle Woogie," *The Glenn Miller Chesterfield Shows*, RCA Victor Records, LSP-3981 (e).

9. Pete Johnson, Albert Ammons, and Meade Lux Lewis, "Cavalcade of Boogie," *From Spirituals to Swing*, Vanguard Records, VRS-8523/4.

CHAPTER

Swing (1932–1942)

"As individual as each era may ultimately be, it cannot be entirely separated from its connections to the past and its links to the future."[1]

Demonstration 12
(cassette 1, side A, track 12; CD 1, track 12)

Swing

:00 Introduction on solo drums using tom-toms.

:04 Ensemble chorus (saxes on melody, brass on riff); full rhythm section keeps $\frac{4}{4}$ rhythm.

:17 Drum solo on tom-toms.

:20 Clarinet solo (one chorus backed by trombones on riff).

:34 Ensemble chorus (same as first chorus except a tone higher).

:49 Ensemble chorus (same except for another half tone higher for still more intensity).

1:01 Clarinet solo break.

1:03 End.

Swing is the name given to the era following boogie-woogie in the development of jazz. In general, *swing* refers to the music of large dance bands that played written arrangements, occasionally using improvised solos. Most noteworthy jazz has a rhythmic drive, or swing. Still, the era of jazz in the 1930s and early 1940s is called the swing era.

Some jazz terms can become quite confusing, and *swing* is one of them. The confusion comes from the fact that some of the most popular swing music did not swing; rather, it involved jazz players doing a jazz interpretation of pretty **ballads.** One unusual aspect of swing jazz is that, though most people remember the **up-tempo** tunes, the swing bands actually played more ballads than anything else. But it should be remembered that those ballads were played by players who were very jazz oriented. Listen, for example, to Benny Goodman, the King of Swing, play his theme, a very pretty ballad called "Good-bye"; jazz trumpeter Harry James plays an **obligato** in the background.[2]

Some listeners today feel that all swing bands sound alike. The swing era saw literally hundreds of name attractions, and so one of the biggest concerns for the leaders was identification. They wanted the fans to be able to distinguish their band from all others after hearing just a few measures of music. Therefore, most bands attempted to have an identifying trademark. For example, Tommy Dorsey probably played with a more beautiful tone and control on the trombone than anyone else, so he played solos on just about every arrangement, and

Benny Goodman.
Courtesy of Popsie and Phoebe Jacobs

the fans recognized his sound.³ Glenn Miller used a clarinet to play lead over his saxophone section, a most identifying feature.⁴ (For an introduction to swing, listen to demonstration 12.)

Beginnings of the Swing Era

Fletcher Henderson, an influential figure in the swing era, is credited with having created, with his brother Horace and with Don Redman, the pattern for swing arrangements.⁵ This pattern was successful, being copied by almost every popular dance band of the era. Henderson is said to have established the independent use of trumpet, trombone, saxophone, and rhythm sections, with the use of soloists. (This exact format is used today by most of the thousands of college and high school jazz bands in the United States. The attitude, also fostered by music publishers, seems to be that this is the easiest avenue for today's jazz education.)

In New York in 1924, Henderson had Louis Armstrong, Coleman Hawkins, and Don Redman among his exclusive personnel. In 1924 in Kansas City, Bennie Moten put together his first saxophone section as such; the idea was simply to create more sonority. Moten added more brass as early as 1931, using three trumpets and two trombones. Henderson had done the same thing in 1929. Some say that the first jazz orchestra to play written arrangements in New York was the Billy Paige Band, with Don Redman as arranger and lead alto sax, in 1922. Redman then joined Fletcher Henderson, stayed with him until 1927, joined McKinney's Cotton Pickers in 1931, and eventually organized his own band. Henderson, Redman, and others took the parts that were generally conceived to be for one trumpet, for example, and harmonized them to be played by three trumpets (For notational examples, see examples 21A and 21B, Appendix B.)

Jazz Arrangements

The general procedure in the creation of a swing jazz arrangement is to write a score that has specific notes for each instrument to play in every measure. (For a notational example, see example 22, Appendix B.) In jazz, the music arranger indicates measures for solo improvisation. After the arranger has decided which musical notations will result in the desired sounds, the score is given to a music copyist who extracts from the score the individual parts for the various instruments. This then becomes a blueprint for each instrumentalist, showing exactly what is to be played while the other instrumentalists play their parts.

Short, repeated refrains or phrases (which are quite typical in African music), or riffs, are common in jazz. Sometimes riffs are used in an ostinato fashion as catalysts that hold the music together. Repeated riffs,

which cause great momentum and impetus, were used extensively by Kansas City musicians such as Bennie Moten (later Count Basie's band) in the 1920s and by New York musicians such as Fletcher Henderson, who was scoring arrangements for blues singers Bessie Smith, Ma Rainey, and others. The use of riffs became standard in the more jazz-oriented big bands, sometimes backing up a soloist and sometimes composing entire selections. Listen to demonstration 12 for the swing excerpt in which the brass section plays a riff behind the saxophones. The trombones also play a riff under the clarinet solo (For notational examples, see examples 24A, 24B, Appendix B.)

Fletcher Henderson

Fletcher Henderson, a schooled piano player from Georgia, came to New York in 1920 originally to do postgraduate study at Columbia University as a chemistry major. Henderson became so involved in music, however, that his other goals were forsaken. Henderson was a pianist, but his most notable talent was his arranging. He wrote most of the library of music that launched the career of the Benny Goodman orchestra.

The personnel of Henderson's own orchestra was most impressive. At one time or another, almost all the important black musicians of the day played in his band: Louis Armstrong, Roy Eldridge, Don Redman, Coleman Hawkins, and Lester Young. Many members from the Henderson band went on either to have bands of their own or to become featured solo attractions.⁶

There always seem to be many controversies concerning jazz. Henderson became deeply involved in one: the split between the advocates of small dixieland bands and those favoring the larger bands heading in the direction of swing. Many thought that the rise of the big bands meant the fall of jazz completely. The small-band advocates considered these large ensembles "top heavy" because of the unusually large number of horn players. Not only was the rhythm section now outnumbered, but, as the ensembles grew in size, the arrangements tended to become more detailed to provide a tighter ensemble sound. With the larger number of musicians, the dixieland texture, which granted each player much individual expression, was no longer possible. The solo areas in a swing band composition offered chances for individual expression, but they were only a small part of the whole composition.

At first, Henderson toyed with sort of an enlarged dixieland group. But with the addition of Redman, who had studied at the Boston and Detroit music conservatories, tighter harmonic control became a major interest. Henderson thought that too much improvisation was almost dreary unless the improvisers were really exceptional. He also thought that the polyphony established in the dixieland styles was too risky and that there should be more control.

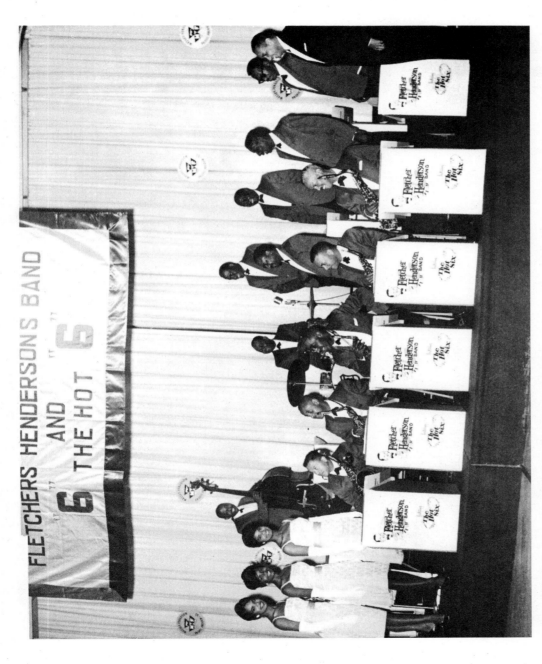

Fletcher Henderson and his orchestra. Henderson is on the extreme right.
Courtesy of Ray Avery

New York

During the 1920s, when Chicago Style Dixieland was the most popular jazz expression, New York and Kansas City were the most important geographic areas for developments leading toward the swing style of jazz. In the mid-1920s, Duke Ellington was becoming a name attraction, King Oliver was playing in the Savoy Ballroom in New York's Harlem, and Fletcher Henderson was at the Roseland Ballroom in Times Square. In New York were located network radio programs, booking offices, and recording studios so that musicians began to migrate to that city from all over the country. One of the most swinging bands to invade New York was William McKinney's Cotton Pickers. This band, with many ex-Henderson personnel, recorded more than fifty tunes between 1928 and 1933 (FJ, "Four or Five Times," vol. 8).

The band of Chick Webb was one of the new bands that kept appearing in New York around 1929 or 1930[7]

(NW, 217, "Heebie Jeebies"). This band could swing while playing lightly and never exploited showmanship at the expense of musical integrity. In the mid-1930s, the teenager Ella Fitzgerald raised that band to prominence. (One of the authors, while participating often in the famous "battle of bands" at the Savoy Ballroom in New York's Harlem, where Chick Webb's band was usually considered to be a house band, was always glad that the Webb band was not one of his adversaries.)

However, the best-known performers who developed swing in New York in the 1920s were Fletcher Henderson and Duke Ellington[8] (S, "The Stampede," side B, band 11; S, "Wrappin' It Up," side B, band 12; S, "East St. Louis Toodle-oo," side D, band 10, S, "New East St. Louis Toodle-oo," side D, band 11; S, "Concerto for Cootie," side E, band 1; S, "Ko-Ko," side D, band 13; S, "Blue Serge," side E, band 4; FJ, "Copenhagen," "Money Blues," "Jackass Blues," and "Down South Camp Meeting," vol. 8).

Demonstration 13 (cassette 1, side A, track 13; CD 1, track 13)

Fletcher Henderson
"Wrappin' It Up"

The structure for each chorus is ABAC.

:00 Introduction: Brass has the theme and saxes respond.

:09 First chorus: Saxes state the main theme, and each phrase is a variation of the previous one; this is structural phrase A.

:19 Structural phrase B.

:28 Structural phrase A as trumpets join the saxes.

:37 Structural phrase C.

:48 Second chorus: Hilton Jefferson plays an alto sax solo backed up by muted trumpets; same ABAC structure for this chorus.

1:25 Third chorus: Red Allen plays a trumpet solo backed up by saxes.

1:34 Whole brass section plays lead.

1:44 Trumpet solo resumes.

2:03 Fourth chorus: Theme is tossed back and forth between brass and reeds (now on clarinets).

2:13 Clarinet solo.

2:22 Saxes take lead.

2:31 Brass join in.

2:39 Ending phrase, which later becomes a big-band cliché.

2:42 End.

Demonstration 14 (cassette 1, side A, track 14; CD 1, track 14)

Duke Ellington Orchestra
"In a Mello Tone"

:00 Piano solo as introduction: 8 measures with unison saxes taking pickups on last measure.

:13 First chorus: Unison saxes with trombones playing an elaborate backup for 30 measures.

1:09 Two-measure piano interlude.

1:13 Second chorus: Cootie Williams on trumpet solo with plunger; saxes back him up; 32 measures with ensemble pickups in the last measure.

2:13 Third chorus: 4 measures, ensemble.

2:21 Alto sax solo by Johnny Hodges: 4 measures plus next 6.

2:40 Two-measure break by Hodges on alto sax.

2:44 Eight-measure solo by Hodges on alto sax.

2:58 Ensemble alternates measures with Hodges on sax for 6 measures.

3:12 Ensemble plays out softly.

3:17 End.

The structure for each chorus is ABAC.

Generally, the New York bands had heavily structured arrangements. But really, no New York school existed as had in New Orleans, Chicago, and Kansas City. There were many important performers in New York in the 1920s, but their styles did not seem to coincide. Regardless, the direction of most was at least toward swing.

Kansas City

"Jazz was literally exploding in myriad new directions—not only musically and stylistically, but geographically as well."

Kansas City was bustling with activity from the early 1920s to about 1938. A political organization known as the Pendergast Machine did much more than encourage the nightclub atmosphere, and so an abundance of employment opportunities for jazz musicians arose. The influx showed that Kansas City had become a jazz

mecca: there was Bill Basie from Red Bank, New Jersey; Ben Webster from Tulsa; Lester Young from Mississippi; and Andy Kirk from Dallas.

The Bennie Moten band was considered to be the top band in the Kansas City area from about 1926 to 1935[10] (S, "Moten Swing," side C, band 2; NW, 217, "Toby," side 2, band 1; FJ, "Kansas City Breakdown" and "Moten's Swing," vol. 8), but the competition was extremely keen from the bands of Andy Kirk (piano and arrangements by Mary Lou Williams), Walter Page, Alphonso Trent, and others. The Kansas City bands were looser in musical setting and relied heavily on blues-based riffs.

Mary Lou Williams

One of the greatest performers to come out of the Kansas City area was undoubtedly the multitalented Mary Lou Williams. She was the first woman in jazz history to compose and arrange for a large jazz band, and she dominated the performances of the great Andy Kirk band with her skillful piano playing.[11] Her eclecticism held her in great stead, and she is considered one of the great jazz pianists. Her compositions were in the libraries of a dozen leading swing bands. The last years of her life (she

Mary Lou Williams.
Courtesy of the Institute of Jazz Studies

died in 1981) were filled with many honors, including a street in Kansas City being named after her. Mary Lou Williams was always a perennial innovator.[12]

Count Basie

Count Basie was in New York in the early 1920s when he joined a road show, the Benny Moten band, that became stranded in Kansas City. He then started his own band, and most of Moten's better players went with Basie. It is therefore natural that some historians believe that Basie took over Moten's band, especially as all these events happened around the time of Moten's death.

When Moten died, Basie became the leading figure in the Kansas City style of swing. He gave the audiences what they wanted while maintaining a true jazz orchestra with extremely high standards for over forty years.

Basie's players used all of the musical advancements developed in the Kansas City territory to good advantage. For example, Basie anticipated bop by freeing the piano from merely keeping time, and his drummer, Jo Jones, added interesting accents to his very moving rhythm. Basie's economic piano style demonstrated the old adage that less is more. The band, with its relaxed swing, was lauded more for its performances than for the compositions it performed. Members were also admired for their consistent ability to swing; hence, the band was often called "the swing machine." Economics forced Basie to go to a small group for two years (1950–52). But "Basie himself is reported to have said in

Count Basie and his rhythm section. Bass: Walter Page; guitar: Freddy Green; drums: Jo Jones.
Courtesy of Bob Asen, Metronome Magazine

1950, if he could just have that old band once again before he died, he would leave this earth a happy man."[13]

Basie died in June 1984. However, the Basie band, now led by the talented woodwind player Frank Foster, still swings as hard as any band today[14] (S, "Doggin' Around," side D, band 5; S, "Taxi War Dance," side D, band 6; S, "Lester Leaps In," side D, band 7).

Swing Becomes Accepted

The depression came in 1929, and a few musicians, including Armstrong and Ellington, left for Europe. Some hotel-type bands, such as Lombardo's, survived, and many of the better jazz players, such as Benny Goodman, were able to find employment in staff radio jobs. But in general, the entire business suddenly failed. Music was a luxury that most of the public simply had to do without.

Many jazz authorities believe that the swing era was launched in 1934 when Benny Goodman left the radio studios and formed his own band, using arrangements scored mainly by Fletcher Henderson. However, swing

was certainly well on its way before 1934. In 1932, Glen Gray and his Casa Loma Orchestra, with many reputable jazz performers, was playing weekly radio shows for Camel cigarettes. (This was a large band featuring precise arrangements laden with riffs often played with a call-and-response format between brass and saxes.) They first recorded as early as 1929 as the Orange Blossoms, then changed their name to that of a Toronto club, Casa Loma, also in 1929. Their first big hit, "Casa Loma Stomp,"[15] was recorded in 1930.

As stated earlier, before 1932 the Fletcher Henderson band was already well established, as was Duke Ellington's, and good, large swing bands were playing in the Kansas City area. The fact that large jazz bands developed in two such diverse areas as New York and Kansas City is another unusual phenomenon, like the diverse origins of the music itself, that surrounds jazz.

The public was trying to forget the stock market crash and the ensuing depression, and one logical manifestation was the great upsurge in dancing. The jazz players of the swing era became highly sought after for their dance music. The speakeasies of the 1920s were enough to hold the six or seven thousand people who would come from miles around to hear their favorite swing bands.

The bands of the swing era produced a fuller sound than that of the dixieland bands mainly because they used two or three times as many players. Because of the number of instrumentalists, the music was organized in a homophonic construction (for Notational examples see Appendix B, #23), making the musical sounds more organized in their effect. At times the music of the large bands even sounded less complex than the polyphonically conceived dixieland music. The **block chords** used by the swing bands are the obvious clues to the homophonic construction of this type of jazz. Most of the orchestras of the swing era returned to the use of a flat-four rhythm to give their music a rhythm distinct from that which immediately preceded it. During the 1920s, the widely imitated Chicago Style Dixieland was played in $\frac{2}{4}$, but the Kansas City musicians at this same time played mainly in $\frac{4}{4}$; swing jazz was usually in $\frac{4}{4}$.

Paul Whiteman

The Original Dixieland Jazz Band had played in New York in 1917, but even more people were made aware of the possibilities of jazz elements when Paul Whiteman introduced George Gershwin's "Rhapsody in Blue" in Aeolian Hall in 1924. This work can hardly be considered jazz as it is defined in this book, but it pointed out some of the idioms of this music to the public and helped focus attention in the general direction of jazz. "Rhapsody in Blue" could conceivably be construed as the first third-stream music effort. (This direction is discussed in chapter 12.)

Obviously, Whiteman's title, the King of Jazz, was a misnomer, merely a publicity name, but Whiteman was a very influential man and a great supporter of jazz players. He hired many name jazz musicians and paid the top salary of the day. Jazz players and critics are too quick to degrade Whiteman's position when they fail to consider that the jazz players joined Whiteman's orchestra of their own free will, often when they were not busy enough to maintain financial stability.

Whiteman had great admiration for these players. Consider, for example, that Bix Beiderbecke was away from the orchestra for nearly a year trying to recover from alcoholism and related problems. During that time, Whiteman retained him on full salary and, it is also reported, paid Beiderbecke's medical bills. During some of that time, Beiderbecke played one-night engagements with competing orchestras.

A look at some of the personnel from Whiteman's roster establishes his regard for, and financial support of, the jazz players of the day: Bix Beiderbecke, Frankie Trumbauer, Red Norvo, Tommy and Jimmy Dorsey, Jack and Charlie Teagarden, Eddie Lang, and Joe Venuti. Most of the recordings of the Whiteman orchestra show

---

Listening Guide 🎵 📼

Demonstration 15
(cassette 1, side A, track 15; CD 1, track 15)

Count Basie
*"Taxi War Dance"**

:00 Introduction consists of 4 measures of piano solo (Basie) in a boogie-woogie pattern followed by 4 measures of brass.

:09 First chorus: Tenor sax solo (Lester Young) for 16 measures (rhythm plays $\frac{4}{4}$ except piano plays accents throughout the record).

:26 8 measures as bridge of chorus, still tenor sax solo.

:35 8 measures to finish up the chorus, same as first 8 measures of this first chorus.

:44 Second chorus: Trombone solo (Dickie Wells), 32-measure chorus with the same chords for the bridge that were used in the first chorus.

1:23 Third chorus: 4 measures of brass.

1:27 Four measures of tenor sax solo (Buddy Tate).

1:32 Repeat of the above 8 measures.

1:41 Eight measures of piano solo on the bridge chords.

1:50 Four measures of brass.

1:55 Four measures of tenor sax solo.

1:59 Fourth chorus: 4 measures of full ensemble (piano playing boogie-woogie pattern).

2:04 Four measures of tenor sax solo (Lester Young).

2:09 Repeat of above 8 measures.

2:16 Eight measures of piano solo on bridge chords.

2:26 Four measures of full ensemble.

2:31 Four measures of tenor sax solo.

2:36 Two measures of piano, 2 measures of tenor sax (Buddy Tate), 2 measures of bass solo (Walter Page), 2 measures of drums (Jo Jones).

2:45 Full ensemble ending.

2:48 End.

*Smithsonian Collection, side D, band 6.

---

fairly small and could not house large bands. But with the repeal of the Volstead Act in 1933, social life so changed that large ballrooms were needed for the thousands who wanted to dance every night and large bands seemed to be the answer to the dance halls. The country was covered with large ballrooms. Bands often played in towns so small that there would be only one house with an indoor bathroom. Yet there would be a ballroom large very little influence of jazz as it is considered in this book. However, there are noteworthy recordings by jazz players made while they were members of Whiteman's band. For example, Whiteman established a group within his larger organization called the Swing Wing. Jack Teagarden and others were featured in this "band within a band."[16]

Among early jazz trombonists Jack Teagarden is *the* outstanding performer. His easygoing manner fostered a style of playing jazz on the trombone that was unique among his predecessors and peers. His playing and his wonderful jazz singing became a lyric style to be imitated for years. He died in 1964, having recorded about a thousand sides (songs) during his lifetime. His long

musical lines, flexible technique, and beautiful tone will probably never be equaled.

The Swing Bands

By the late 1930s, prosperity was returning, and records and radio were extremely instrumental in publicizing jazz. As a consequence, for the first time a segment of jazz was the most-listened-to music in the world, and more excellent musicians were working in this field than during any previous period. During 1937, eighteen thousand musicians were on the road, and the number continued to increase. After having been frequently considered

Benny Goodman and his orchestra. Trumpets (left to right): Harry James, Ziggy Elman, Chris Griffin, Johnny Davis; trombones: Murray McEachern, Red Ballard; saxophones: Vido Musso, Hymie Schertzer, Art Rollini, George Koenig; piano: Jess Stacy; bass: Harry Goodman; guitar: Allan Reuss; drums: Gene Krupa.

Courtesy of Leo Walker

a fairly tawdry occupation, jazz, with the rise of swing, became a respectable, remunerative profession with the "public's embrace of swing as its national music."[17]

The first jazz concert took place in 1936 at New York's Onyx Club. It was called a "Swing Music Concert." The next year, "Hollywood's Second Swing Concert" was held at the famous Palomar Ballroom, featuring Benny Goodman, Louis Prima, Les Hite, Ben Pollack, and a fine all-female big band under the direction of Peggy Gilbert. The Benny Goodman jazz concerts, presented for the first time in Carnegie Hall in 1938, were milestones in the acceptance of jazz.[18]

At this time, Benny Goodman was considered the King of Swing. It was understood that, if a clarinet player did not play the instrument in the Goodman manner, he was not playing clarinet correctly. This of course put great pressure on talented clarinet players who wanted to play in their own style instead of copying Goodman.

By the time Goodman became a success, large black orchestras had already established the format for this size of organization. These were the orchestras of Moten, Kirk, and Trent from the Midwest and those of Henderson, Ellington, McKinney, and Jimmy Lunceford from the East. Goodman's success was not assured at all until he opened at the Palomar Ballroom in Los Angeles in 1935 after a very discouraging tour across the country. But from that moment on, there was no doubt that this next style of jazz was extremely well received by the public.[19] Dave Dexter wrote glowingly of Goodman:

Goodman often did generous things, and his courage in mixing Negroes with what was essentially an all-white orchestra and touring the Southern states can never be

underestimated. He achieved as much in smashing segregation in the arts as anybody in history.

Through the years, Goodman's clarinet remained the model for all beginners. Shaw could play "prettier" notes at times, Barney Bigard added an elusive coloring to Ellington's ensemble and big Irving Prestopnik wove glorious improvisations above the Dixieland blowings of the Bob Crosbyites, but Goodman had a sound all his own, a technique no other could top and a swinging, rhythmic approach that was irresistible.[20]

Artie Shaw claims that his own playing grew from his music, not from his instrument.

The Dorsey Brothers started with a large-band version of dixieland[21] with singer Bob Crosby. When Crosby developed his own band with the help of ex-Pollack saxophonist Gil Rodin, it was only natural that Crosby's band would be dixieland oriented—that was the style he had been weaned on in the early Dorsey Brothers orchestra.

Occasionally, cooperative bands allowed all the members to share in the profits and woes. Glen Gray and the Casa Loma Orchestra operated in this manner[22] (NW, 217, "Casa Loma Stomp," side 1, band 2). In the beginning, the Woody Herman Herds was cooperative, but later it ended this means of operating and went through several distinct changes. At first it was a mixture of an overgrown dixieland band and a Kansas City blues-type swing band. Later it progressed toward the Goodman approach to swing, and later still it became "progressive."[23]

The public decided that the most popular of all the swing bands was that of Glenn Miller. Miller had been involved with jazz in its truest sense since childhood. He

Glenn Miller and his orchestra. Trombones (left to right): Paul Tanner, Jimmy Priddy, Frank D'Anolfo, Miller; trumpets: John Best, Steve Lipkin, Dale McMickle, Billy May; saxophones: Will Schwartz, Al Klink, Skip Martin, Ernie Caceres, Tex Beneke; drums: Moe Purtill; guitar: Bobby Hackett; bass: Doc Goldberg, piano: Chummy MacGregor; singers: Bill Conway, Hal Dickinson, Marion Hutton, Ray Eberle, Chuck Goldstein, Ralph Brewster.

Courtesy of Paul Tanner

had worked with Red Nichols, Ben Pollack, and others in earlier styles and had organized and worked with the Dorsey Brothers, Ray Noble, and others heading toward swing. Miller was a brilliant arranger, an outstanding businessman, and a fine trombone player. When he started his band, he went deeply in debt but within two years was a millionaire. One of the authors found him to be an exemplary employer. The band worked only the best jobs in the country, had a commercial radio program three nights a week, recorded often, and even made motion pictures. It was an ideal job for a young sideman. Today there are Glenn Miller societies all over the world, and at this writing Miller albums record extremely high sales.[24]

It was only natural that new bands continually developed, being fronted by musicians who had been featured as solo artists in someone else's band. For example, from the Benny Goodman band came Harry James, Gene Krupa, Lionel Hampton, Teddy Wilson, and others who became leaders in their own right.

The first recording of a new band would often sound similar to the band that the new leader had just left because the new leader would hire friends from the band from which he had resigned. Because the musician's union had an established minimum salary that had to be paid to the musicians for recordings, new leaders would often hire more capable musicians outside the band for recording purposes.

A word should be mentioned at this time about pianist Stan Kenton's varied career. He organized and wrote arrangements in 1940 for a band to compete with the stylings of other swing bands. His second stage, from 1945 to 1949, featured a series of "Artistry" motifs, or a large band that used harmonic and melodic advancements of the bop era, labeled "progressive." Pete Rugolo was the chief arranger. Next, Kenton had a very large orchestra that included classical woodwinds, horns, and a full string section. Kenton called this phase "Innovations in Modern Music." His next band, in 1954, was a more normal size swing jazz band, but he featured the very modern writing of Bill Holman, Shorty Rogers, Gerry Mulligan, and others. The 1960s saw Kenton in front of what he called his "Neophonic Orchestra," a most interesting experiment involving many talented contemporary arranger/composers. For several more years, Kenton remained one of the most energetic, exciting personalities in jazz with an exceptional band that toured the world. He died at the age of 67 on August 25, 1979.[25]

The overall contributions of different swing bands to the development and future of jazz were varied. Benny Goodman's contribution was drive with an intense $\frac{4}{4}$ rhythmic feeling. The Casa Loma Band featured ensemble arrangements specializing in the call-and-response pattern. Duke Ellington offered new sounds and colors built around the individual talents of his musicians and introduced larger forms into jazz. Glenn Miller proved that unerring precision was a possibility in jazz. Lionel

Hampton played with chaotic swing and uninhibited showmanship plus superior improvisation. Bob Crosby preserved and expanded Chicago Style Dixieland music. Stan Kenton used more complex harmonies and brought recognition to such innovators as Shelly Manne, Shorty Rogers, Gerry Mulligan, and many others. Count Basie contributed a type of relaxed ensemble setting with longer solo opportunities. Woody Herman aided the growth of jazz by continually adapting each new trend, and his bands were always proving grounds for rising young instrumentalists. Herman surprised many people by adding a woman trumpet player in the 1940s, Billie Rogers, who played with as much strength and swung as hard as anyone else in the band.

In the swing era, the role of composer/arranger became important. Such excellent style-setting musicians as Fletcher and Horace Henderson, Don Redman, Duke Ellington, and many others shifted the timbre of jazz from the early Paul Whiteman sounds to the sophisticated, swinging music of the large bands. Today, fine textbooks by Bill Russo, Henry Mancini, George Russell, Russ Garcia, Van Alexander, and others deal with this art.

Benny Goodman (1909–1986)

Rave reviews for an artist (who was probably the universal symbol of jazz thirty-five years earlier) dominated the media in 1975. Although it is true that when Benny Goodman played a concert many of his listeners experienced a great deal of nostalgia, some who thoroughly enjoyed his mastery of the clarinet, his vibrant rhythm feel, and his effervescent improvisations were too young to feel any nostalgia for his music. He was truly a master of his art.

Benny Goodman was born on May 30, 1909, in Chicago, the eighth of eleven children of an immigrant tailor. Just as jazz is a product of America, Benny Goodman's rise from poverty to global fame is a typical American story.

His early musical training was in a synagogue orchestra and at Hull House in Chicago. He next studied privately with Franz Schoepp of the Chicago Symphony Orchestra. By the time Goodman was sixteen, word of his excellent musicianship had spread even to California, and Ben Pollack asked him to join his band. He had built a considerable reputation by the time he left the Pollack band in 1929 at the age of twenty. For the next five years, he played on radio and for recording companies in New York.

In 1934, Goodman organized his first band for a theater restaurant, the Music Hall, owned by Billy Rose. At the same time, Goodman played on a series of Saturday night, three-hour radio shows. The two jobs coincided with his association with Fletcher Henderson, who created most of the musical arrangements that were such an integral part of Goodman's success.

In the winter of 1934-35 Goodman began a tour across the United States that seemed to consist of one failure after another. No one appeared to know or care about his band. The farther the band traveled from New York, the more worried became Goodman, the band, his bookers, and the manager of the Palomar Ballroom in Los Angeles—their destination. In fact, it has often been rumored that had the manager been able to locate Goodman during that tour he would have canceled the booking. Fortunately, the booking was not canceled. Goodman opened at the Palomar Ballroom in May 1935 and was an immediate success. Whether the swing type of jazz started earlier than this is beside the point. Goodman's engagement at the Palomar is designated by most jazz writers as the beginning of the swing era.

Goodman's band played a hard-driving type of swing in comparison to other bands at that time. He often rehearsed the band without the rhythm section, reasoning that, if an arrangement could swing well and have momentum without the rhythm section, the music would offer much more when the rhythm section was added. The band also played a soft, more subtle jazz—a chamber music sort of jazz—by using trios, quartets, quintets, and so on.

The Goodman trio, started in 1935, consisted of Teddy Wilson on piano, Gene Krupa on drums, and Goodman on clarinet. The group was enlarged to a quartet in 1936 with the addition of the exuberant Lionel Hampton on vibraphone, and in 1939 it became a sextet when Charlie Christian on guitar and a bass player were added. These smaller groups also included at various times Red Norvo, Cootie Williams, Roy Eldridge, and Georgie Auld. The small units played during the intermissions of performances by the large band and also recorded separately. Some fans consider these recordings to be as important as those of the large band.

In 1938, the Benny Goodman band became the first swing band to play a concert in Carnegie Hall. Record sales of his Carnegie Hall concerts alone grossed more than a million dollars and continue to sell today.

Mention should also be made of Goodman's classical solo work. He commissioned and recorded a composition by Béla Bartók, commissioned clarinet concertos by Aaron Copland and Paul Hindemith, and performed works by Mozart, Debussy, Brahms, and other composers with such distinguished orchestras as the Boston Symphony, the Rochester Symphony, the NBC Symphony, the Cleveland Symphony, the Budapest String Quartet, and the American Art Quartet. Goodman was one of the few musicians who moved easily between classical music and jazz, becoming distinguished in each field. In 1955, Universal-International Studios made a motion picture based on his life, and Goodman himself recorded the music and acted as musical director.

Goodman toured in many parts of the world on behalf of the U.S. State Department. In 1956, he played to sellout audiences in Hong Kong, Singapore, Tokyo, and Bangkok. In 1958 and 1959, his overseas tours took him to Belgium, Germany, Sweden, Denmark, France, Switzerland, Austria, England, Australia, Central America, South America, and Alaska, and his reception was as great as ever each time. The Goodman band was chosen to be the first band to make a State Department tour of Russia. His triumph there was proof of his artistry, the durability of the swing style, and the worldwide popularity of this American music. Benny Goodman enjoyed truly international popularity. The mere announcement that he was to perform in a country caused great excitement among the jazz enthusiasts there, a fact probably more true about Goodman than about any other living musician.

Since the mid-1960s, Goodman appeared regularly at jazz festivals and even at some of the more plush night spots. At the end of the 1960s, he toured the United States with both jazz and classical groups and recorded in the United States and England. Through the 1970s, Goodman continued to tour Europe, the United States, and Canada. Sometimes he appeared with a full band, sometimes with a sextet, and sometimes with members of his original quartet. The reception was the same: he was the King of Swing, a jazz immortal, and an international celebrity to jazz fans of all ages.

Goodman was the first bandleader to force the issue of integration. Black and white musicians jammed together in after-hours clubs and recorded together, but neither the white nor the black public would go to see a "mixed" band. In 1936, when Goodman hired Teddy Wilson and Lionel Hampton, he had to pretend that they were not regular members of his band but only an act. Finally, he simply acknowledged that these musicians were part of his band and gave notice that the public would have to see and hear his music on his terms. He stated very simply in a non-political way that he was selling not prejudice or integration but music.

Goodman continued to play jazz in a most exemplary manner and led the world on clarinet. He performed a concert at Carnegie Hall in 1974, thirty-six years and eight months after his first concert there. The authors saw and heard Goodman in 1975 at a jazz festival where he received a standing ovation as he walked on stage. As he played, he proved conclusively that he truly deserved the applause.

Beside being the King of Swing, and beside almost single-handedly cutting through racial barriers in music, Goodman was instrumental in making it possible for jazz musicians to earn a decent wage. He brought jazz out of back rooms into the best night spots and into the greatest theaters where young people screamed and danced in the aisles. Still, for a man whose name is synonymous with the big-band era, Goodman was extremely low key, never flamboyant. His playing was a combination of great wit, precise musicianship, beautiful subtleties, and never-ending swing. "In the 1930s he brought American jazz to the attention of his countrymen and to the world in a way that had previously not been accomplished."26

Down Beat magazine nominated Goodman to its All Time Jazz Hall of Fame, and the National Academy of Recording Arts and Sciences placed his recording of "Sing Sing Sing" in its hall of fame. He collaborated on four books: *The Kingdom of Swing; BG—Off the Record, BG—On the Record,* and *Benny: King of Swing.*27 Goodman inspired musicians when he was only sixteen years old, and until he died in June 1986 he continued to inspire them. He did not follow the changing fads in jazz, so he was unique. He attributed his continued overwhelming success to the fact that he simply played "good" music.

Big-Band Soloists

One of the oddities of big-band jazz was that soloists gained importance also. Critic Joachim Berendt wrote of this situation:

Thus, the thirties also became the era of great soloists: the tenor saxists Coleman Hawkins and Chu Berry; the clarinetist Benny Goodman; the drummers Gene Krupa, Cozy Cole, and Sid Catlett; the pianists Fats Waller and Teddy Wilson; the alto saxists Benny Carter and Johnny Hodges; the trumpeters Roy Eldridge, Bunny Berigan, and Rex Stewart.

Often these two tendencies—the orchestral and the soloistic—merged. Benny Goodman's clarinet seemed all the more glamorous against the backdrop of his big band, Louis Armstrong's trumpet stood out in bold relief when accompanied by Louis Russell's orchestra, and the voluminous tone of Coleman Hawkins' or Chu Berry's tenor seemed to gain from the contrast to the "hard" sound of Fletcher Henderson's band.28

Coleman Hawkins

The epitome of swing tenor saxophonists was Coleman Hawkins with his full tone, flowing lines, and heavy vibrato29 (S, "The Man I Love," side 4, band 5). A reassuring example of Hawkins's impeccable taste as an improviser is his recording of "Body and Soul"30 (S, side C, band 6; NW, 274, side 1, band 8). "Hawkins' mesmerizing hold on all who followed—except for Lester Young—was overwhelming, permanent, and unquestioned."31

Hawkins had played with blues singer Mamie Smith's Jazz Hounds in 1922–23 but first gained recognition in the Fletcher Henderson Orchestra, where he played the clarinet and the bass and baritone saxes along with tenor sax, on which he really excelled. In 1923, Hawkins made his first recording with Henderson on "Dicty Blues," demonstrating a great rhythmic feel while playing a slap-tongue solo (considered strictly a comic approach today).

Eventually, his rich tone became one of the most impressive aspects of his playing, as did his long, flowing lines. His solo on "Body and Soul," recorded in 1939, never seems to pause—it just continues on and on.

Lester Young

Of all the great tenor saxophonists competing with Hawkins, only one seemed to be going in a direction all his own: talented player Lester Young. Don Heckman compared the early learning environments of two famous tenor saxophone players—Coleman Hawkins with Fletcher Henderson and Lester Young with Count Basie.32

Hawkins predated Young as an active participant in the jazz scene. As a member of the Fletcher Henderson Orchestra for ten years (1923–33), he was intimately involved with what was probably the most famous jazz ensemble of the time. Henderson's orchestra typified the Eastern approach.

The Henderson, Duke Ellington, and Charles Johnson orchestras all played for a variety of musical events

Listening Guide

Demonstration 16 (cassette 1, side A, track 16; CD 1, track 16)

Coleman Hawkins (playing)
"The Man I Love"

:00 Hawkins enters on tenor sax. He plays for two 32-bar choruses. Notice the long melodic phrases he uses to span each 8-measure subdivision of each chorus.

:19 Second 8-bar phrase of the first chorus. Notice that Hawkins tends to overlap his melodic phrases with the beginning of each 8-bar phrase of the song.

:38 Third 8-bar phrase.

:57 Last eight bar phrase. Notice how he melodically sets up the next 32-bar chorus.

1:15 Hawkins solos another complete chorus; the activity in the rhythm section increases.

1:34 Second 8-bar phrase.

1:53 Third 8-bar phrase. Listen for the flat-four feel in the rhythm section.

2:11 Last phrase of this chorus; back to a swing feel.

2:31 End.

Coleman Hawkins.
Courtesy of the Institute of Jazz Studies

before audiences that frequently were all white. Although they were considered (with the exception of Ellington at the Cotton Club), to be primarily dance bands, the type of dance music they played was considerably more diverse than the bands further west. The Henderson group might be expected on any given night to play popular hits, tangos, Irish waltzes, and original jazz tunes. The music was usually written in complex arrangements, and the bands were carefully rehearsed. With some groups, in fact, well-drilled performances became more important than either improvisation or solos. Fortunately, this never happened with Henderson, who realized the importance of good soloists when Louis Armstrong joined the band in 1924. It was only logical that Hawkins' artistic growth would have been affected by such a musical environment.

. . . Young came into prominence in a completely different milieu. The Count Basie Band was the pinnacle of Kansas City and Southwestern jazz. Its music was blues-oriented, filled with riffing backgrounds, and frequently based on spontaneous head arrangements. The soloists had more opportunity to stretch out than the soloists in the more heavily orchestrated New York bands. Few of the Basie arrangements were very complicated; good intonation and well-drilled performances were not nearly as important as was the creation of a rolling, surging rhythmic swing. Kansas City jazz was dancing jazz, and the beat was the most important element. The revolutionary work of the Basie rhythm section made the Basie band something special. Their ability to generate a free-flowing, almost-alive pulse undoubtedly helped Young develop a rangy horizontal, i.e., melodic, playing style.[33]

Sometimes it is hard for young jazz enthusiasts to see how older players have influenced contemporary favorites, but the influences are there. Both Young's lines and Hawkins's tone can be heard in Coltrane's recordings. Young's rhythmic and melodic outlooks can be heard on Ornette Coleman and Eric Dolphy records. In

---

Listening Guide

Demonstration 17 (cassette 1, side B, track 1; CD 1, track 17)

Benny Goodman Quartet
"I Got Rhythm"
Benny Goodman, clarinet
Teddy Wilson, piano
Lionel Hampton, vibraphone
Gene Krupa, drums

:00   Piano solo: 2 measures.
:01   Clarinet solo: 2 measures.
:02   Vibraphone solo: 2 measures.
:04   Ensemble (all 4): 2 measures.
:05   Ensemble: 34 measures.
:34   Piano solo: 34 measures.
1:01   Another chorus for piano solo: 34 measures.
1:29   Clarinet solo: 34 measures.
1:58   Another chorus for clarinet solo: 34 measures.
2:25   Vibraphone solo: 34 measures.
2:54   Another chorus for vibraphone solo: 34 measures.
3:22   Six measures of ensemble.
3:26   Two measures, complete break.
3:28   Same as last 8 measures.
3:34   Ensemble for 18 measures.
3:48   Six measures of ensemble.
3:53   Two measures, complete break.
3:55   Six measures of ensemble.
4:00   Two measures, complete break.
4:02   Ensemble for 18 measures.
4:17   Ensemble for 34 measures, becoming more exciting.
4:43   Ensemble for 34 measures, even more exciting.
5:10   End.

Listening Guide

Benny Goodman Septet
*"I Found a New Baby"**
Benny Goodman, clarinet
Cootie Williams, trumpet
Count Basie, piano
Georgie Auld, tenor sax
Charlie Christian, guitar
Jo Jones, drums
Artie Bernstein, bass

:00   Introduction: 2 measures of brushes.
:02   Four measures of unison tenor sax and trumpet with cup mute; Goodman on clarinet takes pickups on last measure.
:06   First chorus: Goodman solos on clarinet backed by trumpet and tenor sax for 32 measures; Goodman varies between interpretation and improvisation.
:45   Second chorus: Charlie Christian guitar solo for 32 measures.
1:24   Third chorus: Count Basie piano solo backed by sax and trumpet for 16 measures.
1:43   Bridge of the tune: Basie and Goodman toy with call and response for 16 measures.
1:52   Basie on piano solo for 8 measures.
2:01   Fourth chorus: 16 measures of trumpet solo.
2:20   Sixteen measures of trumpet solo.
2:39   Eight measures of drum solo.
2:47   Ensemble for 8 measures: A complete 6-way jam session.
2:57   End.

*Smithsonian Collection, side D, band 8.

fact, it would not be an overstatement to say that every contemporary saxophonist is indebted to Young, Hawkins, and Parker.

Some good bands pursued the showmanship aspect of the business with great energy, a typical example being Cab Calloway.[34] Scat singing was advanced to an art form by his truly inventive singing in the 1930s. The showmanship aspect of performance was at low ebb in jazz at one time, causing record executive Irving Townsend to proclaim, "For some reason, jazz thinks it doesn't need showmanship; it couldn't be more wrong."[35]

Swing Combos

The small-combo idea was never entirely discarded. Most large bands also had a small group made up of the better jazz players in the band. The smaller combo played during intermissions of the large band, and sometimes the small group built up its own personal following. In his band, Goodman had a trio, quartet, quintet, sextet, and even septet, depending on the personnel in his band[36] (S, Benny Goodman Sextet, "I Found a New Baby," side D, band 8, and "Breakfast Feud" with Charlie Christian, side D, band 9; S, Benny Goodman Trio, "Body and Soul," side C, band 5; NW, 274, "I Found a New Baby," side 1, band 7). Artie Shaw's small "band within a band" was called the Gramercy Five and featured Johnny Guarnieri on harpsichord. Woody Herman

had the Woodchoppers, Tommy Dorsey had the Clambake Seven, and so on. Throughout the swing years, Fifty-second Street in New York, with its numerous night clubs, was a real gathering place for small combos.

In July 1944, Norman Granz organized a jazz concert at the Los Angeles Philharmonic Auditorium to aid in a fund for the defense of some Mexican-Americans who had been sent to San Quentin after a killing in Los Angeles. This concert was recorded and was the first commercial recording made in a public place instead of in a studio. It was a **jam session** recorded live, and it started a whole new phase in recording history. Jazz at the Philharmonic, as Granz's recording and touring package became known, was an extremely successful venture.

Duke Ellington (1899–1974)

Just as Armstrong crystallized and popularized the solo aspect of jazz, Duke Ellington, more than any other single musician, proved that orchestrating jazz was an art of the highest level. However, it should be pointed out that Ellington's music was always a combination of solo and ensemble playing. He, like Basie, drew the thoughts of his soloists together into the orchestral whole, accomplishing the feat from the piano. "He was a born orchestral pianist . . . to lead the orchestra, in other words, from the piano, to galvanize it rhythmically, to inspire it creatively, and to complement it pianistically when needed."[37]

On the other hand, the musicians playing for Ellington did not lose their identity. The Ellington orchestra was always made up of the *individual* talents of his players. It cannot be emphasized enough that listeners are always aware of the personalities of the players (Johnny Hodges, Lawrence Brown, Rex Stewart, Harry Carney, and so on). Yet the band always sounded like Ellington regardless of changes in personnel over the years. This is one of the most important aspects of the band: allowing individuals to retain their own identities and to expand and explore their own directions. Ellington's band always sounded like a well-knit unit expressing the feelings and personalities of Ellington while achieving a wonderful relationship between compositions and the orchestra.

Edward Kennedy ("Duke") Ellington was born in Washington, D.C., on April 29, 1899. He did not come from a poor family, as did Armstrong, and he had educational advantages that many musicians his age lacked. He received his nickname from a high school friend. He was a better-than-average young painter and won a scholarship to study at the Pratt Institute in Brooklyn, New York. His art career was superseded, of course, by music.

Ellington listened to and was influenced by ragtime piano players in the Washington area. It is possible to hear ragtime and stride in Ellington's extended piano

solos, especially at the faster tempos. The influences of Fats Waller, Willie ("The Lion") Smith, and James P. Johnson are evident. Ellington played piano, but most jazz writers agree that the orchestra was his real instrument. By the age of seventeen, he had a five-piece combo called the Washingtonians.

In 1919, Ellington's son Mercer was born. He became a trumpet player, composer, and arranger—a talented musician in his own right. Mercer now leads the Ellington band.

Ellington, with his drummer Sonny Greer and saxophonist Toby Hardwicke, made an abortive attempt to move to New York in 1922 to join the orchestra of Wilbur Sweatman. Financial problems caused Ellington to return to Washington until Fats Waller encouraged him to try to move again in 1923. This time Ellington and his friends went to work in New York's Harlem, where Ellington began his exceptional career as a leader, pianist, and composer/arranger.

Around 1926, the Ellington personnel began to solidify, and as a consequence his style—his sound—was established. Personnel changes were rare from then on. Complete sections of the orchestra remained constant for an entire decade. It is no wonder that they worked so very well together. Baritone saxophone player Harry Carney joined the band in 1926 when he was seventeen and remained in the orchestra until he died in 1974. Johnny Hodges joined the band in 1928 and, except for a period from 1951 to 1955, stayed with the band until his death in 1971.

A move that really established the orchestra was the booking at the Cotton Club in Harlem from 1927 to 1932. Ellington's influence from that point on has always been quite definite. His musical pictures were considerably ahead of their time, and the band could swing. Ellington's band at this time featured what were called "jungle sounds," which included much "growling" on the instruments. As a consequence, the very elaborate floor shows of the Cotton Club were designed around the music that the band played. Once again, the sounds of the individuals were woven into the tonal colors of the entire group, an attribute that was evident throughout Ellington's career.

Ellington had four rather different styles that pervaded his repertoire. One was the previously mentioned "jungle style" built around the raucous playing of Bubber Miley and then of Cootie Williams on trumpet and Tricky Sam Nanton on trombone. Ellington also had a "mood style" that is identified with the beautiful ballads played by saxophonist Johnny Hodges. Some of the selections, such as "Solitude," are well known to the public, but others, such as "Prelude to a Kiss" and

"Lotus Blossom," are known and loved mostly by musicians. Another Ellington style could be called his "concerto style," in which he featured Cootie Williams on trumpet or Jimmy Hamilton or Barney Bigard on clarinet. The other style was a rather "standard style," in which he approached his arrangements in much the same manner as other large bands. However, he always sounded exactly like Ellington, something no one else could accomplish.

Ellington was always concerned about his music being called jazz or at least *merely* jazz. Does a jazz piece have to swing? What about his harmonies? His sounds? His music was often severely criticized for not being that which it was never intended to be. One of his severest critics, John Hammond, denounced Ellington's music as pretentious and not truly jazz.

In 1933, the depression prompted Ellington to make what turned out to be a most successful international attraction. When Ellington first went to England, he was surprised to find out how well known he and other American jazz players were. He realized the importance of jazz as an American export, but he was also aware that popularity at home somewhat determined his effectiveness abroad.

There is no need to expound on his success during the swing era. His band was by far the most colorful of the large bands during a time when large jazz bands were attracting a multitude of followers.

Ellington may not have been quite as popular with the public as he could have been because, compared with some other bands, he did not receive as much radio coverage and did not concern himself as much with the popular tunes of the day.

In 1943, Ellington gave the first of a series of annual concerts at Carnegie Hall in New York, introducing the longer forms into jazz that became a recognized part of his repertoire (an example is "Black, Brown, and Beige," fifty minutes in length). He seemed to expand his thinking without altering his music. Ellington's recording of "Reminiscing in Tempo" in 1935 foreshadowed later directions. He used the concerto form in jazz to write "Barney's Concerto" (for clarinetist Barney Bigard) and "Cootie's Concerto" (for trumpeter Cootie Williams).

Ellington toured constantly, which kept his image alive throughout the world. He recorded historically important works written by himself and Billy Strayhorn. The collaboration of Ellington and Strayhorn led to some of the most charming music in any category of the art. Sometimes while composing a piece of music, either Ellington or Strayhorn would realize that a specific member of the orchestra was in need of a work on which he would be featured, and this fact would influence the composition. Sometimes it worked just the opposite: the work being composed would need a specific player to be interpreted to the greatest advantage.

Duke Ellington.
Courtesy of Ray Avery

Ellington's innovations include the following: the wonderful ensemble sound (developed using individuals in the band), the larger forms in jazz (which often ignored the three-minute limit on recordings that dictated the repertoire of most bands), his more than skillful orchestration, the use of voices as instruments (as far back as 1927 with singer Adelaide Hall on "Creole Love Song"), and many innovative jazz tunes starting with "Mood Indigo" (first recorded as "Dreamy Blues" in 1930), "Sophisticated Lady" (1933), and "Solitude" (1934). Ellington often changed the titles of his tunes. For example, "Rumpus in Richmond" was changed to "Harlem Air Shaft." This puts the liner notes on some albums in a very suspicious light, as some record company employee tried to explain the final titles as if it were Ellington's idea of daily life in New York's Harlem.

Those listeners who challenge all changes disturbed Ellington—to a point. His later music was sometimes compared unfavorably with that which he had played in the past. Ellington's answer to the "time test" (comparing jazz to other music) was that he was not interested in writing or playing music for posterity; he wanted his music to sound good at the very moment it was performed.

The earliest Ellington recording available is an album called *The Birth of Big Band Jazz*. These sides were recorded in 1923 (some writers place the date at 1925). The album called *Early Ellington* comprises recordings made between 1927 and 1931. Most writers feel that Ellington's greatest recordings were made between 1940 and 1942 with such records as "Jack the Bear," "Warm Valley," "Cotton Tail," "Chelsea Bridge," "Take the A Train," "C Jam Blues," and so on. Ellington recorded more than one hundred and fifty albums, although well over half can no longer be purchased. However, the Smithsonian Institution has helped to resolve this situation with sets that fill many of the would-be gaps in collections of Ellington's music.[38]

True, Ellington did perform his "standards"—he was almost required to. But it cannot be said that his repertoire did not have good variety. He performed in so many different situations (dance halls, large clubs, theaters, festivals, concert halls) that he had to diversify.

It is worth noting that Ellington, while feeling that his music was always primarily black music, never felt his ethnic ties to the point of using only black musicians in his band, as witnessed by the white drummer Louie Bellson.

It appears as if the talents and influences of Duke Ellington will always be with us. Today there are Ellington societies, the Duke Ellington Cancer Fund, and even Duke Ellington Boulevard in upper Manhattan and a Broadway play entitled "Sophisticated Ladies" featuring Mercer Ellington conducting the Duke Ellington Orchestra performing his father's music. Ellington's style of arranging and composing is taught at the Berklee College of Music in Boston. In Washington, D.C., students attend Duke Ellington High School of the Arts. At the University of California, Los Angeles, guitarist Kenny Burrell teaches a course called "Ellingtonia."[39]

Ellington's band, his music, and his recordings are proof of his belief that although jazz borrowed from any and every source available, it still remained personal. His ensemble was an integrated whole, yet no one's orchestra has ever been based so much on the talents of its individuals. Some jazz writers actually credit Ellington's success to his brilliant sidemen, but these sidemen always point to Ellington's composing, arranging, piano playing, and leadership in general. In 1962, Leonard Feather wrote of Ellington: "We see him today as the most challenging, most provocative, most brilliant, and most irreplaceable paragon in the sixty-year history of jazz."[40] That statement is still true.

The Demise of Swing

Because of the military draft and problems of transportation, the swing era came to an abrupt end at the beginning of World War II. Swing bands could not function unless they could play one-night stands. Although the bands took a financial loss on location jobs, they fostered the popularity necessary for radio time and gave musicians a chance to record (and a chance to rest from the rigors of traveling). Then the bands went on the road again to recoup their losses. But World War II meant no gasoline and no automobile tires for civilians, so all unessential travel came to a halt in the United States. One other event contributed to the shutdown of employment for musicians when the federal government levied a thirty percent cabaret tax, and most cabarets simply closed their doors.

Big-Band Legacy

"I call myself a coach more than a bandleader, and my teams win."[41]

The big band has often been compared to classical music's symphonic orchestra. Like the orchestra, the big band has offered jazz musicians an ensemble of relatively fixed instrumentation for which to compose. The characteristic common to most large ensembles is the carefully composed arrangements that hold the many players together. Because of the immense popularity of the big bands during the swing era, the grouping of those ensembles—saxophone, trumpet, and trombone sections with a rhythm section—became the established instrumentation for large jazz groups. Although the instrumentation was more or less standardized, the music for those ensembles was not. The most successful bands very often had identifiable leaders that placed their individual stamps on the musical product.

Ghost Bands

Because the big bands spanned such a long period from the very early bands of the 1920s to contemporary big bands of the 1990s, their development reflects much of jazz's history. The bands of the swing era enjoyed a prominence and popularity in America seldom if ever felt by other jazz styles. As a result of this popularity, a nostalgia for that style still exists today and has helped keep several bands actively playing and recording even after the deaths of their leaders. Central among these bands are the contemporary Miller and Dorsey bands, which most often perform the original arrangements that made them popular during the swing era. When new arrangements are written, they are generally restricted to the same stylistic trademarks typical of the original bands. Critics and historians have often referred to these groups as "ghost bands" because of the absence of their leaders and, in most cases, completely new personnel.[42]

Transition Bands

Several of the big bands that began working in the twenties, thirties, or forties performed successfully into the seventies and eighties. These bands vary as to how much stylistic change they have undergone throughout their long careers. Prominent among these bands are those of Duke Ellington (now directed by his son Mercer), Count Basie (now under the direction of Frank Foster), Woody Herman (now under the direction of Frank Tiberi), Stan Kenton, Maynard Ferguson, Gil Evans, Ray Charles, Dizzy Gillespie, Les Brown, Harry James, Buddy Rich, and Tex Beneke. Not all these bands are still playing, and those that are, even without their original leaders, cannot properly be called ghost bands. They constantly introduce new material and are not as tightly bound to the nostalgic expectations of their listeners.

Count Basie's band had a long playing career with Basie at the helm and maintained a rather consistent jazz style. What changes did occur were introduced by contemporary soloists. However, Basie felt that the responsibility for innovation rested with the writers, not the performers. After Basie's death, his band was led briefly by Thad Jones and is now led by Frank Foster, both former members of the band. The new arrangements written by both these men were not necessarily restricted to the original Basie style.

Like Basie's band, Woody Herman's retained a hard, swinging style; however, Herman flirted somewhat with newer musical styles.[43] Maynard Ferguson's band strongly embraced the rock idiom and maintains a large audience.[44] Buddy Rich's band, like both Ferguson's and Herman's, spent most of its time touring, which proved to be very expensive and extremely taxing on the musicians because of the size of the groups. Despite these limitations, the fact that these bands continue to be so active attests to the interest that audiences still have for the big-band medium.

The most varied musical styles during this transition period for big bands were heard in the Ellington and Kenton bands. Kenton explored a more expanded instrumentation with French horns and often took on a truly symphonic sound during the late 1950s and early 1960s (NW, 216, "Mirage," band 4). It is noteworthy that he specified in his will that there be no ghost band under his name after his death.[45] Ellington used the big-band medium to experiment with new compositional structures not before associated with big bands.

Contemporary Large Bands

Not all of today's big bands were carried over from earlier periods. The medium has remained vital enough to support the development of new bands by leaders like Thad Jones and Mel Lewis, Toshiko Akiyoshi and Lew Tabackin, Don Ellis, Doc Severinsen, Quincy Jones, Louis Bellson, and Ed Shaunessy. Although several of these bands exhibit new and very individualized styles, many of them maintain a close tie to the swinging style of the Basie and Herman bands.

Particularly interesting are the compositions by pianist Toshiko Akiyoshi, which feature both a modern and a culture-crossing style.[46] She often rates among the top jazz composers in each year's *Down Beat* critics' poll. The Thad Jones–Mel Lewis orchestra, an East Coast ensemble, began as a rehearsal band that offered musicians a chance to play arrangements for their own enjoyment.[47] It was not long, however, before the freshness of the arrangements and competent playing brought the band to national prominence. Both the Akiyoshi and the Thad Jones–Mel Lewis bands are characterized by carefully crafted arrangements that helped expand the big-band idiom. Although the musicians are of the highest caliber, they play supporting roles to the more dominant statements of the composers themselves.

Don Ellis

Trumpeter Don Ellis offered one of the most radical yet captivating approaches for big bands. While at the University of California, Los Angeles, he studied with talented Indian musicians like Ravi Shankar, who taught at the university in 1965. Ellis and Harihar Rao (from India) formed what they called the Hindustani Jazz Sextet.

It should be noted here that possibly the most intricate rhythmic system is that from India. The amalgam of jazz elements, the **raga**, and certain Eastern rhythms produced truly extraordinary jazz music. A raga is a melodic form, a succession of notes, of which are thousands. Ellis was also intrigued by the Indian tala, a rhythmic series that contains 3 to 108 beats. The particular tala to be played at a given moment is predetermined, but the rhythmic possibilities are almost endless. (Keep in mind that these Indian musical fragments derive from speech patterns. This is also true in the African musical culture.)

Don Ellis

Don Ellis was an excellent trumpet player, and he also soloed well on drums. Not only did Ellis advance rhythmic techniques, become an educated and acknowledged performer of jazz/rock, and introduce interesting uses for electronic devices, but he also devised a trumpet with an extra valve that allowed him to play quarter tones. Such pitches may seem odd when compared to the well-tempered twelve-tone European scale, but in Eastern cultures they are quite suitable. Ellis died in 1978.

Toshiko Akiyoshi.
Courtesy Tom Capi. Insert, K. Abe

Ellis believed that young children in some countries sing and dance in meters unnatural to jazz. This would imply that meter is a matter of conditioning that differs between cultures. Ellis directed a successful large band that featured many unusual meters such as $\frac{19}{4}$ and $\frac{11}{8}$.[48] He then subdivided the measures; for example, the very title of the selection in $\frac{19}{4}$ meter is the subdivision "33221222." Ellis also recorded a number called "New Nine," in which the subdivision (the manner in which the measures are counted and played) varies: 2223, 2232, 2322, 3222, and 333.[49] His "Blues in Elf" (in $\frac{11}{4}$) is counted 3332.[50] "Indian Lady" is in $\frac{5}{4}$ and touches on gospel, rock, and free improvisation.[51]

Summary

Swing is still with us, and much of the jazz we hear today stems directly from the developments of this eight- or ten-year period. The swing era must also be credited with two beneficial side effects: it absolutely rescued the record industry, and it allowed the musical instrument industry to grow to its present strength.

To reiterate, no style ever really dies out. For years, Eddie Condon ran a nightclub that featured nothing but Chicago Style Dixieland.[52] The Early New Orleans Dixieland revival of the late 1930s was mentioned in chapter 5.[53] Swing is still played all over the world. Not only is nostalgia of swing a salable product, but swing itself is a most communicative style of jazz.[54]

Books can be found on the market today that are writen solely about the swing era,[55] and these are generally both interesting and informative. Even books on the activities of just the Glenn Miller band during the swing era can be found,[56] and other books about the band are being written at this time. Bands such as those of Basie, Ellington, and Herman have certainly proven that the big bands can swing as hard as, and maintain all the vitality demonstrated by, the smaller groups of the day. The organized, written arrangements are capable of creating an energy all their own. The controversy that began with Henderson's band—that one ensemble was superior to another—is no longer appropriate.

The big band is the expression of a very long ensemble tradition. From the earliest jazz ensembles, a balance between improvisation and composition has been carefully maintained. The big band represents the fullest expression of jazz composition and arrangement. As jazz evolved, it has tread a delicate line between the improvised flights of individual players and their collective performances as ensembles. Early ensembles, such as the marching bands of New Orleans, were themselves improvised, each player adding what, at the moment, seemed necessary for a complete sound.

Players, in effect, created an extemporaneous arrangement. These ensembles later became the voice of composers and arrangers who found great subtleties in the instrumental groupings. Like the individual players of each stylistic period, the larger ensembles reflected the attitudes and musical sensibilities of the time. Marching jazz bands developed into the early society and swing bands, which were followed later by the bop bands and, finally, the current compositionally based jazz ensembles.

Throughout these periods, the bands have offered a vehicle of jazz expression for both the player and the writer. This band tradition represents the melding of two vital aspects of jazz performance: expression of individuals and ensembles and expressions engineered by the imagination of jazz composer/arrangers and implemented through the creativity of individual performers.

For Further Study

1. In what ways did Fletcher Henderson influence the development of jazz in the swing era?

2. Describe the role of the music arranger in this era.

3. Explain why swing bands produced a fuller sound.

4. What jazz trombonist is considered the outstanding trombone virtuoso of the era?

5. Certain limitations were placed on the recordings of swing bands of the record industry. What were these limitations?

6. Identify the band that was the most popular as well as the most successful.

7. What were some factors that resulted in the end of the Swing Era?

8. Was swing music primarily for listening or for dancing?

9. To enhance your aural perception of the big-band sound, listen to several recordings of thirty-seven top bands playing ten years of top tunes from the album *The Great Band Era* manufactured especially for *Readers Digest* by RCA.

10. Now listen to the swing band recordings in the album *Jazz* (FJ, 2808, vol. 8) and compare the arrangements of these earlier bands with the band sounds in the *Readers Digest* album.

11. The swing era produced many outstanding soloists, among them Benny Goodman and his clarinet. Listen to his sextet playing "I Found a New Baby" (S, side D, band 8) and identify the instrument that follows Benny Goodman's clarinet solo.

12. Listen to Duke Ellington's "Ko-Ko" (S, side D, band 13). Toward the end of the recording you will hear another outstanding soloist on an instrument that was not considered a solo instrument. Can you identify the instrument?

13. In what ways do the contemporary large bands differ from the large swing bands?

14. Describe the differences in the way performers react to one another in big bands and in small ensembles.

15. Discuss the different roles played by the composer/arranger in small-group ensembles and in big bands.

Suggested Additional Listening

Akiyoshi, Toshiko, and Lew Tabackin Big Band. *Insights*. RCA Records, AFL 1-2678.

Calloway, Cab. *Sixteen Calloway Classics*. Columbia Records, J-10.

Casa Loma Band. *Glen Gray's Greatest Hits*. MCA Records, 122.

Herman, Woody. *Giant Steps.* Fantasy Records, 9477.
———. *Thundering Herd.* Fantasy Records, 9452.
Jammin' for the Jackpot. New World Records, 217.
Jive at Five. New World Records, 274.
Little Club Jazz. New World Records, 250.
Severinsen, Doc. *Doc Severinsen's Closet.* Command Records, RSSD-950-S.
Vig, Tommy. *The Sound of the Seventies.* Milestone Records, 9007.
The World of Swing. Columbia Records, F6-32945.

Additional Reading Resources

Allen, Walter C. *Hendersonia: The Music of Fletcher Henderson and His Musicians.*
Basie, Count. *Good Morning Blues: The Autobiography of Count Basie, as Told to Albert Murray.*
Berger, Morroe; Patrick, Edward; and Patrick, James. *Benny Carter, A Life in American Music.*
Charters, Samuel B., and Kunstadt, Leonard. *Jazz: A History of the New York Scene.*
Dance, Stanley. *The World of Count Basie.*
———. *The World of Swing.*
Dexter, Dave. *The Jazz Story,* 56–87, 105–20.
Feather, Leonard. *The Book of Jazz,* 174–91.
Harris, Rex. *Jazz,* 168–74.
McCarthy, Albert. *Big Band Jazz.*
Russell, Ross. *Jazz Styles in Kansas City and the Southwest.*

Duke Ellington

And His Mother Called Him Bill. RCA Victor Records, LSP-3906.
At His Very Best. RCA Victor Records, LPM-1715.
Best of Duke Ellington. Capitol Records, SM-1602.
Birth of Big Band Jazz. Riverside Records, 129.
Concert of Sacred Music. RCA Victor Records, LSP-3582.
Duke Ellington, the Beginning. Decca Records, DL-9224.
Duke Ellington, 70th Birthday Concert. Solid State Records, SS 19000.
Duke Ellington's Greatest Hits. Reprise Records, S-6234.
Duke's Big 4. Pablo Records, 2310703.
Early Ellington. Brunswick Records, 54007.
Ellington at Newport. Columbia Records, CS 8648.
Ellington Era. Columbia Records, C3L 27.
Ellington '66. Reprise Records, 6154.
Historically Speaking—the Duke. Bethlehem Records, BCP 60.
New Orleans Suite. Atlantic Records, SD 1580.
Smithsonian Collection of Classic Jazz, vols. 6 and 7.
This Is Duke Ellington. RCA Victor Records, VPM-6042.
This One's for Blanton. Pablo Records, 2310721.
Togo Brava Suite. United Artists Records, UXS-92.

Benny Goodman

All Time Greatest Hits. Columbia Records, PG-31547.
Benny Goodman. Archive of Folk and Jazz Music Records, 277.
Carnegie Hall Concert. Columbia Records, OSL-160.
The Complete Benny Goodman. Bluebird Records, AXM 2-5515.
From Spirituals to Swing. Vanguard Records, VRS-8523/4.
Great Benny Goodman. Columbia Records, CS 9283.
Greatest Hits. Columbia Records, CS-8643.
Small Groups. RCA Victor Records, LPV 521.
Smithsonian Collection of Classic Jazz, vols. 4 and 6.
This Is Benny Goodman. RCA Victor Records, VPM 6040.

Notes

1. Gunther Schuller, *The Swing Era* (London: Oxford University Press, 1989), 845.
2. Benny Goodman, "Good-bye," *The Great Band Era.*
3. Tommy Dorsey, "I'm Gettin' Sentimental Over You," *The Great Band Era.*
4. Glenn Miller, "Moonlight Serenade," *The Great Band Era.*
5. Nat Shapiro and Nat Hentoff, eds., *The Jazz Makers* (New York: Grove Press, 1957), 118.
6. Fletcher Henderson, *A Study in Frustration,* Columbia Records, C4L-19; *Fletcher Henderson,* vols. 1 and 2, Decca Records, 79227-8; Fletcher Henderson, *Developing an American Orchestra, 1927–1947,* Smithsonian Collection, R-006; *Big Band Jazz,* Smithsonian Collection of Recordings.
7. Chick Webb, "Let's Get Together," *Jazz Odyssey,* vol. 3; *King of Savoy,* Decca Records, DL 9223; *Big Band Jazz,* Smithsonian Collection of Recordings.
8. *Fletcher Henderson,* vol. 8; "Nagasaki" and "It's the Talk of the Town," *The Jazz Story,* vol. 3; "Hop Off," *History of Classic Jazz,* vol. 8; Duke Ellington, *The Ellington Era,* Columbia Records, C3L 27; *Historically Speaking—the Duke,* Bethlehem Records, BCP 60; "Hot and Bothered," *Folkways Jazz,* vol. 8; "Sophisticated Lady," *The Jazz Story,* vol. 3; "Happy-Go-Lucky Local," *The Jazz Story,* vol. 4; "Rainy Night," *History of Classic Jazz,* vol. 8; *Big Band Jazz,* Smithsonian Collection of Recordings.
9. Schuller, *The Swing Era,* 5.
10. Benny Moten, *Big Band Jazz,* Smithsonian Collection of Recordings.
11. Andy Kirk, *Instrumentally Speaking,* MCA Records, 1308; *My Mamma Pinned a Rose,* Pablo Records, 2310819.
12. *Big Band Jazz,* Smithsonian Collection of Recordings.
13. Schuller, *The Swing Era,* 261.
14. Count Basie, *The Best of Basie,* Columbia Records, C3L-33; *E = MC²*; *Count Basie,* Roulette Records, ST 52003; *The Best of Count Basie,* MCA Records, 4050; *Big Band Jazz,* Smithsonian Collection of Recordings.
15. "Casa Loma Stomp," *Big Band Jazz,* Smithsonian Collection of Recordings, cassette 1, band 13.
16. Jack Teagarden (Paul Whiteman's Orchestra) "Aunt Hagar's Blues," Decca Records, 2145; Jack Teagarden, "Giants of Jazz," Time-Life Records, STL-J08.
17. Schuller, *The Swing Era,* 100.
18. *From Spirituals to Swing,* Vanguard Records, VRS-8523/4.
19. Benny Goodman, *The Great Benny Goodman,* Columbia Records, CL-820; *Benny Goodman Carnegie Concert, The Great Band Era,* and *Big Band Jazz,* Smithsonian Collection of Recordings.

Schuller, Gunther. *Early Jazz: Its Roots and Musical Development,* 242–317.
———. *The Swing Era.*
Shapiro, Nat, and Hentoff, Nat, eds. *The Jazz Makers,* 175–86, 218–26.
Simon, George T. *The Big Bands.*
———. *Glenn Miller.*
———. *Simon Says.*
Stearns, Marshall. *The Story of Jazz,* 120–54.
Ulanov, Barry. *Handbook of Jazz,* 15–26.
Walker, Leo. *The Wonderful Era of the Great Dance Bands.*

Note: Complete information, including name of publisher and date of publication, is provided in this book's bibliography.

20. Dave Dexter, *The Jazz Story: From the Nineties to the Sixties*, 1964. Reprinted by permission of Prentice-Hall, Inc., Englewood Cliffs, N.J., 114–15.

21. Dorsey Brothers, *The Fabulous Dorseys Play Dixieland Jazz*, Decca Records, DL8631.

22. The Casa Loma Band, "Casa Loma Stomp," *The Jazz Story*, vol. 4; *Big Band Jazz*, Smithsonian Collection of Recordings, cassette 1, band 13.

23. Woody Herman, *The Thundering Herds*, Columbia Records, C3L–25; "Misty Morning," *The Jazz Story*, vol. 5; *Big Band Jazz*, Smithsonian Collection of Recordings.

24. *Glenn Miller—a Memorial*, RCA Victor Records, VPM 6019; *The Great Band Era* and *Big Band Jazz*, Smithsonian Collection of Recordings.

25. Stan Kenton, *The Kenton Era*, The Creative World of Stan Kenton, ST 1030; *Big Band Jazz*, Smithsonian Collection of Recordings.

26. Schuller, *The Swing Era*, 45.

27. Benny Goodman and Irving Kolodin, *The Kingdom of Swing* (New York: Frederick Ungar, 1939); Benny Goodman and D. R. Connor, *BG—Off the Record* (Fairless Hills, Pa.: Gaildonna Publishers, 1969); Benny Goodman, D. R. Connor, and W. W. Hicks, *BG—On the Record* (New Rochelle, N.Y.: Arlington House, 1969); Stanley Baron, *Benny: King of Swing* (New York: William Morrow, 1979).

28. Joachim Berendt, *Jazz Book: From New Orleans to Rock and Free Jazz*, trans. Dan Morgenstern (Westport, Conn.: Lawrence Hill & Co., 1975).

29. Coleman Hawkins, *The Hawk and the Hunter*, Mira Records, LPS-3003; *Coleman Hawkins*, Everest Records, FS-252; *Bean and the Boys*, Prestige Records, S-7824; *The Real Thing*, Prestige Records, 24083.

30. Coleman Hawkins, "Body and Soul," *The Greatest Names in Jazz*.

31. Schuller, *The Swing Era*, 426.

32. Coleman Hawkins (the Fletcher Henderson Orchestra), *A Study in Frustration*, Columbia Records, C4L–19; Lester Young (with the Count Basie Orchestra), *Lester Young Memorial*, Epic Records, SN 6031.

33. Don Heckman, "Pres and Hawk, Saxophone Fountainheads," *Down Beat* 30, no. 1 (January 1963): 20.

34. Cab Calloway Orchestra, "Pickin' the Cabbage," *Jammin' for the Jackpot*, New World Records, 217; *Singers and Soloists of the Swing Bands*, Smithsonian Collection of Recordings.

35. Irving Townsend, "The Trouble with Jazz," *Down Beat* 29, no. 7 (March 1962): 14.

36. Benny Goodman, *The Great Benny Goodman; Benny Goodman Carnegie Concert*, and *Singers and Soloists of the Swing Bands*, Smithsonian Collection of Recordings.

37. Schuller, *The Swing Era*, 49.

38. Duke Ellington, *Ellington '38*, Smithsonian Records, R003; *Ellington '39*, Smithsonian Records, R010.

39. Kenny Burrell, *Ellington Is Forever*, vols. 1 and 2, Fantasy Records, 79005 and 79008.

40. Leonard Feather, "The Duke's Progress," *Down Beat* 29, no. 12 (June 1962): 19.

41. Woody Herman, *Down Beat* 53, no. 11 (November 1986), 21.

42. Glenn Miller, *In the Digital Mood*, GRP Records, GRP-A-1002. This record is a re-recording of original arrangements with the new digital technology.

43. Woody Herman, *Woody Herman and His Big Band, "50th Anniversary Tour*," Concord Jazz, CJ-302-C.

44. Maynard Ferguson, *Live from San Francisco*, Palo Alto, 8077.

45. From a conversation with the authors.

46. Toshiko Akiyoshi and Lew Tabackin, *Kogun*, RCA Victor Records, 6246.

47. Thad Jones and Mel Lewis, *Central Park North*, Solid State Records, SS 18058; *Mel Lewis and the Jazz Orchestra*, Tel-Arc Records, 10044 (first album since Thad Jones left).

48. Don Ellis Orchestra, "332221222," "Live at Monterey, Pacific Jazz Records, PJ-10112; "Upstart," *The Don Ellis Orchestra Live in 3=9/4 Time*, Pacific Jazz Records, PJ-10123.

49. Don Ellis, "New Nine," *Live at Monterey*, Pacific Jazz Records, PJ-10112.

50. Don Ellis, "Blues in Elf," *Tears of Joy*, Columbia Records, G 30927.

51. Don Ellis, "Indian Lady," *Electric Bath*, Columbia Records, CL 2785.

52. *History of Classic Jazz*, vol. 9.

53. Ibid., vol. 10.

54. Live Concert, *Music Made Famous by Glenn Miller*, Warner Brothers Records, W 1428; *Those Swingin' Days of the Big Bands*, Pickwick Records, TMW-002; *The Great Band Era* and *The Big Bands Are Back Swinging Today's Hits*, RCA Victor Records, RD4-112 (XRIS-9501). *Big Band Jazz*, Smithsonian Collection of Recordings.

55. George Simon, *The Big Bands* (New York: Macmillan, 1967); George Simon, *Simon Says* (New Rochelle, N.Y.: Arlington House, 1971); Schuller, *The Swing Era*.

56. John Flower, *Moonlight Serenade* (New Rochelle, N.Y.: Arlington House, 1972); George T. Simon, *Glenn Miller* (New York: Thomas Y. Crowell, 1974).

CHAPTER 8

Bop (1940–1950)

Example 8.1

BE BOP

Listening Guide

Demonstration 18
(cassette 1, side B, track 2; CD 1, track 18)

Bop

:00 Ensemble chorus (trumpet, alto sax, and electric guitar in unison); bass and drums keep $\frac{4}{4}$ rhythm plus accents on piano.

:11 Trumpet solo: 2 choruses, very frantic style.

:33 Solo break on drums.

:35 Ensemble chorus (same as first chorus).

:48 End.

"When a group of bop musicians had finished with a given tune it would be unrecognizable even to the composer. The musicians acknowledged the distortion by renaming the pieces."[1]

Bop jazz was sometimes called *bebop* or *rebop*, but common usage shortened it to *bop*. One explanation for the name is that players sang the words *bebop* and *rebop* to an early bop phrase, as shown in example 8.1.

The Shift to Bop

Bop was a revolt against the confines of the larger bands. The short, stylized solos typical of the large bands of the swing era minimized the opportunity for exploratory expression. Soloists not only desired more freedom for experimentation but also searched for a fresh, different approach to jazz. The young players were tired of reading written arrangements, tired of the clichés of swing, tired of the limited opportunities for improvisation, and so on. They also felt that many musicians with little creativeness were earning more than their share of fame and wealth and that the time had come for many changes. (For an introduction to bop, listen to demonstration 18.)

Most bop players turned naturally to small combos. A quintet seemed to be the size Charlie Parker found most comfortable. It is interesting that the combos resembled, in appearance at least, the earlier dixieland bands, that is, a rhythm section with a sparse (by comparison to swing) front line. Without a doubt, the bop combo reflected Kansas City jam sessions. Regardless of

Charlie Parker.
Courtesy of Orrin Keepnews

what is claimed, bop or any other style of music surely does or does not "begin" at any one place and at any one time. It could not, for example, have been decided in October 1940, at Minton's Playhouse in New York's Harlem, that bop was to be the next jazz style.

Many unrelated events brought about quite naturally. Just as Early New Orleans Dixieland jazz solidified in New Orleans years before, bop solidified in New York in the early 1940s. Charlie Parker said that an alto saxophone player from Dallas named Buster Smith was playing the beginnings of this free style. In the Southwest, Charlie Christian surely played saxophone-type lines on the guitar. In the St. Louis area, Jimmy Blanton was innovating on the bass. All this activity meant that the bop style developed not only in New York but also in Kansas City, St. Louis, Oklahoma City, and elsewhere.

Bop Arranging

The shift to bop embraced the most radical changes in the development of jazz to this point. The smaller band necessary for these new experimentations was in part an outgrowth of the military draft and the transportation difficulties during World War II. In contrast to the musical arrangements of the swing era, notations for the bop bands were usually confined to **unison** lines for the melodic instruments. A standard format for performing tunes in the bop manner was to play the first chorus in unison (trumpet and saxophone usually), then the improvised choruses, followed by the unison chorus again. Therefore, if the tune had a chorus of thirty-two bars and the form AABA, the first eight bars (A) would be composed, the second eight would be a repetition of the first eight (A), the third eight would be improvised (B), and the last eight would again be a repetition of the first eight (A). This added up to thirty-two bars and constituted the first chorus and the last chorus. Therefore, only one eight-bar strain, the A part, had to be planned beforehand.[2]

Example 8.2

The bop players accented the note between the beats:

Example 8.3

Compare the swing style:

Example 8.4

Musical Expansion

For greater freedom of expression, these players used **extended harmonies** in their improvised choruses. The development of new harmonic resources for the jazz musician followed closely on the heels of experimentations by classical composers. At the turn of the century, harmonies were enriched through the successive inclusion of higher members of the **overtone series**, resulting in an extensive use of **ninth, eleventh,** and **thirteenth chords** and beyond. See notational examples 24, 25 Appendix B. Use of the flatted fifth became so ordinary that from this point on it was considered another "blue note," just as the third and seventh tones of the scale had been.

It was not until the bop era that the use of **higher harmonics** and their resultant complex harmonies

became prevalent. Harmonic sonorities that were complex enough to be designated as polychords were used extensively. This harmonic construction can best be understood as a combination of two conventional chords. As long as these chords have a close relationship, such as common tones, they are perceived as one chord in the same key rather than in two separate keys (see notational example 24 in Appendix B). These new, more complex chords were substituted for the simpler chords used in the standard tunes of the day. The players were greatly stimulated by fresh chords inside of old progressions. This shift to more complex harmonies was significant enough that few successful swing players were able to adopt the new requirements of bop, creating a significant shift in the continuity of jazz's evolution.

Bop playing in general employed faster tempos[3] (S, Dizzy Gillespie and Charlie Parker, "Shaw 'Nuff," side E, band 7; S, Charlie Parker, "KoKo," side E, band 8; NW, 271, Dizzy Gillespie and Charlie Parker, "Shaw 'Nuff," side 1, band 3; NW, Dizzy Gillespie, "Things To Come," side 1, band 8; NW, Dizzy Gillespie, "KoKo," side 1, band 5). To create excitement by merely increasing the tempo would have been impractical with the large, unwieldy bands of the swing era, but it was done effectively in bop. Moreover, bop was the first style of jazz that was not specifically for dancing. Although the early jazz players used primarily quarter notes with four-tone chords or chords of the seventh, the bop players often played sixteenth-note rhythms with harmonies of greater complexity. One of the unusual phrasing idioms in bop occurred when there was a series of eighth notes:

Therefore, if the phrase were counted "one and, two and, three and, four and," the players would accent the "ands." Also bop phrasing was at first heavily influenced by Kansas City–type short riffs, but soon the statements, both planned and improvised, became longer and less repetitive.

There was more tension in the music of this era than in the music of the swing era. Jazz, as well as the other arts, has always been influenced by the mood of the times, and in the 1940s the United States was entering a war. The musical tension, then, was created by **tonal clashes,** unusual harmonies, and fast tempos with complex rhythms. To play bop well, the musicians had to have a good knowledge of harmony plus great technical facility. Even with these attributes, the hectic tempos and rapidly moving chords of many of the works caused some experienced players to merely run the chords (**arpeggios**) instead of creating interesting melodic lines.

One of the major changes that occurred during the bop era was repertoire, the building of which was accomplished mainly by using the chords of a **standard tune** as the framework on which to compose a new melody. An example of this kind of borrowing is found in the selection "Ornithology," which is a melody improvised from the harmonies in the composition "How High the Moon." Both Miles Davis and Thelonious Monk recorded tunes based on "All God's Children Got Rhythm." Davis called his "Little Willie Leaps," and Monk's is titled "Suburban Eyes." Chords from "What Is This Thing Called Love" became "Hot House," "Indiana" became "Donna Lee," "Whispering" became "Groovin' High," "I Got Rhythm" became "Anthropology," "Koko" is from the chords to "Cherokee," "S'Wonderful" became "Stupendous," and so on. Twelve-bar blues had such titles as "Relaxin'" at Camarillo," "Parker's Mood," "Now's the Time," and "Congo Blues." In previous eras, the melody was usually stated in the first chorus, and improvisation began after that. The bop innovators, however, often disregarded the initial statement of the melody and began their improvisation at the beginning of the selection. Beside changing the harmonies, melodies, and rhythms, the bop players changed the approach to phrasing from neat **symmetrical** phrases to phrases that seemed uneven and unnatural compared to earlier jazz.

The Bop Rhythm Section

The assigned parts played by individual members of the rhythm section also underwent radical changes. Instead of the regular $\frac{4}{4}$ steady rhythm heard in swing music, the drummer now used the bass and snare drums mainly for accents and punctuations. He usually maintained an overall sound by playing eighth-note rhythms on the top cymbal. If the accents were not spontaneous, they were played on either the fourth beat of the bar or the fourth beat of every other bar. The more spontaneous punctuations were called **bombs** which had to be played with great discernment to aid the impetus instead of being a distraction. The piano player changed from playing $\frac{4}{4}$ steady rhythm to chordal punctuations (Count Basie had played in this style for some time). These punctuations were played at specific moments to designate the chord changes and thus added to the overall musical excitement. With the advent of the amplifier, the guitar became a melody instrument and took its place with the trumpet, saxophone, and others. This left the sole responsibility for the steady pulse of the beat to the string bass. Although the string bass part now had a more interesting line, this line was secondary to the job of maintaining a rhythmic pulse.

The beauty of the bop rhythm section was that the individual members were freed from duplicating one another's role. In the swing style, all four players were forced mainly to keep the pulse because the bands were quite large and the public wanted to feel the pure, unornamented, uncomplicated beat in order to dance. Generally, these bop approaches were not really new, as shown by Basie's piano work, Jimmy Blanton's bass playing with Ellington, and Charlie Christian's guitar work with Benny Goodman's orchestra. The bop players also added rhythm players from Cuba who not only aided the pulse assigned to the bass player but also brought new rhythmic excitement into jazz through improvised **cross-rhythms.** This addition pointed out the fact that the more intricate aspects of the West African musical tradition had been kept alive much more in Cuba than in the United States. Of course, Latin rhythms, as they were considered, were not new to jazz. For example, there is a tango section in Handy's "St. Louis Blues," which was written about thirty years earlier.

The Performers

Much of the leadership of this era must be attributed to Charlie Parker's fluid alto sax, Dizzy Gillespie's virtuosic trumpet playing, Thelonious Monk's melodies, and the brilliantly accented drumming of Kenny Clarke and Max Roach. The early bop sessions at Minton's Playhouse emerged from a band led by drummer Kenny Clarke. Charlie Parker was not there at first, but he came later. Ex-bandleader Teddy Hill applied the Kansas City formula to Minton's style. As the manager, he hired a good contemporary nucleus of players with whom the performers of this advanced jazz enjoyed jamming. The musicians who played regularly at Minton's devised ways to discourage the unwanted from sitting in on the jam sessions. They would play tunes at such fast tempos, and play what at the time were such strange chords, that those musicians not really in the clique simply could not compete.

Roy Eldridge and Dizzy Gillespie

Dizzy Gillespie, as talented a trumpet player as he is a showman, has combined great technique with fresh thoughts and extensive harmonic knowledge. Along with Parker, he was a leader in the style of jazz that he and his contemporaries labeled bop. Gillespie's trumpet playing stems from Louis Armstrong by way of Roy Eldridge.

Not nearly enough is ever said about Roy Eldridge. He had played in a very fiery style for many years before bop came along,[5] and he first became prominent during his stint with Fletcher Henderson in 1936. He was admired not only for his virtuosic technique and startling use of the extreme upper register of the trumpet but also for his exciting and refreshingly new musical lines. Eldridge was featured with the bands of Gene Krupa (1941–43) and Artie Shaw (1944–45).

Dizzy Gillespie's playing was so modeled on the talents of Eldridge that when Eldridge left the Teddy Hill band, Gillespie was very naturally hired to replace him. Gillespie's first recorded solos were with this band in 1937. "King Porter Stomp" and "Blue Rhythm

Fantasy" reflect the Ellington influence most directly, but "Things to Come" was probably his most important record (NW, side 1, band 5).

Around 1939, with Cab Calloway's band, Gillespie made his first appearance as arranger/composer. These tunes were "Paradiddle" (featuring Cozy Cole on drums) and "Pickin' the Cabbage." He was with Calloway for two years, during which time he improved considerably. "Dizzy, always a prankster and cutup, was finally fired by Calloway, who accused him of throwing spitballs on the bandstand—ironically, the *one time* Gillespie was actually blameless.[6] There is no doubt that Gillespie was the most talked about bop musician at that time.

In 1945, Gillespie organized his first big band, preferring the larger band at a time when all other bop advocates were performing in combos. His first big band, called Hep-Sations, was short-lived. Gillespie became interested in African-Cuban rhythms after having performed with Cuban orchestras around New York. In 1947, he added Chano Pozo to his band to bring Latin American and West African rhythms to jazz. With the addition of Pozo, the gap between bop and the $\frac{4}{4}$ meter of swing became more apparent. The followers of

Dizzy Gillespie.
Courtesy of the Institute of Jazz Studies

Gillespie's trumpet excursions included Fats Navarro, Kenny Dorham, Miles Davis (early in his career), Clifford Brown, Thad Jones, Donald Byrd, Pete and Conte Condoli, Freddie Hubbard, Wynton Marsalis, and Jon Faddis.

It should also be noted that Gillespie was the first to take a jazz band on tour for the U.S. State Department. His band, composed of both black and white musicians, helped relieve diplomatic tension in some parts of the world.

The reactions to Gillespie's style of playing ranged all the way from unqualified enthusiasm to pure indignation. Today he is highly regarded all over the world, and his contributions to modern jazz trends cannot possibly be disputed[7] (S, Dizzy Gillespie, "I Can't Get Started with You," side E, band 6; S, Dizzy Gillespie and Charlie Parker, "Shaw 'Nuff," side E, band 7; FJ, "Groovin' High," vol. 11).

The period from 1944 to 1947 was noted for the great jazz groups that worked in the clubs on Fifty-second Street in New York, where the first actual bop band was formed by Dizzy Gillespie and bassist Oscar Pettiford in January 1944. The Earl ("Fatha") Hines band had experimented in 1942 and 1943, but until the emergence of the Gillespie-Pettiford band in 1944, bop had been confined mainly to Harlem's after-hours clubs, such as Monroe's and Minton's, and to occasional improvised solos in big bands by performers such as Howard McGee, Charlie Parker, and Dizzy Gillespie. These choruses seemed out of context in the big swing bands—Cab Calloway, Andy Kirk, and so on.

Charlie Parker (1921–1955)

Charlie Parker, called "Yardbird"—or more often simply "Bird"—was born on August 29, 1921, in Kansas City, Kansas, and moved to Kansas City, Missouri, at the age of seven. As a youngster, he listened a great deal to saxophonists Lester Young and Buster Smith. An important predecessor of Parker, Smith was from the Kansas City school. After Benny Moten's death, Smith was a co-leader, with Basie, of Moten's group.

As far back as 1932, Buster Smith recordings foreshadow Charlie Parker. There is no doubt about the strong influence that altoist Smith and tenor saxophonist Young had on young Parker. But it is surprising that Parker himself credited five white saxophonists with being the greatest early influences on his playing: nonjazz players Rudy Wiedoeft and Rudy Vallee and jazzmen Frank Teschemacher, Jimmy Dorsey, and Bud Freeman. He definitely surpassed all these players.

In 1936, Parker used to stand around in the alley behind the Reno Club in Kansas City and listen to the Basie band. At fifteen years of age, he was learning in the same way that most jazz players learned their trade: he listened and attempted to imitate. Parker was always curious about advanced harmony, and he worked for and studied with a graduate of the Boston Conservatory, Tommy Douglas, who was ahead of his time in this direction in 1935. Parker's studies with pianists and guitarists furthered this knowledge. He became intensely interested in the use of the higher harmonies of chords as structures on which to improvise new melodies. This approach became one of the mainstays of the bop movement, and many new tunes were created from old chord progressions.

When saxophonist Budd Johnson heard eighteen-year-old Parker in Chicago, he noted that Parker already had some of the elements of bop—such as double time—in his repertoire.

Parker first came to New York in 1939 to search out jam sessions and every other opportunity to listen and learn, supporting himself by washing dishes and other

---

Listening Guide

Charlie Parker's Re-Boppers
"KoKo"*

:00 Introduction: Unison alto sax (Charlie Parker) and muted trumpet (Dizzy Gillespie); drums with brushes using many accents (Max Roach).

:06 Muted trumpet solo, drums continue as before.

:12 Alto sax solo, drums the same.

:19 Alto sax and muted trumpet in parallel harmony, drums the same.

:25 First chorus: Alto sax solo, drums on a fast $\frac{4}{4}$ rhythm plus accents, bass playing a very fast walking style (Curley Russell), piano enters with his own chordal punctuations. If the piano seems a bit late, that is because that is also Gillespie; he had to put his trumpet down.

:50 Bridge of first chorus: change of chords.

1:04 Last part of first chorus.

1:15 Second chorus: Parker still on alto sax.

1:40 Bridge of second chorus.

1:54 Last part of second chorus.

2:07 Drum solo: very intricate as far as the pulse is concerned (this gives Gillespie time to go from piano to the trumpet).

2:27 Alto sax and muted trumpet in unison, drums now on cymbals.

2:34 Muted trumpet solo, drums the same.

2:40 Alto sax solo, drummer a bit lighter on cymbals now.

2:45 Alto sax and muted trumpet in parallel harmony (a reminder of the introduction for the sake of continuity).

2:49 End.

*Smithsonian Collection, side E, band 8.

menial jobs. The first combo job that Parker played in New York was at Clark Monroe's Uptown House on 134th Street. He left town afterward with the Jay McShann band. The first recorded solos of Parker are on transcriptions made by the Jay McShann band in 1940 at a Wichita, Kansas, radio station. The McShann band, besides being blues based, was also riff oriented like Basie's. It was McShann who brought Parker back to New York in 1942, this time as a mature musician.

Today it is hard to locate recordings of Parker with McShann. Folkways pressed "Hootie Blues," recorded in Dallas in 1941, and Decca pressed "Sepian Bounce," recorded in New York in 1942[8] (FJ, Jay McShann, "Hootie Blues," vol. 10). By 1942, mainly because of jam sessions at Minton's Playhouse, Parker and Dizzy Gillespie had become the most talked about musicians in the new style of jazz called bop.

In 1942, saxophonist Budd Johnson was urging Earl Hines to hire Parker from McShann's blues-oriented band. In December 1942, Johnson himself left Hines, Billy Eckstine then talked Hines into hiring Parker and was replaced temporarily by a young teenager named Miles Davis. Thus the association between Davis and Parker began. "The key musicians each produced certain ideas independently and when they came together in New York they discovered their affinities and stimulated each other to further effort. Over a period of several years this produced a synthesis of new elements based on old that became known as modern jazz, or bop."[9]

Parker's first job as leader was in 1944 at the Spotlight Club on New York's Fifty-second Street after he had left Eckstine. His most mature jazz statements are generally conceded to be those recorded in 1945 under his own name as leader: "Koko," "Now's the Time," "Billie's Bounce," "Meandering," "Warming Up a Riff," and "Thriving from a Riff." On these records he shows a rich, expressive tone and unprecedented rhythmic freedom in his phrasing.

Parker's success was demonstrated by the fact that after World War II he was sometimes paid $1,200 a week by the same people who had hired him earlier for $2 a night.

In 1946, Parker spent seven months in Camarillo State Hospital in California. By 1949, because of a combination of ulcers, drugs, and alcohol, his playing began to decline. He was not considered reliable by booking offices, so employment began to be a problem. Some musicians never see the drug and alcohol problems affecting them, but Parker was very much aware that his career had been ruined by these mistakes. He constantly advised against such indulgence. Sonny Rollins tells of conversations along this line with Parker:

Bird befriended quite a few guys. Sonny Stitt before me. With us and a few other cats, especially saxophone players, it was like a father thing. When we were hung up personally, we went just to talk to him, just to see him. The purpose of his whole existence was music and he showed me that music was the paramount thing and anything that interfered with it I should stay away from. Later on I was able to take advantage of his advice, but he died before I had a chance to see him and tell him I had.[10]

In 1950, Parker recorded with strings (as did Gillespie). Although it was the fulfillment of a dream for Parker, his fans screamed that he had "gone commercial." When Parker's young daughter Pree died of pneumonia, he seemed to decline for the last time both musically and physically. He died on March 12, 1955, at the age of thirty-three.

One of the trying aspects of Parker's career is that he knew that even among contemporary musicians only a few understood his music. Parker's abilities and contributions have, of course, been finally recognized. In fact, it would be extremely difficult to find a musician who is more recognized and so little understood.

In 1973, a group called Supersax was featured on an album called Supersax Plays Bird.[11] For this album, saxophonist Med Flory and bassist Buddy Clark put together a library of Parker's recorded solos. Flory and Clark harmonized all these wonderful improvisations and played them using five saxophones—an almost overwhelming sound. The album won a Grammy Award from the National Academy of Recording Arts and Sciences (NARAS) for the best jazz record performed by a group (as opposed to a large band). Supersax has extended these efforts further since their first recording.

In 1974, Onyx Records released an album of the very first works recorded by Parker in his work with Jay McShann.[12] This album, called Original Recordings, also won a NARAS award for the best solo jazz album. Such public recognition came nearly twenty years after Parker's death.

Most young saxophonists feel that Parker's style and melodic and rhythmic thoughts are the "correct" ways to play. Furthermore, in 1969 the Charlie Parker Center for the Performing Arts was established by a group of teachers, musicians, and civic leaders to provide free music instruction for young players.

In February 1942, one Down Beat reporter stated that Parker had a tendency to play too many notes. In July of that year, another reporter from the same magazine noted that Parker used a minimum of notes. To say that there was controversy and a lack of understanding of Parker's work even among his peers would be a gross understatement. Some who write and talk about jazz feel that Parker was the most important catalyst in the advancement of jazz. Surely, no one can doubt that he brought to culmination the many innovations of the 1940s and 1950s, more changes than had previously occurred in the history of jazz.

Listening Guide

Demonstration 19 🔊
(cassette 1, side B, track 3; CD 1, track 19)

Charlie Parker

"Shaw 'Nuff"
Charlie Parker, alto sax
Dizzy Gillespie, trumpet
Al Haig, piano
Curley Russell, bass
Sidney Catlett, drums

:00 Eight measures: Drums, bass, and bass of piano.
:06 Trumpet and alto sax in thirds for 8 measures.
:13 Six measures of unison ending with famous "Salt Peanuts" phrase.
:17 Piano break for 2 measures.
:19 Unison main theme (head): 32 measures.
:47 Alto sax solo by Charlie Parker for 32 measures.
1:14 Trumpet solo by Dizzy Gillespie for 32 measures.
1:41 Piano solo for 32 measures.
2:07 Original theme in unison as first chorus.
2:34 Same as top of record: Drums, bass, and bass of piano for 8 measures.
2:41 Trumpet and sax in thirds again.
2:48 Eight bars of unison as in the earlier part of the record.
2:56 End.

Parker was one of the rare musicians who could play slow blues very well but was also comfortable at extremely fast tempos. Most of what Parker played was based on the blues: "Now's the Time," "Cool Blues," and others.

One of Parker's most impressive assets was his use of rhythmic nuances. "Relaxin' at Camarillo" (NW, 271, side 1, band 6) shows how beautifully these can be applied to the standard blues form. Of course, Parker had an impeccable ear and virtuosity on the alto saxophone that could be exploited unconsciously rather than being contrived. When a musician realizes what Parker was able to invent within the six-note phrase in "Embraceable You," the musician hears developments leading to Sonny Rollins and others. Parker used the phrase repeatedly, but he also changed each time, demonstrating a creativeness worthy of Mozart, Beethoven, and others who composed great music from motifs (NW, 271, side 1, band 7). Most musicians agree that as advanced as Parker's style was, he never seemed to lose sight of the early jazz roots. Some casual observers seem surprised that Parker could appreciate all kinds of music not only melodically and harmonically but also rhythmically. Those who follow him can benefit from this freedom, not necessarily from copying his actual phrases.

Parker thought that there must be something in jazz improvisation that had not been done before because he thought that he could hear things that he could not play. By continually working over his favorite tune, "Cherokee," he finally found that he could play what he had been hearing by developing melodic lines from the higher harmonies of the chords. Parker freed the solo aspect of jazz not only melodically and harmonically but also rhythmically. Those who follow him can benefit from this freedom, not necessarily from copying his actual phrases.

It is true that drummers Kenny Clarke and Max Roach developed new rhythmic approaches, Thelonious Monk new harmonic approaches, Dizzy Gillespie new solo directions, and so on. But it did seem to be Charlie Parker who brought all these elements to maturity in the style known as bop. Parker's playing was the realization of the potential of what was available; Parker's influence, like Armstrong's earlier, extended to all instruments.

Parker's achievements are unique and for a continually sick man almost incredible. It is hard to imagine what he would have accomplished given a long and healthy life. In many ways his admirers got more out of his life than Parker did himself but, in the end, he is not a man to be pitied. On all but his darkest days he experienced the joy of creation that is given few men to know and he enriched the lives of all those who could respond to his work.[13]

There has never been a greater dedication to a jazz musician than "To Bird With Love" by Societo Wizlov (La Cure, 86310, Antigny, France), a 424-page epic on Parker. It is 14½ inches high and 10 inches wide, weighs 8 pounds, and costs $147.

Bud Powell

Bud Powell should rightfully share the honors of the bop era with such luminaries as Parker and Gillespie. Powell, who came from a musical family, won prizes as a schoolboy for his Bach recitals. He brought this advanced technique and his harmonic acuity into the bop community, where he was welcomed most openly. Powell then became an established member of the Fifty-second Street scene before he moved to France in 1959, where he received the recognition to which he was entitled.

Powell's early death did not deprive jazz listeners of a worthwhile legacy. He recorded solo albums and was well represented on many recordings in his chosen style. Powell, a seemingly logical piano heir to Art Tatum's reign, was truly a pioneer in bop piano. He played with the John Kirby and Dizzy Gillespie groups, as well as others, but was constantly plagued by mental illnesses, which began when he was only twenty-one years old. In spite of this, repressings by both Verve and Blue Note

Christian and Blanton

Both Charlie Christian and Jimmy Blanton became national figures on the jazz scene late in 1939. In the short span between 1939 and 1942 (both died of tuberculosis in 1942), Christian and Blanton entirely changed the concept of playing their respective instruments—Christian the guitar and Blanton the bass.

Charlie Christian played mostly around Oklahoma City, Kansas City, and St. Louis before joining Benny Goodman when he was only nineteen years old. Although Christian was influential, speculation remains as to what he would have contributed had he not died prematurely. His guitar playing influenced all subsequent jazz, and he must be placed in the same category as Gillespie, Parker, Lester Young, and Blanton. He elevated the guitar from a strictly rhythm instrument to a solo melody instrument equal to other instruments. This is not to say that other guitarists did not play extremely capable solos, but Christian, who came along about the same time as the introduction of the amplifier, was by far the strongest influence. Although he was involved in a new extension of chords, Christian's main innovation was that he played solos with long lines like those for a saxophone.

Most guitarists possibly felt that the big moving chords of Eddie Lang, George Van Epps, and other earlier players were beyond them. Also, the most perfect listening conditions were necessary for hearing guitar solos. Christian's single-note lines and the advent of the amplifier opened the door for many talented players such as Wes Montgomery, Barney Kessel, George Benson, and Pat Metheny. It should be understood, however, that Christian's approach to solos—single-note lines instead of great moving chords—had been played earlier by the talented Belgian player Django Reinhardt. (There were few Reinhardt recordings at that time to document his technique.)

Even in Christian's original and modern guitar playing, the blues influence was the main feature. But unlike other blues guitarists, Christian pioneered the use of the amplifier as early as 1937 in Oklahoma City. He joined the Benny Goodman band in 1939 in New York, at which time, after his performances every evening with Goodman, he became a regular performer at Minton's. The fact that he died in 1942 meant that he had very little time to develop his impressive legacy. The most mentioned of his recordings today are "Solo Flight" with the Benny Goodman orchestra, "Gone with What Wind" with the Benny Goodman sextet, and "Profoundly Blue" with the Edmond Hall quartet[15] (S, Benny Goodman with Charlie Christian, "Breakfast Feud," side D, band 9).

Until Jimmy Blanton joined Duke Ellington in 1939, the bass player played either two or four notes to a bar and played very simple lines, mainly the roots and fifths of the chords. There was hardly ever a bass solo, as these demanded more technique from players as well as some entirely new techniques from recording engineers. In the Ellington band, Blanton excited the jazz world with his solo "Jack the Bear" and his duets with Ellington: "Mr. J. B. Blues" and "Pitter Panther Patter." Blanton satisfied his listeners with the bass parts that he played, but while accomplishing this he also played tasteful, interesting lines. He used eighth notes and sixteenth notes without ever sounding clumsy on the instrument, and he also proved that he could bow well. Although he died early, Blanton laid the foundations for all bass players who followed. They would assume responsibility for keeping the pulse for the whole combo while weaving their way among the new, advanced chords. Blanton's solo on Duke Ellington's "Jack the Bear" was considered for a long time to be the greatest bass solo on record[16] (NW, 274, "Pitter Panther Patter," side 2, band 8).

One of the fine bass players to follow Blanton was Oscar Pettiford, who, with Dizzy Gillespie, formed the first bop band to appear on Fifty-second Street in 1944. Although there have been many great bass players, two must be singled out: Ray Brown and Charlie Mingus. Brown progressed so quickly that he had been out of high school only two years when he joined the famous Dizzy Gillespie sextet in 1946. Brown's style seems modern today, and although he sounds relaxed, he displays great technical ability and fine taste. The musicianship of Mingus was ever present as he included ostinato figures, **pedal points**, and **double stops** even during accompaniment. When Mingus soloed, you were aware that he was also a good contemporary composer.

Thelonious Monk

Ever since jazz musicians began hearing Thelonious Monk, they realized that he was an important pianist and jazz composer. Works written by Monk have to be considered "compositions" as opposed to the "lines" written by, for example, Charlie Parker. Under some lines the harmony can be changed, and over some chord progressions new lines can be invented. But with Monk's works it seems necessary to use both his lines and his harmony. When Monk improvised, he did not simply play variations; sometimes he fragmented lines and at other times elaborated on them. He often started with a basic phrase and, like Sonny Rollins on the tenor sax, played the phrase in almost every conceivable manner. However, he received recognition for his composing before he was accepted as an innovating pianist.

An example of Monk's strong influence is the effect he had on John Coltrane. When Coltrane joined Monk's combo, he had to struggle with the repertoire. But after his experience in the group, he had the opportunity to become a really great musician and a most important influence himself. It was as if Monk were able to open

record companies, as well as recordings with Parker and Gillespie, attest to his contributions[14] (NW, 271, "Un Poco Loco," side 2, band 2).

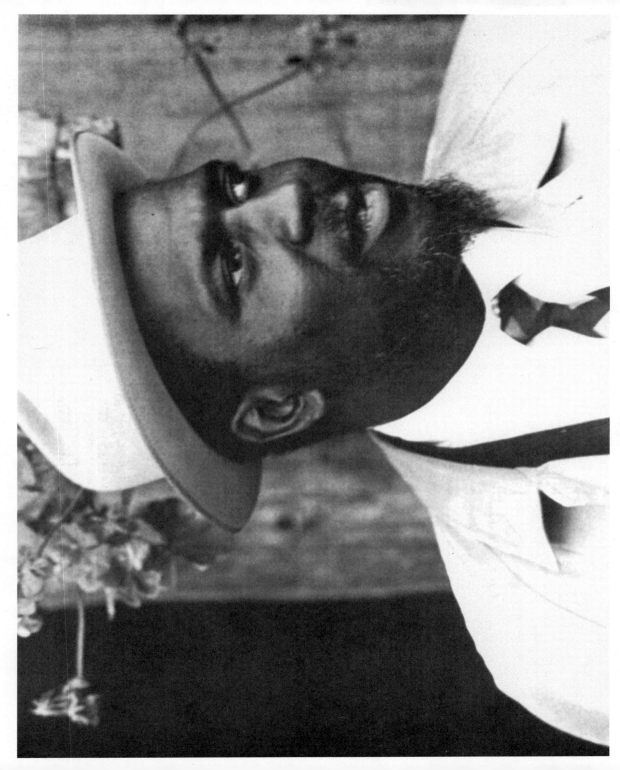

Thelonious Monk.
Courtesy of Ray Avery

Coltrane's ears and point out possible directions as yet unconceived by the saxophonist[17] (S, Thelonious Monk, "Misterioso," "Evidence," "Criss Cross," and "I Should Care," side G, bands 1, 2, 3, and 5; S, Miles Davis's All Stars, "Bags' Groove," side G, band 6; NW, 271, "Misterioso," side 2, band 4).

Thelonious Sphere Monk died in February 1982.

Kai Winding and Frank Rosolino

Trombone playing did not contribute to the beginning of the bop style. Trombone players who had the virtuosity to play this style were not sufficiently interested at first, as it required a highly developed technique as well as understanding. J. J. Johnson proved to trombonists that the style was possible on the instrument. Kai Winding, Frank Rosolino, and many others quickly followed his lead.

Bop and Progressive Big Bands

When large bands used these bop harmonic and melodic developments, this jazz was labeled "progressive." At first, the only contributions in this direction were solos in big bands by such musicians as Gillespie and Parker, but soon entire bands were dedicated to these new directions. The progressive bandleaders included Stan Kenton (who even adopted the label "progressive").[18] Woody Herman, Earl Hines, Billy Eckstine, Boyd Raeburn, and

Demonstration 20 [CD/cassette icons] (cassette 1, side B, track 4; CD 1, track 20)

Thelonious Monk with the Miles Davis All Stars
*"Bags' Groove"**

This excerpt features the piano solo of Thelonious Monk. Listen for the overall shape of the solo created from a single melodic idea. Monk takes an amazingly economic approach to the use of melody throughout the solo but still creates an effective solo structure.

:00 Notice the simple beginning motive and how it begins to be transformed.

:18 Second chorus: Motive becomes more angular.

:37 Third chorus: Motive takes a new shape that is maintained throughout the chorus with scattered chordal support.

:55 Fourth chorus: Motive takes on a harmonic shape developed from the chordal shapes used in the previous chorus.

1:15 Fourth chorus: Very open melody with a lot of silence between the short motivic statements. He begins to introduce some dissonant notes as part of the motive.

1:33 Fifth chorus: Sparse melodic approach continues with the use of unexpected ending notes in the motive that proves to be very dramatic.

1:51 Sixth chorus: Dissonant intervals (2 notes very close together) to accent the motivic statements. This type of melodic activity became a trademark of Monk's style.

2:10 Seventh chorus: The motive is reduced even further in size.

2:29 Eighth chorus: Very simple chord punctuations that are separated by a lot of silence; notice the open quality of the chords and how sparsely they are voiced.

2:48 End.

*Smithsonian Collection, side G, band 4.

bands led by Gillespie himself. The Boyd Raeburn band played music as far removed from the earlier swing bands as could be envisioned.

Billy Eckstine

Billy Eckstine, having built a following as a ballad singer with Earl Hines, formed a band comprising almost every leading bop player at one time[19] (NW, 284, "Good Jelly Blues," side 1, band 6). Between 1944 and 1946, his female singer was Sarah Vaughan. The Earl Hines and Billy Eckstine bands of this type reached their peak during a record ban, so there is not much recorded documentation of them. (Record bans occur when the musicians' union strikes against the record companies, Eckstine's band dates from June 1944 to February 1947. Many of the frustrations included limited audience appeal for the new music, bans on recording by the musicians' union, and lack of sympathy, cooperation, and encouragement from record companies when there was no ban.)

At times Eckstine's band was a financial success, but when the orchestra disbanded, Eckstine was left somewhat in debt. Gillespie was the musical director of Eckstine's band. Their first records sold mainly because of Eckstine's fine vocals. In fact, his vocals, along with those of Sarah Vaughan, were the band's best means of communication with both the public and the recording executives. In 1944, when Gillespie left the Billy Eckstine band, he was first replaced by Fats Navarro and then by Miles Davis, who remained with the band until it disbanded in 1947. George Hoefer of *Down Beat* described what happened when Davis first joined the band for a short stay in 1944:

Trumpeter Anderson was taken seriously ill shortly after the band's arrival in St. Louis and was hospitalized. On the night the band opened at the Riviera, the first customer was a high school student with a trumpet under his arm. Gillespie asked him if he had a union card, and Miles Davis, 16, of East St. Louis, said that he did. The music director told him to go up on the stand and see what he could do.

"Miles," Eckstine said, "he sounded terrible." Davis recalled, "I couldn't read the book, I was so busy listening to Bird and Dizzy." He played a few nights with the band and then headed for Juilliard in New York.[20]

The band eventually recorded a variety of jazz for National Records, including up-tempo works, ballads, and blues. Eckstine can even be heard on valve trombone solos. The trend was for vocalists to be more successful attractions than bands, and Eckstine surely must be considered one of the finest singers to come out of jazz or any other background.

Stan Kenton

Stan Kenton, who was continually an influential pioneer in jazz, had been working as a pianist in Los Angeles before organizing his first band in Balboa, California, in 1941. Kenton stated that the soon became aware of the adventurous excitement of jazz players and began to base his repertoire on the talents of the excellent musicians who passed through his band. Great credit should be accorded Kenton for having never compromised what to him was art for the comfort and safety of more commercial aspects of big bands. Kenton added Jack Costanzo to play Latin rhythms in 1948, furthering this direction in contemporary jazz.[21]

Stan Kenton.
Courtesy of Ray Avery

By 1944, Woody Herman had lost his dixieland trend and some of his Ellington influence as additions in his band began showing a heavy bop emphasis. For example, at one point his trumpet section was composed of Sonny Berman, Neal Hefti, Pete Condoli, and Conrad Gozzo.[22]

Summary

By 1946, bop was being heard even in some commercial dance bands. Today, most good amateur or semi-amateur players improvise in the bop style. Even most name jazz players perform in a manner directly related

Woody Herman.
Courtesy of Ray Avery

to the bop school. Some more than others show the effects of having worked through the cool and funky styles since bop, but the phrases, the harmonies, and the approach still seem to be quite clearly derived from bop.

Bop did not have a chance to emerge gradually for public listening as the other styles had. By the time the differences between the union and the record industry were resolved, bop was well advanced. One reason for its slow acceptance by listeners was that the public was saturated with bad publicity about bop that made the music appear more like a passing fad than an advancement in the development of jazz. An example is the way in which the followers of Gillespie imitated his dark glasses, goatee, and beret. Fan magazines even began advertising "bebop ties."

After World War II, when bop started to be heard by more of the public, its radical departure from swing caused great consternation. Some of the older jazz players accepted the advancements, but most rejected bop, feeling that it lacked the more desirable jazz characteristics: the emphasis on pulse, the theme-and-variations approach, and so on. However, the real opposition appeared to stem from jazz critics, which seems to be the case as each new innovation arrives on the jazz scene. The adverse reaction to bop resulted in the revival of simpler forms of jazz, such as Early New Orleans Dixieland. Oddly enough, Parker and Gillespie were not terribly far from the early roots of jazz. Parker's earliest recordings were blues numbers; Gillespie's earliest recording was "King Porter Stomp," written by Jelly Roll Morton.

These changes in jazz, like the changes in classical music, were reactions against the preceding jazz styles. Musicians were constantly searching for new means of expression, so they intentionally played melodic lines with unusual intervals. The absence of an easily recognizable melody has been one of the main obstacles to the acceptance of bop by the general public. The complexities of the style of jazz demand deeper concentration and more attentive listening. Rex Harris suggests that bop should not be dismissed at first hearing: "No worthwhile form of music will yield its secret so readily as that."[23]

Bop music included some vocals, but bop players primarily thought instrumentally. Earlier players played as they would have sung, seeming to work over a melody. Bop players were much more involved with working over the chord progressions.

For Further Study

1. Explain the term *bop*.
2. In what ways was this direction in the development of jazz a change from the swing era?
3. Compare the arrangements of bop music with those of the swing era.
4. What is meant by "extended harmonies"?
5. Why were bop ensembles able to employ a faster tempo than swing bands?

6. Why is the word *tension* most appropriate in describing the feeling of bop music?
7. In what manner did the percussionist obtain the effect of accent and punctuation?
8. Listen to Dizzy Gillespie's rendition of "Things to Come" (*Dizzy Gillespie,* Galaxy Series, Long play 4811), and in your own words describe your reactions to the music.
9. An excellent example of the true bop sound is found on the album Jazz at Massey Hall (Fantasy, 6003) in the selection "Wee" as played by Charlie Chan, Dizzy Gillespie, Bud Powell, Max Roach, and Charles Mingus. Name the instrument featured in the solo spot that follows the short introduction. Do you hear the ascending and descending melodic playing of the string bass? Is the instrument bowed or plucked? Which instrument improvises next? What would you say about the range of tones this instrument realizes? What instrument is third? Finally, what instrument takes over in the wild climax?
10. Listen to Charlie Parker's Re-Boppers playing "KoKo" (S, side E, band 8), which is not the same as Ellington's blues "Ko-Ko," which borrows its chord changes from the song "Cherokee" and is a classic example of the true bop style of playing. Listen carefully to the interplay between the saxophone and trumpet as they toss the melody back and forth to the accompaniment of the exciting drummer Max Roach.

Suggested Additional Listening

Art Blakey and the Jazz Messengers, "Straight Ahead," Concord Jazz Records, CJ-168.
Bebop. New World Records, 271.
The Be-Bop Era.
Bird and Diz. Verve Records, V6-8006.
Bird Symbols. Charlie Parker Records, PLP-407.
Bird—The Savoy Recordings (Master Takes). Savoy Records, SJL-2201.
Charlie Parker. Everest Records, FS-254.
Charlie Parker. Prestige Records, 24009.
Charlie Parker. Savoy Records, S5J5500.
Charlie Parker in Historical Recordings. Le Jazz Cool Records, JC102.
Charlie Parker Memorial Album. Savoy Records, MG-12000.
Charlie Parker Story, vols. 1-3. Verve Records, V6-8000-1-2.
Echoes of an Era. Roulette Records, RE-105.
Eckstine, Billy. *Mister B and the Band—the Savoy Sessions.* Savoy Records, SJL-2214.
Essential Charlie Parker. Verve Records, V-8409.
The Genius of Bud Powell. Verve Records, VE2-2506.
Genius of Charlie Parker. Savoy Records, MG-12014.
Giants of Jazz. Atlantic Records, 2-905.
Gillespie, Dizzy. *Big 4.* Pablo Records, 23107.
————. *The Great Dizzy Gillespie.* Counterpoint Records, 554.
————. *In the Beginning.* Prestige Records, 24030.
Greatest Jazz Concert Ever. Prestige Records, 24024.
Jazz at Massey Hall. Fantasy Records, 6003.
Jazz in Revolution—the Big Bands in the 1940s. New World Records, 284.

Additional Reading Resources

Berendt, Joachim. *The New Jazz Book*, 17–19, 61–70.

Dankworth, Avril. *Jazz: An Introduction to Its Musical Basis*, 68–75.

Dexter, Dave. *The Jazz Story*, 121–31.

Feather, Leonard. *The Book of Jazz*.

Francis, André. *Jazz*, 107–15, 124–30.

Harrison, Max. *Charlie Parker*.

———. *Inside Jazz*.

———. "Thelonious Monk." *Musician and Musicians*, London, May 1982.

Hodeir, André. *Jazz: Its Evolution and Essence*, 99–115.

Keepnews, Orrin. "The Monk of Jazz: Memories of Thelonious, The Legendary Pianist." *Washington Post*, February 18, 1982.

Reisner, Robert G. *Bird: The Legend of Charlie Parker*.

Russell, Ross. *Bird Lives: The High Life and Hard Times of Charlie (Yardbird) Parker*.

Shapiro, Nat, and Hentoff, Nat, eds. *The Jazz Makers*, 332–48.

Stearns, Marshall. *The Story of Jazz*, 155–72.

Williams, Martin T. *The Jazz Tradition*, 187–213.

Wilson, John S. "Thelonious Monk, Created Wry Jazz Melodies and Harmonies." *The New York Times*, February 23, 1982, D20.

Note: Complete information, including name of publisher and date of publication, is provided in this book's bibliography.

Notes

1. From Henry Pleasants, *Serious Music and All That Jazz*, 1969. Reprinted by permission of Simon & Schuster, Inc.

2. Charlie Parker, "Yardbird Suite," *Bird Symbols*, Charlie Parker Records, PLP-407.

3. Dizzy Gillespie and Charlie Parker, "Wee," *Jazz at Massey Hall*, Fantasy Records, 6003; *Big Band Jazz*, Smithsonian Collection of Recordings.

4. Al Casey, "How High the Moon," *The History of Jazz*, vol. 4; Charlie Parker, "Ornithology," *Bird Symbols*, Charlie Parker Records, PLP-407.

5. Roy Eldridge, *Dale's Wail*, Verve Records, MGV-8089.

6. Gunther Schuller, *The Swing Era* (London: Oxford University Press, 1989), 347.

7. Dizzy Gillespie and the All Stars, "Leap Here," *Dizzy Gillespie, Jazz Story*, vol. 5; *Dizzy Gillespie*, RCA Victor Records, LPV 530; *Essential, Verve Records*, 68566; *The Greatest Names in Jazz*, "Carombola," *History of Jazz*, vol. 4; *Dizzy Gillespie: Composer's Concepts*, Mercury Em Arcy Records, EMS-2-410; *Dizzy Gillespie and Stan Getz*, Verve Records, VE 2-2521; *Benny Carter and Dizzy Gillespie*, Pablo Records, 231-0781; *Bahiana*, Pablo Records, 262-5708; *Big Band Jazz*, Smithsonian Collection of Recordings.

8. Jay McShann, "Sepian Bounce," *Encyclopedia of Jazz*, vol. 3, Decca Records, DL 8400, and *Encyclopedia of Jazz on Records*, vol. 3.

9. Max Harrison, *Charlie Parker* (New York: A. S. Barnes, 1961), 17.

10. Harrison, *Charlie Parker*, 64–65.

11. *Supersax Plays Bird*, Capitol Records, ST 11177.

12. Charlie Parker, *Original Recordings*, Onyx Records, 221.

13. Harrison, *Charlie Parker*, 74.

14. Bud Powell, *The Amazing Bud Powell*, vols. 1 and 2, Blue Note Records, 81503-4.

15. Charlie Christian, *Charlie Christian*, Columbia Records, CL 652, G-30779; (with Edmond Hall's Quartet), "Profoundly Blue," *Three Decades of Jazz (1939–1949)*; *Charlie Christian, Solo Flight*, Columbia Records, CG-30779; *The Harlem Jazz Scene*, Archive of Folk Music, 219E; "Solo Flight," *Singers and Soloists of the Swing Bands*, Smithsonian Collection of Recordings.

16. Jimmy Blanton (Duke Ellington's Orchestra), "Jack the Bear," *Historically Speaking—the Duke*, Bethlehem Records, BCP 60.

17. Thelonious Monk, *Thelonious Monk*, Prestige Records, 24006; *Brilliant Corners*, Riverside Records, RLP 12-226; *Monk's Dream*, Columbia Special Products, JCS-8765; *The Thelonious Monk Orchestra at Town Hall*, Riverside Records, 1138; Miles Davis' Album, "Bags' Groove, Take 1," *Bags' Groove*, Prestige Records, 7109; *Misterioso*, Columbia Records, CS-9236.

18. Stan Kenton, *Kenton in Stereo*, The Creative World of Stan Kenton, ST 1004.

19. Billy Eckstine Orchestra, *Big Band Jazz*, Smithsonian Collection of Recordings.

20. George Hoefer, "The First Big Bop Band," *Down Beat 32*, no. 16 (July 1965): 21.

21. Stan Kenton, *Cuban Fire*, The Creative World of Stan Kenton, ST 1008.

22. Woody Herman, *The Thundering Herds*, vol. 1, Columbia Records, C3L-25.

23. Rex Harris, *Jazz* (Baltimore: Penguin Books, 1956), 188.

Kenton, Stan. *The Kenton Era*. The Creative World of Stan Kenton, ST-1030.

Monk, Thelonious. *Genius of Thelonious Monk*. Prestige Records, 7656.

———. *Memorial Album*. Milestone Records, M-47064.

———. *Straight, No Chaser*. Columbia Records, CS-9451.

Original Recordings. Onyx Records, 221.

Smithsonian Collection of Classic Jazz, vols. 7 and 8.

Strictly Bebop. Capitol Records, ML-11059.

CHAPTER 9

Cool (1949–1955)

Listening Guide

Demonstration 21
(cassette 1, side B, track 5; CD 1, track 21)

Cool

:00 Ensemble chorus (flute lead and flügelhorn harmony); bass, guitar, and drums keep a relaxed $\frac{4}{4}$ rhythm while piano plays fill-ins.

:27 Flute solo (one chorus); listen also for piano fill-ins.

:55 Ensemble chorus (same as first chorus).

1:26 End.

Just as the bop style of jazz was a reaction against swing, the cool style of playing was a reaction against the complexities of bop. "Conservatism and understatement were the keys to this era. Jazz assumed . . . the form of a restrained chamber music."[2] The shock treatment of ten brass and five saxes would have been entirely out of place. What was needed was a truly chamber orchestra. Chico Hamilton, a drummer, was surprisingly a leader in the new direction.[3] Of course, Hamilton was no ordinary drummer, as indicated by his subtle rhythmic control and use of different drum pitches and timbres. One of his surprises was that he featured Fred Katz on cello.[4] (For an introduction to cool jazz, listen to demonstration 21.)

It is often thought that the violin and other stringed instruments do not make satisfying jazz sounds because these instruments, except for the plucked (**pizzicato**) bass, cannot be played percussively; rather, are usually bowed. This attitude reveals an oversight of some good jazz talent such as Jean Luc Ponty, Noel Pointer, Leroy Jenkins, Joe Venuti, Stuff Smith, Eddie South,[5] Ray Nance, and Stephane Grappelly[6] (NW, 250, Joe Venuti, "My Honey's Loving Arms," side 1, band 1; NW, Eddie South, "Hejre Kati," side 1, band 3; NW, Stuff Smith, "Knock Knock," side 1, band 9). Edgar Redmond, a woodwind player, has put forth much effort to enlighten music educators along this line and has produced a very good album to prove his point.[7]

The **tonal sonorities** of these conservative players could be compared to pastel colors, whereas the solos of Gillespie and his followers could be compared to fiery red colors. Marshall Stearns thought of cool as a new "kind of jazz which could be quite easily arranged . . . by conservatory-trained musicians with a real feeling for

Lester Young.
Courtesy of Dave Dexter, Jr.

contrapuntal jazz in an extended form."[8] By the extended form, Stearns refers to the fact that this new style was not restricted to twelve-, sixteen-, and thirty-two-measure choruses. Cool players devised a way to go even further than bop players in the direction of freedom from the square-cut divisions of jazz music. For example, in playing a thirty-two-bar chorus, the soloist would play a little into the next player's chorus, causing the second soloist to play into the third soloist's chorus in order to play thirty-two bars, and so on (see example 9.1). This helped the music flow as a continuous entity and erased the conception of a block type of form. By 1950, the acceptance of the long-playing record made possible the recording of longer works and longer improvisations.

This music sacrificed excitement for subtlety, and the players underplayed their variations. André Hodeir analyzed cool music according to three principal characteristics: "First, a sonority very different from the one adopted by earlier schools; second, a special type of phrase; and finally, an orchestral conception that . . . is not its least interesting element."[9] These three characteristics deserve examination. The most pronounced difference from the preceding eras was the more delicate **attack** used by the cool players. Little or no vibrato was used, and the wind players had a tendency to use the **middle registers** rather than the extremes. The delicate attacks used in the cool era and the lack of vibrato caused the playing to resemble that of classical playing, although relaxation was more salient to this style of jazz than to the classical performances.[10] It should also be noted that increasing numbers of schooled players were entering the jazz field.

In general, cool phrasing did not permit the player to deviate far from the original line. Some critics consider this backtracking rather than an advancement. Even with their melodic charm, these lines often lacked the richness and boldness of music of the bop era. The cool players conceived their harmonic parts polyphonically, an approach that gave the instrumentalist an independence of line not found in the swing era.

The Ingredients of Cool

The chamber-type orchestral groups or combos were usually composed of three to eight players. The introduction of instruments not previously associated with

jazz changed the overall sound: the flute became important as a jazz instrument, as did the French horn, oboe, and cello. Important flute players include Paul Horn,[11] Buddy Collette, Herbie Mann,[12] Bud Shank, Frank Wess, and others. The soft sounds of the French horn fit beautifully with the general feeling of cool jazz. Although Willie Ruff, Johnny Graas,[13] Junior Collins, and Julius Watkins deserve mention, there has nevertheless been a scarcity of jazz French horn players.

Playing jazz on a double-reed instrument is still not common. Bob Cooper began playing jazz on the oboe while he was with Stan Kenton. Today, fresh blues and other jazz formats can be heard on the oboe on records by Yusef Lateef[14] and Rahsaan Roland Kirk. The oboe and other double-reed instruments, new to jazz, fit in very well with the more standard instruments (trumpet, trombone, and saxophone) when the standard instruments are played in a cool manner as individual instruments instead of as parts of a section. The tuba was brought into jazz for the first time since the very early dixieland period and was given slow-moving melodic lines instead of the familiar bass parts of marches.

The **flügelhorn** worked its way into the jazz scene mainly through the efforts of Miles Davis, Clark Terry, and Art Farmer.[15] The flügel, as it is often called, is in the same key and pitch as the B-flat trumpet and cornet. It has a larger bore, and as a consequence, a darker, more mellow sound; it is also easier to play at a low register and harder to play at a high register than the trumpet. The most enjoyable examples are the Clark Terry–Bob Brookmeyer recordings that team flügelist Terry with the very talented and tasteful valve trombonist Brookmeyer.[16]

The cool players established that jazz need not be confined to 4/4 and 2/4 meters and that choruses need not always be divided symmetrically. Many new meter signatures came into use in jazz, including 3/4, 5/4, 9/4, and others. Successful jazz compositions often used an interchange of signatures within a selection. Pianist Dave Brubeck stimulated interest by laying one rhythm or more over another, creating both polyrhythms and **polymeters**.[17] Don Ellis, of course, carried the use of meters new in jazz much further (see chapter 7).

This school of jazz moved closer to classical music, even to the point of adopting such forms as rondos and fugues.[18] Sometimes the use of classical forms in jazz has been categorized as **third-stream music**. Sometimes, however, the Modern Jazz Quartet (and other

Example 9.1

First solo

| 8 bars | 8 bars | 8 bars | 8 bars |

32 bar chorus

Second solo

| 8 bars | 8 bars | 8 bars | 8 bars |

32 bar chorus

Third solo

| 8 bars | etc. |

groups) used the fugue and similar forms just to play good, swinging, subtle jazz and gave no thought to third-stream music. It should also be noted that the quartet played classical forms quite precisely. For example, the fugues it played were truly baroque in form except that the exposition parts were improvised. Critics who feel that the cool era lacked excitement should note that these players were seeking a more subtle means of jazz expression. The Modern Jazz Quartet, although subtle,

had the strength and vitality necessary for longevity; it lasted from 1951 to 1974 and then reassembled in 1981.

The public seemed quite divided in its attitude toward cool players. Some people felt that the musicians were bored and arrogant or disdainful and cold. Others considered the cool players to be creative, hard-working, serious musicians, not clowns trying to be impressive. They understood that the players were in fact saying, "Like my music for itself."

Modern Jazz Quartet. Piano and director: John Lewis; drums: Connie Kay; bass: Percy Heath; vibraphone: Milt Jackson.

Courtesy of Ray Avery

Cool Bands

Cool developed gradually, as did previous styles. For example, saxophonist Benny Carter underplayed his attacks. Teddy Wilson played the piano with a delicate touch, and Benny Goodman stopped using the thick vibrato of Jimmy Noone and other clarinetists. Miles Davis's solo on Charlie Parker's "Chasin' the Bird" in 1947 and John Lewis's piano solo on Dizzy Gillespie's record of "Round Midnight" in 1948 also anticipated the cool era. However, it took Lester Young to prove that great swing could be generated without using any of the aggressive performance practices typical of earlier jazz styles.

Musicians have always been in agreement in their admiration of Benny Carter—his playing, his writing, and his exemplary personality. It has been a mystery why Carter never attained the public recognition due him. He is an excellent player on the saxophone/clarinet and on the trumpet, he arranges music artistically, and he is a fine composer.

Near the end of the 1940s, two large bands that seemed to have entirely different feelings and directions were quite influential in the beginnings of cool: Claude Thornhill's band from about 1946 to 1949 and Woody Herman's band from 1947 to 1949. Both were instrumental in directing the trend away from the hot feel toward the cool feel.

Woody Herman was the type of bandleader who always seemed to make changes in his personnel to keep the band up-to-date. He formed a band in Los Angeles in 1947 after he had disbanded for three months. This band had a saxophone section that influenced the workings of sax sections that followed. He hired Sam Marowitz on alto; Stan Getz, Zoot Sims, and Herbie Steward on tenors; and Serge Chaloff on baritone. From this group (not using alto sax) came the famous "Four Brothers" sound. This was a tightly knit, beautifully blended section of four excellent jazz players who again disproved the theory that good improvisers are too individualistic to coordinate well. (The tune "Four Brothers," incidentally, was written by another talented reed player, Jimmy Giuffre.) Another boost for the cool advocate was the recording by the Herman band of Ralph Burns's "Early Autumn," a record that alone was enough to launch the career of Stan Getz.[19]

The Claude Thornhill band, in addition to a tuba and a French horn player, had such talented musicians as Lee Konitz on alto sax, Gerry Mulligan on baritone sax and as arranger, and Gil Evans also as arranger[20] (NW, 248. Claude Thornhill, "Donna Lee," side 1, band 6). The nucleus of this band made the first Miles Davis-Gil Evans records. One of the several recording bans was lifted in December 1948, and the way was open for the three recording sessions in 1949 and 1950 for an album that was eventually called *The Birth of the Cool*[21] (S, "Boplicity," side F, band 8). An excerpt of a question-and-answer session with Gerry Mulligan throws a little light on these events:

Question: Was this an attempt to get away from the conventional bop format?

Mulligan: No, the idea was just to try to get a good little rehearsal band together. Something to write for.

Question: Was the fact that so many men on the Miles Davis dates came from the Thornhill band coincidental?

Mulligan: No, the Thornhill orchestra was a tremendous influence on that small band. Because the instrumentation, when you get down to it, was a reduced version of what Claude was using at the time.

Question: Then it was more or less regarded as a workshop experiment?

Mulligan: Yes. As far as the "Cool Jazz" part of it, all of that comes after the fact of what it was designed to be.[22]*

The Performers

The leading exponents of cool jazz were Lester Young, Miles Davis (from about 1949 on), and Stan Getz, one of the few tenor saxophone players who compares well with Young in this style.

As for his part in these recordings, Miles Davis believed that at the time he was interested in nothing more original than playing with a lighter sound; it was more expressive, he thought. At any rate, the recordings of this nine-man orchestra did set the tone for the cool era. Mulligan wrote "Jeru," "Venus de Milo," "Rocker," and "Godchild"; Gil Evans contributed "Boplicity" and "Moon Dreams"; John Lewis wrote "Move," "Budo," and "Rouge"; and John Carisi wrote "Israel."

The George Shearing Quintet also influenced the beginning of cool. Shearing, a classically trained pianist originally from England, can play in any style of jazz or classical music that he cares to. One of his favorite approaches is to play bop-type thoughts in a very subtle manner, thus making a good transition from one era to the next.[23]

Lester Young

"And in terms of a revolutionizing and lasting effect on several generations of jazz players, it is an incontrovertible fact that Lester Young was *the* most influential artist after Armstrong and before Parker."[24] Lester Young not only started a new style of playing tenor sax but was also the epitome of an entirely new concept of jazz—hence his nickname Prez, president of the cool era of jazz.[25]

*From Leonard Feather, "Cool," in *Jazz*, 1959. Reprinted by permission of Leonard Feather.

Lester Young

Lester Young was born in Mississippi and matured during the 1930s in Kansas City, where the jam sessions prepared him for all competition. Young first attracted attention when he was with the Count Basie band,[26] but there was much opposition to his playing at first. The big bands were very much oriented to the full-bodied Coleman Hawkins approach to tenor sax. Young seemed light and airy, even out of place, in the big Basie band with his slightly behind the beat swing and unique tone. However, the younger players were more than impressed.

Lester Young, the model for cool tenor saxophonists, played softer than Coleman Hawkins and was more subtle and abstract. This "led directly to a harmonic freeing-up of the language of jazz without which Bop, Modern Jazz, George Russell's Lydian Concept and eventually musicians like Ornette Coleman, John Coltrane, and Eric Dolphy could not have evolved."[27] Young was influenced the most by Rudy Wiedoeft (a nonjazz concert artist), Frankie Trumbauer, and Jimmy Dorsey. Oddly enough, all were white alto saxophone or C melody saxophone players instead of black tenor saxophone players. Young's playing naturally matched his personality—soft spoken and understated.

Young joined the Basie band for the second time in 1936 and stayed with him through 1940, during which time he recorded 105 sides (songs) with Basie and many others with other, small groups. His first job as a leader was in 1941 on Fifty-second Street in New York. However, he did return to the Basie band for a few months in 1943 and 1944 and in the latter year was drafted into the army. Young was associated with Norman Granz's *Jazz at the Philharmonic* from 1946 until his death on March 15, 1959. Young had a beautiful, light, pure sound, but his greatest asset was his phrasing—his linear playing anticipating cool in still another way. He would carry melodic thoughts to their conclusion regardless of the bar lines. Although he recorded many solos with the Basie band that are available in repressings, those most cherished by his army of admirers are the small combo records, including those backing Billie Holiday vocals.[28]

Gil Evans

The transplanted Canadian Gil Evans deserves great credit for the successes of some of the more popular Miles Davis albums. This is not to denigrate Davis at all, but it shifts some of the accolades to the talented, creative, and yet subtle manner in which Evans utilized the large orchestra to highlight Davis's talent.

Because Young's career as a player centers chronologically in the swing era, it may seem somewhat out of place to consider him in our discussion of the cool era. He is perhaps best known playing for the Basie band, but even in that high-energy band he was known for a personal sound that ultimately predicted the later cool sound. This sound was often at its best when he worked with Billie Holiday in smaller, more intimate settings.

Listening Guide

Demonstration 22
(cassette 1, side B, track 6; CD 1, track 22)

Lester Young and Count Basie
"Lester Leaps In"

:00 Four-measure piano introduction.
:04 Eight measures, then repeated: Tenor sax, trombone, and trumpet in cup mute in 3-part harmony.
:19 Bass and piano: 8-measure bridge.
:27 First theme repeated.
:35 Second chorus: Lester Young solos on tenor sax for 32 measures.
1:06 Third chorus: Piano and sax interplay for 8 measures.
1:15 Sax solos alone for 8 measures.
1:22 Eight-measure bridge: Sax solo.
1:30 Sax alone for 6 measures, rhythm comes in on next 2.
1:38 On fourth chorus, piano and sax trade fours, first the piano for 4 measures.
1:42 Sax for 4 measures.
1:46 Piano for 4 measures.
1:50 Sax for 4 measures.
1:53 Piano for 4 measures.
1:58 Sax for 4 measures.
2:01 Piano for 4 measures.
2:05 Sax for 4 measures.
2:09 Fifth chorus is still different—ensemble for 4 measures.
2:13 Sax for 4 measures.
2:18 Ensemble for 4 measures.
2:21 Piano for 4 measures.
2:23 Piano for the 8-measure bridge.
2:33 Ensemble for 4 measures.
2:37 Sax for 4 measures.
2:42 Sixth chorus starts with ensemble for 4 measures.
2:47 Bass solo for 4 measures.
2:49 Ensemble for 4 measures.
2:52 Bass for 4 measures.
2:58 Bass and piano for 8 measures.
3:04 Ensemble for 4 measures.
3:08 Ensemble plays the last 4 measures out in jam-session style.

Gerry Mulligan.
Courtesy of Ray Avery

Listening Guide

Demonstration 23
(cassette 1, side B, track 7; CD 1, track 23)

Miles Davis with the Gil Evans Orchestra
"Summertime" from Porgy and Bess

0:00 Begins with Davis playing the melody with a very light "cool" backup in the orchestra. Listen for the orchestral colors pulled from the unusual instrumentation, which includes French horns, tuba, and flutes as well as saxes, trumpets, and trombones.

0:35 First solo chorus taken by Davis. Motivic response continues in the orchestra.

1:10 Second chorus by Davis. Orchestral colors expand somewhat as the gentle peak of the arrangement is reached.

1:46 Third chorus by Davis.

2:22 Davis returns to the melody for the final chorus.

3:03 Slows down.

3:16 End.

Listening Guide

Miles Davis
"Boplicity"

:00 First chorus (no introduction): Trumpet lead (Miles Davis), bass and drums play a relaxed $\frac{4}{4}$ rhythm throughout; piano plays gentle chordal punctuations.

:27 Bridge: Change of melody and chords.

:42 Last part of first chorus.

:56 Second chorus: Baritone sax solo (Gerry Mulligan), rhythm section continues as before.

1:24 Bridge: Sax unison with French horn, trombone, and tuba.

1:35 Trumpet solo.

1:42 Last part of second chorus: Slight variation on the original 8 measures of the tune, ensemble.

1:58 Third chorus: Trumpet solo, sustained harmonic background.

2:25 Bridge: Piano solo (John Lewis) sustained harmonic background for half of solo (saxes, trombone, French horn, tuba).

2:40 Ensemble with the original melody.

2:57 End.

*Smithsonian Collection, side F, band 8.

Evans's penchant for buoyant, weightless, yet impressive sounds was honed earlier in the Claude Thornhill Orchestra. The albums *Miles Ahead*, *Porgy and Bess*, and *Sketches of Spain* were enough to leave the jazz public wishing the collaboration would go on forever.

Miles Davis

Miles Davis first came to New York in 1945 to study at Juilliard. He has said that when he began playing he tried to imitate anyone he could but that Clark Terry was his main influence. It seems that no matter what Davis plays on his horn, it has a rather sad feeling to it. There is no doubt that he plays with the sound he desires and that he simply would not trust his personal thoughts to any other type of sound. He seems to have a highly developed sense of communicative simplicity. At first, Davis could not play high, loud, or very fast. When he arrived on the New York scene, he was young enough to be in the process of developing strength in his lip muscles, but he felt that he could think better if he were playing with a light sound; he was more relaxed with that approach. The critics of his bop playing with Parker in 1945 should remember that eighteen-year-old Davis was only in his formative years.

Davis was not destined to be known only for his contribution to the development of cool jazz. As we will see, he will continue to be an innovative force in the evolution of jazz. It is true that the only real constant in his career is his unpredictability. Davis was a musician who was always searching for a new, fresh, exciting way to play his music. He did not feel obligated to older fans; after all, they can buy his previous albums and thereby preserve the style that they prefer. Fans of the cool era feel that the collaboration of the talents of Davis and Gil Evans is one of the highlights of music history. For interesting contrasts, compare the feelings on such Davis albums as *Sketches of Spain*, done with Gil Evans, and *Bitches' Brew*, done with an electrified rhythm section as well as with an **amplification** of Davis's trumpet[29] (S, "Summertime," side G, band 7).

West Coast Jazz

During the late 1940s, a cool style was also developing on the West Coast. Although the Miles Davis–Gil Evans collaboration in 1949 was an East Coast expression and is thought to have had a germinal influence on the development of cool, the style moved west and was brought to fruition in the writing and performing skills of players such as saxophonist Jimmy Giuffre and trumpeter Shorty Rogers. These two, joined by drummer Shelly Manne, were all former members of the Stan Kenton

band and proved to be leading influences in the development of the West Coast cool movement.

Just as Minton's was a center of activity for the bop community in New York, so was the Lighthouse at Hermosa Beach for the developing West Coast jazz style. Howard Rumsey, a former bass player for Stan Kenton, organized Sunday concerts in this club in 1948. By 1950, the Lighthouse had become a part of the West Coast jazz definition.

It is difficult to draw any clear distinction between the East and West Coast cool styles. They reflect both an interest in an introverted tone and a commitment to unique instrumentations for which specialized arrangements were made. Unlike big bands, which have sections of like instruments, the cool groups tended to group unlike instruments in search of a new ensemble sound.

The fact that the cool style moved from New York to the West Coast set the two geographical locations in a competition for the attention of the jazz community. The distinction between the two schools was one more of publicity than of style. The players themselves were not restricted to just one style—cool or hot. For example, Stan Getz, who was a leader of cool jazz on the East Coast, was capable of a very spirited bop style.[30] The separation of styles and their geographical locations were not as sharply drawn as the marketing promotion of the day may have suggested. Both cool and bop players could be found on both coasts. However, the West Coast did, undeniably, offer cool players a rich center for their exchange of ideas.

The East Coast did eventually recapture the jazz mainstream as the hard bop style emerged in response to the more intellectual cool style popular on the West Coast. The debate between the two styles was further fueled by the fact that most of the West Coast musicians were white, whereas most of the East Coast hard bop players were black. The white players mostly came out of the swing band tradition, whereas the black players usually were associated with the bop style. The development of hard bop is viewed as both a return to the hotter spirit of jazz and a reclamation of the jazz tradition by the black community.

The writers of cool on the West Coast often worked in the tradition of Duke Ellington by writing arrangements with specific players and specific sounds in mind.[31] The compositions were further customized by the unique grouping of instruments in each ensemble.[32] Both Shorty Rogers and Jimmy Giuffre composed during their tenure with the Kenton band, and they carried these compositional skills into their cool ensembles. Joining these two was Gerry Mulligan, who had been a part of the original "Birth of the Cool" recordings in New York. His quartet without a piano is perhaps one of the more famous ensembles illustrating the cool

Miles Davis.
Courtesy of Les McCann

arranger's interest in finding new approaches. His work in this quartet, with Chet Baker on trumpet, offers some of the best examples of balance between compositional and individual expressions typical of West Coast jazz.[33]

The musicians on the West Coast often made their living by also working in Hollywood studio orchestras. The use of carefully arranged music was also characteristic of their work in the studio and may have influenced their approach to their jazz. Just as many of the East Coast cool players shared a tie to the Claude Thornhill band, many of the players on the West Coast shared one to Kenton's early band; in addition to Manne, Guiffre, and Rogers were other active players such as Art Pepper, Bud Shank, and Bill Holman. Gerry Mulligan bridges the two coasts by bringing his background with the Thornhill band and his work with Miles Davis and Gil Evans to the West Coast. To a certain extent, Dave Brubeck's role on the West Coast, paralleled Lennie Tristano's work on the East Coast. Both brought more esoteric compositional concerns to their work, and each centered small but dedicated groups of players and listeners.

In many cases, the ensemble writing used in the West Coast style showed influences of Western Europe, if not in actual musical content at least in the compositional approach. Brubeck's music reflected his study with the modern classical composer Darius Milhaud. Some of Guiffre's later pieces even approached a type of experimental style not unlike the atonal work of classical composers. This move toward a type of jazz classicism stood in sharp contrast to the developing "regression" to hard bop on the East Coast. (For a more thorough discussion of hard bop regression, see chapter 10.)

Summary

Cool is a style of jazz that even the general public can agree is beautiful music. Very few players contributed more to this beauty than tenor saxophonist Stan Getz. Getz was very heavily influenced by Lester Young, but as time went on he was able to establish an identity of his own that is quite distinctive. His bossa nova excursions brought together a very moving Brazilian rhythm with pure tone and melodic charm, a combination that was readily accepted throughout the world.[34]

As cool jazz drifted farther from bop and all other preceding styles, it reached the apex of subtlety when Jimmy Giuffre, playing low-register clarinet instead of tenor sax, decided to do away entirely with the steady pulse of jazz. Giuffre claimed that the beat of the music could be implicit instead of explicit. But when the listener experiences Giuffre's trio (clarinet, bass, and guitar) playing "Happy Man," the pulse can be felt quite readily even though no instrument is relegated to the pulse alone.[35]

In considering cool jazz in retrospect, one realizes the major problem in performing this style: no matter how cool the jazz becomes, it must always have warmth, a problem the best musicians solved beautifully.

For Further Study

1. What are some words that might be used to describe the feeling and tone of the cool era?

2. How does the cool type of tonal attack and vibrato influence the descriptive terms listed in question 1?

3. What instruments became important in this era that were not prominent previously?

4. What instrument used in early dixieland music became more prominent and was used melodically in this era?

5. What new meters were used in place of $\frac{2}{4}$ and $\frac{4}{4}$?

6. Define the terms polyrhythm and polymeter.

7. Who were the leading exponents of cool jazz?

8. Two selections that are good examples of this jazz era are "Jeru" and "Moon Dreams" from the Miles Davis album *Birth of the Cool* (Capitol Records, DT1974). Compare and contrast these selections by answering the following:

   a. Are the instruments played mostly in the middle range, or do you hear extremely high and low pitches?

   b. Do the instrumentalists use vibrato in solo spots?

   c. Compare the percussion rhythm with that of the bop era. How do you react to the rhythmic pulse of "Moon Dreams"?

9. An example of the use of alternating meters is "Three to Get Ready" in the album *Time Out* by the Dave Brubeck Quartet (Columbia, CL-1397). After the short waltzlike melody, the meter alternates between $\frac{3}{4}$ and $\frac{4}{4}$. Listen carefully and clap lightly two measures of three (heavy-light-light, heavy-light-light) followed by two measures of four (heavy-light-light-light, heavy-light-light-light) and continue to alternate.

10. Listen to "The Morning After" and "I Want to Be Happy" from the album *Chico Hamilton Quintet* (Pacific Jazz Enterprises, PJ-1209) and identify by sound two instruments used in jazz for the first time.

Suggested Additional Listening

Baker, Chet. *Cool Burnin'.* Prestige Records, PR 7496.

Davis, Miles. *Basic Miles.* Columbia Records, C 32025.

———. *Greatest Hits.* Columbia Records, CS-9809.

———. *Greatest Hits.* Prestige Records, S-7457.

———. *Miles Ahead.* Columbia Records, CL 1041.

———. *Miles Davis.* Prestige Records, 24001.

———. *Miles Davis at Filmore.* Columbia Records, G 30038.

———. *Walkin'.* Prestige Records, 7608.

Desmond, Paul, and Mulligan, Gerry. *Two of a Mind.* RCA Victor Records, LSP-2624.

Evans, Gil. *Out of the Cool.* Impulse Records, A-4.

Getz, Stan. *Best of Stan Getz.* Verve Records, V6-8719.

———. *Stan Getz Years.* Roost Records, RK-103.

———. *Greatest Names in Jazz.* Verve Records, PR 2-3.

Modern Jazz Quartet. *European Concert.* Atlantic Records, 2-603.

———. *European Tour.* Atlantic Records, SD 20603.

———. *The Last Concert.* Atlantic Records, 909.

Mulligan, Gerry. *What Is There to Say?* Columbia Records, 16 0258.

———. *Modern Jazz Quartet.* Prestige Records, 24005.

Mulligan, Gerry, and Baker, Chet. *Timeless.* Pacific Jazz Records, PJ-75.

Nica's Dream. New World Records, 242.

Young, Lester. *The Aladdin Sessions.* Blue Note Records, BN-LA456-H2.

———. *Complete Lester Young on Savoy.* Arista Records, SJL-2022.

———. *Young Lester Young.* Columbia Records, J 24.

Additional Reading Resources

Berendt, Joachim. *The New Jazz Book.* 19–24.

Cole, Bill. *Miles Davis.*

Francis, André. *Jazz.* 130–49.

Hodeir, André. *Jazz: Its Evolution and Essence.* 116–38.

Porter, Lewis. *Lester Young.*

Shapiro, Nat, and Hentoff, Nat, eds. *The Jazz Makers.* 243–75.

Stearns, Marshall. *The Story of Jazz.* 167–72.

Williams, Martin T. *The Jazz Tradition.* 219, 233.

Note: Complete information, including name of publisher and date of publication, is provided in this book's bibliography.

Notes

1. Dom Cerulli, Burt Korall, and Mort Nasatir, *The Jazz World* (New York: Ballantine Books, 1960), 206.

2. Barry Ulanov, *Handbook of Jazz* (New York: Viking Press, 1959), 158.

3. Chico Hamilton, *The Best of Chico Hamilton,* Impulse Records, A-9174; *Easy Livin',* Sunset Records, SUS-5215.

4. *Chico Hamilton Quintet,* Pacific Jazz Records, PJ-1209.

5. Eddie Lang and Joe Venuti, "Farewell Blues," *Encyclopedia of Jazz on Records;* Joe Venuti, *The Daddy of the Violin,* BASF Records, BASF-MPS 2120885-0; *Stringing the Blues,* Columbia Records, C2L-24.

6. Stephane Grappelly, Django, Barclay Records, 820105; Django Reinhardt Record, *Djangology,* RCA Victor Records, LPM-2319; *Violin Summit!* 1966 BASF Records, 20 626.

7. Edgar Redmond and the Modern String Ensemble, Disque Phenomenon Records, DP 2696.

8. Marshall Stearns, *The Story of Jazz* (London: Oxford University Press, 1958), 170.

9. André Hodeir, *Jazz: Its Evolution and Essence* (New York: Grove Press, 1956), 118.

10. Woody Herman, "Summer Sequence," *The Thundering Herds,* Columbia Records, C3L-25; "Early Autumn," *History of Jazz,* vol. 4; *Big Band Jazz,* Smithsonian Collection of Recordings.

11. Paul Horn, *Profile of a Jazz Musician,* Columbia Records, CL 1922.

12. Herbie Mann, *Latin Mann,* Columbia Records, CL 2388; *Today,* Atlantic Records, SD 1454; *Stone Flute,* Embryo Records, SD 18035.

13. Johnny Graas, "Mulliganesque," *Encyclopedia of Jazz on Records,* vol. 4.

14. Yusef Lateef, *Eastern Sounds*, Prestige Records, PR 7319.
15. Art Farmer, *Art*, Argo Records, 678.
16. Clark Terry, *Bobby Brookmeyer Quintet*, Mainstream Records, 320.
17. Dave Brubeck, *Time Out*, Columbia Records, CL-1397.
18. Modern Jazz Quartet, "A Fugue for Music Inn," *The Modern Jazz Quartet at Music Inn*, Atlantic Records, 1247.
19. Woody Herman, *The Thundering Herds*; "Early Autumn," *Singers and Soloists of the Swing Bands*, Smithsonian Collection of Recordings.
20. Claude Thornhill, "Snowfall," *The Great Band Era*; Claude Thornhill Orchestra, "Donna Lee," *Jazz in Revolution—the Big Bands in the 1940s*, New World Records, 284; *The Memorable Claude Thornhill*, Columbia Records, KG-32906; *Big Band Jazz*, Smithsonian Collection of Recordings.
21. Miles Davis, *The Birth of the Cool*, Capitol Records, DT 1974.
22. Leonard Feather, "Cool," in *Jazz* (Los Angeles: Pacific Press, 1959), 26.
23. George Shearing, *Best of George Shearing*, Capitol Records, ST 2104; *Touch of Genius*, MGM Records, E 90.

24. Gunther Schuller, *The Swing Era* (London: Oxford University Press, 1989), 547.
25. Lester Young, *Prez*, Mainstream Records, 56012.
26. *Lester Young Memorial*, Epic Records, SN 6031.
27. Schuller, *The Swing Era*, 233.
28. *The Essential Lester Young*, Verve Records, V-8398; *Giant of Jazz*, Sunset Records, SUM-1181.
29. Miles Davis, *Sketches of Spain*, Columbia Records, CL-1480; *Bitches' Brew*, Columbia Records, GP 26.
30. *Stan Getz Plays*, Clef Records, MGC-137.
31. Jimmy Giuffre, *Four Brothers*, Capitol, LP KPL102.
32. *Shorty Rogers Giants*, Capitol, LP LC6549.
33. *Gerry Mulligan Quartet*, vol. 1, Pacific Jazz, Vogue, LP LDE029.
34. Stan Getz, *Jazz Samba*, Verve Records, V-8432; *Jazz Samba Encore*, Verve Records, 68523.
35. Jimmy Giuffre, "Happy Man," *Seven Pieces*, Verve Records, MG V-8307.

Hard Bop, Funky/Straight-Ahead Jazz (circa 1954–   )

"The funky idiom represented an attempt by the

jazzman to rediscover his emotional roots."[1]

Listening Guide

Demonstration 24
(cassette 1, side B, track 8; CD 1, track 24)

Funky

:00 Introduction: Piano solo and bass solo alternate measures.

:06 Ensemble chorus: Flügelhorn lead and alto sax harmony; piano, bass, guitar, and drums play $\frac{2}{4}$ rhythm.

:28 Flügelhorn solo (one chorus): Listen for drums accenting second and fourth beats.

:51 Ensemble chorus: Same as first chorus.

1:16 End.

This style was first called funky hard bop regression, but as the style changed considerably the title was shortened to funky. The word *funky* refers to the rollicking, rhythmic feeling of the style. The term *hard* means a performance that is more driving and less relaxed than cool jazz. The phrase *bop regression* implies a return to the elements of the bop style.

It may well be true that musical styles swing back and forth like a pendulum, but the swinging of that pendulum is not smooth. The swing has been toward more complexity, and it occurs fairly gradually. For example, the players of the swing era added more musicians, the bop players played with extended harmonies and complicated melodies, and the cool players brought in new instruments, time signatures, and extended forms. But the funky style that followed seemed to revert quite suddenly to the most basic of music elements, for example, the "amen chords" from religious services. (For an introduction to the funky style, listen to demonstration 24.)

The term *funky* was often used interchangeably with *soul* during this period. Both the funky and the soul styles are also associated with the music prevalent in the black churches. The term *soul* certainly has a connection to the church and perhaps speaks of the intended emotional content of the music. On the other hand, *funky* has a more earthy association. "Emotional" and "earthy" are both appropriate descriptions of this music.

Funky was a raw-boned type of playing that used highly rhythmical melodies and less complex harmonies than were used in the preceding era. The music had a happy sound and lacked tension and frustration. Performers of this music used bop elements that were generally simplified because of having passed through the cool era. Today, the simplification has gone even further.

Most of the bop sounds have been dropped in favor of elements that tend toward gospel jazz.

The new black awareness developing in the United States no doubt contributed to the development of the funky and gospel styles. During this time, blacks found that the black church, with its use of harmonies and blues inflections, provided a link to their roots.

Some authors even suggest that the funky style was an effort among blacks to recapture jazz as their own expression.[2] Even if this intent did exist, the funky idiom quickly spread throughout the jazz world and was soon played by everyone, from school bands to professional ensembles, regardless of race.

Perhaps even more than an ethnic reaction, the funky idiom can be seen as a reaction to the cool intellectualism that many found in music of the cool period. The lively and emotionally exuberant nature of the funky style stands in strong contrast to the measured and controlled expression of the cool players. Unlike the cool style, which looked to European compositional techniques, the funky style adopted the truly American, and oral, idioms found in gospel and blues.

The distinction between cool and hard bop was also geographical. The cool style was often called West Coast jazz because it seemed centered in California. Shelly Manne even suggested that a more relaxed lifestyle in California might have been a factor in the development of the relaxed cool jazz style in contrast to the more driving bop style he found typical of New York jazz.[3]

The Music

Funky music borrows elements from African American church music of the day. The loose style and the manner in which the melodies were harmonized were quite similar to the manner of performance at work in the church. The scale used in funky is reminiscent of the scale used in early blues but is now refined by its use in the church. The result is a gospel blues sound typified by a consistent use of blue notes.

Although these blue notes are not really the same as the original blue notes heard by church singers, their prevalent use in this style is meant to create the same effect. The original blue notes were slightly mistuned notes (very often the third and seventh of the scale) in a major key. This mistuning created a disagreement between the major key and the almost minor blue notes sung against it. In an effort to re-create the earlier blues sound, players in this period actually played many pieces in minor keys (for notational examples 26, 27A, 27B, see Appendix B).

Gospel Jazz

Gospel jazz is an extension of the funky style. If a distinction can be made between funky and gospel, it is in gospel's more triadic use of harmonies, very much like those associated with the improvisational singing of hymns. As the name implies, gospel jazz uses elements from, and has a definite feeling of, early gospel music.[4] A primary example of these elements is the constant use of the amen chord progression (I, IV, I) (**plagal cadence**). Amen chords were used extensively in Les McCann's "Fish This Week."[5] Although this style represents a return to prejazz music, gospel jazz has also been influenced by all preceding jazz styles, including their harmonies, forms, and advanced musical techniques.[6] Rhythm, as well as emotional intensity, is highlighted in gospel jazz.

Many selections of this form of jazz can be performed in a church as easily as in a nightclub. One is Les McCann's "A Little 3/4 for God and Company."[7] Big gospel bands sometimes perform in a handclapping, "shouting Baptist" manner as they enact a scene of baptism in a work such as "Wade in the Water."[8]

The first edition of this book spoke of gospel jazz as "soul jazz"; since then, the term has been used ad infinitum. If *soul* means *sincerity*, then certainly Armstrong's first recordings, or those of Jack Teagarden, must be included in this category, and no performer was more sincere than Mahalia Jackson. But the term began to have some racial and revolutionary connotations. Therefore, as the music reverted to church roots, the authors have seen the label for this kind of jazz gradually change to "gospel jazz."

The Performers

The funky style was introduced by pianists but was quickly adopted by all instrumentalists. It was brought to public notice by pianist Horace Silver and a group led by drummer Art Blakey called the Jazz Messengers.[9] Silver also made many records with his own combo[10] (demonstration 34). Most pianists who play funky music admit that Silver was its progenitor.

Horace Silver

Joachim Berendt mentions Horace Silver as the beginning:

The pianist-composer Horace Silver—and along with him a few others—has broken through with a manner of playing known as "funky": slow or medium blues, played hard on the beat, with all of the heavy feeling and expression characteristic of the old blues. Jazz musicians of all persuasions and on both coasts have thrown themselves into funk with notable enthusiasm.[11]

A good example of a big band playing in a funky manner is "Hey, Pete" on Dizzy Gillespie's album *Dizzy in Greece*.[12] This album contains part of the music that Gillespie performed on the first State Department—sponsored tour in jazz history. It is also excellent proof that the talented Quincy Jones could write good funky blues works for big bands. In addition, the album

Les McCann.
Courtesy of Ray Avery

demonstrates that the funky melodies were more rifflike and rhythmically and melodically more simple than bop.

Critic Don Don Heckman has some different insights into these changes as he writes about the jazz of the 1960s:

Perhaps the most significant was the music that was called, variously, funk, soul, etc. Its roots in modern jazz could be traced to Horace Silver's efforts to translate the Blues-

based forms, riffs, and rhythms of the Midwestern and Southwestern bands of the late '20s and early '30s into the idiom of the contemporary small group. Its roots in Negro society were less well defined but also important.

Silver's work, however, was soon modified, simplified, and repeated—over and over. And few of the imitators understood the delicate balance of elements that was crucial to the music's artistic success. As often happens,

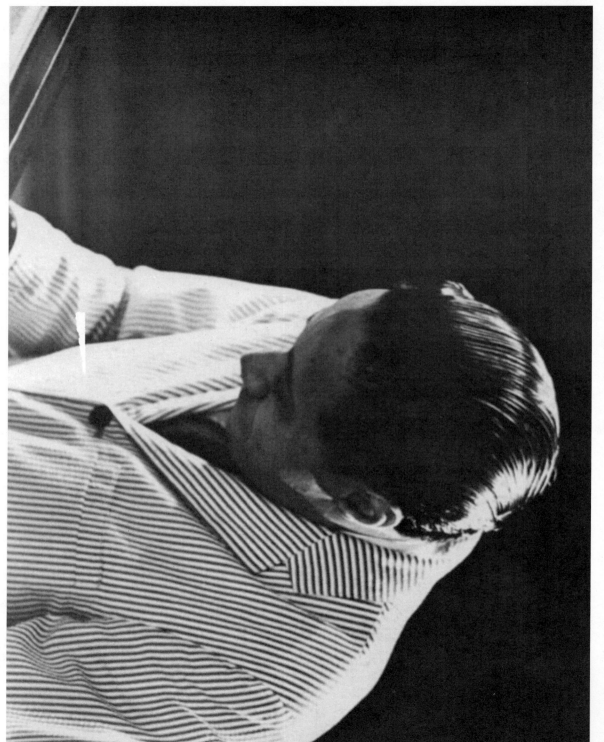

the values Silver was seeking to express were discarded by most of his imitators in favor of the superficialities—the simple rhythms, the reduction of blues changes to their most simple form, and the distortion of Gospel-derived techniques. The relationship between this music, which was considered by many to be a genuine expression of the Negro past, and the growing civil-rights movement was very close.[13]

The return to jazz roots indicated by the less complex harmonies, excessive use of blue notes, and simpler rhythmic feeling emphasized communication between players and listeners and led away from the compositional or technical complexities of cool or bop. It is interesting that on early Horace Silver recordings the bop concept is prominent and the afterbeat accent hardly discernible. In the funky style, the bop elements faded gradually as the accented afterbeat developed.

The Hammond organ had been only rarely used before 1951 (by Fats Waller and Count Basie) when Wild Bill Davis surprised everyone by performing real blues-oriented works on it. Later, Jimmy Smith proved the real potential of the instrument by using a larger variety of organ stops (effects) than any other player in the jazz field and by using incredible technique. The instrument was accepted wholeheartedly in the funky era. A parallel, if not the root of this style of organ playing, can be found in the black church service. This association with the church is not new to the historical development of jazz.

Certainly one of the best funky piano players was Carl Perkins, who died much too soon to leave a legacy,[14] Les McCann paid tribute to Perkins by naming a tune after him.[15] Another notable funky artist is Ramsey Lewis. André Previn adopted the funky style when he came on the jazz scene. When he first entered the jazz field,

Charles Mingus

Charles Mingus approached his composition and performance with an intensity seldom matched in jazz. His emotional style spanned the gap between composition and improvisation. To maintain the intensity and accuracy of his ideas, he would sometimes recite the compositions to the group rather than limit his ideas by writing them down. He would even stop performances to correct compositional ideas or to scold the audience for not listening. His constant experimentation seldom placed him in the mainstream of jazz's evolution, but he exerted a constant influence on that evolution.

of so-called serious music had lost touch entirely with their dwindling audience. "He [the contemporary 'serious' composer] finds it difficult to admit that he is simply not producing music that provokes a sympathetic response in his listeners. He forgets that it is the purpose of music to provoke such a response, and that all superior music in the past has provoked it."[16] The funky players agreed with Pleasants. Communication at the immediate level was truly important.

Charles Mingus

Charles Mingus is perhaps the most difficult player/composer of the bop and post-bop eras to categorize. His musical output covers a wide berth of idioms and styles, from his earliest work with Armstrong and Kid Ory to the later, almost free compositions such as "Pithecanthropus Erectus,"[17] and his efforts became centrally important during the hard bop days. His connection to that idiom may not at first be stylistically apparent. However, his compositional intent was to create a direct, immediate emotional statement. His legacy to this jazz tradition lies in the manner in which he tried to convey the emotion.

Mingus attempted to channel the creative energies of his players into a unified statement. Although he relied on the individual strengths of his players, he also expected them to work toward a common emotional statement during a performance. This approach differs from the traditional bop approach, which encourages players to seek very individual statements during their improvisations.

An example of Mingus's emotional intent can be heard in his recording of "Haitian Fight Song."[18] He has been quoted that it could also have been called "Afro-American Fight Song."[19] He goes on to say that to play it successfully, he must think about prejudice, hate, and persecution. In this regard, Mingus shows his tie to the funky movement and its relationship to the developing black-rights activities.

Demonstration 25
(cassette 1, side B, track 9; CD 1, track 25)

Horace Silver Quintet (with Art Blakey)

"*Stop Time*"*
Kenny Dorham, *trumpet*
Hank Mobley, *tenor saxophone*
Horace Silver, *piano*
Doug Watkins, *bass*
Art Blakey, *drums*

:00 Introductory theme with one repeat at a lower range.
:08 "Head" melody with trumpet and saxophone in unison.
:24 Trumpet solo.
1:11 Tenor saxophone solo.
1:58 Piano solo; listen to the left-hand–punctuated "comping" patterns as Silver solos with his right hand.
2:55 Just as his solo ends, listen for the blues ("funky") melodic references.
2:58 Trumpet solo, at which point the band begins to "trade fours"; each player with solo for 4 measures with 4-bar drum solos in between.
3:02 Four-bar drum solo.
3:06 Four-bar tenor solo.
3:10 Four-bar drum solo.
3:14 Four-bar trumpet solo.
3:18 Four-bar drum solo.
3:21 Four-bar tenor solo.
3:25 Extended drum solo.
3:44 "Head" melody returns with trumpet and saxophone in unison.
3:55 Introductory theme restated.
4:03 End.

*Bebop, New World Records, 271 (originally Blue Note, 45-1631).

Previn generated considerable controversy about the worth or at least the sincerity of his interpretation of that style. However, Previn continued to listen to good players and to associate himself with an excellent rhythm section (Shelly Manne, Red Mitchell, and others), and his playing improved rapidly to the point where it was no longer controversial. Today, Previn is capable of leading an entire tour as a jazz pianist, a classical pianist, or a classical conductor. He is, at this writing, the conductor of a symphony orchestra.

Just about the time that jazz musicians were deciding that they wanted to get back to communicating with the public (about 1953), Henry Pleasants, a reputable critic of symphonic music, opera, and so on, wrote a scathing book emphasizing that present-day composers

Charles Mingus.
Photo by Tony Lane, Courtesy of Fantasy Records

A more direct tie to the gospel idiom can be found in his 1959 recording of "Better Git It in Your Soul" from his album *Mingus Ah Um*.[20] In this recording, the reference to the gospel church is made clear.

Mingus's ties to both the swing and the bop traditions can be heard in his composition "Hora Decubitus"[21] (S, "Hora Decubitus," side 10, band 5). The 1963 recording of this piece shows the balance between individual statement and collective intent that Mingus was able to inspire in his players. The emotional level is high from the beginning to the end of the performance. Only an ensemble that is both loose and secure could successfully support the different solo styles of Booker Ervin (tenor saxophone) and Eric Dolphy (alto saxophone). Also listen to his quintet playing "Haitian Fight Song" for an example of his bass playing and his compositional approach[22] (S, side G, band 8).

Sonny Rollins

Tenor saxophonist Sonny Rollins exercised much influence during the late 1950s. He captured the attention of many of the day's players with his melodic style of improvisation in which he often improvised from a melodic line with apparent disregard for chord structure.[23] As previously stated, an improvising player in the swing era usually had only a few measures in which to express his ideas. Rollins, on the other hand, often improvises for twenty or thirty minutes to develop his musical thoughts, inventing a short phrase, elaborating on it, and expanding the idea in every conceivable direction as Mozart, Haydn, and Beethoven did. The concept is at least five hundred years old.

Rollins's playing shows cool and bop influences repeatedly. For two choruses of "Limehouse Blues" he shows great economy of notes, playing only what he

Listening Guide

Charles Mingus
*"Haitian Fight Song"**

:00 Bass solo: Listen for thematic material to be quoted later.
:50 Mingus sets up a rhythmic pattern that establishes "time".
1:05 Tamborine enters.
1:10 Drums enter with time.
1:18 Trombone enters softly in background with one of the two main motives.
1:32 Alto saxophone enters very softly in background and gets louder.
1:35 Listen for the sax and trombone as they exchange motives back and forth.
1:54 Mingus adds vocal line.
2:07 Trombone solo; first of 5 blues choruses.
2:25 Second chorus.
2:30 Saxophone softly in background.
2:44 Double time feel in both rhythm section and soloist; third chorus.
3:02 Marchlike beat in whole ensemble under the trombone solo; fourth chorus.
3:19 Drum fill.
3:22 Return to original tempo, still trombone solo; fifth chorus.
3:41 Piano solo begins; first of 5 blues choruses.
3:55 Piano solo uses motive from opening section.
4:00 Second chorus.
4:20 March feel returns; third chorus.
4:40 Return to original tempo, still piano solo; fourth chorus.
5:00 Fifth chorus.
5:19 Saxophone solo begins; first of 5 blues choruses.
5:39 Second chorus.
5:58 Double time chorus as in trombone solo; third chorus.
6:16 March feel under sax solo; fourth chorus.
6:33 Drum fill.
6:36 Return to original tempo, still saxophone solo; fifth chorus.
6:55 Bass solo with light piano "comping" underneath and straight time in drums; first of 9 blues choruses.
7:14 Second chorus.
7:34 Third chorus.
7:53 Fourth chorus.
7:58 Gospel chords in piano.
8:13 Fifth chorus: Listen for motive in bass solo.
8:27 Drums drop out.
8:32 Sixth chorus.
8:50 Seventh chorus.
9:08 Eighth chorus, freer style and time.
9:30 Ninth chorus.
9:33 Mingus hints at time with response from drums.
9:52 Mingus again begins rhythmic time pattern used at the beginning.
10:50 Horns again exchange motives back and forth.
11:03 Mingus vocalizes.
11:25 Ensemble slows down.
11:40 Mingus uses bow on bass.
11:55 End.

*Smithsonian Collection, side G, band 8.

Sonny Rollins

An interesting aspect of Sonny Rollins's career was that after he had become a top nightclub attraction he became dissatisfied with his performance. He retired for two years, from the summer of 1959 to the fall of 1961 (and again in 1969), to practice. (Stories are that much of this practicing took place on top of the Williamsburg Bridge in New York.) Such retirement action takes great courage and dedication. The consensus seems to be that Rollins's absence did bring his coordination to real excellence.

thinks the listener needs to hear. Then the bop influences become apparent, and an occasional funky phrase is added.[24] On his recording of "St. Thomas," his solo flows extremely well as he establishes a short melodic melody. Rollins is more concerned with fragments of a thought and elaborates on it, changing it in every way he can.[25] By little phrases he continually brings the listener back to thoughts that he has played earlier. Listen to "Doxy" to hear this approach.[26]

The key in Rollins's advancement is thematic improvisation rather than either improvisation on a chord progression or variations on an established piece than with the whole melody itself, and he uses these fragments for his own personal expression. Many musicians use this approach, but Rollins seems to have brought it to a recognizable, viable level.

This thematic or motivic approach can be heard in the way Rollins works the theme of "St. Thomas." His recording of "Blue 7" is a clear example of how he, sometimes humorously, dissects a melodic line[28] (demonstration 27). It is sometimes noted that this approach stems from the piano playing of Thelonious Monk, at least as far as Rollins is concerned. Therefore, another example of the thematic approach is Monk's development of a little three-note motif in "Bags' Groove"[29] (demonstration 20). Most musicians who had observed Monk's approach considered it valid but pianistic. After Rollins demonstrated that playing such a motif was feasible and logical on a saxophone (which can be played only one note at a time), an entire school of wind players followed his lead.

Art Blakey

Art Blakey's group, first established in 1955, can boast some of the most prominent players in this genre: Horace Silver, Freddie Hubbard, Wayne Shorter, Lee Morgan, Hank Mobley, Kenny Dorham, and both Marsalis brothers, Branford and Wynton.

Blakey described his efforts to pass on the jazz tradition by saying: "I look for the new guys, and I just give them a place to hone their art and they grow. They do it themselves. I just give them a chance. All they need is a little guidance, a little direction, and they're gone. When they get big enough, I let them go and get their own thing. Then I find some more."[30] Blakey died in 1990.

Neoclassical Jazz/Straight-Ahead Jazz

The hard bop school often explained its development as a return to the basics of jazz. It saw the new instrumentation and compositional devices used by cool musicians as gimmicks rather than valid developments of the jazz tradition. Their call was therefore back to a "straight-

---

Listening Guide

Demonstration 26 (cassette 1, side B, track 10; CD 1, track 26)

Charles Mingus
*"Eclipse"**

:00 Cello solo; loose arrhythmic support and atonal horn statements.

:30 Vocal enters; more metric feel; cello plays a countermelody to the vocal; more traditional chordal support but still extended harmonies.

1:32 Instrumental interlude; faster tempo with loose-sounding counterpoint.

1:47 Bass and cello play counterpoint lines that build as other instruments enter; atonal feeling results from the counterpoint.

2:30 Vocal enters with cello obligato; more traditional harmonic support.

2:55 End.

*New World Collection, 216, side 1, band 5.

Listening Guide

Demonstration 27 (cassette 1, side B, track 11; CD 1, track 27)

Sonny Rollins
"Blue 7"

:00 Bass (Doug Watkins) plays a walking solo.

:15 Drums (Max Roach) enter lightly, with mainly second and fourth beats on the foot cymbals.

:43 Tenor sax (Sonny Rollins) enters, establishing the theme.

1:06 Piano (Tommy Flanagan) enters, solving any key problem listeners may have had because of Rollins's angular solo lines.

2:57 Piano solo; the I, IV, and V chords can be detected quite easily.

3:57 Tenor sax returns; very short interlude, just a clue to designate that the piano solo is over and that the drum solo should start.

4:07 Drum solo; lightly and steadily on the foot cymbals (on beats 2 and 4) while playing intricate syncopated work on the snare drum, bass drum, and tom-toms.

6:23 Drummer splashes a definite clue that he has finished his solo.

6:23 Tenor sax solos again.

7:05 Tenor sax softens to accentuate the walking bass as in the beginning.

8:09 Piano and drums soften to feature the bass (demonstration tape fades out here).

8:30 Piano drops out, leaving just the walking bass and afterbeats on the foot cymbals.

9:19 Tenor sax solo reenters; 4 bars, starting a series of trading fours with the drums.

9:26 Four-bar drum solo.

9:33 Four-bar tenor sax solo.

9:40 Four-bar drum solo.

9:47 Four-bar tenor sax solo.

9:55 Four-bar drum solo.

10:02 Four-bar tenor sax solo.

10:44 Tenor sax softens and plays sustained notes.

11:11 End.

ahead" jazz that was more improvisational and emotionally based. In essence, they were charting a traditional line of development for jazz that did not veer from the "mainstream," another expression often applied to this return-to-basics movement. This was more than a mere revival of an older tradition; it was also a recognition by jazz musicians that they had a guiding jazz tradition that was worth preserving.

The Young Lions

As jazz in the 1990s has looked back to the masters and heroes of the bop period, a new generation of players has emerged on the scene. These new players have faced a different set of expectations than the original bop players did. Rather than lead jazz in a new direction, away from the cool sound of jazz, these new players are supporting a revival of an earlier jazz era. This revival, however, looks back to a time defined by musicians still alive and working today. The new generation of lions therefore finds it necessary to earn recognition within the pride of existing mature lions who still have a strong hold on the reins of straight-ahead jazz. This is demonstrated by the fact that a *Down Beat* poll in 1995 still listed established players such as Sonny Rollins ahead of young lions such as Joe Lovano and Joshua Redman.

The young lions differ somewhat from the original straight-ahead players in that they are generally products of formal training at schools such as Berklee. Consequently, their knowledge of jazz, both theoretical and historical, factors into their work and gives them a perspective not shared by the original players of bop. However, a complaint of neoclassical musicians is that in their reverence for a past jazz style they have been robbed of their individual voices, the very attribute that defined the earlier jazz figures being emulated.

As the historical arch from bop to hard bop stretches over the cool period, a similar arch from hard bop spans later stylistic periods, such as free and fusion, to land again in the work of players like trumpeter Wynton Marsalis, who has become one of the dominant voices of neoclassicism. The list of other young lions is long and growing.

Wynton Marsalis

Wynton Marsalis is perhaps the fullest embodiment of mainstream jazz and is often associated with the development of a neoclassical period in jazz. The term *neoclassical* refers to "new" expressions of classical jazz styles. Hard bop was essentially a neoclassical movement that reflected earlier gospel influences in jazz, whereas this later neoclassical style looks to New Orleans for its inspiration. Wynton Marsalis not only speaks respectfully (and often quite strongly) about the legacy of past jazz styles; he is himself a respected performer of the straight-ahead style as it is traced from its origins in New Orleans.

The source of Wynton Marsalis's historical respect for jazz can be attributed to his father, Ellis, a respected player and teacher of traditional jazz. His other sons, saxophonist Branford and trombonist Delfeayo, are also outspoken heralds of traditional jazz.

Wynton Marsalis brings the hard bop period full circle. Like so many other strong players in this tradition, Marsalis worked in his youth under the tutelage of Art Blakey in the Jazz Messengers. The straight-ahead jazz legacy can be heard on *Art Blakey and the Jazz Messengers, "Album of the Year."*[31] The composition by

---

Listening Guide

Demonstration 28
(cassette 2, side A, track 1; CD 2, track 1)

Art Blakey and the Jazz Messengers

Art Blakey, drums
Wynton Marsalis, trumpet
Charles Fambrough, bass
Bobby Watson, alto saxophone
James Williams, piano
"E.T.A."

Each chorus of this piece is 32 measures long with 4 8-bar phrases, making an AABA structure that can be heard most clearly when the theme is played at the beginning and end of the performance.

:00 Drum solo sets up the head.
:26 (A) Band enters playing the head in harmony; (A) repeat of first 8 bars of the head.
:37 (B) Middle 8 bars or "bridge."
:42 (A) Return to first 8 bars.
:48 Alto sax solo; notice bop phrasing and driving walking bass.
:58 (B) section to the chorus.
1:04 (A) return to the A section.
1:10 Second chorus of alto sax solo.
1:32 Third chorus of solo.
1:54 Trumpet solo, also three choruses.
2:15 Second chorus.
2:37 Third chorus.
2:59 Tenor sax solo, only two choruses.
3:19 Second chorus.
3:41 Piano solo, again only two choruses.
4:25 All the horn players play a single chorus in unison, similar to the unison chorus used in the bop era.
4:47 Drum solo.
5:32 Head returns with the two A sections.
5:43 (B) bridge.
5:48 (A) return to last A.
5:54 Slows down with an ending phrase.
6:09 End.

pianist James Williams, "Soulful Mister Timmons," is particularly noteworthy because of its gospel and blues references.

Terence Blanchard et al.

Terence Blanchard represents the breadth of the young lions. Although an accomplished trumpet player, he has also crossed over into film writing, working on several films with Spike Lee. His academic knowledge of music places him in the legacy of other performer/composer/arrangers such as Herbie Hancock and Quincy Jones.

Blanchard's performance is firmly rooted on the practice of former legends such as Clifford Brown and the tutelage of mentors such as Art Blakey. Even his repertoire reflects his interest in the traditions laid down by earlier jazz figures such as Billie Holiday.[32]

Other young lions include saxophonists Joshua Redman and Joe Lovano, guitarist Kevin Eubanks, and trumpeter Roy Hargrove. These musicians have certainly claimed notice among critics of jazz as masterful technicians of jazz. Yet, following the legacy of an earlier tradition does not easily afford them the same opportunities of those that preceded them. They are measured by their ability to re-create the signature voices of their predecessors rather than by the individuality of their own voices. How they survive the historical flow that jazz will follow remains to be seen.

Some musicians have even more specific expectations placed on them. Trumpeters Jon Faddis and Wallace Roney have been given the mantles of Dizzy Gillespie and Miles Davis to carry throughout their careers. The rapid-high-note virtuosity of Faddis mirrors the contributions of Gillespie, and the introspective style of

Terence Blanchard.
Lee Tanner/The Jazz Image

Roney is reminiscent of Davis. As jazz has matured and begun to reflect on its past, musicians must interact differently with one another as well as with their past.

Harry Connick, Jr.

Neoclassical jazz has become popularized by another New Orleans musician, pianist/vocalist/composer Harry Connick, Jr. As a very young player, Connick became immersed in the musical styles of New Orleans. As he matured, his interest moved from contemporary rock and jazz to the classic piano players of jazz and the styles associated with them. As a singer, he is often compared to Frank Sinatra.

His success with the soundtrack for the movie *When Harry Met Sally* not only launched his career at the age of twenty-one but gave a remarkable boost to the public's interest in neoclassical jazz. The soundtrack album features Connick doing the standard love songs sung by the original artists in the movie.[33] Like the Marsalis family, Connick sees his own role in the revival of traditional jazz. "But jazz is becoming popular again! Wynton started it, and Branford, and I'm continuing it."[34] These neoclassical adherents, like those in the hard bop traditions, see their music as a return to the real essence of jazz—revitalized and again entertaining. "In the '40s and '50s, jazz musicians entertained. In the '60s, rock & roll entertained and jazz stopped entertaining. In the '70s, jazz got very obscure. In the '80s, jazz was dead and rock was #1. Jazz was absolutely nothing until Wynton Marsalis came along and pretty much brought it out of obscurity."[35]

The jazz tradition is continually subject to great change. At times like those discussed here—hard bop and neoclassical—jazz's mainstream reappears and works to stabilize the more short-lived excursions in new

Joe Lovano and Joshua Redman.
Lee Tanner/The Jazz Image (both photos)

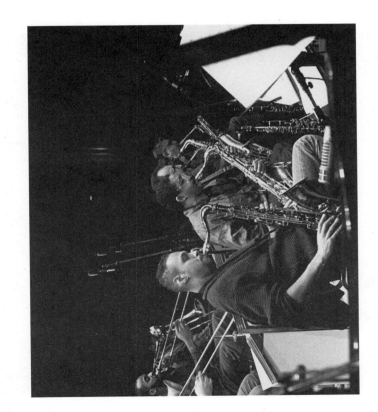

directions. As we will see in later chapters, some of the new influences on jazz will prove more lasting than others, some will lose their identities in the mainstream, and others will work to redefine our understanding of the jazz mainstream itself.

Contemporary Jazz Singers

The first recorded example of the wordless vocal jazz style called scat singing was by Louis Armstrong in his recording of "Heebie Jeebies" in 1926. Dispensing with the lyrics completely, the singer substitutes either nonsense or real syllables for the words. Many jazz and popular singers display virtuosity in this style of singing.

Sarah Vaughan

Sarah Vaughan played piano with the Earl Hines orchestra and later became a featured vocalist. As a pianist, her knowledge of harmony greatly influenced her ability to sing scat as well as ballads. Vaughan sang for presidents and toured the world with rhythm sections, a cappella choirs, jazz combos, large jazz bands, and symphony orchestras. One of her best albums to date—*I Love Brazil*—was recorded in Brazil in 1977[36] (S, "All Alone," "My Funny Valentine," side F, bands 11 and 12; NW, "Key Largo," 295, side 2, band 1).

Vaughan has influenced many singers, and she was considerably influenced by those musicians with whom she worked. This most impressive list includes Dizzy Gillespie, Earl Hines, Charlie Parker, Miles Davis, Clifford Brown, Herbie Mann, Cannonball Adderley, the Count Basie Band, Thad Jones, Jimmy Rowles, Michel Legrand, and Bob James. It is no wonder that her creative vocalizing was so steeped in jazz. Sarah Vaughan died in 1990.

Betty Carter

Another straight-ahead vocalist is Betty Carter, formerly with the Lionel Hampton band. She is an excellent scat singer, and with her rapid execution of nonsense syllables interspersed with the actual lyrics she almost sounds like an instrumentalist playing rapid sixteenth-note patterns.

Carter feels that she is the keeper of a dying flame—the true jazz singer. She agrees that the great jazz singer is linked to the instrumental approach to performing; the lyrics seem to become mere vehicles. Carter was profoundly influenced by Charlie Parker and Sonny Rollins, and these influences probably account for her rhythmic daring and virtuosity. These bop artists are easily detected in her highly creative scat singing[37] (NW, "Moonlight in Vermont," "Thou Swell," and "Can't We Be Friends?" 295, side 2, bands 2–4).

Ella Fitzgerald

The popular and talented Ella Fitzgerald has proven that popular singing and jazz singing can be merged with good taste. "A-Tisket A-Tasket" was a good swing tune that she recorded with Chick Webb in the 1930s. Later, she showed bop influences by scat singing bop to "How High the Moon" recorded in 1948. She wanted to prove that bop performed with the voice could be comparable to instrumental renditions. Although she was a contralto singer, she was able to sing almost three octaves by using her head voice. Her talented delivery was a brilliant example of the voice imitating an instrument.

Her style, tone, and intonation produced no criticism from anyone except the singer herself. By 1982, Ella Fitzgerald had won ten Grammy Awards and the *Down Beat* readers' poll twenty-two times[38] (S, "You'd Be So Nice to Come Home To," side C, band 10).

Summary

The funky hard bop era has proven to be more than merely a return to the bop style. In many ways, it demonstrates the development of an emerging tradition that begins to define itself as a maturing art form. An apparent paradox exists as the players look back to move forward. When looking back they saw the vitality that has always been a part of the jazz tradition and that seemed to come into focus somewhat during the bop period. The black-rights movement, with its search for black roots, no doubt strongly influenced the development of this music. The gospel sound of the black church merged with the energy remembered from the bop period to generate this new style.

This era also offers a window to a continuing jazz tradition. The "mainstream" has continued to flow and coexist with the many styles that have developed since that time. To many players such as Wynton Marsalis, this straight-ahead style represents the true tradition of jazz. Whether it is the purest form of jazz is certainly debatable; however, it must be recognized as perhaps the style most associated with the present jazz community's notion of what is meant by the jazz tradition.

This period, therefore, represents an important time in the history of jazz as a developing art form. As proven by jazz performers passed on their attitudes and abilities to a new generation of performers, they also passed on a respect for the tradition from which they all came.

For Further Study

1. In terms of rhythmic feeling, what does the word funky mean?
2. How would one describe the emotion or feeling of the music of the funky era?
3. What electronic instrument became popular in this era?
4. Listen to the excellent example of the funky style, "The Preacher," on *Horace Silver and the Jazz*

Ella Fitzgerald.
Courtesy of the Institute of Jazz Studies

Messengers (Blue Note Records, BLP1518). Give your reactions to the total sound. Is the melody recognizable? Do you hear the amen chord progression? Which of the two solo instruments, trumpet or saxophone, plays blue notes? Do you hear the musical conversation between the piano and ensemble near the end?

Suggested Additional Listening

Adderley, Cannonball. *The Best of Cannonball Adderley.* Capitol Records, SN 16002.

———. *The Cannonball Adderley Quintet Plus.* Riverside Records, 9388.

———. *Mercy, Mercy, Mercy.* Capitol Records, T 2663.

Additional Reading Resources

Blancq, Charles. *Sonny Rollins: The Journey of a Jazzman.*

Mingus, Charles. *Beneath the Underdog.*

Priestley, Brian. *Mingus: A Critical Biography.*

Williams, Martin T., ed. *The Art of Jazz*, 233–38.

Note: Complete information, including name of publisher and date of publication, is provided in this book's bibliography.

Notes

1. Martin T. Williams, "Bebop and After: A Report," in *Jazz*, ed. Nat Hentoff and Albert McCarthy (New York: Holt, Rinehart & Winston, 1959), 297.

2. James Lincoln Collier, *The Making of Jazz* (New York: Dell Publishing, 1978), 435–53.

3. Shelly Manne, from an interview with Reginald Buckner.

4. McCann, *Les McCann Plays the Truth.*

5. Ibid.

6. The Jazz Brothers, "Something Different," *The Soul of Jazz.*

7. McCann, *Les McCann Plays the Truth.*

8. Johnny Griffin, "Wade in the Water," *The Soul of Jazz.*

9. Horace Silver (Art Blakey), *A Night at Bird Land*, Blue Note Records, vol. 1, 1521; *Horace Silver and the Jazz Messengers*, Blue Note Records, BLP1518.

10. Horace Silver, *Blowing the Blues Away*, Blue Note Records, 4017; *Song for My Father*, Blue Note Records, 4185.

11. Joachim Berendt, *Jazz Book: From New Orleans to Rock and Free Jazz*, trans. by Dan Morgenstern (Westport, Conn., Lawrence Hill & Co., 1975).

12. Dizzy Gillespie, "Hey Pete," *Dizzy in Greece*, Verve Records, MEV-8017.

13. Don Heckman, "Ornette and the Sixties," *Down Beat* 31, no. 20 (July 1964): 59.

14. Carl Perkins, "Too Close for Comfort," *Jazz Pianists Galore*, World Pacific Records, JWC-506.

15. Les McCann, "For Carl Perkins," *Les McCann Plays the Truth*, Pacific Jazz Records, PJ-2.

16. From Henry Pleasants, *Serious Music and All That Jazz*, 1969. Reprinted by permission of Simon & Schuster, Inc.

17. Charles Mingus, *The Best of Charles Mingus*, Atlantic, SD 1555.

18. Ibid.

19. Collier, *The Making of Jazz*, 446.

20. Charles Mingus, *Mingus Ah Um*, Columbus, CS 8171.

21. Charles Mingus, "Hora Decubitus," *Smithsonian Collection of Classic Jazz.*

22. Charles Mingus, "Haitian Fight Song," *Smithsonian Collection of Classic Jazz.*

23. Sonny Rollins, *Sonny Rollins at Music Inn*, Metro Jazz Records, E 1011.

24. Sonny Rollins, "Limehouse Blues," *Sonny Rollins at Music Inn.*

25. Sonny Rollins, "St. Thomas," *Saxophone Colossus*, Prestige Records, LP 7079.

26. Sonny Rollins, "Doxy," *Sonny Rollins at Music Inn and On Man in Jazz*, RCA Victor Records, LPM/LSP-2612.

27. Sonny Rollins, "St. Thomas," *Saxophone Colossus.*

28. Sonny Rollins, "Blue 7," *Saxophone Colossus and Smithsonian Collection of Classic Jazz.*

29. Thelonious Monk (Miles Davis record), "Bags' Groove" (Take 1)," *Bags' Groove*, Prestige Records, 7109.

30. Art Blakey, "Art Blakey in His Prime," *Down Beat* 52, no. 7 (July 1985): 21.

31. Art Blakey, *Art Blakey and the Jazz Messengers*, "Album of the Year," Timeless, SJP 155.

32. Blanchard, Terence, *In My Solitude: The Billie Holiday Songbook*, Columbia, 57793.

33. Harry Connick, Jr., *When Harry Met Sally*, Columbia, CK 45319.

34. Harry Connick, Jr., *Down Beat* 57, no. 3 (March 1990): 18.

35. Ibid.

36. Sarah Vaughan, *Sarah Vaughan*, Archive of Folk Music, FS-250; *Sarah Vaughan*, Trip Records, 5501; *Live in Japan*, Mainstream Records, 401; *Swings Easy*, Trip Records, 5511; *Love Brazil*, Pablo Records, 2312101.

37. Betty Carter, *Finally*, Roulette Records, 5000; *Betty Carter*, Bet-Car Productions, MK 1001; *Betty Carter Album*, Bet-Car Productions, MK 1002; *Now It's My Turn*, Roulette Records, 5005; *Ray Charles and Betty Carter*, ABC-Paramount Records, 385.

38. Ella Fitzgerald, *Best of Ella Fitzgerald*, MCA Records, 4047; *Ella in Berlin*, Verve Records, 6404; *Fine and Mellow*, Pablo Records, 2310829; *Ella Fitzgerald and Count Basie, A Perfect Match*, Pablo Records, 2312110; *Ella Fitzgerald and Joe Pass, Fitzgerald and Pass . . . Again*, Pablo Records, 2310772.

Connick, Harry, Jr. "Trio," *Lofty's Roach Soufflé*. Columbia, CK 46223.

———. *20*. Columbia, CK 44369.

Holmes, Richard. "Groove." *The Best of Richard "Groove" Holmes*. Prestige Records, 7700.

Lewis, Ramsey. *The Best of Ramsey Lewis*. Cadet Records, S-839.

———. *The In Crowd*. Cadet Records, S-757.

Morgan, Lee. "The Sidewinder." *Three Decades of Jazz (1959–1969).*

Rollins, Sonny. *Blue 7*. Prestige Records, LP 7079.

———. *Sonny Rollins* (2 vols.). Blue Note Records, 1542, 1558.

Silver, Horace. *Best of Horace Silver*. Blue Note Records, 84325.

———. *Taking Care of Business*. Prestige Records, 24082.

Smith, Jimmy. "Back at the Chicken Shack." *Three Decades of Jazz (1959–1969).*

———. *Jimmy Smith's Greatest Hits*. Blue Note Records, BST 89901.

CHAPTER 11

Free Form, Avant-Garde

"But is it jazz? . . . Whatever it may be—and one often has the feeling that even the musicians don't quite know what they have hold of; it is a music in flux, if anything—it must not be burdened with comparisons that are unwarranted."[1]

Most new developments in jazz have been extensions of earlier traditions and only modify the musical structures and idioms defined by preceding styles. The avant-garde of a developing art form implies a conscious breaking away from the tradition established by that art form. Free jazz was such a movement. "Free form," also known as **free improvisation** or even the "new thing," breaks sharply with its musical predecessors. It is actually easier to describe what free form is not than to find descriptors for the limitless number of expressions of which it is capable. Most free-form efforts operate in a medium that is not defined by the harmonic and rhythmic forms prescribed by earlier jazz practices.

Even with the new approach taken by bop, the song structure, with its repeating harmonic form, was maintained. The songs were characterized by a steady rhythmic meter that varied little throughout the course of the performance. If a tune were in $\frac{4}{4}$, it would likely remain that throughout the performance. Although the melody to the tune was often absent during the improvised solo areas, the harmonies remained the same. There was therefore a formal, unchanging structure that supported each player's improvisation.

Free-form improvisation sheds these structures of harmonic repetition and rhythmic regularity to allow players to react to one another without restrictions. The musical material for the improvisation comes extemporaneously from the players rather than from a commonly known tune. The greatest empathy possible is necessary for this means of performance to be successful. Also, the old axiom "The more freedom allowed, the more discipline necessary" is pertinent to this style. Without discipline, a performer might merely make unusual, unrelated sounds instead of reacting in a musical way to the other players. (For an example of how two players might interact in a free music environment, listen to demonstration 29.)

In an age when the finished product is the only criterion for judgment, it is refreshing to have a situation in which the process, not the product, is really important. However, this one fact makes free-form jazz difficult to understand—at first. The listener must conscientiously observe, and then attempt to empathize with, the players to appreciate the excitement of this process. It is often easier to understand this style first in a live performance, where the listener can more readily become involved with the players.

This type of music can be compared to action or nonrepresentational painting, such as a Jackson Pollock work. Listen to Red Mitchell (bass) and Shelly Manne (drums) as they attempt to communicate with Ornette Coleman (and vice versa) on "Lorraine."[2] Alto saxophonist Joe Harriott, sometimes called an abstractionist, claims to have worked in this idiom before there could have been any Ornette Coleman influence.

Eric Dolphy.
Courtesy of the Institute of Jazz Studies

Listening Guide

Demonstration 29
(cassette 2, side A, track 2; CD 2, track 2)

Free Form
"Dialogue"
Ann LaBerge, flute
David Megill, alto saxophone

:00 Part I: Saxophone player sings while playing.

:06 Flute player uses breath articulations while saxophone plays soft melodic fragments.

:17 Flute player sings while playing.

:25 Part II: Interchange of repeated notes; flute player uses flutter tongue technique.

:39 Exchange of short punctuated notes between players.

:54 Part III: More lyric tone used by both players; glissando in flute.

1:10 Gradually picks up more melodic speed as short melodic motives are passed back and forth.

1:26 Sharp change from soft, low tones to louder, less lyric sound.

1:36 Soft consonant ending.

1:42 Part IV: Soft, rapid exchange of melodic ideas that grow in intensity and volume.

2:02 Short, very loud, and overblown notes exchanged as piece ends.

2:08 End.

It would not be illogical to feel that the seeds of free-form jazz existed from the beginnings of jazz itself. The very nature of improvisation places great emphasis on spontaneous musical creativity. To some degree, every jazz performance contains an element of improvisation, if only in the rhythm section, where the specific notes are left to the players' discretion. The balance between fixed compositions and improvisatory development has shifted throughout jazz's history. Free-form jazz proves to be the fullest expression of spontaneous composition, and improvisation takes the dominant role.

The leading players and composers in this medium come to it from different musical and philosophical backgrounds that add a distinctive stamp to each of their efforts. As we will see, the traditional musical structures of harmony and rhythm are only two of the many possible glues available to musicians. The effectiveness of free-form performance rests in the individual and collective compositional strengths of the players. The individual musical characteristics of the players carry over into the performance itself; instilling it with its own unique expression. The dominant musical voice in an ensemble helps establish the trademarks that unify and narrow the infinite possibilities of a free-form composition. These trademarks, in turn, help distinguish the performances of Cecil Taylor from those of Ornette Coleman or John Coltrane.

Free-form jazz did not just suddenly appear with Ornette Coleman's "Free Jazz" recording. Composers such as Charles Mingus had already pushed hard on the musical fabric, forcing it into a freer expression. As early as 1956, Mingus had recorded "Pithencanthropus Erectus" and shocked the listening world with his daring use of some free playing. In much the same way, Coltrane broke into a free style as a natural result of his own harmonic and melodic extensions.

It was Ornette Coleman, however, who drew the sharpest line between the traditional jazz idiom as he coined a name for his new expression: free jazz.

Ornette Coleman

Saxophonist Ornette Coleman was one of the most controversial free jazz players. Critics who have examined his work fall into one of two distinct groups. One group is composed of staunch admirers, whereas the other group views his work as unworthy of any consideration. These adverse opinions are due to Coleman's apparent disregard for tradition[3] (S, "Lonely Woman," side I, band 4; S, "Congeniality," side J, band 1; S, "Free Jazz," side J, band 2). It is said that he refuses to comply with restrictions normally imposed by rhythm and meter, chord progressions, and melodic continuity and that he desires the freedom to play any thought that occurs to him at any time, regardless of context.

Score for free-form demonstration 29.

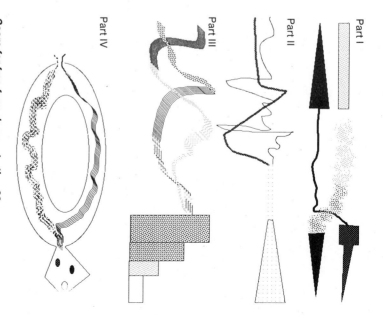

Part I

Part II

Part III

Part IV

Listening Guide

Ornette Coleman
"Free Jazz"*

:00	Introduction.
:10	Melody (from which to improvise later) played in unison at this point.
:22	Alto sax solo (Ornette Coleman); listen for 2 basses and the accenting on the drums.
1:10	Backup horns enter.
3:33	Horns play independently.
4:10	Alto sax plays faster, one bass is bowing.
4:45	Ensemble players now playing very independently.
5:05	Peak.
5:30	Alto sax solos again.
5:40	Everybody is improvising.
6:10	Alto sax solos again.
6:43	Everybody is improvising.
7:45	Everybody plays fast for a moment.
9:46	Original motive played here in unison.
10:00	Fade.
10:03	End.

*Smithsonian Collection, side J, band 2 (excerpt), Atlantic, S-1364.

Ornette Coleman

Ornette Coleman has had a career of controversy. As the first popularly known leader of the jazz avant-garde with his 1960 performance of free jazz, he initiated a controversy of strong, opposing opinions from many of the other established jazz leaders, including Miles Davis and Charles Mingus, who themselves were innovators of jazz styles. Coleman's influence on the development of jazz was rekindled in 1985 with his recording *Song X* with Pat Metheny as well as his introduction of what he calls the "harmolodic theory" that he now employs. This theory centers on the melodic activity of the ensemble that collectively establishes the harmonic texture. "I mean, when you hear my band, you know that everybody is soloing, harmolodically."[5]

There are many misunderstandings concerning Coleman's playing. One is that he turned to free form because he was incapable of anything else. To say that Coleman "doesn't sound good" is too loose a statement. Questions immediately arise: Good compared to what? Compared to other saxophonists? Compared to European scales and harmony?

Coleman shows on "Part 1" that he can play both melodically and rhythmically.[4] Despite the free playing in this cut, much of the melodic rhythms are consistent with those used by traditional jazz players. The melodic lines still swing in a hard bop fashion, but their relationship to the independent bass line is harmonically vague. The steady meter in this cut is not necessarily typical of free jazz performances, but it works well as a support for Coleman's solo and the responses by the other horn players.

In fact, Coleman is very melody oriented. He also phrases freely. He feels no obligation to contain or extend his musical thoughts so that they fit neatly into a certain number of measures, which is logical because he does not use defined chord progressions. Also, he is not involved in keeping a certain pulse; after all, his music is not for dancing. Coleman's melodies have pitch relationships even for the uninitiated, but his metrically invented phrases are placed over a free rhythm with no identifiable chord progressions, an approach that tends to lose those who have not listened to free form. The shift from a steady pulse to a free-flowing rhythm can be traced first to Lester Young and then to Gerry Mulligan and others as they attempted to avoid constraint within the **bar lines.**

Because there is no chord progression, some players feel free enough to avoid a key center and play with an atonal feel. This sense of not being in a key is not quite the same as the **twelve-tone system** of Schoenberg, where each tone has equal importance and no key center

is implied. Rather, these players seem to have no home base, which many listeners evidently need. However, there is no reason to argue about atonality in jazz. Remember that many of the roots of jazz, such as the field holler, were in no specific key. Some authorities consider the lack of a steady pulse or beat to be a new rhythmic concept, whereas others consider it no concept at all. One of the more appreciated concepts of this new music is the way in which musical thoughts and attitudes from the entire world are incorporated. Obviously, these young musicians feel that older musical concepts are too rigid, too predictable, and certainly too laden with clichés.

Coleman was the first player to move all the way into harmonic freedom. This idea had been examined earlier by classical composers but in an entirely different way. Although Coleman approached it through improvisation, to say that he was the first is only partially true. Actually, he was only the first to receive widespread recognition. When Coleman organized a quartet in 1957 in Los Angeles, Cecil Taylor was playing in a free manner at the Newport Jazz Festival. Charlie Mingus had invented free sounds even earlier. The term *free form* first appeared on a Coleman album with Eric Dolphy entitled *Free Jazz.*

Faulty intonation has been one of the criticisms leveled at Coleman, but perhaps the fault lies in the well-tempered scale of European classical music. Reference

Demonstration 30
(cassette 2, side A, track 3; CD 2, track 3)

Ornette Coleman Trio

"Faces and Places"*
Ornette Coleman, alto saxophone
David Izenzon, bass
Charles Moffet, drums

It is particularly useful to listen to the entire recording (as well as the excerpt on the demonstration tape) to hear the energy curve at work in this performance. Throughout the piece, the trio plays very clear hard-driving sections referred to as "straight time." Contrasted with these sections are those with less metric focus. The bass generally maintains a straight four-beat pattern, but the drums use accents that sometimes conflict with the meter. As Coleman moves in and out of time in his solo, he is sometimes supported by a similar move in the drums and at other times by a clear meter. Also listen for how Coleman's solo strikes varying amounts of independence from the harmonic areas implied by the bass. This performance shows the trio's ability both to control the traditional jazz language and to move "outside" that language as they shape their energy curve.

Complete Original Demonstration Tape

:00	Saxophone introduction with intermittent time in bass and drums.
:18	Short use of time in the drums but not yet in the bass.
:26	Time established under saxophone solo.
:33	Bass uses a repeating pattern, establishing an ostinato feel with straight time in drums (with accents).
:47	Bass walks.
1:05	Melodic variation, shifting the whole motive chromatically for each statement.
1:32	Drums fall into a straight-time feeling with walking bass pattern.
1:55	Backup again moves away from straight time, creating a contrast for the harder swinging straight-time areas.
2:13	Walking feeling as time returns.
2:31	Drummer syncopates meter with cross-accents.
2:42	Straight time returns.
2:49	Accents in drums.
3:13	Straight time returns.
3:30	Cross-accents on saxophone.
3:50	Coleman uses more traditional melodic language here
4:01 :00	(Demonstration tape begins here.) Coleman begins moving further from the harmonic area established by the bass. He also begins moving at an accelerated pace. His solo at this point has moved to a higher energy level, which he began to set up during the first part of the solo.
5:10 1:09	Listen for the exchange of rhythmic ideas between the saxophone and the drums.
5:20 1:17	Chromatically shifting lines that are more independent harmonically.
5:30 1:29	Rhythmic and harmonic independence in the saxophone.
5:55 1:54	Short double-time saxophone section.
6:10 2:09	Motivic exchange between saxophone and drums.
6:40 2:39	Rhythmic line passed from Coleman to drums; steady, fast tempo maintained by drums (with accents) and bass.
6:55 2:54	Rhythmic and metric cross-accents to set up return to time.
7:05 3:04	Straight time.
7:15 3:14	Listen for rhythmic exchange between the saxophone and drums.
7:35 3:34	Cross-accents on drums setting up drum solo and bringing the saxophone solo to a climax.
8:00 3:59	Return to straight time; drum solo begins.
9:05 4:04	Coleman enters with a double-time saxophone break followed by a fast metric support. Saxophone motivic lines even more independent of the harmonic area suggested by the bass. Drumming also gradually becomes more accented.
9:48 4:47	Double-time melodic lines.
10:01 5:00	Half-time melody; melodic lines become more chromatic and developmental.
10:39 5:38	Solo breaks with drum responses; melodic material is the same as at the beginning.
11:08 6:07	End.

*At the "Golden Circle," Stockholm, vol. 1, Blue Note Records, 842242.

could be made to the blue areas or blue notes and questions raised about the cultures that do not subscribe to the European concept. Possibly, there is faulty intonation in any emotional music in which notes are constantly pushed this way or that way.

Martin Williams quotes Coleman on this issue: "You can play sharp in tune and flat in tune," pointing out that the intonation for any note depends on the musical context.[6]

In the late 1980s, Coleman continued to push into new theoretical and philosophical areas with his proposed "harmolodic theory." His pursuit of such new ideas is a trademark of his continuing career.

Cecil Taylor

Unlike Coleman, pianist Cecil Taylor did not have an extensive background in blues bands. Rather, his contribution was an integration of a conservatory technical facility and European-based compositional practices. However, like Coleman he is interested in a free improvisatory arena for the players. Taylor is often considered an avant-garde expression of third-stream jazz. His music is perhaps a more effective fusion of classical compositional practices and jazz improvisation than the traditional third stream itself. Taylor was able to blend his conservatory background and the raw energy typical

Cecil Taylor playing.
Copyright Tom Copi/Michael Ochs Archives, Venice, CA

of the freest improvisation into a seamless whole. He found an intersection in which his music can be heard as either classical or jazz, depending on the vantage point of the listener.

Unlike Coleman's music, Taylor's does not usually reveal traditional jazz idioms, although the spirit of jazz improvisation is clearly evident. "Enter Evening," recorded in 1966, is an example of Taylor's free-form style. Notice how the players react to one another in a manner not only free of harmony and meter but also free from many of the usual melodic jazz idioms[7] (S, side 1, band 2). Taylor's use of an oboe and a bass clarinet in the ensemble is consistent with the third stream's earlier use of traditionally classical instruments.

The variety of musical textures used in Taylor's music can be heard on "Idur" and "Serdab"[8] (NW, 201). "Idur" is a very high energy composition made up of fragmented and punctuated statements that are characteristic of much of Taylor's percussive style. He often approaches his piano as a drummer might, striking clusters of notes for their percussive effect. The sequence of musical textures leads the listener through a series of energy levels that are shaped by Taylor's compositional skill. Throughout these pieces, the interchange between musicians is the propelling force. What any one player does at any one time is seldom as important as the composite musical statement. It is often helpful when listening to this type of free-form music to step back from the detail of individual players and listen to the whole musical fabric that the players weave collectively. Notice that many of the transitions between musical areas are carried by Taylor himself as he sets up each new collective effort.

"Serdab" offers the listener some contrasting musical textures, although there are still several high-energy sections. In this composition, although the players have many occasions to work out melodic ideas individually, the composite sound is still dominant. In several of the more open areas, Taylor is willing to use traditional jazz idioms, only to move quickly back into a more dense percussive style. The interchange between players is more clearly audible in the less dense areas, where the melodic fragments are given more length and often accompanied by other similar (or contrasting) melodic lines.

Taylor's music often requires stamina from listeners and players alike. His concerts are notorious for their long, uninterrupted compositions. Holding such long compositional structures in a free-form manner attests to Taylor's strength as a composer. "3 Phasis," a single piece, runs over fifty-seven minutes, spanning two sides of a record[9] (NW, 303). The fact that this recording was the last of six efforts made that day to record this piece demonstrates the ensemble's intensity and stamina. Perhaps more than any other trait, Taylor's intensity is the hallmark of his music, an intensity more typical of jazz than the European counterpart with which it was fused. Few composers have been as successful as Taylor at blending the two musical worlds so completely.

John Coltrane (1926–1967)

Saxophonist John Coltrane combined great emotion with excellent musicianship and discipline with freedom. Like Parker, he did not have an extensive career (compared to Armstrong and Ellington), which lasted about twelve years, from 1955 to 1967.

John Coltrane was born in Hamlet, North Carolina, on September 23, 1926. He studied saxophone in Philadelphia, where he began playing professionally. Coltrane started to attain recognition while playing with Miles Davis from 1955 to 1960. In 1960 he formed his own quartet, and in 1965 Alice McLeod (Coltrane's wife) joined the group. Coltrane's short career ended with his death on July 1, 1967, at the age of forty.

Musicians disagree about other contemporary players such as Ornette Coleman, but there were few disagreements about John Coltrane. He was a fine saxophone player (tenor and soprano) in every sense. The prime concern of most musicians is the tone that a player produces, as there is no way to imagine a musical sound without considering the quality of the tone. Coltrane produced a large, dark, lush sound from his instrument. A brief listen to "Ogunde" verifies this.[10] On the album Giant Steps (Coltrane's first album under his own name), his beautiful, solid tone is most evident in "Naima."[11] This record shows his confidence at this time in his career and reveals deeper feeling and conviction than when he worked for Davis. His drive is very apparent on "Cousin Mary."

Coltrane's chief legacy was his beautiful tone and his control of the upper register. (He had equal strength in all registers of the instrument—an unusual trait.) Wayne Shorter, Charles Lloyd, Pharoah Sanders, and Eddie Harris all show traces of this legacy. The influence of Coltrane's very passionate approach appears in unlikely places, as in an occasional near scream from cool saxophonist Stan Getz. Coltrane said that Sidney Bechet was an important influence on his own playing.

Coltrane advanced jazz improvisation harmonically through long excursions into the higher harmonics of chords on an instrument (tenor saxophone) that is sounded where a trombone, or a man's voice, is pitched.

Coltrane had great coordination between his fingering of the saxophone and his tonguing. This coordination allowed him a fast technique, and he played arpeggios so rapidly that they are referred to as Coltrane's "sheets of sound." These can be heard as early in his career as "All Blues" with Miles Davis as well as in "Cousin Mary" with his own quartet. Coltrane's creativity with his sheets of sound was actually homophonically constructed music that had been carried to a higher level. He thought of these runs as if they were chords on top of chords. His fast arpeggios have great emotional impact, and he was an expert in the use of sequences.

A logical starting place for those uninitiated in Coltrane's music is Miles Davis's recording of Kind of

Blue.[12] On "All Blues," "So What," and "Freddie Freeloader," the listener can hear Coltrane when he was working for a fairly conservative leader. Therefore, he had not expanded his directions very much and is quite easy to understand and appreciate immediately. It is interesting to compare the Coltrane of this album with Cannonball Adderley. On both "So What" and "Freddie Freeloader," Adderley shows a more direct association with Parker while playing some very funky phrases not to be found in Coltrane's playing. In "Freddie Freeloader," Coltrane is blowing aggressively and melodically at the same time.

Coltrane played rhythmically but counter to that which was being played by what would normally be the rhythm section; so the music became **arrhythmic.** This effect freed the rhythm players to play whatever occurred to them according to the melodic thoughts they were hearing. Coltrane could play "on top of the beat" whenever he wanted to, but he liked to play differently from the rhythm players with the idea that this freed them from having to play with him. His counterrhythms can be heard on both "Countdown" and "Spiral" on *Giant Steps.* He seemed to fuse melody and rhythm in "The Father and The Son and The Holy Ghost."[13]

Eventually, Coltrane turned toward emphasizing the melodic line above all else. Chords were used only as they related to the melody. Instead of melody being improvised out of harmony, melody was improvised from melody, an approach used by classical composers quite early in the history of music but seldom by jazz performers. Coltrane had the advantage of working with Thelonious Monk, from whom he was able to establish a mature, consistent relationship between the chords and his melodic thoughts. Monk stimulated Coltrane's interest in wide intervals, although it is very possible that his interest in various types of scales came from his time with the Miles Davis group.

Coltrane broke away from the format of theme, solos, theme. His recording of "The Father and The Son and The Holy Ghost" has no real theme before his solo, and the ensemble portion has no theme at all. This is very disturbing to jazz listeners who expect only traditional approaches to jazz. In "Countdown," Coltrane shows his great coordination. The work sounds free, yet when chords are brought in under his solo, he is exactly where he should be harmonically.

An example of Coltrane's innovation is a selection called "India," recorded before the Beatles received credit for "discovering" Ravi Shankar. In this album, one hears influences such as Indian scales and rhythms.

Coltrane opened the path for others such as Archie Shepp through his conviction that improvisation could continue past all existing melodic considerations, harmonic considerations, and rhythmic flow. Free form seemed to need another leader beside Ornette Coleman. Coltrane became this leader with his long improvisations (sometimes forty minutes), his sheets of sound, his tone,

and his technique. He was looked on as a spiritual leader. Coltrane and his followers have often been criticized for playing solos that were too long, but their answer was that they needed the time to explore the music in depth.

At first, Coltrane was admired more as a technically complete musician than as a creative artist. He showed speed as he cascaded chords with his powerful moving tone. But his recording *A Love Supreme* seemed to change the attitude toward his playing,[14] as it is a very emotional record that does away with some earlier excesses and is more a work of art than an exhibition. Coltrane tried to explain (in his music) the wonderful things that the universe meant to him. Playing jazz was a spiritual experience to Coltrane, and he always felt that he should share his feelings with his listeners. There is no doubt about his strong religious motivation.

Coltrane continually experimented. Even when listeners were well acquainted with Coltrane's recordings, they would still be constantly surprised and amazed at each live performance. His fans learned to expect only the unexpected.

In 1965 Coltrane won four *Down Beat* polls: Record of the Year (*A Love Supreme*), Jazzman of the Year, Hall of Fame, and Number-One Tenor Saxophonist.

"Coltrane came, and he made music. He built on existing foundations. He and his music lived in inexorable relation to other lives, other ideas, other musics. But how he built! The musical structures are changed forever because of him."[15]

The Coltrane Legacy

Despite Coltrane's relatively short career, he charted one of the most direct, continuous courses from the **modal jazz** of the Miles Davis quintet to his own late albums, rich with free improvisation. Rather than declare independence from traditional form and harmonic practice as Coleman did, Coltrane extended the traditional harmonic chords until they no longer functioned tonally. The resulting **atonal** medium offered Coltrane a free environment in which he could develop his melodic ideas.

Coltrane used the modal jazz approach as a springboard for his characteristic melodic extensions. His melodies were often based on modes played over slow-moving harmonies. Rather than using the lower notes of a chord (i.e., the root, third, or fifth), Coltrane centered his melodies on higher **harmonics** such as the ninth, eleventh, and thirteenth. The result was a more complex harmonic sound that could, when pushed harder, develop into atonal passages characteristic of free-form jazz. The slow-moving harmonies of modal jazz actually contained the seeds of atonality because they fostered a melodic approach toward improvisation and allowed time for the player to explore more complex harmonic extensions. Coltrane uses this modal jazz approach on his recording of "Alabama" (S, side I, band 3). Notice the relationship of his melody to the harmonic underpinning. He is able to consistently maintain an extended distance from the basic harmony. The opening and closing statements use only one chord, over which Coltrane plays a modal melodic line.

Coltrane's sense of melody is displayed in one of his most celebrated performances on a Rodgers and Hammerstein tune, "My Favorite Things," performed with his quartet.[16] His solo on this recording shows how he applied his modal and extended harmonic techniques to the more traditional song form. As his solo develops, it becomes so extended harmonically that it seems only vaguely related to the ongoing and apparently frozen harmonic center below it. At several points the quartet collectively weaves musical textures not dissimilar to those heard in Ornette Coleman's free expressions.

Coltrane completes his transition toward free form in performances like "Manifestations," in which his later quartet operates in a very free interchange.[17] Even with

Listening Guide

Demonstration 31
(cassette 2, side A, track 4; CD 2, track 4)

John Coltrane
"A Love Supreme, Part I—Acknowledgement"*
John Coltrane, tenor sax
McCoy Tyner, piano
Jimmy Garrison, bass
Elvin Jones, drums

Complete Original Demonstration Tape

:00 Saxophone fanfare with cymbal accompaniment.

:30 Melody of 4 notes played by bass.

:38 Drums start making "time."

:46 Piano enters.

1:02 Sax enters with new melodic material (still motivic in nature); piano generally keeps 2-note movement taken from opening bass motive as the "comping" pattern.

1:29 Example of ascending and descending chromatic chord patterns used by the piano; listen for constant motivic variation by the saxophonists.

2:01 Bass begins to move toward 4-beat patterns instead of variations of the motive; loose references to the motive are maintained most of the time and passed between the various players.

3:08 Example of bass 4-beat pattern that still reflects motive.

4:05 Example of soloists using short, fragmented statements of the motive.

4:45 A return to the simple melodic motive, continually repeated.

5:53 Players sing to motive, "A Love Supreme."

6:23 Motive moves down a step.

6:37 Saxophone drops out and ensemble begins to fade.

6:53 Piano drops out, only bass and drums remain.

7:07 Only bass remains, playing the motive.

7:32 End.

*A Love Supreme, Impulse Records, AS-77.

Listening Guide

World Saxophone Quartet
"Steppin'"*

:00 Ostinato in baritone saxophone and soprano saxophone.

:10 Theme enters (A section).

:26 Extended harmonic and legato theme (B section).

:41 Return to A section ostinato.

:51 Theme A returns.

1:07 Repeat of B section legato theme.

1:23 Swing feel setup with variation of ostinato and collective improvisation in the other saxophones; listen for the interchange of ideas and the passing around of the ostinato.

2:32 Starts getting freer as ostinato is passed around.

2:55 Very free section; bass voice joins the collective improvisation.

3:10 Legato bass changes character of style.

3:20 Staccato bass returns; still free in upper parts.

3:35 All parts are free again.

3:58 Bass voice is temporarily featured; interchange from top to bottom of ideas—very free; ostinato still referenced by several members; intensity increases.

4:43 Double-time feel in baritone saxophone while upper voices pull back rhythmically.

4:58 Free section with more space in the texture; hints at opening ostinato.

5:30 Very frenetic with fast melodic lines.

5:40 Fragmented ostinato enters in baritone saxophone.

6:06 Slow to stop, then return to opening ostinato.

6:16 Theme A.

6:32 Theme B.

6:48 Return to A section and beginning to fade with chord punctuations in upper saxophones.

7:07 Final chord.

7:14 End.

*Smithsonian Collection, side J, band 3.

the freedom allowed the players, Coltrane's guiding influence can be heard. The long but disjunct melodic lines, frozen harmonic centers, and emotional intensity characterize the later Coltrane performances.

Chicago Style of Free Jazz

Sun Ra

The first popular expression of the new avant-garde school of jazz in Chicago can be found in the work of composer/pianist Sun Ra. After a somewhat mysterious childhood, Sun Ra worked as arranger/pianist for theater orchestras such as Jesse Miller and Fletcher Henderson. His own career as leader began in 1953 with the organization of a quartet that later was expanded into a big band called Arkestra, with which Sun Ra is best known.

Sun Ra's work has been quite controversial. He is lauded by some as a great innovator, carefully balancing the musical worlds of composition and improvisation. By others he is seen as nothing more than a charlatan. Critics of Sun Ra cite his own musical defense as grounds for dismissing his music.

Music is a universal language. The intergalactic music in its present phase of presentation will be correlative to the key synopsis of the past and to the uncharted multi-potential planes outside the bounds of the limited earth-eternity future. The intergalactic music is in hieroglyphic sound: an abstract analysis and synthesis of man's relationship to the universe, visible and invisible first man and second man.[18]

Despite his controversial posture as a musical scientist, he was certainly the first composer in Chicago to employ techniques of collective improvisation in big-band compositions. Even Sun Ra's success with big-band jazz has not spawned many other groups like it. The only other such group is the Jazz Composers' Orchestra led by Carla Bley and Mike Mantler.

Sun Ra's *Heliocentric Worlds* (vols. 1 and 2) demonstrates his effectiveness with composing for a large ensemble and still maintaining an allegiance to collective improvisation. His success here is based on the nature of his compositional process, which allows the structure to emerge as a result of the extraordinary musical communication established among his players.[19]

Association for the Advancement of Creative Music

Throughout jazz history, musical styles have been associated with geographical locations, such as New Orleans and Chicago Dixieland, West Coast jazz, and East Coast hard bop. In the 1960s, Chicago was again a center for a developing jazz style. A new, more world-based music was being explored by a group called the Association for the Advancement of Creative Music (AACM). The group was founded by composer/pianist/clarinetist Richard Abrams, whose work focused largely on a group called the Experimental Band, which was itself made up of smaller units. This band had no permanent membership; rather, it changed to meet whatever composition and performance demands were required for concerts and recordings. The personnel for the AACM included other prominent players of new music such as trumpeter Leo Smith, saxophonist Anthony Braxton, and violinist Leroy Jenkins.

Art Ensemble of Chicago

Out of the Experimental Band came many important innovators of avant-garde jazz. Saxophonist Joseph Jarman developed into a leading composer for AACM and worked often in multimedia formats. Jarman came to the AACM from a rock and blues background. Woodwind player Roscoe Mitchell came to the AACM from a bop background by way of Ornette Coleman. Trumpeter Lester Bowie also worked in the Experimental Band before joining forces with Jarman, Mitchell, and bassist Malachi Favors in 1968 to form the Art Ensemble of Chicago. In 1969, the Art Ensemble moved to Paris and recorded some of their most notable albums.[20]

The work of the Art Ensemble, like that of AACM, is very difficult to describe in detail because of the variety of compositional and performance tactics they employed. The diversity of intent is perhaps their most defining trademark, but some general descriptors can be applied across their work:

1. an emphasis on collective interaction,
2. a wide range of tone colors,
3. the exploration of sound structures, and
4. a suspension of fixed rhythmic support (no drummer).

The Art Ensemble is capable of a wide range of musical styles that still hold to these general characteristics, ranging from the reciting of poetry to the quoting of traditional jazz idioms. Their use of tone color, instrumental technique, language, and traditional jazz styles may be presented in quite unexpected ways. They are able to suspend traditional musical elements, such as harmony or rhythm, and still maintain a cohesive performance because of their sophisticated ensemble skills. For example, because there is no drummer, the percussion is performed collectively; the equipment is spread throughout the group and players move to equipment as needed.

Like most of the music of AACM, that of the Art Ensemble has a firm compositional base. The compositional detail describes not the notes to be played but rather the way in which the performance is to proceed. Although individual performances follow the charted composition, they also respond to the evolving collective improvisation. This balance between compositional intent and free improvisation is the foundation on which AACM operates.

AACM/M-BASE/Black Artist Group

The history of jazz centers mainly around the virtuosic expressions of individual players. Even name musical groups are most often defined by the individuals in them and most often by the leadership of just one individual. The Association for the Advancement of Creative Musicians (AACM), Macro-Basic Array of Structured Extemporizations (M-BASE), and the Black Artists Group work outside this more traditional definition.

The AACM was established in Chicago during the 1960s by Richard Abrams to act as a support group for musicians working in new and experimental music. This group influenced the avant-garde of jazz through groups such as the Art Ensemble and individuals such as Anthony Braxton.

It is difficult to characterize the nature of the music that AACM has fostered since the 1960s because it has been so experimental. However, a common consensus exists that the composers/performers should be free to explore not only traditional elements of pitch and meter but also the more general notions of sound and time. All sounds are considered appropriate musical material, and their placement in time is completely free.

The Black Artists Group, formed in 1968 in St. Louis, was organized in much the same manner as AACM. Out of this group came three saxophone players who would later develop the World

Saxophone Quartet: Oliver Lake, alto sax; Julius Hemp-hill, alto sax; and Hamiet Bluiett, baritone sax. The quartet was complete when they added David Murray on tenor sax in 1976. Their compositions strike a balance between free improvisational textures (typical of Ornette Coleman) and more structured compositional passages. The quartet is capable of a wide range of compositional approaches and stylistic moods, from complex interweaving of lines to light, humorous pieces ("Steppin'," S, side J, band 3).

During the late 1980s, another group of black musicians, M-BASE, developed in Brooklyn. Parallels have been drawn between it and AACM. Greg Osby, Geri Allen, Steve Coleman, and Robin Eubanks are among those who spearheaded the development of the organization. Although AACM and M-BASE each operate as collectives for the advancement of their ideas, the groups differ in their musical heritage. Whereas AACM has a strong alliance with the avant-garde (normally associated with classical and world music), M-BASE works at an experimental intersection between jazz and popular music forms such as rhythm and blues and soul. And, whereas AACM represents a search for new music that is often free from traditional forms and practice, M-BASE explores possible musical blends between various jazz and popular traditions.

Anthony Braxton

The jazz and classical avant-garde streams are in many ways practically indistinguishable. The **chance music** promoted by John Cage, although free in term of harmony, timbre, and meter, finds its cohesion in the intellectual restrictions imposed by the composer. Without containing the traditional musical idioms to support the free use of sound and rhythm, compositions are based on the composer's ability to creatively mold the musical elements into an understandable whole. As in the highly emotional music of Mingus, Coleman, and Coltrane, the emotional theme and the players' collective understanding of that theme can be used to hold large expanses of music together. The classical approach toward new music is often based not on emotional unity as such but on an intellectual premise that explores and develops new musical areas.

Cecil Taylor maintained a careful balance between emotional and intellectual composition. Multifaceted woodwind player Anthony Braxton also maintains this kind of balance. His compositions are based on well-crafted notions about timbre and time relationships yet develop freely in an improvisational environment.

Braxton spent the mid-1960s in Chicago with AACM. He has been productive as both an author and a

composer, writing a great deal about his view of creativity in music and basing his musical compositions on well-developed theories. His 1974 album *Anthony Braxton, New York, Fall 1974* offers several examples of his compositional approach.[21] Each cut from the album is represented with an enigmatic geometric design that guided the performance. Contrast the almost boplike idiom of "Side One, Cut One" with the much freer "Side Two, Cut Three." The first side clearly reflects a jazz heritage in its use of meter and melodic inflection, but the second has very few obvious ties to traditional jazz.

Although similar to Taylor's more classical approach, Braxton's music presents a more specifically composed image than that of Taylor. This is not to say that Braxton's music lacks the improvisational energy that is characteristic of Taylor's or Coleman's. Braxton has often performed fully improvised solo concerts which would be difficult to match in technique or intensity. His music, however, tends to show the more measured qualities associated with more fully composed music. "Side Two, Cut One" demonstrates his ability to maintain such a controlled yet free-sounding environment. His clarinet lines are effectively intertwined with the timbres produced by Richard Teitelbaum on the Moog synthesizer.

Anthony Braxton.
Photo by Carl Baugher

Contemporary Avant-Garde

Greg Osby

Although the avant-garde school of jazz reached its zenith during the 1960s, its legacy is played out today by contemporary jazz performers. Many of these composers and performers were also connected to the Chicago school and to AACM and M-BASE in particular. Prominent among this new generation of free-thinking jazz players is saxophonist Greg Osby, who has played with Lester Bowie, David Murray, and the World Saxophone Quartet.

Osby, like previous avant-garde players, challenges the neoclassical jazz school as having lost the true spirit of jazz by looking back at previous styles and possibly sacrificing the chance to find an individual voice. In this regard, Osby proves to be truly connected to the original avant-garde school of the 1960s. By definition, "avant-garde" means to stand against the status quo. Ornette Coleman did this when he introduced free jazz, and Greg Osby does this today in both his own playing and reasoning.[22]

Henry Threadgill

Perhaps even more of an iconoclast than Greg Osby is composer Henry Threadgill, who also came from the experience of the AACM in Chicago. He sees the world as his venue, has a musical palette wider than jazz, and like Osby takes issue with the emerging neoclassical school of jazz: "There's an incestuous esthetic in jazz right now, and the ramifications come through in neoclassicism and all of these things that are retro. . . . When one starts thinking on the basis of culture, and then to justify an esthetic that is retro and anti-evolutionary inside of that idea of culture, I think that's very destructive."[23]

Like the first generation of avant-garde jazz players and composers, Threadgill approaches his music from a philosophical approach that values the change in jazz's

Greg Osby (right) and Jon Faddis.
Courtesy of Ray Avery

evolution and looks to external influences for fresh material. The avant-garde jazz musician looks back in history to embrace the context of jazz but not necessarily the content. Threadgill's work with Very Very Circus, one of his ensembles, shows his interest in pushing jazz's front edge by asserting his own individualism and interest in global music.[24]

The Free Jazz Controversy

Some performers who gain recognition today make no pretense of any connection with past musical styles. They specify that they play "emotion," which is entirely different from playing lines, keys, modes, and rhythms.[25] Players of free form are considered the most radical musicians since the bop era. They feel that music in general and jazz in particular should show the emotion of the player, something they believe was not adequately done with the older types of jazz. Coleman and other free-form players think that jazz should also express feelings not previously reflected. After an interview with Archie Shepp, Leonard Feather wrote, "Shepp's music—impassioned, fierce, often atonal, almost totally free of rules of harmony, melody and tone that have governed most music of this century—reflects the turmoil and frustrations that bedevil him."[26] Whether free form is "hate music," "love music," or something else, it is still a means of expression.

Left to right: Steve McCall, Henry Threadgill, and Fred Hopkins.
Frank Driggs Collection

We suspect that it is mainly the critics and musicians who simply cannot go along with these new expansions who call free-form jazz hate music. Some of the music on Coltrane's recordings is in fact quite religious. There were many jazz critics who would neither support nor condemn free form for fear of eventually being proven wrong or at least foolish. No matter what it is called, and although many claim that it is chaotic, this music has found an audience.

Free-form players thrive on controversy. Free-form advocates who acknowledge that this style has not developed a large following argue that a person should have the right to fail. But failure is not always the result for free-form players. There are even those who are financially successful—witness Ornette Coleman's Guggenheim Foundation grant.

Because free-form jazz does not adhere to established rules, the question is often asked whether free form is jazz and, indeed, whether it is music. Each listener must decide. When free form was still fairly new in jazz (in comparison to most styles), Dan Morgenstern took a perceptive look at the controversy:

But is it jazz? Some of the main elements are lacking. There is little of what we have come to know as "swing." There is often none of the formal organization found in most jazz—rhythm section and melody instruments, solo versus ensemble, strict time, etc. Yet, the sound and feeling is often of a kind peculiar to jazz as we have become accustomed to it, and it is certainly not "classical" music in any sense of that ill-defined word. Whatever it may be—and one often has the feeling that even the musicians don't quite know what they have hold of; it is a music in flux, if anything—it must not be burdened with comparisons that are unwarranted.

To accuse a drummer of not swinging when he doesn't want to achieve swing in the sense that his critic has in mind is unfair and pointless. To demand adherence to formal patterns that the musicians are obviously rejecting is as foolish as taking a painter of geometric abstractions to task for being nonrepresentational.[27]

Summary

In spite of the debate as to whether the performance is jazz, the free-form manner of expression proves to be the ultimate in improvisation. Coleman was the leader in this direction, but followers—notably Eric Dolphy and Ken McIntyre—extended this experimentation much further.[28]

Coltrane was a tremendous help in furthering the careers of other contemporary free jazz players such as Archie Shepp and Pharaoh Sanders. Coltrane and Coleman were at the top of most musicians' polls in the mid-1960s, especially in Europe.

McCoy Tyner played piano for Coltrane for almost six years (1960–65), and it took him almost eight years after that to free himself to the point where he was an individual expressing his own thoughts. When he started his group, they played set forms but later became much more flexible and free.[29]

Some contemporary groups deserve special mention because of their highly experimental nature: the Archie Shepp Quintet, the New York Art Quintet, the Albert Ayler Quintet, and the Jazz Composers Workshop (later Jazz Composers Orchestra) with Carla Bley and Mike Mantler. There is also much of this type of activity in Europe. There have been innovators of avant-garde jazz in Los Angeles, but the main strongholds are New York and Europe. However, there is a "catch-22" in that the club owners will not hire these musicians until they have recordings, and record companies are reluctant to give them a recording date until they have proven that their music is commercial enough to appeal to the expanding jazz audience.

It appears as though at least the freer aspects of jazz have somewhat reduced the freedom acquired in the 1960s. Most successful recording artists today construct their works by beginning with a strain with which listeners can relate, following with an entirely free portion, and then returning to the recognizable strain. The pattern may occur several times in a long selection, giving listeners pivotal points to cling to. At this time, listeners accept this: they can recognize the selection while appreciating the freedom of the player in other portions. Players, meanwhile, are tending toward retaining a key center for the seemingly free parts. It is as if the musician has learned that entire freedom is not an answer to expression—that the player needs boundaries, or bases, from which to explore. Some players with this attitude are Miles Davis, Cecil Taylor, John Klemmer, Keith Jarrett, Chick Corea, Pharaoh Sanders, McCoy Tyner, Alice Coltrane, Wayne Shorter, Anthony Braxton, Don Cherry, and Sun Ra.

The free-form player places the importance of individuality of self-expression considerably ahead of popularity or acceptance by general audiences. His or her claim to musical artistry is often through music unrelated to any previous approach to music.

For Further Study

1. What relationship exists between the attitude one has toward free-form jazz and one's understanding of the way the musical elements are used by the performer in expressing musical thoughts?
2. Explain two variations of free-form technique used by performers playing this type of jazz.
3. Describe the fundamental difference between John Coltrane and Anthony Braxton in terms of their approaches to free jazz.

Suggested Additional Listening

Art Ensemble of Chicago. *The Third Decade*, ECM/Warner Brothers Records, 25014-1.

———. *Urban Bushman*, ECM/Warner Brothers Records, ECM 2-1211.

Ayler, Albert. *Vibrations*. Arista Freedom Records, AL 1000.

Bowie, Lester. *Numbers 1 and 2*, Nessa, n-1.

Braxton, Anthony. *New York, Fall 1974*.

Cherry, Don. *El Corazon*. ECM/Warner Brothers Records, ECM 1-1230.

———. *Old and New Dreams*. Black Saint Records, BSR-0013.

Coleman, Ornette. *At the "Golden Circle" Stockholm*. Blue Note Records, 842242.

———. *Science Fiction*. Columbia Records, KC 31061.

Handy, John, III. *Quote, Unquote*. Roulette Records, R 52124.

Jarman, Joseph. *Song For*, Delmark, 410.

Jazz Composers Orchestra. JCOA Records, 1001/2.

Mitchell, Roscoe. *Sound*, Delmark, 408.

Murray, David. *Morning Song*. Black Saint Records, BSR-0075.

Sanders, Pharaoh. *Deaf Dumb Blind*. Impulse Records, AS 9199.

———. *Journey to the One*. Theresa Records, TR 108/109.

Shepp, Archie. *Four for Trane*. Impulse Records, A-71.

———. *On This Night*. Impulse Records, A-97.

Sun Ra. *The Futuristic Sounds of Sun Ra*, Savoy, MG 12138.

———. *Sun Song*, Delmark, 411.

Taylor, Cecil. *Silent Tongues*. Unit Core Records, 30551.

———. *Unit Structures*. Blue Note Records, 84237.

World Saxophone Quartet. *W.S.Q.* Black Saint Records, BSR-0027.

Additional Reading Resources

Budds, Michael J. *Jazz in the Sixties*.

Jost, Ekkehard. *Free Jazz*.

Litweiler, John. *The Freedom Principle of Jazz After 1958*.

Note: Complete information, including name of publisher and date of publication, is provided in this book's bibliography.

Notes

1. Dan Morgenstern, "The October Revolution—Two Views of the Avant Garde in Action," *Down Beat* 34, no. 30 (November 1964): 33.

2. Ornette Coleman, "Lorraine," *Tomorrow Is the Question,* Contemporary Records, M3569.

3. Coleman, *Tomorrow Is the Question.*

4. Ornette Coleman, *Free Jazz,* Atlantic Records, 1364.

5. Howard Mandel, "Ornette Coleman," *Down Beat* 54, no. 8 (August 1987): 17.

6. Ornette Coleman, *Smithsonian Collection of Classic Jazz,* liner notes, 1973: 43.

7. Cecil Taylor, "Enter Evening," *Smithsonian Collection of Classic Jazz.*

8. Cecil Taylor, "Idut" and "Serdab," *New World Records, 201.*

9. Cecil Taylor, *3 Phasis,* New World Records, 303.

10. John Coltrane, "Ogunde," *Expression,* Impulse Records, A-9120.

11. John Coltrane, *Giant Steps,* Atlantic Records, 1311.

12. John Coltrane (Miles Davis album), *Kind of Blue,* Columbia Records, CL 1355.

13. John Coltrane, "The Father and The Son and The Holy Ghost," *Meditations,* Impulse Records, A-9110.

14. John Coltrane, *A Love Supreme,* Impulse Records, A-77.

15. Gordon Kopulos, "John Coltrane: Retrospective Perspective," *Down Beat* 38, no. 14 (July 1971): 40.

16. John Coltrane, *The Best of John Coltrane,* Impulse Records, AS-9200-2.

17. John Coltrane, *The Best of John Coltrane: His Greatest Years,* Impulse Records, AS-9223-2.

18. Ekkehard Jost, *Free Jazz* (New York: Da Capo Press, 1981), 181.

19. *Heliocentric Worlds of Sun Ra,* vol. 1, ESP 1014 (vol. 2, ESP 1017).

20. Art Ensemble, *A Jackson in Your House,* Affinity, AFF 9; *People in Sorrow,* Nessa, 3.

21. Anthony Braxton, *Anthony Braxton,* New York, Fall 1974, Arista Records, AL 4032.

22. Greg Osby, *3-D Lifestyles,* Blue Note, 98635; *Man Talk for Moderns* Vol. 10, Blue Note, 95414.

23. *Down Beat* 62, no. 3 (March 1995): 18.

24. Henry Threadgill, *Carry the Day,* Columbia, 66995.

25. Albert Ayler, *Bells,* E.S.P. Disk, 1011.

26. Leonard Feather, "Archie Shepp Jazz: Portrait in Passion," *Los Angeles Times,* 10 April 1966, 23.

27. Dan Morgenstern, "The October Revolution—Two Views of the Avant Garde in Action," *Down Beat* 34, no. 30 (November 1964): 33.

28. Eric Dolphy, "Out to Lunch," *Three Decades of Jazz (1959–1969);* Ken McIntyre and Eric Dolphy, *Looking Ahead,* Prestige Records, 8247.

29. McCoy Tyner, *Sama Layuca,* Milestone Records, M-9056; *Together,* Milestone Records, M-9087; *Reflections,* Milestone Records, M-47062.

CHAPTER

12

Crossover,
Third Stream,
Latin Jazz

"The greatness of jazz lies in the fact that it never ceases to develop and change."[1]

The evolution of musical styles is often metaphorically referred to as a collection of streams that share a common source but have branched to create individual identities. However, unlike its river analogue, once a musical stream branches from its source it is still subject to the influences of all other musical streams around it. Musical streams, in essence, share a common riverbed: the cultural milieu of the day. Because they often share listeners, performers, and critics, elements of each style tend to cross over into one another, creating even newer streams.

Musical crossovers are certainly not new to jazz. The players of jazz have always borrowed from anywhere and everywhere. The terms **crossover** and **fusion,** however, became especially prevalent during the late 1950s and into the 1970s, after rock and roll had captured the attention of the public, opening new doors for the development of jazz itself.

The fact that jazz's art status was certain led many to question whether it was foul play to assimilate the characteristics of other clearly delineated musical styles. How classical can jazz become and still remain jazz? Likewise, where does one draw the line between jazz and rock expressions? Questions such as these have unsettled, time and again, our efforts to fix a firm definition of jazz. As frustrating as this constant assimilation of other idioms is for historians, it is also the driving force behind the evolving jazz musical stream. The very fact that jazz is unique and indigenous to America demonstrates the multiplicity of cultural influences at work here and absent in the same proportions anywhere else. Jazz is a carefully blended style that depends on its past, but now it also depends on the fertile crossovers from the various musical styles around it.

The degree to which the crossover occurs and the directions in which it moves influence any newly emerging musical style. Sometimes the crossover is one sided, as when one stream assimilates much but exports little. In contrast, a more equal fusion can occur that creates a new style capable of being claimed by each of the contributing streams. Third-stream music is more typical of the former. Jazz has continually borrowed from the European classical model, but the reverse—the classical use of jazz idioms—has been only sporadic and short lived. Jazz/rock fusion has proven to be a more equal exchange. Successful rock groups such as Blood, Sweat and Tears or Sting have borrowed jazz idioms and even players for their mainly rock sound. Jazz groups, as early as the Ramsey Lewis Trio, have in turn imported the more frozen harmonic structure and rhythmic insistence typical of rock to open new doors for improvisational freedom.[2]

The two most dominant jazz crossover areas of the 1960s and 1970s occurred with the classical and rock

Gunther Schuller (standing) and Dizzy Gillespie.
Courtesy of Ray Avery

163

streams. Since that time, the rock stream has itself become even more multifaceted, creating new opportunities for jazz crossover. This chapter deals with one of the earliest recognized crossovers to influence jazz: third-stream and Latin jazz.

Third Stream

Throughout jazz's history, composers have struck a balance between the fully composed pieces typical of Western European models and the more open improvisatory structures characteristic of the oral tradition. The cool era marked a move toward the more fully composed and formally defined works. The hard bop period was, in contrast, a call for a return to the more individual and spontaneous oral tradition. Third-stream jazz can be seen as an extension of the cool compositional style and can be linked to Gunther Schuller, who participated with Miles Davis on the *Birth of the Cool* album. In fact, the phrase *third stream* is usually attributed to Schuller, although writer John S. Wilson is also credited with inventing it.

Third-stream jazz shares both the instrumental sound and the instrumental variety first employed during the cool era. The jazz musicians play their instruments in a manner closely resembling the technique used by symphonic players, which employs a precise tonal attack and a minimum of vibrato. Third stream, also like cool, introduces more exotic and typically classical instruments, such as the French horn, oboe, bassoon, and cello. The harmonies used in third-stream music are similar to those associated with contemporary jazz; however, musical forms—such as the fugue, canon, theme and variations, and other extended types—were borrowed from classical music.[3] The use of these forms by third-stream composers resulted in a return to a more polyphonic type of composition. Classical music markedly differs from jazz in its use of meter and rhythmic pulse. Although present in both, jazz has always given it great prominence. Third-stream jazz often uses a more classical notion of rhythm, which gives more weight to the melodic and harmonic activity than to a strong rhythmic pulse. For this reason, some contend that third-stream music cannot be considered jazz.[4]

Gunther Schuller

Gunther Schuller was a French horn player with the Metropolitan Opera in New York and has composed both classical and third-stream pieces. From 1967 to 1977 he was the director of the New England Conservatory of Music in Boston. He therefore brought much of his classical training to his efforts in third-stream jazz. Schuller's "Abstraction" and Larry Austin's "Improvisation for Orchestra and Jazz Soloists" are good examples of early third-stream music.

Robert Freedman's "An Interlude" is an example of a third-stream composition that uses classical models of polytonal and polymodal techniques.[5] Leon Dallin defines a polytonal composition as one that clearly emphasizes two or more tonal centers at the same time.[6] Polymodal music uses two modes (major and minor) with the same tonic or two forms of the same chord simultaneously. Dallin calls it "dual modality".

Jazz as an art form has also been embraced by the classical art world through commissions of jazz works for performance by symphony orchestras, for example, Brubeck's *Dialogues for Jazz Combo and Symphony Orchestra*,[7] Rolph Lieberman's *Concerto for Jazz Band and Symphony Orchestra*, and John Graas's *Jazz Symphony No. 1*. These compositions fall into two distinct groups: (1) compositions that contain jazz elements intended for performance by large symphonic orchestras using traditional instrumentation and (2) concerto grosso approaches that place a small jazz group of seven or eight players within a large symphonic orchestra.

Too often, however, the concerto grosso format offers a little jazz and a little of the classical ensemble but no integrated effect. John Lewis's "Sketch" is an example of a third-stream composition that combined the Modern Jazz Quartet and the Beaux Arts String Quartet.[8] During this performance, neither of the two groups seem to lose their identities, but an integrated feeling is still created.

During the late 1950s, the Modern Jazz Quartet proved to be a pivotal group between cool and third stream. John Lewis's classical training can be seen in the composed nature of the ensemble passages and the formal compositional structures used. His use of Renaissance brass sounds and his own characteristic improvisatory style offers yet another third-stream blend in his composition "Piazza Navonna"[9] (NW, 216, side 2, band 4). In a manner similar to Lewis's "Sketch," Chuck Mangione also merged his jazz quintet with a symphony orchestra as well as a full choir on the album *Land of Make Believe*.[10]

On closer inspection of third-stream techniques, particularly the use of more fully composed compositional forms, we find that composers throughout the history of jazz have been importing classical techniques. Scott Joplin used quite strict forms for his rags, and Jelly Roll Morton was a master of the compositional concept of theme and variations. Duke Ellington's music certainly reflects the power of a classical compositional approach in a strictly jazz medium. Only during the third-stream period, however, was such a conscious effort to assimilate classical music idioms evident.

The Sauter-Finegan Orchestra was an earlier attempt to bridge the gap between jazz and classical music. The orchestra was originally organized strictly as a recording orchestra and was strongly influenced by the impressionistic music of Debussy and Ravel. Eddie Sauter was as well known an arranger for the Benny Goodman orchestra as Bill Finegan was for the Glenn Miller orchestra. Their most ambitious effort was the

COLORPLATE 1   PRESERVATION HALL JAZZ BAND, NEW ORLEANS, 1989.
LEFT TO RIGHT: LOUIS NELSON, TROMBONE; FRANK OXLEY, DRUMS; "KID
SHIEK" POLA, TRUMPET; MANNY CRUSTO, CLARINET; CHESTER ZARDES,
BASS; JEANETTE KIMBALL, PIANO; LES MUSCUTT, BANJO. Photo by Jan
Steele.

COLORPLATE 2   TODAY THERE ARE JAZZ FESTIVALS ALL OVER THE WORLD.
Photo by Jan Steele.

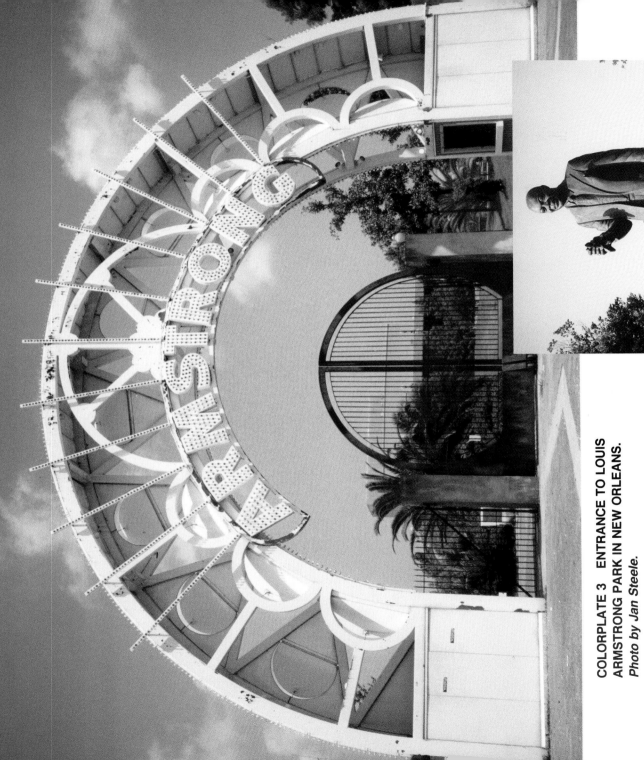

COLORPLATE 3   ENTRANCE TO LOUIS ARMSTRONG PARK IN NEW ORLEANS.
Photo by Jan Steele.

COLORPLATE 4   STATUE OF ARMSTRONG IN LOUIS ARMSTRONG PARK, NEW ORLEANS.
Photo by Jan Steele.

COLORPLATE 5   JOE "KING" OLIVER'S ORCHESTRA. PICTURE TAKEN AT THE NEW ORLEANS JAZZ MUSEUM. LEFT TO RIGHT: HONORE DUTREY, TROMBONE; WARREN "BABY" DODDS, DRUMS; JOE "KING" OLIVER, TRUMPET; LOUIS ARMSTRONG, SLIDE TRUMPET; LIL' HARDIN, PIANO; BILL JOHNSON, BANJO (ALSO BASS). *Photo by Jan Steele.*

COLORPLATE 8 ORNETTE COLEMAN.
Photo by Carl Baugher.

COLORPLATE 10
JULIUS HEMPHILL.
Photo by Carl Baugher.

COLORPLATE 11 HAMIET BLUIETT.
Photo by Carl Baugher.

COLORPLATE 13
JOSEPH JARMAN.
Photo by Carl Baugher.

COLORPLATE 14   LESTER BOWIE.
Photo by Carl Baugher.

COLORPLATE 16 CHICK COREA.
Photo by Mitchell Seidel.

Listening Guide

Demonstration 32
(cassette 2, side A, track 5; CD 2, track 5)

Modern Jazz Quartet

Milt Jackson, vibes
John Lewis, piano
Percy Heath, bass
Kenny Clarke, drums
"Django"

This composition is named in memory of the French gypsy guitarist Django Reinhardt, who died in 1953.

0:00 (A) Piano and vibraphone statement of the theme on which the work is based. The first 2 measures offer the motive that generates the entire theme and piece.

0:14 Second 4-bar phrase that answers the first. Still uses the same motive.

0:26 Third 4-bar phrase that extends the second and leads to the second part of the opening theme, which is itself derived from the first part used in these 3 opening phrases.

0:39 (B) Second section of the opening theme. The new motive is just 3 notes shared between bass, piano, and vibes.

0:52 Concluding 4 bars of this second section, which slows down before solos begin.

1:06 (A) Vibe solo. 2 choruses of ABA. Tempo picks up with a light swing feel. Listen for the light comping in the piano behind the solo (12 bars).

1:33 (B) Motivic use of the theme in vibe solo as a set up to the next chorus (8 bars).

1:50 (A) Return to swing feel to close the first chorus.

1:59 Motivic bass line under the soloist.

2:16 (A) Second chorus follows the same formal design as the first. Return to straight time (first of 2 6-bar phrases).

2:29 Second 6-bar phrase to complete the 12-bar section.

2:42 (B) Middle phrase of the second chorus (8 bars).

2:59 (A) Return to swing feel for final 12 bars of the second chorus. Motivic bass line reappears.

3:25 A double-speed statement (diminution) of the second part of the opening theme used as an interlude between solos.

3:34 (A) Piano solo begins (demonstration tape fades out here). The same formal structure used for the vibe solo is followed for the piano solo—2 choruses of ABA.

4:00 (B) Listen for repeated notes in bass (demonstration tape fades out here).

4:17 (A) Same bass motive used under solo.

4:43 (A) of second chorus.

5:10 (B) Same repeated notes in the bass.

5:27 (A) Last 12 bars with bass motive underneath.

5:53 Opening theme is repeated at the same tempo as the beginning.

6:30 Second section of opening (now closing) theme.

7:00 Slows down and ends.

Jazz in Classical Composition

Classical composers were actually first in their efforts to cross over the classical/jazz line. The most lasting and popular attempt to include jazz idioms in classical music occurred in France in the 1920s. Composers such as Darius Milhaud, in his travels to the United States, actually obtained firsthand knowledge of the New Orleans jazz style as heard in Harlem.[14] As a result of his trip, he composed a work, *La Création du Monde,* about which he writes, "I adopted the same orchestra as used in Harlem, and I made wholesale use of the jazz style to convey a purely classical feeling."[15]

Rhythmic and harmonic jazz elements were consciously used in France as exotic music references to the free-spirited music of the African American. This interest in jazz was also promoted among literary leaders such as Jean Cocteau, who, in his essay, *Le Coq et l'arlequin,* holds up American jazz as an example of the

Lieberman work, which was extremely well received when performed and recorded with the Chicago Symphony Orchestra.

The Stan Kenton orchestra showcased several third-stream compositions. William Russo's compositions for this orchestra were often bold and adventuresome in their blend of classical, avant-garde, and jazz elements[11] (NW, 216, "Mirage," side 1, band 4, NW, 216, "Eldon Heath," side 2, band 1).

"All About Rosie" from the *Modern Jazz Concert* album demonstrates how George Russell developed an extended jazz (or third stream) work from a children's song-game.[12]

Yet another approach to third-stream music is the actual use of classically composed music in a larger jazz work or the complete statement of a classical work with jazz interpretation. The Swingle Singers used many of Bach's pieces, and Hubert Laws effectively recorded Stravinsky's *Rite of Spring.*[13]

virtue of indigenous and more accessible music that should be assimilated by classical composers.

Ernst Krenek, an Austrian composer, looking to the success of jazz in Paris, wrote a "jazz opera" called *Jonny Spielt Auf* that was popular all over Europe. It was translated into eighteen languages and performed in over a hundred cities. The leading character was, appropriately, a black jazz musician. Stravinsky's *Ragtime for Eleven Instruments* is another example of a classical composer adopting jazz idioms for use in a classical composition.

Stravinsky crossed over in the reverse direction when he wrote the *Ebony Concerto* for the Woody Herman band. This piece is unique in that it is written by a classical composer for a traditional jazz ensemble.

In the United States, composers such as Gershwin and Gould also worked in a classical medium that reflected jazz influences. These composers remained classical in their form and style but made use of the jazz idioms in a generalized sense. Claude Bolling's *Suite for Flute and Jazz Piano* serves as a clear example of this type of fully composed yet jazz-imbued composition. On his own recording of this piece with the renowned classical flutist Pierre Rampal, the use of jazz inflections and idioms helps create a spirit of improvisation even though the composition is completely notated.[16]

These classical works, although greatly influenced by jazz, are not considered to be third stream because they originate from, and maintain their allegiance to, the classical idiom. The deciding feature seems to be

Listening Guide

William Russo
"Eldon Heath"

0:00 Brass counterpoint lines in a free-flowing meter; vague tonal area.
0:28 Transition melodic figures in brass.
0:45 Sax/brass ostinato, more metric.
1:03 Trombone solo with ostinato background.
1:40 Soft and increasingly loud low brass punches; fading ostinato.
2:07 Cymbal roll leading to rhythm section and brass in tempo with jazz phrasing and accents.
2:36 Saxophone solo with very light rhythm; long-tone chordal support in other instruments; muted trumpets.
3:09 Strong brass chords.
3:15 Trombone solo returns.
3:22 Sax and brass ostinato return.
3:47 End.

*New World Collection, 216, side 2, band 1.

Listening Guide

Demonstration 33 (cassette 2, side A, track 6; CD 2, track 6)

Tito Puente
"Donna Lee"

This is an arrangement of the Charlie Parker classic "Donna Lee."

0:00 Drum introduction; notice the interlocking drum patterns.
0:24 Horn players enter with an introductory section that will appear again later as interludes between solos. Notice the cross-rhythms between the trombones (and bass player) and the other horn players (alto saxophone, trumpet, and piccolo).
0:32 The melody (head) is played in unison by the saxophone, trumpet, and piccolo while the trombones and bass play an accompanying cross-rhythm.
0:46 The second part of the head over the same chords.
0:57 Alto saxophone lead-in to a solo over the same chords as the head. Notice the change in the rhythmic backup characterized by heavily syncopated cross-rhythms.
1:11 Second part of the solo chorus.
1:24 Second chorus with a new stop-time backup in the other horn players.
1:37 Horn players drop out, and solo continues for the second part of the second chorus.
1:50 Trumpet solo begins. Same backup is maintained.
2:02 Second part of first chorus.
2:15 Flüegelhorn solo with the stop-time backup.
2:28 Second part of flüegelhorn chorus.
2:40 Interlude similar to the introduction. Complex cross-rhythms are used.
2:50 Piccolo lead-in to solo.
2:53 Solo actually begins. Notice the bop phrasing and accents.
3:06 Second part of solo chorus.
3:19 Second chorus begins with the addition of the stop-time backup.
3:31 Second section of the second chorus.
3:44 Repeat of introduction.
3:50 Repeat of the opening head.
4:03 Second part of the head.
4:14 Drums alone to end the performance.
4:30 End.

the direction in which the crossover moves. A composer who is associated primarily with jazz but who uses classical models or idioms is considered a participant in the third stream. On the other hand, classical composers who fuse jazz expressions in their works are generally excluded, most likely because the third stream is a notion belonging primarily to jazz historians. Despite the shading in terminology, it is worth noting that the crossover between the classical and jazz worlds is a two-way street. Both stylistic streams have been enriched by their association with each other. As we saw in the previous chapters, these two musical streams will again interact as the avant-garde school of jazz emerges.

Latin Jazz

Another important area of jazz crossover involves the music of Latin America. The resulting blend of Latin rhythms and jazz is often referred to as **salsa,** which in translation means "a hot, piquant sauce." The term was adapted to **soulsa** to describe a further crossover of Latin jazz and soul music. Salsa is recognized today as a distinctive style by the jazz community as a whole. An example of infectious, sensitive salsa is *Machaca,* featuring Clare Fisher and Salsa Picante.[17]

Latin rhythms have been a part of the jazz scene almost from the beginning. In fact, this element can be traced back easily to prejazz (see chapter 2). Jelly Roll Morton, for example, often used the tango as a means of expression, and W. C. Handy's "St. Louis Blues"

contains a tango section. Both Dizzy Gillespie and Stan Kenton featured Latin rhythms in the 1940s, and the bossa nova in the 1950s and 1960s brought Brazilian rhythms to public notice.

Kenton disbanded briefly in the 1950s, and many of his musicians were absorbed by Rene Touzet and his band. Touzet used what were primarily vocal musical patterns on which the rhythm section could build to ecstatic heights. The jazz-oriented, powerful brass section from Kenton's band soon made these patterns a driving force.

Reggae, a Jamaican brand of rhythm and blues, is another major influence. Artists as diverse as Paul Simon, Eric Clapton, Elton John, and Stevie Wonder use reggae's captivating beat. Audiences are now showing their willingness to accept the "real thing" in reggae. Like jazz with rock, jazz with reggae has gained public acceptance.

Because the interrelationships among Latin, African, and Cuban rhythms are so technical and complex, it is impossible to fully distinguish among them. Yet each offers distinctive elements as they fuse with jazz.

Jazz even has a defector from Cuba among its ranks in saxophonist Francisco (Paquito) D'Rivera, who is possibly one of the foremost new contributors in the type of jazz that displays both Cuban and American cultures.[18] He had been playing in Cuba with musicians who eventually organized a group called Irakere. This band plays a combination of fiery jazz, rock, and Cuban sounds.

In New York especially, Latin bands mix African-Cuban rhythms, jazz improvisation, and other contemporary jazz thoughts with exciting results. Carlos Santana, Willie Bobo, Tito Puente, Johnny Pacheco, and

Tito Puente.
Lee Tanner/The Jazz Image

Willie Colon are recognized leaders in the field, but Ray Barretto, an energetic percussionist, receives the most publicity. His audiences are mainly bilingual and are very much at home with jazz and such rhythms as the mambo.

Carlos Santana is a dynamic leader whose playing of both Latin music and jazz is accepted by fans of both idioms. If it were possible to hear only two examples of Santana's exciting music, we suggest that they be *Caravanserai* and Barretto's *Carnaval*.[19]

Summary

Crossover is a very general term that applies to the fusion of any two types of music. As we have seen, jazz has fused, or crossed over, quite successfully with classical and Latin music. As we will see in the next chapter, the vitality of jazz continued to fuse with rock. As new musics develop, jazz will no doubt continue to import those qualities that it finds interesting and useful from new emerging musical styles. As jazz matures and becomes an ever-increasing musical force, it will also export a larger number of those idioms that it has developed throughout its history. We will always know that jazz is successfully crossing over as long as new styles emerge that tend to defy categorization yet help shape the developing jazz tradition.

For Further Study

1. Present-day jazz is a potpourri of many years of continuous development. Name the sources and kinds of music jazz musicians adopt today.

2. What are some characteristics of third-stream music? Name the jazz era from which it stemmed.

3. Listen to the Modern Jazz Quartet playing with a string quartet to produce third-stream music in the selection "Sketch" from the album *Third Stream Music* (Atlantic, 1345). How would you describe the total effect? What musical elements seem to be most prominent in the string quartet's part? What jazz elements are most prominent in the Modern Jazz Quartet's part?

Suggested Additional Listening

Dankworth, Johnny, and the London Philharmonic Orchestra. *Collaboration.* Roulette Records, SR 52059.

Evans, Bill. *Bill Evans Trio with Symphony Orchestra.* Verve Records, V6-8640.

Leviev, Milcho. *Music for Big Band and Symphony Orchestra.* Philippopolis Records, PH-101.

Lewis, John. *European Windows.* RCA Victor Records, LPM-1742.

McCann, Les. *Beaux J. PooBoo.* Limelight Records, LS-8625.

Martin, Skip. *Scheherajazz.* Somerset Records, P-9700.

New Wave in Jazz. Impulse Records, A-90.

Orchestra. Capitol Records, ST-484.

Additional Reading Resources

Megill, Donald D., and Demory, Richard S. *Introduction to Jazz History.*

Notes

Note: Complete information, including name of publisher and date of publication, is provided in this book's bibliography.

1. Gunther Schuller, *The Swing Era* (London: Oxford University Press, 1989), 846.

2. Julie Coryell and Laura Friedman, *Jazz-Rock Fusion* (New York: Delta Books, 1979), ix.

3. Harold Shapero, "On Green Mountain," *Modern Jazz Concert,* Columbia Records, WL127.

4. Gunther Schuller, "Transformation," *Modern Jazz Concert.*

5. Robert Freedman, "An Interlude," *Jazz in the Classroom,* Berklee Records, BLPIA.

6. Leon Dallin, *Techniques of Twentieth Century Composition* (Dubuque, Iowa: Wm. C. Brown, 1974), 132.

7. The New York Philharmonic Orchestra with the Dave Brubeck Quartet, conducted by Leonard Bernstein, *Bernstein Plays Brubeck Plays Bernstein,* Columbia Records, CL 1466.

8. The Modern Jazz Quartet, *Third Stream Music,* Atlantic Records, 1345.

9. The Modern Jazz Quartet, "Piazza Navonne," New World Records, 216.

10. Chuck Mangione, *Land of Make Believe,* Mercury Records, SRM 1-684.

11. William Russo, "Mirage" and "Eldon Heath," New World Records, 216.

12. George Russell, "All About Rosie," *Modern Jazz Concert.*

13. Swingle Singers, *Bach's Greatest Hits,* Philips Records, 200-097; Metropolitan Pops Choir with Robert Mandel, *More of the Greatest Hits of Bach,* Laurie Records, LLP 2023; The Jacques Loussier Trio, *Play Bach Jazz,* London Records, 3289; Hubert Laws, *Rite of Spring,* CTI Records, 6012; Nina Simone, "Love Me or Leave Me," *Little Girl Blue,* Bethlehem Records, 6028.

14. Darius Milhaud, *Notes without Music* (New York: Alfred A. Knopf, 1953), 136.

15. Ibid., 148.

16. Claude Bolling, *Suite for Flute and Jazz Piano,* Columbia Records, M33233.

17. Clare Fisher and Salsa Picante, *Machaca,* Discovery Records, DS-835.

18. Paquito D'Rivera, *Paquito Blowin',* Columbia Records, FC 37374.

19. Carlos Santana, *Caravanserai,* Columbia Records, KC 31610; Ray Barretto, *Carnaval,* Fantasy Records, 24713.

Outstanding Jazz Compositions of the Twentieth Century. Columbia Records, C 2S 831/C2L 31.

Russell, George. *Jazz in the Space Age/New York, New York.* RCA Records, 2-4017.

———. *Outer Thoughts.* Milestone Records, M-47027.

Schuller, Gunther. *Jazz Abstractions.* Atlantic Records, S-1365.

Stoltzman, Richard. *Begin Sweet World.* RCA Victor Records, 1-7124.

CHAPTER 13

Crossover, Jazz Fusion

"A hamburger and a hot dog deserve an equally important place in history as caviar and champagne, because we can't do without any of it. We have to have all of it. We have to have french fries. They have to be part of the culture at a certain time in history because they represent the culture."[1]

Early Jazz Rock

By the late 1960s, rock had captured the attention of America's listeners. It was quickly becoming the most influential musical style in the United States, perhaps even the western world. Jazz found in this popular music yet another opportunity for the assimilation of new musical idioms, sounds, and concepts. This crossover with rock is most commonly referred to as "jazz/rock fusion" or just "fusion." Although fusion is not new to jazz's development, it became a popularized notion during the 1960s, and the term itself became specifically associated with groups that crossed over the jazz/rock line.

Miles Davis proved to be a central figure in the development of jazz/rock fusion. After his impact with the *Birth of the Cool* record, he continued to effect change in the development of jazz. His albums *In a Silent Way* (1969) and *Bitches' Brew* (1970) added an impetus to the jazz/rock crossover movement that is still being felt. The list of personnel who worked with Davis during these years reads like a Who's Who of jazz/rock fusion for the 1970s and 1980s: Herbie Hancock, Chick Corea, Wayne Shorter, John McLaughlin, Joe Zawinul, Tony Williams, and Lenny White. These musicians later formed or participated in the most influential fusion groups of the 1970s and early 1980s, particularly Chick Corea with Return to Forever, Joe Zawinul and Wayne Shorter with Weather Report, and John McLaughlin with the Mahavishnu Orchestra.

Jazz, throughout its history, has always cut a careful course between an orally developed tradition and the more schooled, literate tradition characteristic of European classical music. As third-stream jazz was a move toward the literate classical tradition, jazz/rock fusion at first offered a balancing gesture toward the more improvised oral tradition. Rock in the 1950s and 1960s had a raw energy that offered a new rhythmic backdrop for jazz improvisation. Although the harmonic activity in rock was somewhat primitive with respect to jazz, its rhythmic intensity offered a different type of cohesion for extended jazz improvisation.

In addition to the newer electronic instruments and greater amplification, jazz also borrowed the new and increasingly complex rock rhythms. These rock patterns make use of straight eighth notes instead of the uneven eighth notes more typical of swing or bop. It is not uncommon for fusion groups to use both straight and swing eighths simultaneously, with rock patterns in the rhythm section as soloists play bop lines against it.

The changes in the rhythm section are as definite as those made in the bop era when the means of displaying the pulse was also revolutionized. Rock and jazz/rock bass players now usually play an electric bass or bass guitar instead of a traditional stand-up string bass. This

Herbie Hancock.
AP/Wide World Photos

allows them to play faster, invent more complex lines, and use electronic **effects** to alter their sound. The bass player also takes a more prominent position in the ensemble, often offering solo lines as well as basic harmonic support.

The rhythm guitar in most fusion groups plays the chordal punctuations that had been previously assigned to the piano, and the drums, like the bass, move to a more prominent position in the ensemble. Don Ellis explained the manner in which the drummer plays in this idiom:

In the drums, whereas in bebop the sound went to the cymbals, in rock music, (although the cymbals are still used) the opposite has happened, and the basic patterns have gone back to the drums. One of the reasons, I suspect, is that because of the high level of volume at which a great deal of rock is played the cymbals give no definition to the time and merely add a blanket to the overall sound. So the burden of time-keeping has now come back to the snare and bass drums. This also gives it a more solid rhythmic feel. For anyone who likes to swing hard, I think this is a definite step in the right direction.

The patterns the snare drum and the bass drum are playing, instead of being sporadic, are now more regular in the sense that they are played continually.[2]

In later fusion groups, the rhythm section is further expanded with multiple keyboards and electronic effects for most all the other instruments. The commitment to a dominant rhythm section is a central feature of most jazz/rock fusion.

Miles Davis (1926-1991)

Perhaps no figure in the history of jazz has influenced as many different styles over as long a time as Miles Davis has. His prominence in the jazz scene was not paralleled by the stereotypical attributes, poverty, and prodigious talent normally associated with leading jazz players. He was born of a relatively affluent family in 1926 and was even able to attend Juilliard for a short time in 1944. He was never a highly polished trumpet player in technical terms, but he had an aggressive nature that continually pushed him to the forefront of jazz developments. He reigned there despite dramatic musical changes inside and outside the jazz world.

The forthright approach that characterized Davis much of his career began as early as 1944, when he convinced Billy Eckstine to allow him to "sit in" with Earl Hines during a tour through St. Louis.[3] At that time, Hines's band, later Eckstine's band, represented the front edge of the big-band bop style and no doubt captured Davis's attention. In 1945, after his short stay at Juilliard, Davis sought out Charlie Parker, the leading bop player of the day, and actually roomed with him. His association with Parker gave him an unusually early (for his age) start in the top echelons of the jazz community. He even took over Fats Navarro's prestigious chair in Eckstine's band when he was only twenty. Before

Navarro, this chair was defined by Gillespie himself as the showplace for trumpet virtuosity. Although following in the Gillespie tradition, Davis was not the technician necessary for the bravura bop style. Whether this incongruity between style and ability had anything to do with Davis's later, more fragmented and slower melodic style has been much debated.

Davis left Eckstine to play with Parker from 1947 to 1949, at which time he began working with members of the Claude Thornhill band. His association with these players led to the famous Birth of the Cool recordings. Davis assumed leadership during the work on this album, which featured the cool style initiated by Gerry Mulligan, Gil Evans, and John Lewis. Fronting the band catapulted Davis to a newly found prominence among jazz players that endures today.

By 1954, Davis had begun to develop the playing style that characterizes much of his later work. Rather than the high-energy, note-filled melodic lines typical of the bop era, Davis borrowed the softer tone of the cool era and slowed down the melodic activity. His phrasing became fragmented, leaving open spaces for just the rhythm section. He set himself apart from the rhythm section by playing scale-oriented rather than chord-oriented long notes. When responses are made to the energy of the rhythm section, they are usually in the form of short motivic fragments.

By 1958 Davis's playing style was freed further by his use of modal scales and slower-moving harmonies. Rather than weave a melody through complex bop or funk harmonies, he suspended his melodies, based on early modes, above the harmony. The lack of harmonic movement and the scalar concept of improvisation seemed to disassociate the melody from whatever rhythmic underpinning there might be. His Milestones recording demonstrates this modal and almost arrhythmic melodic approach.[4] Davis's collaboration with Gil Evans on "Summertime" produced a particularly effective demonstration of the fragmented and plaintive style to be Davis's trademark (demonstration 23). The backup riffs from the rest of the group plug the open spaces in Davis's solo, and Gershwin's slow melody could not be more appropriate for Davis's penchant for long tones.

Davis's 1959 recording of "So What" clearly demonstrates his new modal approach toward improvisation (S, side H, band 5). There are really only two different harmonies in the entire piece. During the solos, the first harmony lasts sixteen measures (approximately twenty-five seconds), and the second harmony is a half-step higher and lasts eight measures. The solo chorus is completed with a return to the first chord for another eight measures. The fact that the two harmonies are related by only a half-step is itself a move away from tradition, which would more properly dictate a move of four or five scale tones away for the contrasting harmony. The solos above this almost frozen chord progression are usually marked by an introspective and motivic melodic style.

Davis had successfully carried music through the transition from bop to cool and again on to a modal jazz that would launch players like John Coltrane (heard on the "So What" recording). He was to face yet another turn in music with the advent of rock. As rock began to dominate the popular music culture, Davis faced the dilemma confronted by most leaders in jazz: that of maintaining leadership as styles change. Just as Davis was not held to his bop heritage or trapped in the cool idiom, he would not blindly hold to his modal jazz expression and ignore the growing activity in the rock world.

In 1964 Davis made his move by calling on younger names in jazz: Tony Williams, Ron Carter, Herbie Hancock, and Wayne Shorter. He found players who were not as closely tied to the past bop and funky traditions. His *Nefertiti* shows his early efforts at assimilating some of the rock idioms.[5] But it was his 1969 album *In a Silent Way* that first truly addressed the rock issue.[6] He took on John McLaughlin, a guitarist known also to the rock world, to grant a greater integrity to his jazz/rock approach. In 1970 his next album, *Bitches' Brew,* brought his effort into focus and, with the aid of a Grammy, gained him much popularity. His rhythm section, which was characterized by rock patterns and electronic instruments, supported his already well defined modal jazz approach.[7] The cuts on this album even show a relationship to the other quickly developing jazz style: free jazz. The title cut alternates between a free, arrhythmic opening theme and hard-driving rock solo areas. Davis had again discovered a musical forefront and aggressively placed himself in the middle of it. Jazz/rock fusions were already at hand in other bands—Gary Burton, Billy Cobham (Dreams), Larry Coryell, and others —but Davis had created the dominant statement for the developing genre.

Performers of Davis's stature do not make major stylistic moves without generating controversy. Those who hold to previous styles once led by Davis might find his flirtations with newly developing styles somewhat disconcerting. In a career as dynamic as Davis's, not all musical efforts carry the same weight in his stylistic evolution. Many albums fall between the gaps of the giant steps made by *Birth of the Cool* and *Bitches' Brew.* These other albums might often lack the surprise and power of the giants, but they show a musician who continues to experiment while maintaining an individual identity. His 1985 album *You're Under Arrest* shows a new interest in commercial music and its allied recording studio sound.[8] The musical mix is more commercial, and some of the musical material is even drawn from the popular music scene (a song by pop singer Cyndi Lauper). Despite the new format, Davis is still recognizable through his melodic style: plaintive, fragmented, and somewhat isolated from its musical underpinning.

Davis was unique in his ability to sense new directions, assimilate their attributes, and then popularize the newly fused style. As a personality, his outspoken nature was sometimes as strident as his music was definitive. In many ways, he was a maverick among jazz musicians. His intensely introspective if not melancholy playing style was characterized by expressions that can be perceived as technical blunders when contrasted to the lineage of trumpet virtuosos such as Armstrong and Gillespie. Yet these same flaws in techniques offered Davis a personalized style that was conducive to his very intimate expression. His half-valved notes and broken pitches supported the glimpse he often gave us of the raw emotional world often emanating from his music.

Davis's legacy is one of melodic phrasing that breaks holes in the solo fabric while freeing the soloist from the bondage of harmonic movement. Rather than long, unbroken lines, the detail of short melodic motives took center stage. The melodic lines born of these motives then floated above the static harmonic support.

Miles Davis: Bitches' Brew

The early use of electronic instruments can be heard in Miles Davis's *Bitches' Brew.*[9] Dave Holland shares his bass role with Harvey Brooks who plays electric bass. John McLaughlin plays electric guitar, not necessarily new to jazz, and Joe Zawinul, Larry Young, and Chick Corea join in with electronic piano. Beside the horn players—Wayne Shorter on soprano sax, Bennie Maupin on bass clarinet, and Miles Davis on trumpet—the ensemble is completed with percussionist Jim Riley and with three drummers: Lenny White, Jack DeJohnette, and Charles Alias. Like rock groups do, Davis gives the rhythm section a central role in the ensemble's activities. His use of such a large rhythm section offers the soloists wide but active expanses for their solos. The title cut from this record offers a good example of how the soloists can interact with the rhythm section. They sometimes hold sustained lines in contrast to the rhythm section's activity, and at other times they act as just another member of the rhythm section and add only punctuated statements.

The harmonies used in this recording move very slowly and function modally rather than in a more tonal fashion typical of mainstream jazz. Each harmonic center appears almost frozen as the players, both independently and collectively, pull away from it, only to return and reaffirm it. The home key is established more by insistence than by the traditional tonal chord relationships. The static harmonies and the rhythm section's collective embellishment create a very open arena for improvisation. The musical result flows from basic rock patterns to hard bop textures, and at times passages are even more characteristic of free jazz. The cut entitled "Spanish Key" offers a more direct example of how a fusion rhythm section can establish a steady rhythmic drive over slowly moving harmonies. The harmonic changes occur so seldom that they create major articulation points in the composition.

Listening Guide

Demonstration 34
(cassette 2, side B, track 1; CD 2, track 7)

Miles Davis

"Bitches' Brew"*

Miles Davis, trumpet
Wayne Shorter, soprano sax
Lenny White, Jack DeJohnette, and Charles Alias, drums
Bennie Maupin, bass clarinet
Chick Corea and Joe Zawinul, electronic piano
Harvey Brooks (Fender) and Dave Holland, bass
John McLaughlin, electric guitar
Jim Riley, percussion

Complete Original Demonstration Tape

:00	Bass solo.
:07	Keyboard striking a chordal cluster with percussion.
:13	Bass solo.
:22	Keyboard cluster with percussion.
:28	Guitar enters.
:32	Bass solo.
:37	Keyboard cluster with percussion.
:40	Trumpet enters (Miles Davis) with much reverberation; section goes between trumpet entrances and keyboard clusters.
2:45	Bass solo.
2:50	Bass clarinet enters, establishing its motive.
3:27 :00	(Demonstration tape begins here.) Steady rhythm, bass clarinet and keyboard prominent, guitar playing punctuations.
3:44 :21	Trumpet solo fully integrated with the ensemble.
5:46 2:13	Listen for chromatic "comping" patterns in keyboard behind soloist.
6:10 2:46	Trumpet gives way to keyboard and guitar; plenty of heavy rhythm on drums.

7:16	3:52	Softens (Davis says "Like that—nice").
7:40	4:16	Keyboard, guitar, and drums building again; keyboard and drums very rhythmic.
8:20	4:56	Softens again, showing that music should have highs and lows.
8:42	5:18	Trumpet enters.
10:20	6:56	Rhythmic feel changed to suit Davis's new explorations.
11:06	7:42	Trumpet out. (Demonstration tape fades out here.)
11:18		Soprano sax solo backed by forceful rhythm.
12:12		Soprano sax fades.
12:15		Only rhythm with sparse keyboard interjections but building from there.
13:05		Everyone softens to build again; keyboard featured.
14:17		Keyboard clusters and bass solo alternates several times as in the beginning of the selection.
15:22		Trumpet again with lots of reverberation, alternating with the clusters as near the beginning of the selection.
16:45		New subtle rhythmic feel to back bass solo.
17:31		Add bass clarinet; intensity building again.
18:37		Trumpet enters, driving forward.
19:27		Trumpet exits; group softens only to rebuild.
20:27		Trumpet enters, rather subdued, but quickly reaches out further.
21:15		Bass alone—joined by drums, guitar, and keyboard (soon an ensemble with these players and the bass clarinet)—a long rhythmic interlude.
23:15		Bass alone, alternating with keyboard clusters several times.
23:52		Trumpet enters forcefully, as at the top of the selection, jabbing at openings.
26:03		End.

*Bitches' Brew, Columbia Records, GP 26, CS 9995.

Fusion

The fusion of jazz and rock took a new turn in the 1970s and 1980s as members of Miles Davis's *Bitches' Brew* ensemble formed their own groups: Chick Corea with Return to Forever, Joe Zawinul and Wayne Shorter with Weather Report, and John McLaughlin with the Mahavishnu Orchestra. Although all these new leaders are associated with Davis, they did not necessarily receive their musical direction solely from his influence. Corea cites the formation of the Mahavishnu Orchestra and

McLaughlin's use of the electric guitar as equally important to his own movement toward electric jazz fusion.[10]

These new groups were not characterized by the same modal harmonies and expansive solo areas as was characteristic of their work with Davis. They now showed a tighter compositional approach and a wholesale adoption of the new electronic technology. However, unlike some of the groups to follow, their performance was still based on a live ensemble interaction. The new stylistic shift common to these new groups also emphasized a virtuosic playing style. Much like bebop, the

McLaughlin has always demonstrated virtuosic technique and high-energy musical flights. He contributed the sound of rock to the jazz mainstream. In addition, he was among the first to adopt the volume and metallic tone color more typical of rock performers and place them in a more traditional jazz setting. He has influenced the current generation of guitar players, both jazz and rock, in much the same way Wes Montgomery did a generation earlier.

fusion groups demonstrated a virtuosity that was accentuated by a new but characteristic melodic angularity. The virtuosity often permeated the entire ensemble and extended the performance expectations of all the instrumentalists in the group, including the rhythm section.

The rock influence appeared most dominantly in the workings of the rhythm section. The meters and accents were often a highly developed extension of rock patterns. The volume level also moved significantly toward that common to rock groups. The soloists, however, often played boplike lines above the fast-driving textures established by the rhythm section.

There was a certain amount of controversy surrounding these new groups. Many saw the changes being made as a commercialization of jazz and a significant move away from the jazz ideal. The rock instrumentation, the increased volume, and the rock-based rhythmic feel were sometimes viewed as denials of the jazz tradition. But there were also some undeniably jazz-rooted traditions: rhythmic complexity, commitment to improvisation, virtuosic and individual expression, and syncopated ensemble passages.

John McLaughlin: The Mahavishnu Orchestra

Guitarist John McLaughlin was perhaps most responsible for the "sound" of rock heard on the Miles Davis albums *In a Silent Way* and *Bitches' Brew*. McLaughlin played in British rock bands as he was growing up, and the sound appropriate in those early groups can be heard in his later ensembles. In 1969 he made his first appearance in the American musical arena with Tony Williams's Lifetime. This same year he also joined Miles Davis to record *In a Silent Way* and later *Bitches' Brew*. After his stay with Davis, he formed the Mahavishnu Orchestra and recorded several high-energy albums. The first few albums with this group—*Inner Mounting Flame, Birds of Fire,* and *Between Nothingness and Eternity,*—clearly demonstrate the virtuosity and energetic sound associated with McLaughlin and his groups.[11]

After the second version of the Mahavishnu Orchestra disbanded, McLaughlin worked on some Indian-flavored albums with the group Shakti. Particularly notable after his work with that group was a collaboration with two other virtuoso guitarists, Paco De Lucia and Al Di Meola, and the resulting albums *Passion, Grace & Fire* and *Friday Night in San Francisco.*[12]

In addition to his formidable acoustic guitar playing, McLaughlin also embraced a newer synthesized guitar that is interfaced with the Synclavier Digital Music System. His work with this high-tech instrument can be heard on his 1985 album *Mahavishnu*, a return to the earlier Mahavishnu format. When asked why he called this new group by the same name as his previous orchestra, he said, "Personally, the kind of spirit that was established in my first ensemble with that name, something I love very much, is now present in the new band."[13]

Listening Guide

Chick Corea
"Musicmagic"*

:00 Introduction: Acoustic piano (Chick Corea).
:06 Flute enters.
:20 Piano interlude.
:31 Flute reenters.
:42 Piano alone.
1:09 Ritard and hold.
1:10 Low bass note on synthesizer and trombone.
1:17 Brass enters.
1:20 Keyboard with special effects.
1:44 Guitar featured.
2:05 Hold and introduction to newer section.
2:20 Ensemble.
2:33 Fretless sound.
2:50 Guitar solo.
3:21 Fender Rhodes solo.
3:30 Mellotron introduction for vocal.
3:43 Vocal duet—swinging background with ensemble.
4:35 Hammond organ solo—very funky.
5:25 Stop time plus Fender Rhodes.
5:36 Fender Rhodes solo.
6:23 Brass enters.
6:30 New section.
6:41 Brass enters.
6:48 Repeat of sound from 6:30.
7:02 Fender Rhodes solo over stop time, then straight funky solo.
7:52 Brass enters.
8:24 Drum solo over stop time.
8:32 Vocal returns.
8:50 Soprano sax over vocal.
9:01 Soprano sax solo.
9:17 Acoustic piano solo.
9:28 Brass enters.
9:34 Ensemble.
9:52 Piano solo.
10:02 Ensemble.
10:20 Piano solo.
10:25 Ending.
10:48 End.

*Musicmagic, Columbia Records, AL 34682.

Chick Corea.
Courtesy of Glen Wexler

Chick Corea: Return to Forever and Elektric Band

One of the most prominent and popular fusion groups of the 1970s and 1980s, Return to Forever, was led by Chick Corea, formerly with Miles Davis. Corea, a well-schooled piano player, began to use the electronic piano while with Davis. After working with his own avant-garde group, Circle, he formed Return to Forever in 1970. His move to electronic piano soon led to a complete involvement with synthesizers of all kinds.

Corea's music demonstrates a virtuosic skill in both technique and ensemble. His themes are often quite angular and complex rhythmically yet quite accessible to the listener. And despite their complexity, his records prove to be commercially successful. His music flows smoothly between up-tempo jazz, complex rock, and a more commercial rock style.

Return to Forever's 1977 album *Musicmagic*, demonstrates Corea's ability to fuse many quite distinct musical styles into a single composition.[14] The title cut moves from a very smooth commercial sound, through jazz interludes, and to "funky" rock passages. The fusion trademark—an active rock rhythmic underpinning supporting a soloist with jazz phrasing above it—appears throughout the cut. Corea opens and closes the

arrangement with acoustic piano but uses an electronic piano and synthesizers in the body of the piece.

Corea's later albums became more electronic as the instruments themselves became more accessible and more complex. With the advancing technology, outstanding keyboard players such as Corea often experiment with much smaller groups, replacing the usual complement of musicians with sophisticated electronic instruments. Unlike the seven musicians who performed for *Musicmagic*, Corea used only two or three at one time for his 1986 album *Elektric Band*.[15] The title proves to be a play on words: on the surface a reference to a poem called "Elektric City" and secondarily a reference to his heavy use of electronic instruments. Even his drummer, Dave Weckl, used an electronic drum set (Simmons) and drum synthesizer (Linn) on some of the cuts.

Corea wields this equipment quite effectively. His virtuosic keyboard technique and compositional skill showcase the potential for the new technology. His approach is still quite similar to that heard in the Return to Forever albums: rhythmically complex themes, tight ensemble, colorful orchestrations, and virtuosic display. His selection "Got a Match," from the *Elektric Band* album, offers an effective juxtaposition of jazz and rock phrasing. The solo areas again use the high-energy rock backdrop with a more typically bop solo in the foreground.

Listening Guide

Demonstration 35
(cassette 2, side B, track 2; CD 2,
track 8)

Chick Corea, Elektric Band

"Stretch It, Part I"*

Chick Corea, keyboards
John Patitucci, bass
Eric Marienthal, saxophone
Frank Gambale, guitar
Dave Weckl, drums

:00   Piano lead-in joined later by the
      saxophone.
:05   Irregular metric feel.
:09   Return to opening motivic material.
:22   Listen for the ensemble accents during this
      short contrast section.
:29   Return to irregular motivic material with
      drum fills between the disjunct melodic
      fragments.
:39   Beginning of buildup to final chords with
      irregular accents; listen for how the
      melodic fragments are accented as a part
      of the active drumming.
:51   End of Part I.

*Inside Out, GRP Records, GRD-9601.

Listening Guide

Demonstration 36
(cassette 2, side B, track 3; CD 2,
track 9)

Joseph Zawinul and Weather Report

"Birdland"*

Joseph Zawinul, Oberheim Polyphonic, Arp
2600, acoustic piano, vocal, Melodica
Wayne Shorter, soprano, tenor saxophone
Jaco Pastorius, bass, mandocello, vocals
Alex Acuna, drums
Manolo Badrena, tambourine

:00   Analog synthesizer bass line.
:18   Bass guitar with introductory motive.
:43   Synthesizer melodic rifflike motive with
       saxophone.
:55   Interlude: Long, low notes with a new
       rifflike motive above it.
1:02   Short motive over low synthesizer notes—
       builds energy.
1:31   Saxophone enters with synthesizer to
       increase energy.
1:45   Interlude to set up melody.
1:59   Main melody enters with saxophone and
       synthesizer; bass guitar plays fill-ins in
       answer to melody; repeat of melodic
       motive builds energy.
2:36   Long-held-note interlude with synthesizer
       line and some vocal sounds.
3:07   Descending chords with saxophone solo
       over them to build energy.
3:34   Return to opening bass guitar motive as
       synthesizer enters with opening synthe-
       sized bass line and some saxophone
       fills.
3:59   Saxophone and synthesizer riff as in
       opening section.
4:11   Interlude: Long notes and riff motive.
4:15   Melody returns to begin a buildup;
       the melody repeats over and over with
       increasing interplay between players.
5:48   Fade out and end.

*Heavy Weather, Columbia Records, 34418.

On his next album, *Light Years*,[16] Corea tried to
make music that would fit the radio format, that is, four-
minute songs with a consistent rhythm. This style is
more characteristic of other, more commercial groups
such as Spyro-Gyra or the Yellowjackets. He moved
away from that approach on his 1988 album *Eye of the
Beholder*[17] and returned to a live recording process that
allowed more room for performer interaction. Corea
returned to his Elektric Band in 1990 after making an
acoustic album, *Akoustic Band*.[18] On his later album
Inside Out,[19] he uses both acoustic piano and synthesizers. Some of the compositions are made up of several
smaller parts that form structures larger than are usually
found in this style. The playing and melodic design continues in the complex, angular, and virtuosic style normally associated with fusion jazz. Listen to "Stretch It"
or "Tale of Daring" (it is made up of four chapters) from
this album to hear an example of the tight ensemble and
virtuosic interplay that are increasingly associated with
Corea's compositions.

Joe Zawinul and Wayne Shorter: Weather Report

Like Chick Corea, Joe Zawinul and Wayne Shorter
worked with Miles Davis when *Bitches' Brew* was

recorded. Also like Corea, they formed one of the most
commanding fusion bands of the 1970s and 1980s:
Weather Report. A special chemistry seems to have
existed between Zawinul and Shorter that gave their band
a distinctive, popular sound. In an article by George
Varga, Zawinul credits an even earlier Miles Davis
recording with influencing his writing style: "The record
was 'Birth of the Cool,' and it had a great impact on me.
I like to write in that sound-spectrum style."[20] A majority
of the writing during Weather Report's fifteen-year

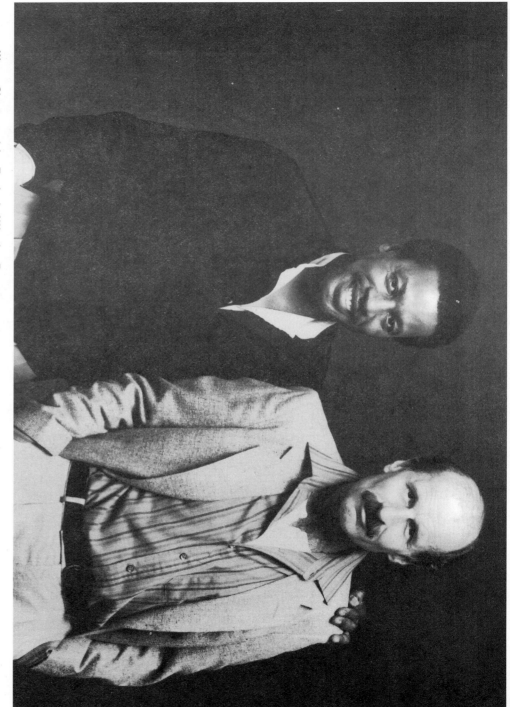

Wayne Shorter and Joe Zawinul of Weather Report.
Courtesy Randee St. Nichols

existence was done by Zawinul; his respect for the composed approach to jazz typical on *The Birth of the Cool* can be heard in his own compositions. Like Corea, Zawinul is an accomplished pianist who moved comfortably into the electronic medium of synthesizers.

Weather Report's 1980 album *Night Passage* offers several examples of fusion at different points along the jazz/rock line.[21] "Rockin' in Rhythm" is based on an Ellington tune and uses synthesizers to fill out a saxophone section sound under Shorter. The rhythm and style are mainly swing, and very little is borrowed from the rock idiom. "Fast City" offers the soloists an energetic arena for a type of virtuosity often associated with fusion groups. The thematic material is again rhythmically complex and punctuated with ensemble motives. Very often even the bass player, Jaco Pastorius, joins the ensemble in the complex unison lines.

The song most associated with Weather Report is Zawinul's "Birdland" from the album *Heavy Weather.*[22] This composition is a beacon of 1970s fusion and reappeared later in settings by the Manhattan Transfer and Quincy Jones.[23]

Zawinul and Shorter's last record together as Weather Report, *This Is This,* came out in 1986 and showed another personnel shift.[24] Victor Bailey (bass) and Mino Cinelu (percussionist/vocalist who had been playing with Weather Report) remained, but Peter Erskine returned on drums, and, more important, John Scofield was added on guitar. Scofield replaced Shorter, and the group continues work as Weather Update.

Zawinul also came out with a solo album in 1986, *Dialects,* on which he used four synthesizers and four drum machines.[25] The only other performers on the album are four vocalists, one of whom is Bobby McFerrin. "All the pieces are improvised," Zawinul told George Varga, "each sound is a personality. It's like a conversation in which I'm the focus."[26] Each piece on the album represents an exotic theme such as "6 A.M./Walking on the Nile" and "The Great Empire" (Japan). Although there is often a rhythmic rock underpinning to the pieces, the musical idiom shifts sharply from piece to piece, reflecting the exotic themes. The compositions might better be thought of as jazz/rock tone poems similar in concept to classical overtures or music for film.

Listening Guide

Demonstration 37
(cassette 2, side B, track 4; CD 2, track 10)

Michael Brecker
"*Itsbynne Reel*"*

Michael Brecker, tenor saxophone and Akai EWI
Mike Stern, guitar
Don Grolnick, piano
Charlie Haden, acoustic bass
Jeff Andrews, fretless electric bass
Jack DeJohnette, drums
Mark O'Connor, violin

Complete Original Demonstration Tape

:00	Melody on Akai EWI controller (A section of melody).
:08	Violin enters and doubles the EWI.
:15	Piano enters.
:31	New middle section (B).
:38	Repeat of B section.
:46	Return of A section.
:54	New melodic section with a development of previous melodic material with counterpoint between the violin and EWI; a sustained note creates a drone, like the frozen harmonic areas to be used later.
2:12	Bass and drums enter with jazz/rock phrasing.
2:21	Listen for synthesized brasslike "punches" on normally unaccented beats.
2:31	Melody repeats.
2:47	New ensemble-like section.
3:01	More staccato and accented phrasing.
3:17	Slow ascending bass and piano; unison notes playing a cross-rhythm.
3:48	Ensemble material for transition to solo.
4:18	Saxophone enters for a solo over the slow cross-rhythm notes in bass and piano.
4:47	Saxophone line joins slow bass and piano notes for unison transition; listen to rhythmic activity in the drums.
5:00	Solo breaks free over a frozen harmony (drone).
5:21	Harmony changes slightly (first time since 5:00); bass ascends and descends by step.
6:09	Double-time melodic ideas move to climax.
6:17	Return to original melodic idea with variations.
6:30	Violin joins the saxophone in unison over the harmonic pedal (drone), very active drumming.
7:01	The two soloists play independent lines in counterpoint.
7:40	End.

Don't Try This At Home, Impulse Records, MCAD-42229.

On his next recording, *Black Water*,[27] Zawinul returned to material more typical of his prefusion days. He also joined forces with Quincy Jones on his very popular 1989 album, *Back on the Block*, with an arrangement of his already popular composition "Birdland." This composition was performed originally by Weather Report and later set to lyrics by Jon Hendricks and performed by Manhattan Transfer. Zawinul continues to write music for a variety of media, including film and classical ensembles. His success in diverse musical arenas allows him to say of himself, "Not jazz, not rock, just me. I am my own category."[28]

Michael Brecker

Saxophonist Michael Brecker is certainly not new to the jazz/rock/fusion scene. He and his brother Randy were at the forefront of the development with their first band, Dreams, in 1970. Like many fusion players, Brecker's early musical experience includes a good deal of experience in rock bands. He later joined Steps Ahead, a group organized and led by vibist Michael Mainieri.

It was not until 1987 that he stepped out to lead his own group with the album *Michael Brecker*.[29] It was at this time that Brecker showed that the EWI (electronic wind instrument) could be a viable jazz instrument.

Brecker further established himself as a leader of a high-energy jazz strongly influenced by blues (often with a backbeat funk style) on his next album, *Don't Try This at Home*.[30] His work with Michael Stern (previously with Miles Davis on *Tutu*) resulted in high-energy virtuosic flights over driving rock as well as up-tempo jazz backups.

Stanley Jordan

Stanley Jordan has taken the electric guitar popularized by rock and turned it to a unique jazz expression. With the use of amplification, Jordan developed a touch technique on the fingerboard of the guitar that allows him to play complex contrapuntal lines not normally possible on a guitar. By using both hands to press the strings to the fretboard, he is able to create individual notes without having to pluck the strings. The normally very soft sound of the string hitting the fret is amplified enough so that the strings do not need to be strummed or picked. Without amplification this playing technique would be virtually impossible. The result is so startling that guitar

players have had to reevaluate the very potential of the instrument. Jordan's album *Magic Touch* even contains a notice to the listener that there is only one guitarist playing all the parts without the use of recorded overdubs.[31]

Jazz: A New Popularity

The controversy in the jazz world that surrounded the new jazz/rock fusion was accentuated by the new generation of players and groups who further embraced stylistic and sound ideals often found in the popular music of the 1980s. These new groups also gained a popularity not enjoyed by jazz musicians since the swing era. This new interest in jazz does not necessarily spill over to the more traditional straight-ahead jazz groups. In fact, many listeners may have virtually no knowledge of the earlier jazz traditions from which these groups evolved. As a result, a new dichotomy has developed in the jazz community between those who hold a strong allegiance to the jazz tradition (embodied in performers like Wynton Marsalis) and those whose music is sometimes called jazz but in reality may have roots more directly tied to the rock or pop tradition.

Through it all, the players themselves apparently see the larger picture and work in their new arena with a firm respect for those who preceded them. Yet they are also excited by the new prospects available in other musical styles around them. Many of these players sport backgrounds not necessarily in jazz. Rather than jazz players importing rock attributes, we have for the first time in fusion performers with backgrounds equally, if not mainly, in rock.

David Sanborn

David Sanborn is an individual positioned between these two emerging definitions of jazz. He is viewed by many as the new saxophone sound in jazz, importing strong blues and rhythm and blues influences. Contrary to the opinion held by his followers, he continues to state, "Even when I do think in categories, I never think of myself as a jazz musician. I've never called myself a jazz musician in the public forum or privately."[32]

Despite this denial, Sanborn has figured prominently in the promotion of jazz's new popularity. He has hosted a jazz radio program called *The Jazz Show* and a late night television show featuring leading jazz personalities. He also enjoys a popularity that extends beyond the traditional jazz community. His work with Bob James on *Double Vision*[33] demonstrates his improvisatory style in a more pop-sounding environment. Sanborn's use of the very high range of the saxophone, called the altissimo register, is one of the trademarks of his sound. The use of this register, although not new to saxophonists, is now widely used by most players. Also on this album is a recording called "Since I Fell For You," with vocalist Al Jarreau, which demonstrates the type of sound and style perhaps controversially called jazz by the newest listening audience of jazz/pop. This audience has only recently moved to jazz and carries with it a pop/rock background. Sanborn, like other performers in this style, offers a stylistic bridge connecting the very commercial world of pop with the jazz tradition.

Pat Metheny

Guitarist Pat Metheny has gained a great deal of popularity because of his proficiency on the instrument as well as his blend of jazz, rock, and Latin influences. His 1978 album *The Pat Metheny Group* gained for him a wider audience than that enjoyed by other otherwise successful jazz musicians. Unlike McLaughlin, Metheny's early background was primarily jazz based. His sound is therefore more in keeping with the more lyrical tradition established by Wes Montgomery.

In 1986 Metheny collaborated with Ornette Coleman to create an album, *Song X*,[34] that offers a blend of the two players' backgrounds. As the title suggests, the sounds of this album were to be viewed as songs that cannot be named, only experienced for their imagination and creativity. Metheny's most recent albums include a Grammy Award winner, *Still Life (Talking)*,[35] released in 1987. It was followed by *Letter from Home*,[36] in which Metheny makes use of sophisticated rhythmic settings that show strong Brazilian influences.

Spyro-Gyra and Yellowjackets

Since the impact of Return to Forever and Weather Report, a second generation of groups has appeared that reflect many of the first generation's rhythmic and ensemble innovations. Most prominent of these groups are Spyro-Gyra and the Yellowjackets.

Spyro-Gyra, led by saxophonist Jay Beckenstein, offers a type of jazz/rock/Latin fusion. Although pianist Jeremy Wall was later replaced by Tom Schuman, he continued as producer/composer/arranger and studio pianist. Beckenstein and Wall, together with guitarist Chet Catallo, bassist David Wolford, drummer Eli Konikoff, and percussionist Gerardo Velez, created a sound that falls somewhere between the complexities of groups such as Weather Report and a more pop style. They first became popular with their album *Morning Dance*.[37] A Latin feel characterizes many of their performances, yet they are still quite effective at establishing their own type of jazz groove with a rock underpinning. "Swing Street," from their album *Point of View*,[38] demonstrates a characteristic jazz/rock feel. Although

Stanley Jordan.
Courtesy David Barr

the title implies a swing style, the meter has definite rock attributes. It begins with a straight-ahead feel but soon develops a half-time rock **backbeat**, leaving the swing feel to the smaller beat subdivisions. This rhythmic feel is often a trademark of fusion groups. Over this backbeat, the soloists adopt a boplike melodic style as they improvise.

The Yellowjackets were formed in 1980 and, like Spyro-Gyra, follow the legacy established by Weather Report. The four members of the group—Russell Ferrante on piano and synthesizers, Jimmy Haslip on bass, Marc Russo on saxophones, and William Kennedy on drums—create complex, energetic arrangements that not only borrow from several previous jazz styles but also blend in sounds more accessible to the popular listening audiences.

The angularity of the melodic lines and the harmonic punches used by the Yellowjackets are particularly reminiscent of Weather Report. The harmonic accents work in much the same fashion that brass punches do in big-band ensembles. "Out of Town," from their 1987 album *Four Corners*,[39] exemplifies their use of synthesizers to give the impression of brass sections and their use of bop solo lines over the intricate jazz/rock–flavored backup. The Yellowjackets also blend Latin influences into their music, generally including a rock feel.

On a later album, *The Spin*,[40] the Yellowjackets move in a different, more acoustic direction. This move brought them closer to the performance tradition common to earlier jazz ensembles. Their previous recordings took a studio approach in which they used sequencers to lay down the first tracks and then build the song through successive overdubs. This album not only took an acoustic approach but also used a sequencer on only one song. "The new album required more blowing, more of a band performance." Their effort on this album was consciously directed toward "trying to keep some sort of traditional direction alive."[41]

Vocal Jazz

In the *Down Beat* readers' polls, vocal groups have been taking their place with instrumentalists and vocal soloists since 1944. The Pied Pipers won for the first six years, then the Mills Brothers for three years, and then the Four Freshmen and the Hi-Lo's. From 1958 through 1963, it was Hendricks, Lambert, and Ross Trio, then three years of the Double Six of Paris. The category was then altered to include nonjazz groups.

The tradition of Lambert, Hendricks, and Ross began in the 1950s. They developed to a high degree the art of taking old jazz records and setting lyrics to just about everything on them—not only the tunes themselves but also the improvised solos. This technique is labeled "vocalese art." Now Annie Ross has been replaced by Yolande Bavan, and Hendricks uses his

wife, Judith; his daughter, Michelle; and Bruce Scott. Their work is a contemporary form of onomatopoeia.[42]

Manhattan Transfer

Following closely in the tradition of Lambert, Hendricks, and Ross is Manhattan Transfer. They have always employed jazz overtones and used many excellent jazz instrumentalists on their recordings. However, their *Extensions* album[43] came as a revelation with the arrangement of Zawinul's "Birdland" and the lyrics by

---

Listening Guide

Demonstration 38 (cassette 2, side B, track 5; CD 2, track 11)

Yellowjackets
"Out of Town"*
Russell Ferrante, keyboards
Jimmy Haslip, bass
Marc Russo, saxophones
William Kennedy, drums

:00 Four-beat jazz feel in the bass with slow rock feel backbeat in bass drum and hand claps.

:19 Melody enters on saxophone.

:37 Piano/synthesizer enters.

:51 Synthesizer and saxophone unison melody line.

1:33 Listen for how the drummer accents ("kicks") the melody and synthesizer harmonic accents.

1:38 Return to the melody.

1:54 Transition area, backbeat accents in bass and drums (on beats 2 and 4).

2:10 Big-band ensemble style punches with saxophone, synthesizers, and drum accents.

2:22 Extended sax "fill" leading to next chorus.

2:32 New chorus with piano solo (MIDI coupled?); listen to how the ensemble "tightens" at the start of the chorus as the bass starts to walk in four and the drums settle in the straight time.

3:34 Synthesized brasslike punches with drum accents.

4:07 Transition with backbeat feel.

4:15 Saxophone and synthesizer unison line returns, with straight-time backup.

4:31 Drum solo.

4:38 Melody returns.

5:02 End.

*Four Corners, MCA Records, MCAD-5994.

Listening Guide

Demonstration 39
(cassette 2, side B, track 6; CD 2, track 12)

New York Voices (Peter Eldridge, Kim Nazarian, Sara Krieger, Darmon Meader, and Caprice Fox)
"Top Secret"*

Original Recording Demonstration Tape

:00	Synthesized ascending melodic motive.
:09	Electric bass enters.
:19	Vocal enters with melody.
1:00	Repeat of melody; listen for choral "punches" in background.
1:41	Staccato vocal section.
1:52	Contrasting legato vocal section; listen for the synthesizer support.
2:01	New chorus with more developed vocal backup punches.
2:43	Legato interlude.
3:03	"Time" returns in rhythm section.
3:14	"Scat" solo begins (Caprice Fox).
3:54	Synthesizer doubles scat solo line.
4:15	Synthesized backup becomes more animated.
4:34	Staccato section returns.
4:44	Legato section returns.
4:54	Return to "head."
5:34	Repeat of final phrase to end.
5:55	Synthesized chords with saxophone solo fades to end.
6:19	End.

*GRP Records, GRD-0589

Jon Hendricks, arranged by the group's own Janis Siegal. The album also included lyricization of "Body and Soul" by the great bop singer Eddie Jefferson. This version was a harmonized transcription of Coleman Hawkins's famous 1939 improvisation.

Manhattan Transfer's 1985 album *Vocalese* marshalls impressive jazz forces in the vocalese style.[44] It makes use of players like McCoy Tyner, Dizzy Gillespie, and the entire Basie band as well as singers such as Jon Hendricks and Bobby McFerrin. "To You" on this album demonstrates the vocalese art. The music comes from a Basie and Ellington session, *First Time*, and the solo is one originally played by Butter Jackson on trombone. The lyrics for the solo were written by Jon Hendricks and sung by Alan Paul, who described the technique: "It was hard, but Jon said if you're doing somebody's solo you've got to do it right. . . . I really listened to Butter's solo and the certain way he shaped the sounds, and Thad Jones came up and said 'Yeah, Butter!'"[45]

New York Voices

New York Voices, a group often compared to Manhattan Transfer, produced an album in 1989, *New York Voices*,[46] that boasts a wide range of styles and developed instrumental accompaniments. Most of the material is the work of two of the vocalists: Darmon Meader and Peter Eldridge, and the group is completed with Kim Nazarian, Sara Krieger, and Caprice Fox. The intricacy of the instrumental backups can be heard on the opening rock-flavored track, "National Amnesia." Both voices and the synthesizer voicings combine to offer harmonic punches much like those associated with big-band arrangements. In "Top Secret," Caprice Fox offers an effective scat solo over a funky background. The album also offers a variety of Latin arrangements and a setting of Monk's "Round Midnight."

Take 6

In 1988 a group of six men under the name of Take 6 burst on the music scene and captured the attention of the jazz community. Although they first began singing together in 1980, they did not gain national prominence until 1988, at which time their success seemed immediate. Their arrangements are a cappella and show a blend of traditional gospel, soul, pop, and jazz. Their arrangements and stylistic delivery reflect influence from earlier groups such as Lambert, Hendricks, and Ross; the Hi-Lo's; and the Mills Brothers. The musical director is Claude V. McKnight III and the principal arranger Mark Kibble. The group is completed with Mervyn Warren, Cedric Dent, David Thomas, and Alvin Chea.

The musical training of the members is demonstrated clearly in the sophistication of the arrangements. Although the arrangements are quite polished and often rich in vocal display, the presentation of the material emanates clearly from the oral gospel tradition. Listen to the sextet's recording of "Get Away, Jordan" on their album *Take 6*.[47] The performance, rooted in the gospel expression, is full of individual and ensemble vocal nuances.

Bobby McFerrin

Bobby McFerrin has proven to be a singer of unusual talent. Although he follows in the scat singing tradition of Louis Armstrong, Ella Fitzgerald, Mel Torme, and Clark Terry, his ability to scat involves more than improvised syllables with jazz inflections. He also makes percussive sounds as accompaniment to his improvisations. McFerrin is particularly effective in solo performance. He is able to re-create all the essential parts of a jazz standard by himself. By dividing his time between the melody and the bass line, he is able to give the impression that both are continually present. He complements

Take 6.
Courtesy of Empire Studio

Bobby McFerrin.
Photo by Carl Baugher

the performance with percussive sounds created by striking his chest while he sings. His album *Spontaneous Inventions* clearly demonstrates his versatility.[48]

Jazz/Pop

Popular music is, without a doubt, the fastest changing of all musics today. Because of the short life of so many of the emerging styles, their impact on jazz is difficult to immediately assess. At the height of disco's popularity, it was tempting to say that no music would be free from its influence, but now, years after its decline, very little of its impact is being felt. It certainly strengthened the move toward a greater use of synthesizers and a refinement in studio techniques, but as a musical idiom it has almost entirely vanished.

Despite the unstable nature of popular music, several notable jazz musicians have taken active roles in its creation. Their jazz heritage and notoriety often carry the jazz label into the new medium even when the music incorporates very little recognizable jazz. Quincy Jones and Herbie Hancock are two such figures. Both composers have worked in the most diverse musical fields—from jazz to film scores—primarily in the rock idiom.

Quincy Jones

Quincy Jones's 1989 album *Back On the Block*[49] offers a wide cross-section of styles meant to represent the many diverse musical areas in which he has worked during his career. The album swings from rap to jazz fusion with singers such as Ella Fitzgerald, Sarah Vaughan, Ray Charles, and Take 6; rappers Ice-T and Melle Mel; instrumentalists Dizzy Gillespie, Miles Davis, George Benson, Joe Zawinul, and Herbie Hancock; and on and on. The blend of individual and commercial styles is impressive and a tribute to Jones's production skills. Particularly interesting is the arrangement of Zawinul's "Birdland," which blends fusion and pop elements quite effectively. Miles Davis, Dizzy Gillespie, George Benson, and James Moody are featured soloists. The underlying rhythm arrangement, which contains electronically generated sequences as well as programmed drum parts, is commercially consistent with the other cuts on the album.

Herbie Hancock

Herbie Hancock is particularly interesting because of his earlier association with the Miles Davis quintet. While working on his many other projects, he found time to reorganize this earlier group, with himself on piano, Ron Carter on bass, Tony Williams on drums, and Freddie Hubbard taking the place of Davis. The group called itself VSOP and featured mainstream jazz. VSOP 2 followed with the Marsalis brothers several years later.

While maintaining his jazz definition with excursions of this kind, Hancock is also producing albums with the Rockit band. He says of these efforts, "Most people who come from a jazz background and do anything in an area of electric or pop music still maintain a lot of the character of jazz in their pop stuff. So it's a true fusion kind of thing. I did that for a while, but I've been trying to take the pop stuff more into the pop area, and leave out the jazz. I think I've pretty much succeeded at that, because the last few records I don't consider jazz records at all."[50]

What Hancock does carry to these later albums is the technical skill and approach more typical of an accomplished jazz player. The music of his album *Sound-System* falls more into the category of beat or breaker music, a rather specific type of music for a popular dance known as break dancing.[51] Hancock may have very well accomplished what he had intended: to clearly leave the jazz out.

Jazz/Pop Blend

Not all musicians have attempted to draw such clear stylistic lines in their work. George Benson was among the first to blur the lines between jazz and popular music with his record *Breezin'*, the first such record by a jazz-

associated musician to go platinum and hold first place in pop, jazz, and rhythm and blues at the same time.[52] Chuck Mangione has also gained a similar popularity with his fusion groups, his most popular piece being his 1978 instrumental "Feels So Good."

Miles Davis's 1985 album *You're Under Arrest* is a rather unusual blend of pop and jazz.[53] He even rearranges a song written and performed by Cindi Lauper, a prominent pop music star at the time, for this album. Despite this more commercial sound, the musical approach is similar to Davis's earlier albums, which tend to place the soloists in sharp contrast to a steady rhythmic underpinning.

Jazz in Rock

In 1971, Irving L. Horowitz, a professor of sociology at Rutgers University, wrote the following about the merging of jazz and rock:

Many recent bands [e.g., Blood, Sweat and Tears, Chicago, and Cold Blood,] are highly reminiscent in their instrumentation of such earlier groups as Miles Davis' Tentet in the late '40s. And the loud, brassy arrangements are direct descendants of Count Basie. A promising new group, Ten Wheel Drive, provides a mixture of Big Mama Thornton blues and a tenor sax reminiscent of Coltrane, all set to tight arrangements that remind one of the Jazz Messengers with Art Blakey and Horace Silver.[54]

Rock from its beginnings shared much in common with jazz, particularly its strong commitment to rhythm. In its earlier days, rock, like jazz, based much of its music on the twelve-bar blues progression (NW, 249, "Shake Rattle & Roll" and "Every Hour," side 1, band 9). However, it was not until the late 1960s that groups like Blood, Sweat and Tears and Chicago (Chicago Transit Authority) consciously incorporated jazz instrumentation and idioms into their work. By that time the rock harmonic idiom was becoming more modal and the rhythmic patterns more complex. The jazz crossover was therefore most apparent in the added instrumentation—saxophones, trumpets, and trombones—to the more usual guitars. These horns did more than back up the traditional rock band. They were an integral part of the ensemble and were even given open areas for jazz solos.

The musicians in the group Chicago say that they incorporated jazz first but that the *Blood, Sweat and Tears* album was produced ahead of their own album. Both bands used horn players and more composed ensemble practices. "Spinning Wheel," from the *Blood, Sweat and Tears* album, was a particularly popular example of their type of jazz/rock fusion. Bobby Colomby's drumming on this album proves to be a forerunner of the drumming heard in prominent fusion groups in the 1970s and 1980s. This particular piece worked its way into the jazz community when Maynard Ferguson used it as a basis for an exciting arrangement for his own band.[55]

The material for the *Blood, Sweat and Tears* album shows both classical and jazz crossover. The use of tra-ditional jazz tunes like "God Bless the Child" on the one hand and an Erik Satie theme from "Trois Gymno-pedies" on the other potentially qualify this album as both fusion and third stream.[56]

More recently, Sting formed a band that attempted to fuse the worlds of rock and jazz. His approach was to import top jazz players and place them in a rock medium. The jazz players were already established jazz musicians: Branford Marsalis, formally with Art Blakely; Daryl Jones, who worked with Miles Davis; Kenny Kirkland, keyboard player for Wynton Marsalis; and Omar Ham-kim, drummer for Weather Report. After working with many young jazz players, Sting picked those whom he considered to be the best young jazz musicians in the world: ". . . on the understanding that we weren't going to play jazz. What I wanted was a flavor. I didn't want to go off and give Branford 120 bars to explore a theme; I was gonna say, 'You're going to have 16 bars and you're going to burn from the first bar.' "[57]

Sting's credentials as a rock musician and song-writer were established while he was with the very pop-ular rock group Police. His new band was a hybrid coun-terpart to most other fusion groups, which are led by prominent jazz leaders. Whereas he imported jazz into a rock medium, bands like Weather Report and Return to Forever imported rock idioms into a jazz medium.

As Sting formed and rehearsed his new group, he recorded the process on videotape and produced a movie documentary that offers some insight to the excitement and dilemma associated with crossover bands. The concluding filmed concert shows a blend of both rock and jazz mate-rial. A couple of the numbers are blues in the traditional jazz sense, whereas other songs, written originally for Police, are adapted for the newer jazz/rock medium.[58]

Summary

The list of crossover musicians, all along the jazz/rock/pop line, is long and growing as fast as the music itself changes. To know which of these will leave legacies remains for time to decide. During the 1970s and 1980s, jazz began to import heavily from the increasingly popular rock styles. This crossover gener-ated some controversy in the jazz community. Was the jazz tradition being forsaken? Was this new music jazz at all?

By the 1980s, a new shift had taken place within this crossover group, and a new popularity in jazz was devel-oping. However, there were also some controversial aspects to this new popularity. By this time, previously controversial groups such as Weather Report and Return to Forever had established themselves as jazz expres-sions, and now the next generation of players was chal-lenging the jazz definition. Because of the popularity that often accompanied these new groups, an accusation of commercial sellout was heard. Also, many of these new players are not protégés of the jazz art world but often come out of the rock or pop style. Although they may not be of the jazz tradition, it is obvious that the players have a great respect for it. The current controversy will no doubt be settled, but for now we must wait and listen.

For Further Study

1. Select two recordings in your school record library that you think would be good examples of jazz/rock. Give reasons for your selections.
2. What is meant by the terms *crossover* and *fusion* as they relate to jazz/rock? Be specific.
3. Who led the way for a fusion of rock rhythm and free-form jazz?
4. In a jazz/rock percussion section, what rhythmic role is assigned to the snare and bass drums in contrast to the electric bass or bass guitar? Why?
5. Identify two of the earliest rock-and-roll groups that featured jazz solos.

Suggested Additional Listening

Adderley, Cannonball. *Cannonball Adderley Quintet and Aman-dia.* Warner Brothers Records, 25873-2.

Aura. Columbia Records, CK 45332.

Basic Miles. Columbia Records, PC-32025.

Best of Miles Davis (2 vols.). PDL Records, 2-1095E.

The Birth of the Cool. Capitol Records, N-16168.

Bitches' Brew (2 vols.). Columbia Records, GP 26.

Chicago Transit Authority. *Chicago.* Columbia Records, GP8.

Collector's Items (with Parker and Mingus) (2 vols.). Prestige Records, 24022E.

———. *Chicago Transit Authority.* Columbia Records, KGP24.

ESP (with Shorter, Hancock, Carter, and Williams). Columbia Records, PC-9150.

"Four" and More (with Hancock). Columbia Records, PC-9253.

Green Haze (with Coltrane) (2 vols.). Prestige Records, 24064.

In a Silent Way. Columbia Records, PC-9875.

Jazz Classics (with Coltrane). Prestige Records, 7373E.

Kind of Blue (with Coltrane and Evans). Columbia Records, PC-8163.

Lewis, Ramsey. *The In Crowd.* Argo Records, LP-757.

The Man with the Horn. Columbia Records, PC-36790.

McCann, Les. *Beaux J. PooBoo.* Limelight Records, LS-8625.

Miles Ahead (with Gil Evans Orchestra). Columbia Records, PC-8633E.

Miles Ahead (with Parker, Lewis, and Silver). Prestige Records, 7822E.

Milestones (with Coltrane and Adderley). Columbia Records, PC-9428E.

My Funny Valentine (with Hancock). Columbia Records, PC-9106.

Nefertiti (with Shorter et al.). Columbia Records, PC-9594.

Porgy and Bess (with Gil Evans Orchestra). Columbia Records, PC-8085.

Quiet Nights (with Gil Evans Orchestra). Columbia Records, PC-8906.

'Round About Midnight (with Coltrane). Columbia Records, PC-8649E.

Seven Steps to Heaven (with Hancock). Columbia Records, PS-8851.

Sketches of Spain (with Gil Evans Orchestra). Columbia Records, PC-8271.

Some Day My Prince Will Come. Columbia Records, PC-8456.
Tutu. Warner Brothers Records, 25490-1.
You're Under Arrest. Columbia Records, FCT 40023.

Additional Reading Resouces

Carr, Ian. *Miles Davis.*
Cole, Bill. *Miles Davis.*
Coryell, Julie, and Friedman, Laura. *Jazz-Rock Fusion.*
Courlander, Harold. *Miles Davis: A Musical Biography.*
Davis, Francis. *In the Moment: Jazz in the 1980s.*
Davis, Miles, and Troupe, Quincy. *Miles.*
Megill, Donald D., and Demory, Richard S. *Introduction to Jazz History.*

Note: Complete information, including name of publisher and date of publication, is provided in this book's bibliography.

Notes

1. Herbie Hancock, *Down Beat* 55, no. 6 (June 1988): 18.
2. Don Ellis, "Rock: The Rhythmic Revolution," *Down Beat* 36, no. 24 (1969): 32.
3. James Lincoln Collier, *The Making of Jazz* (New York: Dell Publishing, 1978), 427.
4. Miles Davis, *Milestones,* Columbia Records, PC-9428E.
5. Miles Davis, *Nefertiti,* Columbia Records, PC 9594.
6. Miles Davis, *In a Silent Way,* Columbia Records, PC 9875.
7. Miles Davis, *Bitches' Brew,* Columbia Records, GP 26.
8. Miles Davis, *You're Under Arrest,* Columbia Records, FCT 40023; *Tutu,* Warner Brothers Records, 25490-1.
9. Miles Davis, *Bitches' Brew,* Columbia Records, GP 26.
10. *Down Beat* 55, no. 9 (September 1988): 19.
11. Mahavishnu Orchestra, *Inner Mounting Flame,* Columbia Records, 31067; *Birds of Fire,* Columbia Records, 31996; *Between Nothingness and Eternity,* Columbia Records, 32766.
12. *Passion, Grace & Fire,* Columbia Records, 38645; *Friday Night in San Francisco,* Columbia Records, 37152.
13. *Down Beat* 52, no. 3 (March 1985): 17.
14. Return to Forever, *Musicmagic,* Columbia Records, AL 34682.
15. Chick Corea, *Elektric Band,* GRP Records, GRP-A-1026 (compact disc, GRP-D-9535).
16. Chick Corea, *Light Years,* GRP Records, GRP-1036.
17. Chick Corea, *Eye of the Beholder,* GRP Records, GRP-1053.
18. Chick Corea, *Akoustic Band,* GRP Records, GRD-9582.
19. Chick Corea, *Elektric Band,* and *Inside Out,* GRP Records, GRD-9601.
20. George Varga, *The San Diego Union,* 9 March 1986.
21. Weather Report, *Night Passage,* CBS Records, 36793.
22. Weather Report, *Heavy Weather,* Columbia Records, 34418.
23. Manhattan Transfer, *Extensions,* Atlantic Records, SD 19258; Quincy Jones, *Back on the Block,* Warner Brothers Records, 0 26020-2.
24. Weather Report, *This Is This,* CBS Records, CK-40280.
25. Joseph Zawinul, *Dialects,* Columbia Records, FCT 40081.
26. George Varga, *The San Diego Union,* 9 March 1986.
27. Joseph Zawinul, *Black Water,* Columbia Records, CK 44316.
28. Leonard Feather, *Los Angeles Times/Calendar,* 18 February 1990.
29. Michael Brecker, *Michael Brecker,* Impulse, 5980.
30. Michael Brecker, *Don't Try This at Home,* Impulse, MCAD-42229.
31. Stanley Jordan, *Magic Touch,* Blue Note Records, BT 85101.
32. *Down Beat* 53, no. 8 (August 1986): 18.
33. *Double Vision,* Warner Brothers Records, 25393-4.
34. Pat Metheny, *Song X,* Geffen, 24096.
35. Pat Metheny, *Still Life (Talking),* Geffen, 24145.
36. Pat Metheny, *Letter from Home,* Geffen, 24245.
37. Spyro-Gyra, *Morning Dance,* Infinity Records, INF9004.
38. Spyro-Gyra, *Point of View,* MCA Records, MCAD-6309.
39. Yellowjackets, *Four Corners,* MCA Records, MCAD-5994.
40. Yellowjackets, *The Spin,* MCA Records, MCAD-6304.
41. *Down Beat* 56, no. 11 (November 1989): 22.
42. *The Best of Lambert, Hendricks and Ross,* Columbia Records, KC-32911.
43. Manhattan Transfer, *Extensions,* Atlantic Records, SD 19258.
44. Manhattan Transfer, *Vocalese,* Atlantic Records, 7 81266-1.
45. Michael Bourne, *Down Beat* 52, no. 11 (November 1985): 24.
46. New York Voices, *New York Voices,* GRP Records, GRD-9589.
47. Take 6, *Take 6,* Reprise, 9 25670-2.
48. Bobby McFerrin, *Spontaneous Inventions,* Blue Note Records, BT 85110.
49. Quincy Jones, *Back on the Block,* Warner Brothers Records, 9 26020-2.
50. Howard Mandel, *Down Beat* 53, no. 7 (July 1986): 17.
51. Herbie Hancock, *Sound-System,* Columbia Records, 39478.
52. George Benson, *Breezin',* Warner Bros. Records, BSK-3111.
53. Miles Davis, *You're Under Arrest,* Columbia Records, FCT 40023.
54. Irving L. Horowitz, "Rock on the Rocks Bubblegum Anyone?" Reprinted from *Psychology Today,* January, 1971. Copyright 1971 by Ziff-Davis Publishing Company. All rights reserved.
55. Maynard Ferguson, "Spinning Wheel," *M. F. Horn II,* Columbia Records, KC 31709, CBS 65027.
56. Blood, Sweat & Tears, *Blood, Sweat and Tears,* Columbia Records, CS9720.
57. Art Lange, *Down Beat* 52, no. 12 (December 1985).
58. Sting, *Bring on the Night,* Karl/Lorimar Feature Films, A&M Films, a division of A&M Records Inc., 1985, YHS 344. The music can be heard on *The Dream of the Blue Turtles,* A&M Records.

Listening Suggestions

Techniques of perceptive listening improve as you develop an understanding of the musical vocabulary of jazz (and of other music). The jazz listening guide on page 11 was developed to give you a systematic aid to use in identifying what to listen to and for. This identification leads to the development of effective listening habits.

A valuable aid in developing perceptive listening is to listen to a composition with other persons. After the first hearing, freely exchange ideas with the other listeners about what you have heard and then replay the record. This experience tends to improve your ability to concentrate as well as to pick up previously missed nuances.

Read the listening guide before listening to be sure that you understand what the various items in the guide mean. After the first hearing, quickly respond to the items you can identify easily. Do not labor over items about which you are unsure. After the second hearing, go back and fill in all the remaining items on the guide. Obviously, some items may not apply to every listening experience. Effective listening takes practice by a listener as well as guidance by an instructor.

Passive listening will not aid in developing understanding and enjoyment of jazz. Listeners must train themselves to listen *to* and *for* the content of the music and to respond actively—not only emotionally but also intellectually. The next step is for each listener to develop a specific set of references to use in deciding whether he or she enjoys and understands jazz.

Jazz Interpretation

Jazz interpretation is illustrated by examples 1A and 1B, the first without jazz interpretation and the second with suggested jazz interpretation. Listen to the differences in the performances (demonstrations 40 and 41, cassette 2, side B, tracks 7 and 8; CD 2, tracks 13 and 14) on the recording that accompanies this book. Today, two completely diverse directions in jazz interpretation are very active. One kind of interpretation seems to be closer than ever to classical music. This trend started around 1950 and continues as more schooled musicians enter the jazz field. The other direction is toward avant-garde jazz, in which some players disregard all earlier approaches to musical lines. These musicians maintain that instead of interpreting lines per se they are playing emotions such as rage or pain.

In contrast with interpretation, example 1C (demonstration 42, cassette 2, side B, track 9; CD 2, track 15) is an improvisation (written out) of the same melody used in example 1A. Listen to the recording and compare examples 1A, 1B, and 1C.

Example 1A *Recorded Demonstration 40 (cassette 2, side B, track 7; CD 2, track 13)*

Example 1B *Recorded Demonstration 41 (cassette 2, side B, track 8; CD 2, track 14)*

Example 1C *Recorded Demonstration 42 (cassette 2, side B, track 9; CD 2, track 15)*

Example 2A

(Beat)

Example 2B

What to Listen For in Jazz

Persons who can bring to the listening experience a fund of musical knowledge have an advantage in gaining insight into jazz. But *knowledge about* music and an *understanding of* music are not the same. Simply stated, the first deals primarily with information (vocabulary), whereas the second relates to direct musical experiences involving concepts and possession of the vocabulary to express understanding of the concepts. The term *concept* suggests a mental image or a complete thought that has been acquired through the senses: hearing, seeing, touching, tasting, and smelling.

As you listen to music, you will find that the concepts of melody, rhythm, harmony, texture, design, and tone color are common to all music. However, some concepts of rhythm, for example, are treated differently or at least more prominently in jazz than in other types of music.

As a preparatory exercise for listening to jazz, you will find it helpful to list under each main musical element words and concepts that you identify with that musical element. For example, (1) under *melody:* high, low, smooth, jagged, **scale**, skips, **key**, diatonic, and chromatic; (2) under *texture:* thick, thin, few instruments, many instruments, homophonic, and polyphonic; (3) under *form:* repetition, contrast, theme, variations, imitation, section, part, three parts, and improvisation; (4) under *harmony:* tension, relaxation, rounds, and chords; (5) under *rhythm:* fast, slow, weak accents, strong accents, beat, **tempo**, pattern, and meter; and (6) under *tone:* piano, soprano, contralto, bass, trumpet, sax, clarinet, and bass drum.

Jazz Ensembles

An initial consideration in listening to jazz **ensembles** is the size of the instrumental group. Does it sound like a large group of more than ten players or like a small combo of instrumentalists? If the group is a large band

and there is a soloist, the listener has very few real clues to the size of the organization unless the soloist is supported by some other part of the band beside the rhythm section. An example is a saxophone solo backed up by a trombone section, consisting of three or four trombones, or by the entire brass section, including trumpets and trombones. While the ensemble is playing, listen for the "bigness" or "thickness" of the overall sound. Sometimes the total sound may be so full that it is almost overwhelming, such as the ensemble portion of Kenton's "Commencement." Listen for complete sections of instruments: saxophone, trumpet, and trombone sections. The sections are quite easy to determine on most albums by bands such as Count Basie's[2] (S, side D, bands 5 and 6). Almost always, both large and small jazz groups have rhythm sections consisting of piano, **bass**, guitar, and drums. Some rhythm sections do not use all four, but rather use only piano with bass or bass and drums with piano.

Another problem with listening is that sometimes a small group or combo may confuse the ear by sounding larger than a full band if the playing and recording techniques are purposefully planned to give that illusion of sound. However, in a combo, listen for the individual instruments. Instead of the saxophone section, listen for the saxophone player; do this for other instrumentalists such as the trumpet or trombone player[3] (S, side E, bands 7 and 8; S, side B, band 2).

Some Musical Concepts in Jazz

Melody

It is important that listeners of jazz music attend to the melodic inventiveness or improvisation on a given melody or the musical interpretation of a given melody. The emotional tone communicated by the jazz performer often reveals the temperament of the player and of society in general at the time of the playing. Usually, music is quite accurate in mirroring the temperament of the times (war, peace, and so on).

Listen as the performers create. Is the emotional tone excitement? Is it calm? (Can calm music be exciting?[4]) Performing music is extremely personal to be sure, but so is listening. One person cannot listen for another. Sometimes big bands are very outgoing, or hot, such as Basie's in "Jumpin' at the Woodside" or "Every Tub"[5] (NW, 274, side 1, band 1; S, side D, bands 5 and 6). However, this is not an exclusive element of large groups. Combos can produce the same feeling—listen to such recordings as Kenny Clarke's "Be a Good Girl"[6] (S, side F, band 2; S, side F, bands 7 and 8). The same outgoing big band can sometimes produce an extremely calm, even introverted feeling. Such an example can be heard in Basie's "Blue and Sentimental" and "Lil' Darlin'" and in Woody Herman's "Misty Morning."[7]

A person who has little technical knowledge of music and who cannot name individual pitches on the staff still may be able to hear the differences between two melodies by feeling ascending tones as they move in steps and descending tones as they skip in varied moves.

Texture

The term *texture* as it is used in music refers to the different ways melodies and harmonies interact. Some textures may give the impression of being open and airy, whereas others may seem quite dense. Textures include not only the various ways of filling the octave and various ways of using the beat but also the many possibilities of repeating the same melody at different pitch levels, of combining two or more different melodies, or of providing a single melody with accompanying chords or harmonies.

A single melody with neither accompanying melodic part nor harmony is known as a **monophonic** construction. The field hollers of the slaves is a good example of a short melodic motive without any accompanying musical sounds.

Another way of treating a melody is to have two melodies start at the *same time* on *different pitch levels*. Another version starts two melodies at *different times* on the *same pitch level*. The combination of two voices singing or playing the same melody but entering at different times is called a **canon**. A canon repeated without a break is called a **round** (i.e., the melody chases itself around and around). The simultaneous sounding of one melody heard in imitation in another voice or instrument and the use of two or more different melodies of equal importance is known as polyphonic construction. Listening to polyphonic, or **horizontal**, texture in music is somewhat analogous to watching a three-ring circus. You realize something important is going on in each of the three rings, but it is difficult to concentrate on them simultaneously. However, it all adds to the excitement of the moment.

A third way of treating a melody is to have all the voices or instruments move together with a single melody, usually in the highest voice part. Harmony in the form of chords in the lower voices acts as an accompaniment to the single melody. This is called homophonic, or vertical, texture. Hymns and spirituals are excellent examples of this type of melodic treatment.

Form

The basic units of form in music are often compared to the basic units in written language. The individual musical note is comparable to the single alphabetical letter in written language. The musical **motive**, or figure (two or more tones forming a distinctive rhythmic-melodic pattern) is the equivalent of a language syllable or word. The first appearance of a **phrase** (usually four measures in length) denotes a language phrase. The extension of the phrase into two phrases, or **periods** (eight measures in length), denotes a language sentence. Sometimes language sentences are longer. In music, long phrases are called double periods, or phrase groups.

For easy identification, phrases and periods are designated by letters. The first phrase is called A, and as each new phrase appears, it is given a different letter (B, C, D, etc.). The forms used extensively in jazz are the twelve-bar (measure) blues strain and the sixteen- and thirty-two-bar choruses that are usually designated ABAB or AABA (see example 4 below).

The twelve-bar blues strain has two similar phrases of four measures each and a third phrase that is different. In the blues melody given in example 3 below, measures 1 through 4 are the first phrases, or A part.

Since the 1940s, some jazz players have combined the AABA and blues forms. The performer does this by playing the first strain (A), repeating it (A), following with a different strain of usually only eight measures (B), and ending with the original strain (A). The first, second, and fourth parts all have twelve measures.

Since the advent of the long-playing record, some modern jazz players have tended to adopt extended musical forms such as the **theme and variation**, fugue, and rondo.[8] The Modern Jazz Quartet offers several albums with examples of extended forms, such as the excellent recording *Collaboration*, in which they perform Bach's "Fugue in A Minor" with guitarist Laurindo Almeida.[9] In fact, jazz players have used the theme-and-variation form since the beginning of this art. The tune is established, and then each repetition is given a variation, whether improvised or planned, to constantly create new interest as the work progresses. This form is often compared to the **chaconne**, in which a series of improvisations is played from a predetermined chord progression.

The authors have considered the possibility that the most important element in all jazz—that of emotion—is overlooked. There is no question that emotional force has been the strongest ally of jazz throughout its history. Jazz can make one contemplate deeply, dance with joy, or weep with sadness. However, because the authors are involved in the performance of music, we are totally convinced that emotion is too necessary an element of all types of music to be considered the exclusive element of any one kind of music. Any music without emotion simply does not seem worth listening to.

Harmony

Closely related to the need to recognize the melodic line is the necessity of response to the musical element of **harmony** in jazz. Harmony is the simultaneous sounding of two or more tones. Two tones sounding together make an interval. The effect produced by the interval depends on the ratio between the two tones. In general, simple ratios tend to be more harmonious and complex ratios more dissonant. For example, for most listeners the sound of three-tone chords with intervals of thirds seems pleasingly consonant and restful, whereas six- or seven-tone chords with intervals of thirds having more complex ratios seem to give listeners feelings of dissonance and tension.

A listener must decide whether the harmonies are too simple, have little variety, and thus are of little interest. In more academic terms, the harmonies or chord progressions should have a sense of forward motion. Sometimes a composition has a pleasing melodic line but is quite dull harmonically. The opposite situation occurs when the composer-arranger or piano soloist is so intent on playing interesting harmonies that the music sounds contrived. This seemed to be prevalent with some large bands in the 1940s and again in the 1960s. Rather than complex harmonies with very little melodic originality, a balance between the two is usually more acceptable.

Rhythm

Rhythm is the very heart of nature and of humanity. It is the pulse of life and is found in all kinds of physical activity. We unconsciously use rhythm—in walking, dancing, running, skipping, and so on. However, *rhythm* is a generic term with many meanings.

In music, one basic element of rhythm is the repetition of sound, either felt or heard, called the beat (or pulse) of the music. To feel the beat, listen and tap or clap the regular repetitions generated by the musical sound.

Although beat is a constant force in every composition, the speed of the beat varies greatly and depends on the feeling, tone, and mood of the music. In some music the beat is fast; elsewhere it is quite slow. The speed of the beat is called the tempo. Thus, to say that the rhythm is slowing is to say that the beat is moving at a slower rate.

Occasionally, a great rhythmic pulse is felt but no melodic line is realized; the rhythm section merely sets a mood. These sections are usually called **vamps.** Some contemporary musicians play on melodic instruments but avoid the usual concept of melody. They say that they are playing a mood or an attitude. Listen to Joe Harriott's "Shadows."[10] There are many situations in which there is a definite melody, but it is subservient to the rhythmic sounds. It is primarily this rhythmic pulse, or juxtaposition of patterns, that expresses the emotion. The technique is quite common in many rock and jazz/rock recordings.[11]

One of the most important elements of rhythm is duration. The performing musician is concerned with translating the symbols on a page of music into sounds and silences (tone pauses, or rests). These sounds and silences may be of any duration. For this reason, clapping the rhythmic pattern does not accurately represent a melody, as the claps are all of equal duration.

Listen to the ticking of a clock. Do some of the ticks seem to be stronger than others? Try tapping on the table with your hand, imitating the regularity of the sound of a clock. Next, tap one beat louder than the following beat. Alternate between loud taps and soft taps. Try tapping one loud beat followed by two soft beats. You should find that in one case the beats occur in groupings of twos and in the other case in groupings of threes. The easiest approach to understanding accent, the basis of meter, is to study the grouping of louds and softs into twos, threes, fours, or more. Meter is the regular (or irregular) grouping of beats according to accent.

In musical notation, the **time signature** located at the beginning of a composition tells a player that the music moves in groupings of threes, fours, or whatever. There are complete styles of jazz that stay primarily in one meter grouping, and the listener should be able to detect these groupings fairly easily. The feeling of 4/4, or flat four, is used by players of Early New Orleans Dixieland, by most swing players, and by many bop and cool players.

When 2/4 meter is designated in jazz music, it denotes something different from 2/4 meter in classical music, in which it means there are two beats to each measure and quarter notes receive one beat. In jazz, however, it means that there are four beats to the measure but that the second and fourth beats are accented. Thus, a jazz player never snaps the fingers or claps the hands on the first and third beats but always the second and fourth, as shown by the accents in examples 5A, 5B, and 5C below. This is the only time when meter interpretation (time signature) in jazz is different than in other music.

The 2/4 beat in jazz is heard most prominently in ragtime and Chicago Style Dixieland music. When funky-style jazz music has four beats to the measure, the second and fourth beats are accented. Sometimes, however, funky is played in 3/4 meter. Rock drummers accent the second and fourth beats, feeling that it adds interest and momentum. Very good jazz, by both small combos and large orchestras, is also performed in 3/4 meter.[12]

The style of jazz called boogie-woogie is performed in 8/8 meter, eight beats to each measure (see chapter 6). In fact, it is the identifying feature of this style, whether it is a piano solo or a large band[13] (S, "Honky Tonk Train," side C, band 4; FJ). Rock players make excellent use of 8/8 meter without actually playing boogie-woogie, seeming to use 4/4 meter in a **double-time** fashion.[14]

Syncopation

Jazz often shifts the melody so that it does not always align itself with the basic beat. This displacement of melodic and harmonic accents off the strong beats in a given meter is called syncopation. As a result of this shift, accents end up on weak beats in a measure, namely the second and fourth beats in a $\frac{4}{4}$ meter, or on the weak part of individual beats. The following two examples illustrate this technique: example 2A above has no syncopation; example 2B does.

Example 2B above shows syncopated notes that have been shifted off the beats so that many of the melodic notes begin in between the four metric beats in each measure. The melodic move from the third to the fourth measure shows how the first beat of the fourth measure is anticipated with a syncopation. The weight of the normally strong first beat of a measure is then out of synchronization with the last note of the melodic line. These syncopated notes are often accentuated by the performer to heighten the syncopated feel. Certainly there is syncopation in all musics, but in jazz syncopation is used often and becomes highly intricate.

There is very little jazz that does not use syncopation. As a consequence, syncopation is more natural for the jazz musician and is more closely connected with jazz in the mind of the public. Of the many examples, we suggest something like Count Basie's "Jumpin' at the Woodside."[15]

Gunther Schuller has defined the syncopation of jazz as "no more than an idiomatic corruption, a flattened-out mutation of what was once the true poly-rhythmic character of African music."[16]

Tone

Another important consideration in listening to music is tone. As a consequence, syncopation is more natural for the jazz musician and is more closely connected with jazz in the mind of the public. Of the many examples, we suggest something like Count Basie's "Jumpin' at the quality to lack intensity, sincerity, and even confidence. These listeners prefer to hear the type of tone made by, for example, a very strong trumpet player. Listening is very personal, almost as personal as performing. Which sound do you find more interesting: a smooth, pretty tone or a rough, aggressive sound?

One of the most important points to be considered is the creativeness of individual players. Do their thoughts sound interesting and fresh, or are they playing clichés that should be forgotten? Players have been known to improvise several consecutive choruses on just one tone. This kind of playing lacks all imagination. On the other hand, some players improvise lines so far ahead of their contemporaries that acceptance and acclaim come too late to be of much satisfaction.

The real judge, of course, is the listener, who must hear the melodies, perceive the rhythm, detect the tone, and so on. Jazz observers are not particularly impressed by classical correctness. They hear enough excellent

piano from Art Tatum to consider him a genius. They are not disturbed at all that Tatum's fingering was atrocious. Jazz listeners hear creativeness from Gillespie's trumpet and are not disturbed by the way he puffs out his cheeks. Present-day jazz observers actually appreciate the primitive approach to playing of many early jazz performers, most of whom had little or no musical schooling. Their lack of schooling—of knowing how to perform "correctly" by European standards—gave the early players a freedom that endears them to most jazz listeners.

One should be reminded that the "test of time" commonly used to judge music is not appropriate for jazz. It is true that there are jazz classics (Armstrong's, "Savoy Blues," Hawkins's "Body and Soul," Parker's "Ornithology," and many others), but jazz players are much more concerned with immediate communication. In fact, many players do not like to compare their present playing style to works they have done in the past; they like to think that they have improved their style by fresher, more contemporary inventiveness and creativity.

Summary

Listening to music is a very personal experience. Because involvement, as opposed to passive listening, is an important key, the authors have offered guides, in this appendix and in other chapters, to help the listener appreciate and understand jazz.

One of the more obvious aspects of the recorded sound is the size of the performing group. The listener can analyze such elements as the type of melody, the texture (thick or thin), the type of form (repetition, contrast, and so on), the tempo, and the instruments. The realization of these considerations will make jazz listening more pleasurable.

For Further Study

1. In your own words, define the following: melody, harmony, rhythm, design, and timbre (or tone color).

2. Skilled listeners should be able to focus on different musical elements. Listen several times to "Yancey Stomp" by Jimmy Yancey, pianist (*Folkways Jazz Series,* vol. 10), and answer the following:

   a. Does the music have an introduction?

   b. Is the left hand at the piano (the bass part) realizing mostly harmony or a repeated melodic figure?

   c. Is the right hand realizing a distinguishable melodic line or short figures that seem almost harmonic in total effect?

   d. Is the meter in duple or triple feeling?

3. Listen to the three-part form of "Fish This Week" as played by Les McCann (*Les McCann Plays the Truth,* Pacific Jazz Records, PJ-2). Listen for the expanded improvised bridge part: A, B (bridge), A.

Example 3 *Blues Melody*

When the notes in the second line of a song look the same as in the first line or phrase they also sound the same. As you can tell, the second phrase of the song (measures 5 to 8) looks and sounds like the first phrase. This phrase may also be indicated by an "A":

The third phrase (measures 9 to 12) is obviously different. Therefore, it is indicated by the letter "B":

When the notes in the second line of a song look the same as in the first line or phrase, they also sound the same. As you can tell, the second phrase of the song (measures 5 to 8) looks and sounds like the first phrase. This phrase may also be indicated by an "A." The third phrase (measures 9 to 12) is obviously different. Therefore, it is indicated by the letter "B."

Next, examine carefully the AABA song (example 4). Look at the first period (measures 1–8). This is the A part. Now

compare the second part (measures 9–16) with the A part. You will discover that the A part and the second part are identical. Thus far we have AA. Examine measures 17–24. You will discover that this part is different from the A part and is therefore called B. Look at the remainder of the song (measures 25 to 32). As you can see, this is the same as the A part, with a slight variation in the ending. This is the most commonly used form in jazz, that is the three-part form, or AABA thirty-two-bar chorus.

Example 4 *AABA Song*

Example 4 AABA Song cont'd.

Example 5A

4/4 or flat four

Example 5B

2/4 in classical music

Example 5C

2/4 in jazz

4. Name the six elements of jazz that distinguish it from other types of music.

5. Give a definition of syncopation.

6. Clap the following 4/4 rhythm: While tapping the beat with your foot, clap an example using a syncopated pattern.

7. Sing or play the melody of the song "Swanee River." Sing or play this melody with a jazz interpretation. What did you alter or perform differently to change the style of your performance?

8. It is fun to improvise. With little musical knowledge, you can make up your own melody at the piano keyboard. Using only the black keys on the piano, start with the black-key C-sharp and play any series of tones with the rhythmic patterns found in the familiar song "Twinkle, Twinkle, Little Star." Repeat the same melody you made up and vary the rhythmic patterns.

9. Listen to "The Kid from Red Bank" from $E = MC^2$ (Roulette, ST-52003). In your own words, describe some of the improvisational techniques the pianist uses. For example, does the player use primarily melodic or harmonic configurations?

10. Classical composers have frequently used the theme-and-variations form in their compositions. Listening to a number of compositions that use this form will help a listener identify the various elements of jazz and how they can be altered or changed in jazz performances.

a. Ravel uses the theme-and-variations design in his composition *Bolero*. Listen to this piece and discover which musical element is used most in the eighteen variations: melody, rhythm, harmony, or tone color (instrumentation).

b. Rimsky-Korsakov uses four variations in his composition *Spanish Caprice*. The theme is in a two-part form, each part being nine measures in length. How does Rimsky-Korsakov treat the variations?

c. Listen to Lucien Cailliet's *Variations on the Theme "Pop! Goes the Weasel."* You will have to be somewhat of a musical detective to follow Cailliet's musical variations on this well-known melody. In which of the variations do you hear at least two of the jazz elements just described? Name the elements.

11. Jazz performers and composers often base their variations on themes of other composers. Compare the different ways that themes are treated in the following examples:

a. *The Great Benny Goodman*, "Let's Dance," Columbia Records, CL-820.

b. *Big Band Beat*, "Strike Up the Band," Richmond Records, B-20034.

c. *Four Freshmen and Five Trombones*, "You Stepped Out of a Dream," Capitol Records, T-683.

d. "Scheherajazz," Somerset Records, P-9700.

e. *Barney Kessel Plays 'Carmen'*, Contemporary Records, 3563.

f. *Dizzy in Greece*, "Anitra's Dance," Verve Records, MEV-8017 ("Anitra's Dance," Grieg, *Peer Gynt Suite*).

Notes

1. Stan Kenton, "Commencement," *The Jazz Story*, vol. 5; Buddy Rich, "Westside Story," *Swingin' New Band*, Pacific Jazz Records, PJ-1013.

2. Count Basie, *The Best of Basie*, Roulette Records, ST-52003.

3. Charlie Parker and Dizzy Gillespie, "Shaw 'Nuff," *Smithsonian Collection of Classic Jazz*; Charlie Parker, "KoKo," *Smithsonian Collection of Classic Jazz*; Louis Armstrong, "Struttin' with Some Barbecue," *Smithsonian Collection of Classic Jazz*; Charlie Parker, "Another Hair Do," *Charlie Parker Memorial Album*, vol. 1, Savoy Records, MG-12000; Louis Armstrong, "I Gotta Right to Sing the Blues," *The Essential Louis Armstrong*, Verve Records, V-8569; Cannonball Adderley, "I Can't Get Started with You," *The Jazz Story*, vol. 5.

4. Count Basie, "Blue and Sentimental," *The Best of Basie*, Roulette Records, RE118; Gerry Mulligan and Ben Webster, "Chelsea Bridge," *The Greatest Names in Jazz*, Verve Records, PR 2-3.

5. Count Basie, "Doggin' Around" and "Taxi War Dance," *Smithsonian Collection of Classic Jazz*; "Every Tub," *Jive at Five*; Count Basie, "Jumpin' at the Woodside" and "Every Tub," *The Best of Basie*; and "The Kid from Redbank," *E = MC²*, "Jumpin' at the Woodside," *Big Band Jazz, Smithsonian Collection of Recordings*, cassette 3, band 12.

6. Kenny Clarke, "Be a Good Girl," *The Jazz Story*, vol. 5; Dizzy Gillespie and Charlie Parker, "Wee," *Jazz at Massey Hall*, Fantasy Records, 6003; "Shaw 'Nuff," *Smithsonian Collection of Classic Jazz*; Charlie Parker, "KoKo," *Smithsonian Collection of Classic Jazz*; "Little Benny," *Smithsonian Collection of Classic Jazz*.

7. Count Basie, "Blue and Sentimental," *The Best of Basie*; "Lil' Darlin'," *E = MC²*; Woody Herman, "Misty Morning," *The Jazz Story*, vol. 5.

8. Gunther Schuller, "Variants on a Theme of Thelonious Monk," *Jazz Abstractions*, Atlantic Records, 1365; "A Fugue for Music Inn," *The Modern Jazz Quartet at Music Inn*, Atlantic Records, 1247; "On Green Mountain" (chaconne form) *Modern Jazz Concert*, Columbia Records, WL127; Dave Brubeck Quartet, "Blue Rondo a la Turk," *Time Out*, Columbia Records, CL-1397.

9. Modern Jazz Quartet with Laurindo Almeida, "Fugue in A Minor," *Collaboration*, Atlantic Records, 1429.

10. Joe Harriott, "Shadows," *The Jazz Story*, vol. 5; Archie Shepp, "The Chased," *The Definitive Jazz Scene*, vol. 3; "The Mac Man," *On This Night*, Impulse Records, A-97.

11. Blood, Sweat and Tears, "Spinning Wheel," *Blood, Sweat and Tears*, Columbia Records, CS9720.

12. Clark Terry, "Hammer-head Waltz," *The Definitive Jazz Scene*, vol. 1; Les McCann, "A Little 3/4 for God and Company," *Les McCann Plays the Truth*, Pacific Jazz Records, PJ-2; Tommy Vig, "Sunrise Sunset," *The Sound of the Seventies*, Milestone Records, 9007.

13. Meade Lux Lewis and Will Bradley, "Beat Me Daddy, Eight to the Bar," Columbia Records, 35530; Count Basie, "Boogie-woogie," Columbia Records, 35959; Tommy Dorsey, "Boogie-woogie," RCA Victor Records, 26054; Benny Goodman, "Roll 'Em," RCA Victor Records, 25627.

14. Spirit, "Topanga Windows," *Spirit*, Ode 70 Records, Z18-4404.

15. Count Basie Orchestra, "Jumpin' at the Woodside," *The Best of Basie*, Roulette Records, RE118; *Big Band Jazz, Smithsonian Collection of Recordings*, cassette 3, band 12.

16. Gunther Schuller, *Early Jazz* (New York: Oxford University Press, 1968), 15.

Chapter 2

B

APPENDIX

Notational Examples

Example 6A *Recorded Demonstration 43 (cassette 2, side B, track 10; CD 2, track 16)*

Example 6B *Recorded Demonstration 44 (cassette 2, side B, track 11; CD 2, track 17)*

Example 6C *Recorded Demonstration 45 (cassette 2, side B, track 12; CD 2, track 18)*

Example 6D *Recorded Demonstration 46 (cassette 2, side B, track 13; CD 2, track 19)*

Example 7

GRUNT

GRUNT

Example 8A *Polyphonic*

Example 8B Homophonic

Examples 8A and 8B demonstrate the difference between polyphonic and homophonic (vertical) harmonization. Example 8A is polyphonically constructed and shows the independence of the harmonic line. Example 8B is homophonically constructed and demonstrates the extreme dependency of the harmony part on the melody.

Chapter 3

Example 9A Recorded Demonstration 47 (cassette 2, side B, track 14; CD 2, track 20)

Example 9B Recorded Demonstration 48 (cassette 2, side B, track 15; CD 2, track 21)

The Blues Form

Eight-bar, twelve-bar, and sixteen-bar blues forms all developed, but by the beginning of World War I the twelve-bar construction had become an accepted form.[1] The blues, like all music, has built chords from the scale tones. If a chord starts on the first note of the scale and then uses every other note (scale tones 1, 3, and 5), the roman numeral I is used to define it. A chord built up from the fourth note would be given the numeral IV, and so on. The seventh tone (or flatted seventh) can be added and designated, such as V_7. These harmonic symbols can be used to describe the harmonic construction of various musical forms.

Most blues researchers claim that the very early blues were patterned after English ballads and often had eight, ten, or sixteen bars.[2] An example of eight-bar blues is "Trouble in Mind," sometimes called "Troubled in Mind," with the following chord progression: I, V_7, I_7, IV, I, V_7, I, I. Another eight-bar blues is "How Long Blues," using a different chord progression: I, I_7, IV, IV, I, V_7, I, I. Among the sixteen-bar blues one can find long lists of songs such as "Careless Love" (I, V_7, I, I—I, I, V_7, V_7, —I, I, IV, IV, —I, I, V_7, I, I), "Basin Street Blues" (I, III$_7$, VI_7, VI_7, —II_7, V_7, I, V_7, —I, III$_7$, VI_7, VI_7, —II_7, V_7, I, I) and sixteen-bar blues tunes that have the standard twelve-bar progression plus a four-bar tag (I, I, I, I_7, —IV, IV, I, I, —V_7, V_7, I, I, —and the the **tag**—II_7, V_7, I, I). Few researchers attempt to notate these early blues, perhaps because there are so many different structures.

The Accepted Chord Progression

Today, the blues is a particular harmonic sequence, a definite musical form in much the same manner that the sonnet is a poetic form. The blues now contains a definite set progression of harmonies and consists of twelve measures. The harmonic progression is as follows: I, I, I, I_7, IV, IV, I, I, V_7, V_7, I, I. Each roman numeral indicates a chord built on a specific tone in the scale. Since about 1960, because of the influence of rock-and-roll artists, the chord in the tenth measure in the progression of harmonies has been changed to IV_7. This alteration is now considered standard.

Each roman numeral as specified in the foregoing harmonic progression designates a chord to be played for one measure, resulting in a **twelve-measure** chorus. Examples 10A, 10B, and 10C are in the key of C.

The Blues Scale

Some theorists designate a "blues scale" as the **Dorian mode** (the white keys of the piano from D to D) or the **Mixolydian mode** (the white keys of the piano from G to G). The false logic in this theory is that the blue areas cannot be pinpointed. The Dorian implies a lowered third and lowered seventh; the Mixolydian implies a natural third and a lowered seventh. These blue tonalities are not on definite notes. The problems of analysis result from the rigidity of the **well-tempered scale** and the fluctuations of the blue tonalities themselves.

Example 10A C Diatonic Scale

Example 10B I, IV, and V_7 Chords in the Key of C

Example 10C Basic Chords Used in the Blues in the Key of C

Example 11 "When To The Sessions of Sweet Silent Thought"
"Lord, Lord, Lord"

When To The Sessions of Sweet Silent Thought

Text by William Shakespeare

Lord, Lord, Lord

Refrain

Spiritual

For Further Study

1. Play the hymn "Lord Jesus Christ, With Us Abide" or any other hymn that contains the harmonic construction of the blues. Listen carefully and identify the blues chord progressions.

2. Select a sonnet and write a blues melody to the words (see the example above: "When To The Sessions of Sweet Silent Thought," text by William Shakespeare).

3. Sing the C-major scale and note the location of the half steps. Next sing only the tones C, D, F, G, and A. You have just sung a pentatonic scale. Explain the difference between a major diatonic scale and a pentatonic scale.

4. Sing the spiritual "Swing Low, Sweet Chariot" in the key of F-major. What scale does this melody use? Explain your answer.

5. Give some titles of blues melodies that do not follow the usual harmonic construction but have the word blues in their titles.

Chapter 4

In example 12A, the accompaniment consists of the bass part confined to the first and third beats and the chords played on the second and fourth beats, or off-beats. Because of the physical action of the left hand, it became the practice for pianists to accent these off-beats, a technique that led to the new rhythmic style of the following era.

Example 12A

Example 12B

Example 13

In example 13, twelve measures are scored in Early New Orleans Dixieland style to point out musically the role assigned to each instrument.

Example 14

Clarinet

Trumpet

Trombone

Composite
Rhythm

Clarinet

Trumpet

Trombone

Composite
Rhythm

Clarinet

Trumpet

Trombone

Composite
Rhythm

Example 14 illustrates the involved syncopation that
causes the accents to shift constantly among the three
lines being played by the trumpet, clarinet, and
trombone.

Example 15

Early New Orleans Dixieland (no accents—flat four, or $\frac{4}{4}$)

Banjo

Tuba

Drums

Example 16

Guitar

Piano

String Bass

Drums

Chicago Style Dixieland (accented second and fourth beats—$\frac{2}{4}$)

Chapter 6

Example 17A

Example 17B

Example 17C

Example 17D

Example 17E

Examples 17A and 17B demonstrate the use of full chords. There are various means of outlining the chords with a melodic bass line. Examples 17C, 17D, and 17E illustrate three of the most common.

In examples 17A and 17B, the bass line originally played by the third guitar is omitted; however, this is not apparent because the moving chords cause the music to sound very full and complete. In examples 17C, 17D, and 17E, the left hand plays the bass line while actually outlining the chords.

Example 18A and B

4 Quarter Notes

8 Eighth Notes

Boogie-woogie has also been called "8 over 4." Example 18A shows the logic of this label in printed music where the meter signature is indicated correctly as $\frac{4}{4}$. The boogie-woogie pianist superimposes eight beats in the same $\frac{4}{4}$ measure because the individual eighth notes are felt as single beats. It would be most correct to say that the pianist plays and feels the music as eight beats to the bar, or written with $\frac{8}{8}$ meter, as shown in example 18B.

Example 19A

Example 19B

The notes in example 19A are outlined in 19B.

Example 20

The theme (example 2A) is now used as a basis for improvisation in the boogie-woogie style. Example 20 shows the bass pattern used by the pianist on demonstration 10.

Chapter 7

Example 21A

Example 21B

original line

{ added 2nd & 3rd
{ trumpet parts

Example 22

1st Alto Saxophone
2nd Alto Saxophone
1st Tenor Saxophone
2nd Tenor Saxophone
Baritone Saxophone
1st Trumpet
2nd Trumpet
3rd Trumpet
4th Trumpet
1st Trombone
2nd Trombone
3rd Trombone
4th Trombone
Guitar
Piano
Bass
Drums

Example 23A

Example 23B

Chapter 8

Example 24

	3rd	5th	7th	9th	11th	13th	etc.

Bb	Gm7	Cm7	F7	Gm7	E dim.	Cm7	F7	Bb
↓	↓	↓	↓	↓	↓	↓	↓	↓
Bb9M7	Db7	Cm7	B9	Bb9M7	Gm9	Cm7	F13	Bb9M7

or

Bb9M7	E9	EbM7	Ab13	Bb9M7	etc.

HIGHER HARMONICS

At the turn of the century, harmonies were enriched through the successive inclusion of higher members of the overtone series.

Example 25

An A-major chord is placed directly over a G7 chord to create an A13 chord.

Substitute chords also became important during the bop era. For example, C to C7 to F could just as well be played C to G7 to F, and it sounded more interesting at the time.

Chapter 10

Example 26

The funky idiom embraces homophonic harmonic construction. Although the lines appear to be invented independently, as can be seen in example 26, they are actually planned homophonically. The lower note is played because of the sound of the specific interval produced when it is played against the melodic note above it. Example 26 also points up the excessive use of the fourth and fifth intervals. Another identifying feature is the use of many blue notes—the E-flats and B-flats in example 26.

Example 27A

Example 27B

The homophonic construction of the swing era and that of the funky era are compared in examples 27A and 27B. Swing music was harmonized in a closed manner, as shown in example 27A, by the blocks of chords. The funky players, while planning their music homophonically, developed a more open, loose setting, as demonstrated in example 27B.

Notes

1. Gunther Schuller, *Early Jazz* (London: Oxford University Press, 1968), 37.
2. LeRoi Jones, *Blues People* (New York: William Morrow, 1963), 62.

Glossary

A

a cappella
Vocal music without instrumental accompaniment.

accent
To stress a melodic note, rhythm, or harmony by playing it louder and with a sharper attack.

accompaniment
Performing with another performer or performers, usually in a less prominent role (e.g., playing the piano accompaniment for a trombone soloist).

amplification
The process of electronically making a sound louder.

analog
The type of audio signal produced by early synthesizers. Voltage rather than numbers is used to describe the musical sounds.

appoggiatura
A musical ornament consisting of a single tone moving to an adjacent tone that is harmonized.

arpeggio
The individual tones of a chord are not sounded simultaneously but are performed like a melody (single tones), nearly always starting at the bottom, or lowest, tone.

arrangement
An adaptation of a musical composition (often called *charts* in musical slang). In a written arrangement, the musical arranger writes out the notes each performer is to play. In a head arrangement, the arrangement is made up out of someone's head, not written down.

arranger
One who writes musical compositions for particular groups of performers.

arrhythmic
Seemingly without meter; music that lacks a definite beat.

atonal
Lacking in tonal centers; free jazz often has atonal areas that avoid the chord and melodic relationships normally associated with the major-minor system.

attack
The manner in which the tone or tones are first sounded.

avant-garde
A term that refers to composers and performers who break away from traditional practices and push for radical change; used primarily to describe post-bop jazz.

B

backbeat
In a $\frac{4}{4}$ measure, the second and fourth beats are sometimes referred to as the backbeats; also, a song that has strong accents on those beats is said to have a backbeat.

ballad
A simple song, usually romantic in nature, that uses the same melody for each stanza.

bar line
A vertical line drawn down a music staff dividing it into bars or measures.

bar of music
A means of dividing music; also called a *measure of music*.

bass (brass)
The member of the brass family sounding the lowest tones; generally referred to as the *tuba*.

bass (string)
An instrument that looks like a very large violin; also called the *bass violin*. The string bass is played either by plucking the strings with the fingers (*pizzicato*) or by bowing (*arco*).

beat or breaker music
A musical style characterized by electronic drum machines and a heavy beat; designed for a dancing style called *break dancing*.

block chords
Usually, chords with many notes that move in parallel motion.

blue tonalities
The alteration of the third and seventh tones of the major scale by a flatting inflection.

bombs
Spontaneous punctuations by the drummer.

break
A short interruption in the flow of the music; an interlude in which a solo player improvises or an accompanying group interpolates.

bridge
The name given to the third eight-bar section in the most common construction of a thirty-two-bar chorus. In an AABA construction, the B is the bridge.

C

call-and-response pattern
A musical pattern common to much jazz and African music in which a "call," usually by a solo singer or instrumentalist, is followed by a "response" from one instrument, an ensemble, or the assembled participants in a ritual. In religious

canon
A form of contrapuntal writing in which the melody, announced by one voice, is imitated by an answering voice.

chaconne
Movement composed with a repeating bass line usually written in form of variations.

chamber music
Music intended for small groups performing in intimate surroundings, as distinct from large groups performing in concert halls, theaters, and so on.

chance music
Music based on chance or random relationships such as the throwing of dice.

Charleston
A dance form that was extremely popular during the 1920s.

chord
The simultaneous sounding of three or more tones.

chord changes
A series of successive chords; also called *chord progression*.

chorus
The main body or refrain of a song as distinct from the verse, which comes first. Very often an arrangement contains many choruses played by individual instrumentalists.

chromatic
Refers to the scales or the alteration of scale tones by using half-steps.

collective improvisation
A situation in which all members of a small group improvise simultaneously.

combo
A small instrumental group consisting of three to eight players.

comp or comping
The rhythmic pattern used by keyboard or guitar players as they accompany soloists. Comping generally makes use of short rhythmic statements of the harmony, leaving room for the soloist to be heard.

compact disc
A disc smaller than vinyl records that holds digital information describing the musical sounds.

concerto grosso
A composition consisting of interplay between a large body of instruments (orchestra) and a small group of instrumentalists (combo).

Congo Square
A large field in New Orleans where slaves gathered to sing and dance.

ceremonies, the congregation may respond to the "call" of the preacher.

contrast
The introduction of different musical material.

contrived
Music that is planned beforehand.

Creole
A person with Negro and French or Spanish ancestry.

crossover
A style of music that appeals to more than one type of listener; usually refers to jazz/rock *fusion*.

cross-rhythm
Two or more rhythmic patterns played simultaneously.

cutting contest
Individual musicians attempting to outplay one another, usually in a jam session situation.

D

diatonic
Pertains to the precise arrangement of tones as found in the major and minor scales.

digital
The use of numbers to describe a sound. The numbers can then be processed by computers or effects. The digital information is converted back to analog form for human hearing.

digital recording
Computer method of recording sound through the use of numbers.

distortion
The alteration of a sound, normally by overamplifying it, to create a rougher sound.

Dorian mode
The arrangement of tones found in the scale using only the white keys of the piano from D to D.

double stop
Two tones stopped by the fingers on a stringed instrument and sounded simultaneously.

double time
When the tempo of the music becomes twice as fast.

drum machine
An electronic device used to create drum patterns similar to those played by traditional set or trap drummers.

E

editing
Cutting or reassembling a recorded tape. Editing was originally done by actually cutting the tape. It can now be done electronically as the final mixdown is made.

effects
Electronic devices that alter electronic sounds (e.g., reverberation, delays, and distortion).

eleventh chord
A chord consisting of six different tones, each separated by an interval of a third.

embouchure
Disposition of the lips and tongue in playing wind instruments.

ensemble
Usually a small group of performers, as distinct from an orchestra or choir.

extended harmony
Tones added to a chord.

F

field hollers
A secret means of communication among slaves while they worked in the fields; sometimes called *field cries*.

fill-in
Originally, a short interlude in a song (such as a blues song) played by an instrumentalist.

flatted fifth
Lowering by a half step the fifth degree of the scale or chord.

flatted tone
Used to lower the pitch one half-step.

flügelhorn
A type of brass instrument with valves, similar to a trumpet.

free improvisation
A descriptive term that emphasizes the complete improvisational nature of free jazz; also called *free form*.

form
Refers to the design of a musical performance. Free jazz's lack of traditional restrictions in form and structure is called free form.

fugue
A type of contrapuntal composition for a given number of parts. Each part is introduced individually, and successive parts are heard in imitation.

fusion
A style of music that appeals to more than one type of listener; usually refers to jazz/rock (see *crossover*).

G

gospel song
A song whose lyrics recount passages from scripture.

guitorgan
A guitarlike instrument with an organ sound.

H

harmonics
The frequencies that collectively create a single tone; also used to refer to the higher chord tones in an extended chord.

harmonizer
An electronic device that creates a parallel melodic line to accompany the original melody.

harmony
Simultaneous sounding of two or more tones.

head voice
Technique of singing in the high range (not falsetto).

higher harmonics
See *extended harmony.*

homophonic
A single melody, usually in the highest voice part, with harmony in the lower voices acting as an accompaniment.

horizontal texture
Polyphonic texture; a simultaneous combination of melodies; the opposite of homophonic texture, which consists of a single melody with harmonic accompaniment.

hymn
A congregational song, with words not taken directly from the Bible, sung in praise of God.

I

iambic pentameter
A type of poetry consisting of an unaccented syllable followed by an accented one, with five of these combinations in each line of poetry.

improvisation
The performing of music that is made up (created) at the moment, not performed from memory or from written music; a manner of playing extemporaneously.

instrumentation
The different types of instruments that make up an ensemble.

J

jam session
An informal gathering of musicians playing on their own time and improvising just for the fun of it.

K

key
A classification given to a particular arrangement of tones in a scale. The first degree of the scale is the tonal center, or key name, and the necessary flats or sharps for a particular key form the key signature.

L

liturgical
Pertaining to the rites of a religious service.

M

Mass
The principal service of the Roman Catholic Church. The part that does not vary is called the Ordinary, or common, of the Mass and consists of the Kyrie, the Gloria, the Credo, the Sanctus with Benedictus, and the Agnus Dei.

master
The name of the final recorded product used to make records.

measure
See *bar of music.*

melisma
A melodic ornamentation; one syllable sung on more than one tone of a song.

melody
A succession of single tones varying in pitch and rhythm and having a recognizable musical shape.

meter
The division of beats into accented and unaccented groupings of two, three, or more.

middle register
The middle part of the complete range of the voice or instrument.

MIDI
Musical Instrument Digital Interface. An established electronic standard used to carry musical information between synthesizers and computers.

Mixolydian mode
The arrangement of tones found in the scale using only the white keys of the piano from G to G.

modal jazz
A jazz style that typically has slow-moving harmonies and older modal scales. The chord relationships are generally not typical of the major-minor system.

monophonic
A single melody with neither accompanying melody nor harmony.

mordent
A rapid movement from one tone to an upper or lower scale tone and back again to the principal tone.

motive or motivic
Short melodic fragments that are used for developing a solo. Motives are often taken by soloists from the song's melody. Some entire pieces are built on short motives (e.g., *A Love Supreme* by Coltrane).

multi-tracking
The ability to record several different sounds on separate parts (tracks) of the recording tape (see *overdub*).

N

new thing
An alternate name, used primarily by jazz players, for free jazz.

ninth chord
A chord consisting of five different tones, each separated by an interval of a third.

O

obligato
An accompanying or free melody played by a second instrument that is less prominent and secondary to the main melody played by the lead instrument.

offbeat
Second or fourth beat in $\frac{4}{4}$ meter.

ostinato
A clear melodic and/or rhythmic figure that is persistently repeated.

overdub
To record over existing record sound.

overtone series
Tones that are related to the first (fundamental) tone sounded. A series of higher tones, or upper partials, that, when the first (or fundamental) is sounded, make up a complex musical tone.

P

pedal point
A tone sustained below while harmonies change.

pentatonic
A scale consisting of only five tones as represented by the five black keys of the piano.

period
A grouping of melodic phrases to form a larger melodic section.

phrase
A small unit of a melody.

pizzicato
A manner of playing stringed instruments by plucking rather than by bowing.

plagal cadence
A specific chord progression, namely, the IV chord resolving to the I chord (e.g., amen chords).

polymeters
Simultaneous use of several meters.

polymodal
The simultaneous sounding of several different modes.

polyphonic
The simultaneous sounding of two or more melodies of equal importance.

polytonal
The simultaneous sounding of tones in more than one key.

portamento
The movement from one tone to another higher or lower tone without any break in the sound.

Q

quadrille
A square dance of five figures that was popular in the nineteenth century.

R

raga
A particular scale in Eastern music.

real time
Musical changes or events that are performed live rather than programmed earlier.

reggae
A Jamaican style of rhythm and blues.

repetition
Presentation of the same musical material in two or more parts of a composition.

reverberation
A series of rapid echoes that follows a sound.

rhythm section
The section of an instrumental ensemble that provides the most prominent rhythmic feel of the music, usually consisting of drums, piano, bass, and guitar.

riff
A short pattern of sounds repeated and played by a soloist or group.

rim shots
Produced by striking the edge, or rim, of the drum and the drumhead simultaneously.

rondo
A musical form in which one section of a composition recurs intermittently with contrasting sections coming between each repetition (e.g., ABACADA).

root tone
The lowest note or tone of a chord when that chord is in its basic, or root, position.

round
A vocal canon for several voices.

rubato
A fluctuation in the tempo of the music for the purpose of giving music an additional element of expression.

S

salsa
A combination of jazz and African-Cuban rhythms.

sampler
An electronic device that analyzes a sound and converts the analog voltage into a digital description that can be altered by a computer. The sampled sound can then be played back using a synthesizer keyboard.

sample
The individual number that describes the strength of a sound at any given moment. Samples can be taken of an analog sound up to approximately 40,000 times a second.

scale
A precise progression of single tones upward or downward in steps. A chromatic scale is a twelve-tone scale with intervals of a half-step; a diatonic scale is an eight-tone scale with a repetition of the eighth degree, pertaining to the major and minor scales; and a pentatonic scale consists of five tones.

scat singing
The use of nonsense syllables while improvising vocally.

Schoenberg's twelve-tone system
A technique of composition in which all twelve half-steps in an octave are treated as equal. A method used by Schoenberg in the form of a "tone row," in which all the twelve tones are placed in a particular order, forming the basis of a musical composition. No tone is repeated within a row. The tone row becomes a "tonal reservoir" from which the composition is drawn.

sequencer
An electronic device that stores a musical series of notes to be played back later. Sequencers can be used to build up a performance by storing several musical sequences, one after another.

tango
A dance of Spanish-American origin commonly in $\frac{4}{4}$ meter.

sharped tone
Raises the pitch one half-step.

sideman
A player in the musical ensemble as differentiated from the leader.

sonata allegro
An instrumental composition with three large sections (ABA)—exposition, development, and recapitulation.

soulsa
A combination of Latin jazz and "soul" music.

speakeasy
A nightclub in the 1920s.

spiritual
A name given to a type of religious folk song of the American Negro, usually of a solo-and-refrain design.

standard tunes
Familiar, well-established popular or jazz tunes. Copyright can be renewed for a certain number of years after the death of the composer.

stock arrangement
A published commercial arrangement, usually simplified and standardized.

Storyville
Red-light district in New Orleans that figured in the origin of jazz.

string bass
A bass violin.

symmetrical
Exhibiting a balance of parts.

syncopation
Accenting a normally weak beat or the weak part of a beat.

T

tack piano
A piano with thumbtacks on the felts of the piano hammers to make it sound older and more authentic for playing ragtime and similar music.

tag
A short addition to the end of a musical composition.

tailgate trombone
A name deriving from the practice of early trombone players sitting on the tailgate of a wagon so that their slides could operate freely out the rear. The phrase became associated with the trombone part in a dixieland ensemble.

tape loop
A loop of magnetic recording tape that is used to repeat a sound. The speed of the tape determines how fast the repeats occur.

tempo
Refers to the speed of the underlying beat. The speed is determined by the number of beats counted over the span of sixty seconds.

theme and variation
A musical form in which the theme is introduced and successive repetitions of the theme, changed or altered in some manner, follow.

third-stream music
A combination of classical music and jazz.

thirteenth chord
A chord consisting of seven different tones, each separated by an interval of a third.

time, making time, or straight time
Often after rhythmically contrasting interludes or a rhythmically complex "head," the rhythm section will fall into a very solid metric feel to launch a solo section. A straight-time feel has very few unusual accents.

time signature
Sign at the beginning of a composition indicating the grouping of beats for each measure. The meter signature 3/4 means that there are three beats in a measure and that a quarter note gets one beat.

Tin Pan Alley
The industry centered in New York that published popular music.

tonal clash
Tones played simultaneously that produce a discordant or clashing effect.

tonal sonorities
The overall effect of the juxtaposition of tonal sounds.

trading fours
Two solo instrumentalists alternating in playing four measures each.

twelve-measure chorus or **twelve-bar strain**
A composition or a part of a composition consisting of twelve measures.

twelve-tone system
A compositional system designed to avoid tonal centers, thereby creating a balanced atonal music.

U

unison
Two or more instruments or voices sounding on the same pitches (tones) or an octave apart.

up-tempo
Fast tempo.

V

vamp
A transitional chord or rhythmic progression of indefinite duration used as a filler until the soloist is ready to start or continue.

verse
The introductory section of a popular song as distinguished from the chorus. The latter consists commonly of thirty-two bars, whereas the verse may have an irregular number of bars and be sung or played in a free tempo.

vertical texture
Block chords that accompany a melodic part; opposite of horizontal thinking.

vibrato
The pulsating effect produced by small, rapid variations in pitch. Most jazz uses vibrato for warmth and interpretation in imitating the human voice.

vocoder
An electronic musical device that allows the player to choose the pitch of any syllable sung, and that can blend two sounds at will.

W

walking bass
The bass part that was originally introduced in boogie-woogie in ostinato form. It concisely spells out the notes in the chords being used and is usually played in eighth notes.

well-tempered scale
Refers to the tuning system found on a keyboard.

Bibliography

A

Albertson, Chris. *Bessie.* New York: Stein & Day, 1972.

Allan, William Francis; Ware, Charles Pickard; and Garrison, Lucy McKim. *Slave Songs of the United States.* New York: Peter Smith, 1867.

Allen, Walter C. *Hendersonia: The Music of Fletcher Henderson and His Musicians, Jazz Monograph no. 4.* Highland Park, N.J.: Walter C. Allen, 1973.

Allen, Walter C., and Rust, Brian. *King Joe Oliver.* London and New York: Sidgwick and Jackson, 1958.

Apel, Willi. *Harvard Dictionary of Music.* Cambridge, Mass.: Harvard University Press, 1955.

Armstrong, Louis. *Swing That Music.* New York: Longmans, Green, 1936.

———. *My Life in New Orleans.* New York: Prentice-Hall, 1954.

———. *Louis Armstrong: A Self Portrait.* New York: Eakins Press, 1971.

B

Baird, David. *From Score to Tape.* Boston: Berklee Press, 1973.

Balliett, Whitney. *The Sound of Surprise.* New York: E. P. Dutton, 1959.

———. *Dinosaurs in the Morning.* Philadelphia: J. B. Lippincott, 1962.

———. *American Musicians.* New York: Oxford University Press, 1986.

Basie, Count. *Good Morning Blues: The Autobiography of Count Basie, as Told to Albert Murray.* New York: Random House, 1986.

Bechet, Sidney. *Treat It Gentle: An Autobiography.* New York: Hill & Wang, 1960.

Berendt, Joachim. *The New Jazz Book.* Translated by Dan Morgenstern. New York: Hill & Wang, 1962.

———. *Jazz Book: From New Orleans to Rock and Free Jazz.* New York: Lawrence Hill, 1975.

Berger, Morroe; Patrick, Edward; and Patrick, James. *Benny Carter: A Life in American Music.* Metuchen, N.J.: Scarecrow Press, 1982.

Bernstein, Leonard. *The Joy of Music.* New York: Simon & Schuster, 1959.

Berton, Ralph. *Remembering Bix: A Memoir of the Jazz Age.* New York: Harper & Row, 1974.

Blancq, Charles. *Sonny Rollins: The Journey of a Jazzman.* Boston: G. K. Hall, 1983.

Blesh, Rudi. *Classic Piano Rags.* New York: Dover Publications, 1973.

Blesh, Rudi, and Janis, Harriet. *Shining Trumpets—a History of Jazz.* New York: Alfred A. Knopf, 1946.

———. *They All Played Ragtime.* New York: Grove Press, 1959.

Bloom, Eric, ed. *Grove's Dictionary of Music and Musicians.* 9 vols. New York: St. Martin's Press, 1959.

Brask, Ole, and Morgenstern, Dan. *Jazz People.* New York: Harry N. Abrams, 1976.

Brooks, Tilford. *America's Black Musical Heritage.* Englewood Cliffs, N.J.: Prentice-Hall, 1984.

Broonzy, William, and Bruynogle, Yannick. *Big Bill Blues.* London: Cassell, 1955.

Brown, Charles T. *The Jazz Experience.* Dubuque, Iowa: Wm. C. Brown, 1989.

Budds, Michael J. *Jazz in the Sixties.* Iowa City: University of Iowa Press, 1978.

Buerkle, Jack V., and Barker, Danny. *Bourbon Street Black.* London: Oxford University Press, 1973.

Buszin, Walter E., ed. *Anniversary Collection of Bach Chorales.* Chicago: Hall McCreary, 1935.

C

Calloway, Cab, and Rollins, Bryant. *Of Minnie the Moocher and Me.* New York: Crowell, 1976.

Carr, Ian. *Miles Davis.* New York: William Morrow, 1982.

Cerulli, Dom; Korall, Burt; and Nasatir, Mort. *The Jazz World.* New York: Ballantine Books, 1960.

Charles, Ray, and Ritz, David. *Brother Ray.* New York: Dial Press, 1978.

Charters, Samuel B. *The Country Blues.* New York: Doubleday, 1958.

———. *Jazz: New Orleans (1855–1963).* New York: Oak Publishers, 1964.

Charters, Samuel B., and Kunstadt, Leonard. *Jazz: A History of The New York Scene.* New York: Doubleday, 1962.

Chase, Gilbert. *America's Music from the Pilgrims to the Present.* New York: McGraw Hill, 1955.

Chilton, John. *Billie's Blues.* New York: Stein & Day, 1975.

———. *Who's Who of Jazz.* New York: Da Capo Press, 1985.

Cole, Bill. *John Coltrane.* New York: Schirmer, 1976.

———. *Miles Davis.* New York: William Morris, 1976.

Collier, Graham. *Inside Jazz.* London: Quartet Books, 1973.

Collier, James Lincoln. *The Making of Jazz.* New York: Dell Publishing, 1978.

Coryell, Julie, and Friedman, Laura. *Jazz-Rock Fusion.* New York: Delta Books, 1979.

Courlander, Harold. *Miles Davis: A Musical Biography.* New York: William Morrow, 1974.

D

Dahl, Linda. *Stormy Weather: The Music and Lives of a Century of Jazz-women.* New York: Pantheon, 1984.

Dale, Rodney. *The World of Jazz.* Cambridge: Basinghall, 1980.

Dance, Stanley. *The World of Duke Ellington.* New York: Scribner, 1970.

———. *The World of Earl Hines.* New York: Scribner, 1974.

———. *The World of Count Basie.* New York: Scribner, 1980.

———. *The World of Swing.* New York: Scribner, 1975.

Dankworth, Avril. *Jazz: An Introduction to Its Musical Basis.* London: Oxford University Press, 1968.

Davis, Francis. *In the Moment: Jazz in the 1980s.* New York: Oxford University Press, 1986.

Davis, Miles, and Troupe, Quincy. *Miles.* New York: Simon and Schuster, 1989.

Davis, Nathan. *Writings in Jazz.* 3d ed. Scottsdale, Ariz.: Gorsuch Scarisbrick, 1985.

Dexter, Dave. *The Jazz Story: From the Nineties to the Sixties.* Englewood Cliffs, N.J.: Prentice-Hall, 1964.

Dineen, Janice D. *The Performing Women* (26910 Grand View Ave., Hayward, Calif. 94542).

Drake, Russell; Herder, Ronald; and Modugno, Anne D. *How to Make Electronic Music.* Pleasantville, N.Y.: EAV Inc., 1975.

E

Ellington, Duke. *Music Is My Mistress.* New York: Doubleday, 1973.

Ellington, Mercer, and Dance, Stanley. *Duke Ellington in Person: An Intimate Memoir.* New York: Houghton Mifflin, 1975.

F

Feather, Leonard. *Inside Jazz.* New York: J. J. Robbins, 1949.

———. *The New Edition of the Encyclopedia of Jazz.* New York: J. J. Robbins, 1960.

———. *The Book of Jazz: A Guide from Then til Now.* New York: Horizon Press, 1965.

———. *The Encyclopedia of Jazz in the Sixties.* New York: Horizon Press, 1966.

———. *From Satchmo to Miles.* New York: Stein & Day, 1974.

———. *The Encyclopedia of Jazz in the Seventies.* New York: Horizon Press, 1976.

———. *Pleasures of Jazz.* New York: Horizon Press, 1976.

———. *The Encyclopedia of Jazz.* New York: Da Capo Press, 1984.

Finkelstein, Sidney. *Jazz: A People's Music.* New York: Da Capo Press, 1975.

Flower, John. *Moonlight Serenade.* New Rochelle, N.Y.: Arlington House, 1972.

Francis, André. *Jazz.* Translated and revised by Martin Williams. New York: Grove Press, 1960.

Friend, David; Perlman, Alan R.; and Piggott, Thomas G. *Learning Music with Synthesizers.* Winona, Minn.: Hal Leonard, 1974.

G

Gammond, Peter, ed. *Scott Joplin and the Ragtime Era.* New York: St. Martin's Press, 1975.

George, Don. *Sweet Man: The Real Duke Ellington.* New York: Putnam, 1981.

Giddins, Gary. *Satchmo.* New York: Doubleday, 1989.

Gillespie, Dizzy, and Fraser, Al. *To Be, or Not . . . to Bop.* Garden City, N.Y.: Doubleday, 1979.

Gitler, Ira. *Jazz Masters of the Forties.* New York: Macmillan, 1966.

———. *Swing to Bop.* New York: Oxford University Press, 1986.

Gleason, Ralph. *Celebrating the Duke.* New York: Dell Publishers, 1975.

Goddard, Chris. *Jazz Away from Home.* London: Paddington Press, 1979.

Goffin, Robert. *Jazz: From the Congo to the Metropolitan.* New York: Da Capo Press, 1975.

Gold, Robert S. *A Jazz Lexicon.* New York: Knopf 1964.

Goldberg, Joe. *Jazz Masters of the Fifties.* New York: Macmillan, 1965.

Gridley, Mark C. *Jazz Styles.* 3d ed. Englewood Cliffs, N.J.: Prentice-Hall, 1985.

H

Hadlock, Richard. *Jazz Masters of the Twenties.* New York: Macmillan, 1965.

Handy, W. C. *W. C. Handy: Father of the Blues.* New York: Collier Books, 1970.

Harris, Rex. *Jazz.* Baltimore: Penguin Books, 1956.

Harrison, Max. *Charlie Parker.* New York: A. S. Barnes, 1961.

———. *A Jazz Retrospect.* Boston: Crescendo, 1976.

Haskins, Jim. *Black Music in America.* New York: Thomas Y. Crowell, 1987.

Hentoff, Nat. *Jazz Life.* New York: Da Capo Press, 1975.

———. *The Jazz Years: Earwitness to an Era.* New York: Da Capo Press, 1987.

———. *Jazz Is.* New York: Random House, 1976.

———. *Boston Boy.* New York: Alfred A. Knopf, 1986.

Hentoff, Nat, and McCarthy, Albert, eds. *Jazz: New Perspectives on the History of Jazz.* New York: Da Capo Press, 1975.

Hickok, Robert. *Exploring Music.* Dubuque, Iowa: Wm. C. Brown, 1989.

Hodeir, André. *Jazz: Its Evolution and Essence.* Translated by David Noakes. New York: Grove Press, 1956.

———. *Toward Jazz.* New York: Grove Press, 1962.

Holiday, Billie, and Duffy, William. *Lady Sings the Blues.* New York: Doubleday, 1965.

J

James, Michael. *Dizzy Gillespie.* New York: A. S. Barnes, 1959.

Jewell, Derek. *Duke: A Portrait of Duke Ellington.* New York: W. W. Norton, 1977.

Jones, LeRoi. *Blues People.* New York: William Morrow, 1963.

———. *Black Music.* New York: William Morrow, 1965.

Jones, Max. *Salute to Satchmo.* London: Longacre Press, 1970.

Jones, Max, and Chilton, John. *Louis: The Louis Armstrong Story.* New York: Little, Brown, 1971.

Jost, Ekkehard. *Free Jazz.* New York: Da Capo Press, 1981.

K

Kaminsky, Max. *My Life in Jazz.* New York: Harper and Row, 1963.

Kaufman, Frederick, and Guckin, John P. *The African Roots of Jazz.* Sherman Oaks, Calif.: Alfred Publishing, 1979.

Keepnews, Orrin, and Grauer, Bill, Jr. *A Pictorial History of Jazz.* New York: Crown Publishers, 1955.

Keil, Charles. *Urban Blues.* Chicago: University of Chicago Press, 1966.

Kennington, Donald, and Reed, Denny L. *The Literature of Jazz.* 2d ed. Chicago: American Library Association, 1980.

Kimball, Bob, and Bolcum, Bill. *Reminiscing with Sizzle and Blake.* New York: Viking Press, 1973.

Kinkle, Roger D. *The Complete Encyclopedia of Popular Music and Jazz.* New Rochelle, N.Y.: Arlington House, 1974.

Kirkeby, Ed. *Ain't Misbehavin': The Story of Fats Waller.* New York: Da Capo Press, 1975.

L

Lee, William F. *People in Jazz: Jazz Keyboard Improvisors of the 19th and 20th Centuries.* Hialeah, Fla.: Columbia Pictures Publications, 1984.

Leonard, Neil. *Jazz and the White Americans.* Chicago: University of Chicago Press, 1962.

———. *Jazz: Myth and Religion.* New York: Oxford University Press, 1987.

Levine, Lawrence W. *High Brow/Low Brow.* Cambridge: Harvard University Press, 1988.

Litweiler, John. *The Freedom Principle of Jazz after 1958.* New York: William Morrow, 1984.

Lomax, Alan. *Mr. Jelly Roll.* New York: Grosset & Dunlap, 1950.

———. *The Folk Songs of North America.* Double Day and Inc.

M

McCarthy, Albert. *Louis Armstrong.* New York: A. S. Barnes, 1959.

———. *Big Band Jazz.* New York: Putnam, 1974.

Marquis, Donald. *In Search of Buddy Bolden: First Man of Jazz.* Baton Rouge: Louisiana State University Press, 1979.

Martin, Henry. *Enjoying Jazz.* New York: Schirmer, 1986.

Martin, John H., and Fritz, William F. *Listening to Jazz.* Fresno: University of California Press, 1969.

Meeker, David. *Jazz in the Movies: A Guide to Jazz Musicians, 1917–1977.* New Rochelle, N.Y.: Arlington House, 1978.

Megill, Donald D., and Demory, Richard S. *Introduction to Jazz History.* 2d ed. Englewood Cliffs, N.J.: Prentice-Hall, 1989.

Mehegan, John. *Jazz Improvisation.* New York: Watson-Guptill Publications, 1959.

Milhaud, Darius. *Notes without Music.* New York: Alfred A. Knopf, 1953.

Miller, Hugh Milton. *History of Music.* New York: Barnes & Noble Books, 1957.

Mingus, Charles. *Beneath the Underdog.* New York: Alfred A. Knopf, 1971.

Morgenstern, Dan. *Jazz People.* New York: Abrams, 1976.

Muro, Don. *An Introduction to Electronic Music Synthesizers.* Melville, N.Y.: Belwin-Mills, 1975.

Murray, Albert. *Stompin' the Blues.* New York: McGraw Hill, 1976.

N

Nanry, Charles. *The Jazz Text.* New York: Van Nostrand, 1979.

O

Ogren, Kathy J. *The Jazz Revolution.* New York: Oxford University Press, 1989.

Oliver, Paul. *The Meaning of the Blues.* New York: Macmillan, 1960.

———. *Bessie Smith.* New York: A. S. Barnes, 1961.

———. *The Savannah Syncopators.* New York: Stein & Day, 1970.

Ostransky, Leroy. *The Anatomy of Jazz.* Seattle: University of Washington Press, 1960.

———. *Jazz City.* Englewood Cliffs, N.J.: Prentice-Hall, 1975.

———. *Understanding Jazz.* Englewood Cliffs, N.J.: Prentice-Hall, 1977.

P

Panassie, Hughes. *The Real Jazz.* Translated by Anne Sorrelle Williams. New York: A. S. Barnes, 1960.

———. *Louis Armstrong.* New York: Scribner, 1971.

Placksin, Sally. *American Women in Jazz.* Wideview Books, 1982.

Pleasants, Henry. *The Great American Popular Singers.* New York: Oxford University Press, 1959.

———. *Serious Music and All That Jazz.* New York: Simon & Schuster, 1969.

Porter, Lewis. *Lester Young.* Boston: Twayne Press, 1985.

Priestley, Brian. *Mingus: A Critical Biography.* New York: Da Capo Press, 1984.

R

Ramsey, Frederic, Jr., and Smith, Charles Edward. *Jazzmen.* New York: Harcourt, Brace, Harvest, 1939.

Reisner, Robert G. *The Jazz Titans.* New York: Doubleday, 1960.

———. *Bird: The Legend of Charlie Parker.* New York: Da Capo Press, 1975.

Roach, Hildred. *Black American Music: Past and Present.* Boston: Crescendo, 1973.

Roberts, John Storm. *Black Music of Two Worlds.* New York: William Morrow, 1974.

Rose, Al. *Eubie Blake.* New York: Schirmer, 1979.

Russell, Ross. *Jazz Styles in Kansas City and the Southwest.* Berkeley: University of California Press, 1971.

———. *Bird Lives: The High Life and Hard Times of Charlie (Yardbird) Parker.* New York: Charterhouse Books, 1973.

Russell, Tony. *Blacks, Whites and the Blues.* New York: Stein & Day, 1970.

S

Sales, Grover. *Jazz: America's Classical Music.* Englewood Cliffs, N.J.: Prentice-Hall.

Sanders, Ruby W. *Jazz Ambassador Louis Armstrong.* Chicago: The Childrens Press, 1973.

Sargeant, Winthrop. *Jazz, Hot and Hybrid.* 3d ed. New York: Da Capo Press, 1975.

Schafer, William J., et al. *The Art of Ragtime.* Baton Rouge: Louisiana State University Press, 1973.

Schenkel, Steven M. *The Tools of Jazz.* Englewood Cliffs, N.J.: Prentice-Hall, 1983.

Schuller, Gunther. *Early Jazz: Its Roots and Musical Development.* London: Oxford University Press, 1968.

———. *The Swing Era: The Development of Jazz 1930–1945.* London: Oxford University Press, 1989.

Scott, Allen. *Jazz Educated, Man.* Silver Spring, Md.: Institute of Modern Languages, 1973.

Shapiro, Nat, and Hentoff, Nat, eds. *The Jazz Makers.* New York: Grove Press, 1957.

Simon, George T. *The Big Bands.* New York: Macmillan, 1967.

———. *Simon Says.* New Rochelle, N.Y.: Arlington House, 1971.

———. *Glenn Miller.* New York: Thomas Y. Crowell, 1974.

Simpkins, C. O. *Coltrane: A Biography.* New York: Herndon House, 1975.

Skowronski, Jo Ann. *Women in America: A Bibliography.* Metucken, N.J.: Scarecrow Press, 1978.

Southern, Eileen. *Music of Black Americans.* New York: W. W. Norton, 1971.

Spellman, A. B. *Black Music: Four Lives in the Bebop Business.* New York: Schocken, 1970.

Standifer, James A., and Reeder, Barbara. *African and Afro-American Materials for Music Educators.* Washington, D.C.: Music Educators National Conference, 1972.

Starr, S. Frederick. *Red and Hot, the Fate of Jazz in the Soviet Union.* New York: Oxford University Press, 1983.

Stearns, Marshall. *The Story of Jazz.* London: Oxford University Press, 1958.

Stewart, Rex. *Jazz Masters of the '30s.* New York: Macmillan, 1972.

Stewart-Baxter, Derrick. *Ma Rainey.* New York: Stein & Day, 1970.

Strange, Allen. *Electronic Music: Systems, Techniques, and Controls.* Dubuque, Iowa: Wm. C. Brown, 1972.

Sudhalter, Richard M., and Evans, Phillip R. *Bix: Man and Legend.* New York: Harper & Row, 1974.

Swenson, John. *The Rolling Stone Jazz Record Guide.* New York: Random House, 1985.

T

Tallmadge, William. *Afro-American Music.* Washington, D.C.: Music Educators National Conference, 1957.

Taylor, Billy. *Jazz and Piano: History and Development.* Dubuque, Iowa: Wm. C. Brown, 1982.

Thomas, J. C. *Chasin' the Trane.* New York: Doubleday, 1975.

Tirro, Frank. *Jazz: A History.* New York: W. W. Norton, 1977.

U

Ulanov, Barry. *Duke Ellington.* New York: Farrar, Strauss & Young, 1946.

———. *Handbook of Jazz.* New York: Viking Press, 1959.

Ulrich, Homer. *Music: A Design for Listening.* 2d ed. New York: Harcourt, Brace, & World, 1962.

Unterbrink, Mary. *Jazz Women at the Keyboard.* Jefferson, N.C.: McFarland, 1983.

W

Walker, Leo. *The Wonderful Era of the Great Dance Bands.* New York: Doubleday, 1972.

Werner, Otto. *The Origin and Development of Jazz.* Dubuque, Iowa: Kendall/Hunt, 1984.

Williams, Martin T. *King Oliver.* New York: A. S. Barnes, 1960.

———. *Jazz Masters of New Orleans.* New York: Macmillan, 1965.

———. *Jazz Masters in Transition (1957–69).* New York: Macmillan, 1970.

———. *The Jazz Tradition.* New York: Oxford University Press, 1983.

———. *Jazz Heritage.* New York: Oxford University Press, 1985.

———, ed. *The Art of Jazz.* London: Oxford University Press, 1959.

Wilson, John S. *The Collector's Jazz: Tradition and Swing.* Philadelphia: J. B. Lippincott, 1958.

———. *The Collector's Jazz: Modern.* Philadelphia: J. B. Lippincott, 1959.

———. *Jazz: The Transition Years, 1940–1960.* New York: Appleton-Century-Crofts, 1966.

Index